Africa

Africa

Endurance and Change
South of the Sahara

Catherine Coquery-Vidrovitch

Translated by David Maisel

UNIVERSITY OF CALIFORNIA PRESS

Berkeley • Los Angeles • London

Originally published as
Afrique noire: permanences et ruptures
© 1985 Editions Payot, Paris

University of California Press
Berkeley and Los Angeles, California

University of California Press, Ltd.
London, England

© 1988 by
The Regents of the University of California

Library of Congress Cataloging-in-Publication Data

Coquery-Vidrovitch, Catherine.
  Africa: endurance and change south of the Sahara.

  Translation of: Afrique noire.
  Bibliography: p.
  Includes index.
  1. Africa, Sub-Saharan—Economic conditions.   2. Africa, Sub-Saharan—Population—
History. 3. Africa, Sub-Saharan—Colonial influence—History.   4. Africa, Sub-Saharan—
Politics and government.   5. Africa, Sub-Saharan—Rural conditions.   6. Labor and
laboring classes—Africa, Sub-Saharan—History.
HC800.C67513   1988   967   87–15316
ISBN 0–520–05679–5 (alk. paper)

Printed in the United States of America
1 2 3 4 5 6 7 8 9

Contents

Maps

Preface and Acknowledgments

This book really began for me over twenty years ago. Since that time I have visited almost all the African countries (excepting only Tanzania, Angola, Burundi, Uganda, Malawi, Lesotho, and Guinea-Bissau) making two journeys a year, on the average. To some—Senegal and the Congo, among others—I have returned often and have stayed for long periods. I am well aware that the vision I have gained, though constantly reworked, remains incomplete, an outsider's; yet so many observations, so many images, so many reflections demand organization.

Nearly always, I started from a city, by any of a number of means of transport—the canoe, the Land Rover, often the train (one sees a lot and has plenty of conversation), and even the air-taxi—alone and carrying a backpack, or, more recently, with graduate students engaged in their own research. I have known the village hut, the government lodging, and the chance hazards of the bush more often than the luxury hotel. I saw, over these years, what had changed (and not only in the cities, where the leap was prodigious) and what had remained immutable.

Aside from professional colleagues and a few others, chosen as much by affinity as by chance, I had little to do with European residents other than superficially; the most colorful were undoubtedly the sometimes friendly adventurers I discovered when I was studying colonial businesses, who often possessed a better knowledge of the country than many present-day "agents de cooperation." But many of my African friends, colleagues, and students will recognize, in the examples, anecdotes, and reflections with which this work is strewn, cases we observed, stories I was told, and questions we discussed together. In my book, I have put much of myself, but more of these associates. As much for their sake as for mine, I wished to address some problems that torment them. What forces shaped the African states, made the African peoples what they are today, and created the problems Africa faces? How much is due to history, to nature, to others, to themselves? And what does their future hold? My hope here is to contribute to answering these questions, and to convey to the reader a little of the affection I feel for that part of the world.

Finally, I must stress the importance of the innovative viewpoints offered by my colleagues in our Institute on Third World Comparative Studies in Paris and of the comments of my students over the years (particularly in my research seminar). They have been my foremost critics, whose reactions have often guided or changed my itinerary. I also owe thanks to Marc Ferro for his attentive rereading of the work and valuable suggestions, to readers of the French edition, especially Jean Suret-Canale, who detected a number of errors and omissions, and to Josette Reux-Kiamenga for the care with which she typed the entire manuscript and for her patience with my corrections.

The American edition records some of the developments that have occurred since the publication of the French edition in 1985.

Without the encouragement of Allen Isaacman and Immanuel Wallerstein the present edition might never have been written. My colleagues at the State University of New York at Binghamton helped to foster in me a "non-francophone" worldview, and my graduate students again provided valuable insights. Special thanks are due to David Maisel for his work in translating the French text, and to Jane-Ellen Long for her admirable skill and patience in shaping the English into colloquial form.

Introduction

This book starts with the premise that the upheavals in Africa today occur too frequently to be merely the result of chance. In Chad, Somalia-Ethiopia, the Sudan, the western Sahara, Nigeria, Zaire, Angola, and all around South Africa, conflicts rage incessantly, with more than sixty apparently spontaneous putsches in the last thirty years.[1]

My research was begun with the hypothesis of a "second partition" of Africa by the major powers—this one economic and military, as the first, just a century ago, about the time of the Berlin International Conference of 1884–1885, was political. This beginning led into a wide-ranging investigation in which imperialism came to assume a prominent role. Underlying the process of underdevelopment is found a long and continuous history of external domination—by both Islam and the West—over the evolution of African societies, and this imperialism, by its expedition, has thrust contemporary capitalism upon these societies.[2] The impact of imperialism on Africa has been persuasively presented in a series of recent essays.[3] The debate has now gone on for at least twenty years, and little is left to be said. At the same time, "imperialism" must not be offered unthinkingly as an explanation of every problem.

I have therefore assumed that the external factors of foreign intervention and domination—the slave trade, the impact of the colonial laws or, more generally, the continuous pressures on the African continent of the Mediterranean and Atlantic economies for the past ten centuries—have been sufficiently documented. But in my travels and through my interviews and reading I have learned the necessity of understanding how these factors were felt, interpreted, absorbed or rejected by the Africans themselves, in the course of a particularly violent and traumatic history and in terms of the original structures, continually refashioned, of their traditional societies.

Therefore I say comparatively little about those social elements that have been acquired from outside: the civil servants, the bureaucratic bourgeoisie, the new entrepreneurs, and the acculturated elite that occupies the center of the political stage. They are undoubtedly important, for they manage the mechanisms of dependence, but they constitute only a tiny, primarily urban minority and their attempts to control and dominate the interior are thwarted by a milieu that demonstrates an extraordinary capacity for absorption, inertia, and resistance.

Similarly, the influx of foreign politics and ideologies fails to solve Africa's problems. The results of liberal capitalism are by no means conclusive. The "miracle" of the Ivory Coast, overdependent on world coffee and cocoa prices that are now well below their 1975–1977 peaks, has come to an end. Zambia faces bankruptcy now that copper, almost its sole source of revenue, has lost its strategic and hence its commercial value. Deeply impoverished Kenya relies exclusively on international tourism, and Senegal owes its survival to French subsidies. In short, the force of the capitalist crisis is being experienced continent-wide.

The immediate results of socialism seem no more promising. The curious phenomenon of a European model of scientific Marxist-Leninism in the Third World—in the Congo, Benin, Angola, Mozambique, and Ethiopia—seems explicable only in terms of an elite of soldiers or intellectuals imbued with European culture, whose behavior stems from political and diplomatic considerations rather than genuine social needs.

The issue of Islam, the third force ready to play an international role in Africa, is more complex, for Islam existed in Africa long before colonization. The question is whether religion is about to break into the political domain in sub-Saharan Africa, removing the management of the society from the hands of humans so as to put it into the hands of God. For lack of any clear political model, the recent Islamic revival has not yet been reflected in the structures of the state. This may yet come, but for the moment, as we shall see, Islam serves principally as a strategic tool: even in Chad and the Sudan, Islam as a political force plays only a secondary role. As Jean-Louis Triaud once said so succinctly, Islam in Africa is "more manipulated than manipulating."

It seems that governmental or international approaches fail to address the issues adequately. If we are to understand its roots, the African reality has to be approached from a different viewpoint. The dominant characteristic of these societies is that the vast majority of the population are peasants. These country-dwellers of whom so little is said still constitute—even if the percentage is beginning to change—nearly three-quarters of the population of sub-Saharan Africa, and it is they who, uprooted from the rural areas, today congregate in what appear to be limitless cities. These men and women form the substratum of this book. I have attempted to describe the processes by which their social systems have broken down when confronted with situations and problems to which they were not in a position to provide answers.

The current disturbances have resulted from the almost total collapse of everything on which, a century ago, these people's existence had appeared to be founded.

Until recently, African societies, while showing extreme divergences, possessed a number of factors in common. First of all, they were, taken as a whole, rural, precapitalist societies, deriving most of their subsistence from the soil, whether they were cultivators, herdsmen, or hunters and gatherers. They also shared the characteristic—less precise, but rich in implications—of constituting original cultural entities, sometimes with a common linguistic foundation (proto-Bantu in the whole central and southern part of the continent). Above all, throughout their history, thanks to frequent migrations, interchanges with distant peoples have been reported. For centuries these rural societies, suffering an extraordinary acceleration of history which has culminated in the violent but relatively brief trauma of colonization followed by the chaos of an as yet new independence, have had to confront the problem of domination and dependence, of an opening-up to the West within a context of rural resistance, the outcome of which has been an unavoidable loss of traditional values.

This background explains the attempt made here to analyze this development over the long run, from four perspectives. The first is that of demography. Research into African demographic history is just beginning, but it already suggests fascinating hypotheses about the connection between the vicissitudes of African demography and the political development of Africa in relation to the other continents. How far do the students of demography take Africa's history into account?

The second is that of government. Present-day African political systems result from the succession and, even more, the overlapping of models of statehood that had no a priori connection: the precolonial kinship system, the coercive colonialist regime, and the contemporary nation-state more or less inspired by the Western democratic model. How do rural Africans today regard the nation-state that is coming into being and to which they must adapt? From what cultural points of reference, with what psychological orientation and what conceptual myths of origin do they approach and, consequently, practice government?

The third perspective concerns the facts of rural life, its continuities and its constraints, and the inevitable changes in the agricultural economy in spite of rural traditionalism and resistance to change. All this raises the question of the capacity for adaptation, let alone revolution, of the rural masses.

Finally, the rural population is being massively transformed into a labor force. Still largely attached to the countryside—through the perpetuation and the reinforcement of migrant labor—it is nonetheless increasingly being drawn into the orbit of Western capitalism, of which the rapidly expanding

African cities are the sign and symbol. Is it, then, from urbanization, from labor unions, from industrialization, that future upheavals will come?

The approach taken here, of building comprehensive structures out of a wide variety of individual cases, may perhaps be found disconcerting. It must not be taken to imply, however, that sub-Saharan Africa is one vast entity in which all the societies are similar: ethnologists know full well that this is not the case. No attempt has been made to reduce all African societies to a single pattern or model, nor to be exhaustive.

This book offers, however, if not the answer itself (who would dare to predict it?), at least a number of elements that could enter into an answer to the following urgent question: in view of the past which has made them what they are today, what future awaits these African masses who are daily experiencing highly accelerated social, economic, ideological, and cultural changes in a continent in transition?

PART I

African Demographic Growth

The Most Erratic Development in History

1

Demography, Ecology, and History

Africa's demographic history is the least studied in the world, yet it is perhaps the richest in contrasts, and it lies at the very heart of the historical process. It has been suggested that the emergence of political systems depends on population density: states would be unlikely to form or would break up if that density fell below a certain level.[1] The fact that the exercise of power in Africa has taken fairly specific forms without necessarily involving the territorial framework of a state suggests that it may be worthwhile to trace the periodic drainage of population on the African continent in precolonial times, affected—but just how is a matter of controversy—by the slave trade; in the colonial period, under a coercive system; and in the postcolonial period, with its recurrent famines. These changes are ultimately connected to the issue of the relationship among the history of the climate, the history of the fragile ecology, and the history of the people—both of the societies and of the political systems.

THE ECOLOGY

Climate

In societies whose low level of technological development renders them particularly vulnerable to the effects of imbalances of nature such as droughts, accidents of climate may be closely related to great social and political mutations. A case in point is the area of west-central Africa today known as Angola, an area of poor soil and great variations in rainfall where, in addition to frequent, relatively insignificant short periods of drought, major droughts occur in almost every decade and a drought of seven years or more comes nearly once in a century.[2] Between 1550 and 1830, some 170 droughts and epidemics (which are usually a consequence of drought) have been recorded. Social revolutions of a structural kind seem to have corre-

7

sponded to the major periods of drought: thus, at the close of the sixteenth century, the Jaga revolution, coinciding with a breakdown of agriculture, encouraged the emergence of the Imbangala, warriors who adopted pillage as a way of life and were much used by the Portuguese in the conduct of the slave trade. Were these not, in fact, hordes of desperate marauders, forced to move onto areas less affected by aridity? This hypothesis is corroborated by oral tradition in the form of a myth of origin employing a metaphor of food: once a group of desperately hungry travelers were able to find relief only by taking the sorghum and millet found in the gizzard of a bird (a reference to the return of part of the group to agriculture once the drought had ended). Moreover, the conduct and ideology of the Imbangala seem to derive from their extreme penury; for example, the ritual murder of children and cannibalistic rites could be expedients to which major periods of famine had reduced them. At any rate, the Imbangala raids resumed when a drought occurred (in 1630–1640 and again in 1650).

Similarly, the drought that lasted from 1784 through 1793 favored a renewal of precolonial Portuguese domination, for those affected flocked to less densely populated areas—the kingdoms of Kasanje and Matamba, the central Kwango valley, and the Ovimbundu states of the central plateaus. Therefore, hunger delivered many victims into the hands of the slave-traders, sold by their masters, or even by their parents, as a means of surviving scanty harvests.

A similar relationship among drought, demography, and migrations can be reconstructed in the northern interlacustrine region of present-day Uganda.[3] During the last millennium, political history has been affected by climate. Research into the dynastic chronologies handed down by oral tradition (going back to the tenth or eleventh century), an examination of the water levels recorded by the Egyptians from the eighth century onward, and the succession of droughts (identified by determining the lowest levels of the White Nile) together reveal that in the history of Uganda—the rise, climax, and decline of clans and tribes and, even more tellingly, of dynasties—political crises were due, above all, to the ecological disorders produced by lack of water.

The Effects of Agriculture

The revolutionary introduction of cassava and maize by the Portuguese had considerable demographic consequences in the fifteenth and sixteenth centuries: in the short run, at least, the spread of cassava, an easy plant to cultivate, increased the demographic capacity of the Congo Basin, although in the long run this was counterbalanced by the higher rates of sickness and mortality caused by the low nutritional value of the new plant.

Much earlier, the diffusion of crops had permitted Bantu expansion from the Congo Basin at the expense of the hunters and gatherers (Pygmies, Bushmen) who had inhabited those areas. Later, the adoption of maize, red beans, sweet potatoes, and then regular potatoes—all plants of American origin—played similar roles at different periods, and these revolutions continued until very late. Thus maize, which reached the northern Congo Basin after 1830, became a major Zande crop only in about 1900. Unknown in Kenya until about 1880 and cultivated only on the east coast until the end of that century, maize has just recently become important in central Africa, and yet today the whole of eastern and southern Africa, from Kenya to the Cape, appears to the traveler to be an agrarian civilization based on the association of maize and livestock.

The landscape of the tiny country of Rwanda, despite its sheltered position as a mountain refuge tucked away among the lakes of the Rift at the very heart of the continent, has likewise been transformed. Still cultivated using almost Neolithic methods, that is, with a preindustrial technology, today all the land is devoted to nonnative crops (leaving virtually no pasture for cattle). With the exception of bananas (which arrived via the Indian Ocean about the tenth century) and pyrethrum (which probably came from China), Rwanda subsists entirely on crops of American origin—red beans, maize, cassava, potato—even though local species of beans and eleusine once existed there. In the northwest, in association with the Institute of Peru, the cultivation of a variety of potato specially suited to the volcanic mountains there has brought about a kind of "green revolution," competing successfully with the "cash crop" of tea even though the latter is of world-renowned quality. The high population density of the country may well be a direct result of this success.

Similarly, it was only in the twentieth century that cassava cultivation spread rapidly in western Africa, at first on the coast and then, after 1920, in the interior. On the Nigerian coast, its success from that time forward at the expense of the yam, which is far more labor-intensive, reflected the magnitude of the crisis of subsistence created by the disorganization of agriculture and shortage of food, compounded by World War I and the epidemic of Spanish influenza in the years 1918–1919. At that time, of the nine million inhabitants of southern Nigeria, as many as two hundred and fifty thousand people died: adults were more vulnerable than children, the young than the old, the men than the women. Thus, the major losses were of young adult males, with a consequent decline in the labor force and in productivity: markets, roads, and "native courts" were closed; schools and churches were transformed into makeshift hospitals. Oral accounts confirm that the widespread cultivation of cassava coincided with this tragic episode,[4] and its rapid spread also matched the new urban growth. Town-dwellers appreciated the virtues of *garri* flour, which was cheap and was easy to prepare and, especially, to store. The arrival of commercial trucking and the completion of the railway in central and western Nigeria facilitated transport from the area of production to the areas of consumption—mining, administrative, and commercial centers.

Still more recently, rice has taken hold on the Ivory Coast. Whereas the colonizers never succeeded in imposing its cultivation, nowadays the smallest piece of low ground is used for growing rice—at present, it is true, for sale rather than for subsistence.

Despite these examples, one should not attempt to account for events in the precolonial period entirely by meteorological determinism or to explain demographic crises solely in terms of colonial coercion. One basic question remains unanswered: Have demographic expansions been caused by such changes in production as the introduction of new plants by the Arabs or the Portuguese, or is demography an independent variable, situated more or less outside the sphere of history?[5]

The problem first arises in connection with the Neolithic revolution of the sixth millennium B.C., which brought about the spread of agriculture south of the Sahara toward Ethiopia and West Africa some three thousand years ago. Did the transition to agriculture promote demographic growth which in turn favored the diffusion of new techniques? Or, on the contrary, did a disturbance in the demographic equilibrium of the hunter-gatherers force them into a new and, generally speaking, less attractive way of life that involved more work and a more stringent organization of labor? The Neolithic revolution can hardly be explained by the inadequacy of the size of the population in relation to its environment; on the contrary, the first agricultural settlements appeared at a period of favorable climatic conditions both in Egypt and in southwestern Asia. The disequilibrating factor was, if anything, an independent increase in the population, in much the same way—if I may offer such a bold analogy—as in England in the eighteenth century a demographic revolution gave rise to an agricultural revolution which in turn brought about the industrial revolution.

In ancient Africa, demographic growth over the long term was in all probability very slow for many centuries at a time, as is indicated by archeological sources, which date the relatively intense population of the sub-Sahara not from the beginnings of agriculture or of ironworking, but from much later, scarcely more than a thousand years ago, at the beginning of what in Bantu Africa is called the Later Iron Age.[6] This acceleration was intensified with contacts with foreigners—first Arabs, and then Europeans.

DEMOGRAPHIC DISCONTINUITY IN THE
TWENTIETH CENTURY

In demography, as in other spheres, the twentieth century has been a time of marked historical change. This change has taken place in two stages: a relatively sharp demographic decline at the time of the European conquest of

Africa, and an unprecedented population explosion beginning in the 1930s and culminating after World War II.

The decline can be explained as resulting from a number of afflictions of unprecedented intensity, unleashed on the precolonial world by the clash of two types of society: epidemics on a scale hitherto unknown in Africa (even if advances in hygiene generally prevented disasters like the one that decimated the American Indian population four or five centuries previously), ecological upheavals (resulting from the exploitation of virgin forest or the spread of speculative cultivation), and, finally and perhaps primarily, the dislocation of society. Opinions as to the precise chronology vary, but it is clear that there was a marked population decline in the last third of the nineteenth century and often in the first quarter of the twentieth.

The recovery may in turn be explained by the first sanitary measures, including the campaign against the great epidemic diseases such as sleeping sickness, and the first vaccinations (against smallpox and yellow fever), which greatly reduced the rates of mortality.

Previous to this, the evolution was much less clear. Were there or were there not sudden drastic changes? Much has been said about the negative demographic effects of the slave trade, which from the mid-seventeenth to the mid-nineteenth century were no doubt considerable but were probably diffuse, uneven. They doubtless took effect more over the medium and even the long term (owing to the changes brought about in the ratio between the sexes and in reproductivity) than as a sudden break at any given moment.

More rapid, from the sixteenth century on, were the consequences of the African contact with the American Indian world as expressed in the "cassava revolution." From that time on, the agricultural frontier of the forest was continually pushed forward by the combined efforts of the forest-dwellers and the agriculturalists. This resulted in a drastic change in demographic centers. The forest, until the end of the fifteenth century, was a relatively unpopulated area, inhabited by hunters and gatherers and, along the edge of the coast and by the side of the lagoons, by fishermen. Their major resources were fish and yams, plus leaves, fruits, and small animals.

The population of the forested area increased at first very slowly and then accelerated as time went on. Five hundred years ago, the forest zone contained perhaps a quarter of the total population of the continent and two-fifths of sub-Saharan Africa, increasing to two-fifths and nearly half, respectively, by about 1850. At the present time the situation has been reversed, with half the population of the continent and five-eighths of that of sub-Saharan Africa living in the forested areas. In the last five centuries, the population of the forested areas may have grown by a factor of twenty, compared to only six or seven in the rest of Africa. The rate of increase in the population of these areas today is tremendous, encouraged as it was by the colonizers, who tended to regard the rainy and forested areas as the "useful" ones (except in southern Africa), and accentuated by the increasing disparity between the "underdeveloped" (particularly Sahelo-Sudanese) states of the interior and the states that are said to be "developing" due to their coastlines (for example, the Ivory Coast and Nigeria).

THE RHYTHM OF DEMOGRAPHIC FLUCTUATIONS

Demography touches the very foundation of humanity. Not only does it correspond to man's biological need to survive and to prosper, but it is connected with his metaphysical realization that survival is ultimately impossible. Right from the start, demographic reactions must be interpreted in both economic and ideological terms.[7]

The Forces of Life

At the present time, the average number of children born alive to each woman in Africa is close to seven, and the general birthrate is about 50 per thousand, although certain areas, such as the east coast and Central Africa (northern Zaire, the Central African Republic, Gabon, Cameroon, Rio Muni), do have lower rates (the phenomenon of the relative sterility of women in these areas is probably recent and is as yet ill explained). Overall, however, Africa at present has the highest birthrate of any continent.

It is a common belief of the African peoples that children are the greatest goods; the worst fate for a woman is to be sterile. A woman is also the greatest possession to acquire, as she represents the forces of production and, above all, of reproduction. These facts lead us to suppose that the forces of life affecting the birth and possible survival of children were perhaps greater in Africa than in the West.[8]

One key to the understanding of the history of development in the West is the initiatory role played by a demographic upsurge that brought an economic progress which was in the long run never nullified or swamped by an equal or greater increase in the number of consumers. Progress thus depended on a long-lasting general prosperity, guaranteed by the capacity of the European societies to regulate their numbers in each period in accordance with the productive forces of the moment. It is true that the Middle Ages were afflicted by a number of "natural" calamities that resulted at times in the reintroduction of a drastic demographic control which population acceleration over too long a period had been in danger of obliterating; the Black Plague of the mid-fourteenth century, which probably wiped out a third of the population, was the prototype of these calamities. Another, though less extreme, factor seems to have been changes in outlook that reinforced or even replaced control by the ecology. Thus, in the thirteenth century, at the end of the long period of medieval demographic growth, a sud-

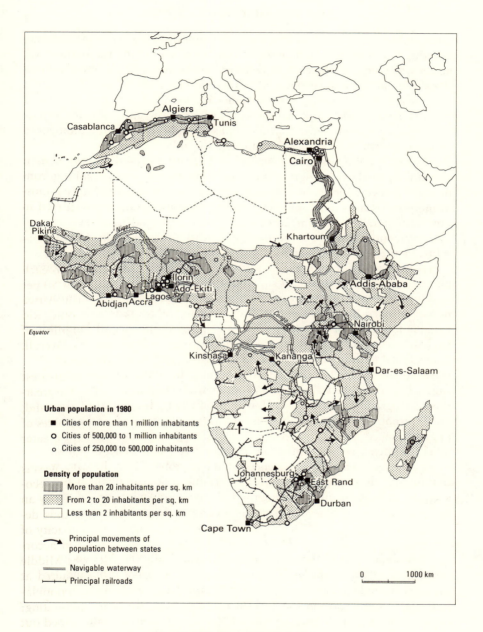

Urban population in 1980

- ■ Cities of more than 1 million inhabitants
- ◉ Cities of 500,000 to 1 million inhabitants
- ○ Cities of 250,000 to 500,000 inhabitants

Density of population

- More than 20 inhabitants per sq. km
- From 2 to 20 inhabitants per sq. km
- Less than 2 inhabitants per sq. km

➤ Principal movements of
population between states

══ Navigable waterway

├──┤ Principal railroads

0   1000 km

Map 1. The Population of Africa

den ideological reversal came about. One sign of this was the Albigensian doctrine that the world of men was the creation not of God but of the devil, and it was therefore the duty of believers to end the renewal of the generations. Similarly, the recurrence of witch-hunts at the end of the sixteenth century and the beginning of the seventeenth seem to have expressed a sort of fury against women and their power of procreation; and under the impact of famine, even the Irish, so Catholic and so prolific, ceased for a moment to regard the birth of a child as the supreme social blessing.

Thus the premodern world experienced cycles of growth that were periodically arrested by demographic catastrophes at least partly resulting from this very growth. Clear objective causes such as wars of conquest by groups in the process of demographic expansion, famines (produced by crop failures and aggravated by meteorological events), or epidemics (exacerbated by famine-induced malnutrition) ought not to render us oblivious to more subtle factors, to social processes and currents connected with the history of ideas and ways of thinking. We must explore whether this type of control played a role in Africa, and, if so, what form it took.

Before the twentieth century, demographic demands in Africa probably never exceeded the means of subsistence available. Moreover, accompanying this low level of population was a relative abundance of land, which probably accounted for the lack of technical progress in agriculture. The Africans failed to develop agricultural techniques not because they were backward (as the colonizers claimed), but because their low technological level sufficed for their needs. Technical progress was superfluous in this extensive itinerant agriculture, which was low in productivity but constituted an adequate response both to fragile soils and irregular rains and to the problems of subsistence.[9]

This evidence reinforces the idea that the forces of life encouraging maximum procreation almost never encountered any obstacle in the African way of thinking (although, on a local level, certain rites of cannibalism and child sacrifice such as one finds among the Imbangala of Angola or the Manja of Central Africa may have been signs of a contrary tendency).

The Forces of Death

Only slightly lower than that of today, historically the African birthrate could generally be considered invariable: about 47.5 per thousand, on the average. It might be expected that this would have resulted in a relatively long-standing increase in the African population, a display of remarkably strong forces of life. It must be acknowledged, however, in order to explain the present demographic weakness, that the forces of death have proved to be even stronger, and it is the modulations of the deathrate that have decided the rhythms of natural demographic variations.

A hypothesis of relative demographic stability would presuppose a deathrate similar to the birthrate, implying a life expectancy of about twenty-one years, but this is exaggerated. All the evidence indicates slow growth over a long period, which on a number of occasions gave rise to local demographic pressures that were sufficient to make a considerable mark on historical evolution.

An average slow growth-rate of about 0.5 percent a year would make the mortality rate drop to 45 per thousand with a life expectancy of twenty-two years. By comparison with the rates existing today in the areas farthest removed from modern sanitary services, that rate still seems too high. The most plausible hypothesis, then, is that of a far more pronounced rate of growth, for limited periods or regions sometimes reaching 2 percent a year. This would be compensated for by the periodic occurrence of phases of disequilibrium accompanied by natural or social cataclysms—in short, in a perhaps somewhat harsher version, the classic pattern of premodern Western demography.

Although in general the demographic pressure remained low, that did not rule out local or regional imbalances. Every time the period during which land was allowed to lie fallow was shortened, the demographic pressure was accompanied by a corresponding rise in the deathrate, for high population density led to malnutrition, which in turn promoted the spread of infectious diseases. It is a fact that, from the sixteenth century onward, periods of drought in Angola in which the population had to group together in the dampest areas were always accompanied by epidemics.

Finally, an increase in population inevitably involved an escalation of conflict between rival groups. Wars aimed at increasing the area a group controlled, and consequently mortality rose, especially for the vanquished group, either as a direct result of the war or, over a longer period, because of the resultant reduction in lands and crops. As for the victorious group, even if, for the moment, it could maintain its natural rate of growth or even improve it by spreading into new territory, this did not necessarily guarantee a positive rate for the entire area. Thus, at the end of the eighteenth century and the beginning of the nineteenth, the Zulu expansion in southeast Africa involved conquest of the high lands of the inner Rand which emptied them of their inhabitants and thus left them wide open to the advance of the Boer colonizers. Later, we shall see in the nineteenth and even the twentieth century the frequency of a correlation between the occurrence of droughts, famines, scarcities, and epizootic diseases, on the one hand, and demographic rhythms, on the other. The latter were made up of an alternation between phases of high mortality and a following compensatory leap in the birthrate (a phenomenon well known to demographers)—for instance, through a lowering of the age of marriage, greater freedom for girls, and an extension of polygyny.[10] All these phenomena were intensified in Africa south of the Sahara by the tropical natural conditions (later aggravated by hasty colonizer actions), since the critical threshold of population density beyond which the sickness ratio could become disastrous—threatening to reduce the population for decades—was remarkably low. A case in point can serve to illustrate our argument by showing both the slowness and the difficulties of the demographic growth of a certain subgroup, the Ani-Ndenye of the southeast Ivory Coast.[11]

From an initial nucleus of two thousand to three thousand inhabitants— a density lower than one per square kilometer—the population probably quadrupled in two centuries, a far from negligible increase. One sign of this growth was the appearance, in three successive waves, of new villages which one after another filled in the vacant spaces between the others, while always remaining under the political control of the dominant families.

But the cost was great: most of the time, natural population growth was almost nil. Mortality, especially infant mortality, was very high: this can be seen from the behavior of the group, which tended to minimize the value of children, regarding them as incomplete persons; only a woman's fourth dead child had the right to a funeral. Whereas the death of an adult was always felt as a mutilation and an abnormality, since it could have been due to other than natural causes, the death of a child at birth or in infancy was regarded as a quite natural phenomenon. The chronic demographic malaise can also be seen in the number of "demographic accidents" that interrupted the normal line of succession in the royal families. On several occasions, a dynasty lacked any male heir, a particularly serious situation in this matrilinear society in which, if women transmitted power and goods, it was the men who wielded the power and disposed of the goods. And yet the reproductive potential of the women of royal lineage seems to have been exploited to the full. They enjoyed the greatest freedom in their choice of a partner; he could even be a captive or a passing stranger.

At last the only remedy was to violate the laws of sanctity of the group, by turning to foreigners who had either come of their own free will, been taken by force, or been adopted through marriage. Thus, the phenomenon of migration was originally indissociable from the demographic phenomenon, a fact which was particularly evident in Africa, where displacements of peoples were a constant factor of history.

AN OVERVIEW OF AFRICAN POPULATION

Starting with these preliminary observations, we can attempt to evaluate the size of the sub-Saharan African population in history, and to identify its major fluctuations. Was Africa perhaps once the most highly populated continent in the world?

The facts and figures most frequently given are not necessarily the most accurate. Even the United Nations, in a retrospective view, refers to B. Riccioli's assessment in the seventeenth century.[12] Riccioli, a Jesuit who attached much importance to the mystical value of numbers, estimated the population of the world at roughly one billion, divided among the continents. This estimate has more or less as much value as the rough-and-ready one concerning the slave trade given by an American journalist at the end of the nineteenth century, which has been cited as authoritative and slavishly recopied in one work after another up to some of the most recent studies of the question.[13] It is true that Riccioli's figures were challenged half a century ago in Willcox's works, which themselves were corrected shortly afterward by Saunders and then more recently by Durand, who finally arrived at a compromise between the previous estimates.[14] The historians of demography, both of Africa and of the rest of the world, have, needless to say, accepted these figures only with reservations.

What, nevertheless, should we think of Riccioli's estimate of a hundred million Africans in 1650? If this number is accurate, Africa must have been one of the most highly populated areas in the world (together with China, with a hundred and thirteen million, and India, with a hundred million), whereas today it is comparatively little populated (it would have accounted for nearly 20 percent of the world's population in 1650, compared to only 13 percent in 1750, 10 percent in 1800, and 9 percent in 1960).[15] Archeology has begun to come to our aid (showing, for instance, that Mali, south of the Niger Basin, was once a cultivated area, at least at the beginning of our era), but proof remains scarce. Such evidence as exists is founded on the idea that, by and large, until about a century ago the population enjoyed a remarkable stability of long duration. However, a very slow rate of growth—around 0.25 percent—could have permitted the population to double or even to quadruple over half a millennium, if the deathrate, as is in fact very likely, was only 2.5 per thousand lower than the birthrate.

If this population growth failed to occur—with all the implications of stagnation this holds for history—it was because the forces of death were stronger in Africa than elsewhere. Two factors contributed to this: a relative hostility, or at least vulnerability, of the natural environment, which was at any rate harsher than elsewhere; and external factors that heavily affected the demography of Africa (the slave trade, colonial coercion).

NATURAL HANDICAPS

Without falling into geographical determinism, we may legitimately ask why agriculture, which appeared in the Sudan about 4000 B.C., took five millennia to become the dominant mode of subsistence further south, in the dry savannas; or why the wheel, known to the ancient Egyptians and attested to in the Sahara, was not adopted further south. It was no doubt because the environment was hardly suitable, probably because of insufficient rainfall and unfavorable soil, while, still further south, the wet savannas and forests, which potentially had more to offer, were the foci from which radiated parasitic diseases especially weakening for the human organism. The people of the Pleistocene age were already familiar, notably, with malaria, viral hepatitis, and herpes, and they had probably learned to avoid areas infested with the tsetse fly, the carrier of sleeping sickness.[16] The spread of this disease in wet areas, as well as of malaria (transmitted by Anopheles mosquitoes) and onchocerciasis may explain why, since valleys were avoided in ancient Africa, irrigated agriculture was rarely practiced.[17] This is very different from the idea, formerly held, that the Sahelo-Sudanese peasant societies stagnated because the "barbarian prosperity" of the country provided them with a comparatively luxurious existence which did not encourage them (as conditions did for those in medieval Poland, for instance) to experiment with difficult technological innovations. On the contrary, everything leads us to believe that if the response was weak, it was because the "challenge" of the natural environment then seemed insurmountable.[18]

If, however, we were now to fall into a geographical determinism, giving it the quality of inevitability, that would no doubt be going too far. The African continent was the only one to undergo such a long drawn-out demographic stagnation (the population fell to 95 million in 1750 and remained at that level for another century), while the population of China tripled from 1600 to 1850, reaching at least 350 million, that of Western Europe increased considerably despite the general drop in the seventeenth century (when the figures for the French population once more became what they had been in the thirteenth century), and the population of India grew from 100 to nearly 150 million in the same period.[19] To explain these figures we must seek further. It is in this context that we should assess the significance of the controversy concerning the demographic implications of another phenomenon which—is it coincidence?—is also peculiar to sub-Saharan Africa: the slave trade.

2

The Effects of the Atlantic
Slave Trade

Two interpretations of the demographic effects of the slave trade, one minimalist and the other maximalist, have been offered, and these tend to correspond with the ideological positions of their proponents. Everyone today agrees about the total number of slaves transported across the Atlantic, but there is a difference in viewpoint between the Third Worldist "progressives," for whom these figures are deeply significant for African demography, and the "moderates" or conservatives—nearly all of whom are non-African—who insist on their relative unimportance. Let us examine the record.

THE DATA ON EXPORTATION

In 1969 was published an assessment based on an exhaustive quantitative analysis of data on slaves who disembarked in America (from the archives of the various countries of the New World for ports, customhouses, and so forth).[1] Although they have been debated and sometimes amended,[2] the conclusions then reached have not been seriously challenged—except in a partisan manner—and a very recent assessment, arrived at by a scholar rather ideologically different from the previous one, through a very different process of inquiry ends by confirming the essential accuracy of the initial estimate.[3]

About 11.7 million people were exported toward America between 1450 and 1900, with an average deathrate on the slave ships of about 13 percent. The distribution of this trade over the centuries was very uneven: more than half of the slaves (52 percent) left in the eighteenth century, less than 20 percent before then (mostly in the seventeenth century), and nearly 30 percent in the nineteenth century, which was dominated by the illegal slave traffic and the revival of the Arab slave trade. Almost the same number, although over a longer period (from the eighth to the nineteenth century) were ex-

19

TABLE 1.   The Atlantic and Saharan Slave Trade from Africa,
1450–1900

	Atlantic slave trade (in millions)	% of total	Saharan slave trade (in millions)	% of total	Total (in millions)
1450–1600	0.367	3.1%	0.9	25.5%	1.3
1601–1700	1.868	16.0	0.710	20.1	2.6
1701–1800	6.133	52.4	0.715	20.3	6.8
1801–1900	3.330	28.5	1.2	34.1	4.5
Total	11.698	100.0%	3.525	100.0%	15.2

SOURCES: P. E. Lovejoy, "The Volume of the Atlantic Slave Trade: A Synthesis," *Journal of African History* 23 (1982): 473–501; R. Austen, "The Trans-Saharan Slave Trade: A Tentative Census," in H. A. Gemery and S. J. Hogendorn, eds., *The Uncommon Market: Essays in the Economic History of the Atlantic Slave Trade* (New York, 1979), pp. 23–76.

ported in slave trade from the Sahara (including the Nile valley) toward the Mediterranean countries (7.4 million plus 1.4 million who died on the journey, half of this trade taking place from the tenth to the beginning of the sixteenth century), and 5 million were taken over the Indian Ocean, more than a third of them in the nineteenth century (see Table 1).

We should add, in an attempt to bring this debate to at least a provisional conclusion, that the correctness of this general estimate is corroborated by a technical factor: the number and the capacity of the transport ships available during these years. There is no point, therefore, in trying to stress the sheer wickedness of the slave trade by inventing fantastically high figures—a hundred or two hundred million slaves transported—as used to be done not so very long ago.[4]

The Atlantic figures were probably negligible until the seventeenth century. Before that time, slaves were still comparatively rare, used locally in the mines (especially in the Caribbean) or as luxuries (as domestic servants, for example). It was from the time that they became major instruments of production that they were imported in large numbers: the growth of the slave trade coincided with the development of the sugar plantations, which began about the middle of the seventeenth century in Brazil and spread to the British Antilles (Jamaica, Barbados) and, in the eighteenth century, to the Caribbean Islands (to the English, to the French—Guadeloupe and Martinique—and finally, at the beginning of the nineteenth century, to the Spanish possession—Cuba). The main demand for slaves thus existed from the 1660s to the first decades of the nineteenth century, culminating in the

century of maximum extension of the sugarcane industry, roughly from 1740 to 1830.[5]

This division into periods enables us to answer those who utilize macroeconomic arguments in order to minimize the demographic effects of the slave trade. Over the period as a whole, to be sure, the loss of population appears small—less than 0.5 percent a year—but this figure is not valid for any length of time within that period.

It is surely more reasonable to suppose that this drainage of millions of individuals (more than 10 percent of the total population in scarcely two centuries, after all) could not fail to have had demographic and social effects: demographic because, without this drainage, not only would the size of the African population have been larger, but also its distribution—by age, by sex and, above all, by region—would have been completely different, with immeasurable political and social consequences.[6]

AN UNKNOWN FACTOR: THE TOTAL DEMOGRAPHIC LOSS

The dimensions of this factor are difficult to determine and will probably remain so. The number of slaves who left for America can be calculated, but not the total number of people lost in the traffic, including those who went astray on the African continent and the slaves who died before having even set foot on the ship, either in the unhealthful barracoons on the coast where they waited, sometimes for several months, to be taken across the Atlantic, or in their cross-country journey to get there, or—to go back even further—in the events surrounding their capture, which generally took place in the course of local or regional intestine wars of incursion. In short, to gain an idea of the deathrate incurred by the system, the whole of the economic, political, and military context must be taken into account. In this area, however, statistics are infinitely malleable. The results differ greatly depending on whether we hypothesize, for instance, that for every slave transported there was one who died in Africa, or five. Take, for example, West Africa, where we know the figures for the eighteenth century with some accuracy: by regression we can estimate the population of West Africa at that time at about twenty million inhabitants, since there were twenty-eight million around 1850.[7] Between 1760 and 1840, slave-traders transported a maximum of 60,000 people a year. If we take these figures at face value, the population loss, at about 0.2–0.3 percent, may seem fairly limited, since it was considerably lower than the rate of natural increase of the population (perhaps 1 percent),[8] but if we suppose that for every slave who was transported at least two or perhaps as many as five were lost—in wars, in the resultant disorders, and through the demographic consequences of deporting a large segment of the most fertile age group—this phenomenon, if only because it was so long-lasting, was sufficient to arrest demographic growth, at least locally, and thus to upset the political evolution of the region enough to bring about major demographic changes. Where the comparative evolution of the continents was concerned, to arrest demographic growth was a particularly serious matter in the eighteenth century, for it was at that time that Western Europe was undergoing its demographic revolution preliminary to the industrial revolution. To conclude from this that the slave trade underlay African underdevelopment requires only a single step more, and one that has recently been taken.[9]

Two separate lines of argument point to this conclusion. One, a study by L. M. Diop, attempts a retrospective evaluation of sub-Saharan Africa population losses, using a simple scheme of mathematical calculation that may surprise demographers. Starting with the known population of about 120 million in 1948, after deducting the 70 million lost through the repercussions of the colonial conquest (we shall return to this), the population of Africa around 1850 was estimated at 190 million. Assuming, once again quite arbitrarily, and yet plausibly—though probably with some exaggeration—that some 70 million in all were lost through the slave trade, Diop concludes that on the eve of the European voyages of discovery, sub-Saharan Africa must have had a minimum population of 190 to 200 million inhabitants: about double the figure usually given. At the very least, many microeconomic hints in Arab and Portuguese sources suggest that in ancient West Africa there was a far larger and denser population than is generally supposed by Western scholars. Despite some obvious oversimplifications (it is not enough, in order to estimate the size of a population at some period in the past, simply to restore its demographic losses without taking into account accompanying effects such as a rise in the birthrate or deathrate) and gross exaggerations (such as giving sixteenth-century Africa, regardless of the geographical evidence relating to soil and rainfall, an average population density similar to that of southern Asia, or, without substantiation, multiplying the accepted figure for exportation prior to 1700 by five), as well as a bland ignorance of the literature on the subject in English, it remains a fascinating hypothesis. It presents the history of African demography as an evolution that was not simply slowed down or even stagnant, but was positively eaten away by the inroads of outside intervention—first by slave-trading and then by colonization. She reaches this striking conclusion: "Black Africa in 1500? An unknown population. In 1930? An explicable underpopulation. In 1980? An unbalanced repopulation."[10]

This idea seems, at any rate, to be supported in a parallel study by J. E. Inikori, who claims that in the mid-nineteenth century, sub-Saharan Africa (again, he is extrapolating from West Africa) displayed every sign of being underpopulated.[11] He believes that three factors contributed to this state of affairs: the unfavorable ecological conditions, the Atlantic slave trade, and the disturbed political situation worldwide, itself in large part traceable to the numerous social consequences of the slave trade. In two centuries, according to Inikori, the drainage of the population through the slave trade, both toward the south (between 6 and 8.5 million) [12] and toward the north (2 million), had risen to 8 or 9 million people altogether, or more than a third of the total. Had these remained in Africa, it seems reasonable to say that they would have become 45 million by about 1870, or, on the continent as a whole, the 25 million deported—taking all the slave trades together—would by 1880 have constituted an additional population of more than 100 million. This, then, would prove a considerable decline in the African population between the seventeenth and the nineteenth century.

Both these lines of argument we have examined have a serious disadvantage: they ignore or downplay the laws of cyclic demographic control through an increase in the deathrate, which could have brought the African population down to a lower level even if the slave trade had not been operative. Still, nothing prevents us from supposing that the demographic pressures which might then have exerted themselves could have had as dynamic an influence on the history of precolonial Africa as they had in the West.

DIFFERENTIAL EFFECTS:
THE DEMOGRAPHIC FACTOR

In fact, an overall assessment of the demographic losses due to the slave trade has little more value than any other continent-wide average such as rainfall or the density of the population per square kilometer. It may be more instructive to analyze the demographic differences in relation to the specific political, social, and demographic contexts of the slave trade.

The effects of the slave trade might be very different, depending on whether the captives were taken from an over- or an underpopulated area. It may be asked whether in West Africa, once again, the regions most affected had or did not have a population density that could recuperate without too much difficulty. As the slave trade preferred young adult males, an extended practice of polygyny could have constituted a demographic response as long as the ratio between the sexes did not become hopelessly unbalanced. It has been estimated that, in order to maintain a very low rate of increase—about 0.2 percent—in a population in which the ratio had fallen to eighty men per hundred women, a group providing 1,000 slaves would have had to have consisted of at least 368,000 individuals.[13] Using this as a model, we must now examine the calculated—or at least estimated—threshold of population density of the regions most affected by the slave trade at the height of their involvement. These figures suggest the uncertainty of our knowledge of the context: to endure the slave trade, the population density around 1800 would have had to exceed 5.2 per square kilometer in Senegal, 11.7 in Guinea, 16.5 in Angola, 31.2 in Ghana, 37.1 on the Ivory Coast, and up to 40 in the Bay of Biafra. Although not impossible, these figures, which still represent an overgeneralized approach, are by no means indisputable.

What *is* indisputable is that wherever the slave trade entered, the structure and demographic habits of the population were altered. A good illustration of this point is Angola at the end of the eighteenth century. We are fortunate in having, for two consecutive years, 1777 and 1778, records of a census of the Angolan population under Portuguese domination according to age, sex, social status (freeman or slave), and race (White, half-caste, Black). Even if the demographic analysis suffers from this remarkable record's very localized character (as it deals with a somewhat ill-defined region roughly subdivided into three areas, the urban area of Luanda, the area of Portuguese plantations, and the area of indigenous agriculture), the results provide food for thought.[14] They show, first of all, a preponderance of women, particularly adults, and, even more, of slaves: a ratio of forty to forty-three male to every hundred female slaves. Thus, women of childbearing age were twice as numerous as men as a result of the intensity with which the slave trade was carried on from the end of the sixteenth century onward.

Nevertheless, this disequilibrium had little effect on the colony's potential for demographic growth, since it was compensated for by a maximum rate of reproduction—about 3.2 percent, or one child every three years for every woman of childbearing age. This resulted in a very high rate of demographic growth, 2.6 percent (12,000 people a year), which could have doubled the population in thirty years. This number could have permitted the slave trade to take some 16,000 people a year, if one adds the probable migration of people to Luanda owing to the desertification of the rural areas most threatened by the slave raids—a process accelerated during the recurrent droughts, which forced the affected populations to come on their own initiative and offer themselves as dependents and slaves. This happened in the years 1780–1790 in Luanda and Benguela and again in 1857, when there was mention of children sold for three or four plates of maize flour or five or six measures of cotton cloth—in other words, for less than in normal times.[15]

Here, it seems, as in West Africa, the slave trade stopped a demographic upsurge rather than significantly reducing the population. Even if it is permissible to wonder whether, considering the prevailing economic system, the low technological level, and the ecological difficulties, the region would have been able to support without grave demographic risks the individuals who were taken as slaves, Thornton takes the argument too far, interpreting the slave trade less as the cause than as the consequence of a necessarily low level of population and claiming that each recurrent phase of aridity, following a period of expansion, could only give rise to emigration, violence, and death. The problem is badly stated: the relatively strong demographic increase could equally well be seen as a response to the aggression of the slave trade. The commonly accepted correlation between the slave trade and depopulation may be mistaken. One of the favorite arguments of the minimalists is that the Nigerian coast, for instance, long a major source for the slave trade, is today one of the most populated areas of Africa. Demographic history could well be approached from an opposite and more dynamic point of view. We might rather ask, since the continual drainage had developed powers of reaction among the affected populations, which considerably augmented their ability to respond to challenges, what happened when, relatively suddenly, the slave trade was prohibited (even if it continued illegally for a period)? The compensatory demographic mechanisms, whose force of inertia is even greater than that of the socioeconomic mechanisms, could be expected to continue to operate, with the high density of population of the Nigerian coasts (the Ibo country) deriving at least in part from this new disequilibrium. Thus, certain regions of Africa that are quite densely populated today may be so not *in spite of* but *because of* the slave trade.[16] Other areas, such as the Gabon hinterland or the Nigerian Middle Belt, were by their deficient demographic potential placed in the position of being unable to cope with the aggression represented by the slave trade, and their underpopulation thus became irreversible.

REGIONAL DIFFERENCES

It is also a mistake to think that the social consequences of the slave trade were distributed uniformly. The effects depended on the prevailing conditions, on whether the coastal populations, who acted as the agents of slavery (that is to say, who used slave labor and participated in the slave trade) are under discussion, or whether it is the enslavable populations of the interior who are being considered: the raiders, or the raided. P. Manning has proposed a model that would respect these regional differences. He hypothesizes one raid a year, exporting 1 percent of the total population of the region, with 1.7 people captured on the coast and 2.5 in the interior for every slave who reached America. The figures given in parentheses correspond to this model—which, however, requires modification since the true rate was well below 1 percent.[17]

On the coast, on the one hand, the Atlantic trade mainly required male slaves for work in the fields, and the raiders also captured women to use as concubines or domestic servants. One can estimate, altogether, that all the men and half of the women captured were exported. Taking into account the additional factor of the reproductive capacity of the women captured in raids, it can be said that the population of the coastal areas, where they co-operated with the slave trade, had a tendency to increase slightly (+ 0.7 per-cent), while because of the abductions and deaths, that of the raided areas tended to diminish (− 3.3 percent). In the Sahelo-Sudanese hinterland, on the other hand, women were more expensive and more in demand, so two-thirds of the women were probably exported either to the south or the north, compared to only one-third of the men, who provided the basis for the local armies. In this case, again, the population of the raided areas di-minished (− 4.9 percent, even more than in the previous case), while the conquering populations increased (+ 2.2 percent). Even if we hypothesize that the rate of exportation in the eighteenth century was no more than 0.2 percent in the coastal regions and 0.05 percent in the hinterland, it is never-theless true that in the course of the century the population of the coastal areas would have declined by at least 15 percent. The totals for the hinter-land probably still stand, but, against this, we see a demographic shift in favor of the raiding peoples.

A recent archeological discovery supports this hypothesis. In a small area of southern Ghana, excavations have revealed that at the end of the eigh-teenth century a recent pottery tradition replaced a much older culture, which in the period between 1540 and 1740 itself succeeded a civilization that was probably millennial.[18] This was precisely the period when the re-gion became a major source of supply for the slave trade, providing first gold and then slaves. About eighteen thousand Africans left the Gold Coast be-tween 1690 and 1700, and the number tripled in the years 1741–1750. It is conceivable that within one or two generations almost the entire population of the valley was sold, despite the fortifications that were erected to defend against repeated raids. A complex process of colonization then took place, allowing the surrounding populations increasingly to attract new immi-grants by means of matrimonial alliances, this time without coming into conflict with the other peoples of the forested regions of South Ghana. We have no reason not to suppose that this radical demographic and social change due to the growth of the Atlantic slave trade happened several times in an area in which waves of migration and settlement have been recorded continually from the sixteenth and, particularly, the seventeenth and eigh-teenth centuries.

POLITICAL AND SOCIAL EFFECTS

Through the demographic upheaval combined with the institution of a new economic system, the slave trade clearly had a considerable impact on the African societies. In some areas, the slave-traders continuously handled a large number of people: this was the case on the equatorial coast from Gabon to the north of Angola which, from the fifteenth to the beginning of the nineteenth century, remained the area of exportation par excellence. In Senegambia, however, the slave trade, although it began early and maintained an even level, was relatively limited in scope. Other exporting areas had peak periods; the Bay of Benin, for example, was one of the chief sources of supply in the second half of the seventeenth century. In the eighteenth century, the slave trade became general, reaching both the west (it was flourishing on the Gold Coast around 1700) and the east (in the Bay of Biafra, center of the trade around 1740); the trans-Saharan slave trade began again with the progressive closing of the other markets, in the Mediterranean area; finally, East Africa, exploited by the Portuguese from the earliest days from their base on Mozambique, played a role of paramount importance with the rise of the abolitionist movement because, being at a distance, it escaped supervision and was consequently less vulnerable.

Just as the main areas of exploitation shifted over time, so the slave trade in the nineteenth century declined at different rates according to time and place. The decline began in the Gold Coast at the beginning of the century, but it scarcely affected the Bay of Biafra before the 1830s. It did not reach the Benin coast and Equatorial Africa until after 1850, and in the Indian Ocean the slave trade persisted until the end of the century.

Even those historians who seek to minimize the demographic impact of the slave trade agree on the importance of its social and economic consequences.[19] A parallel chronology might be made of the evolution of the slave trade and the mutations of the precolonial African societies—not only the economic mutations (involving groups and factors directly involved in the slave trade) but, above all, political and social ones. From the sixteenth century on states arose whose prosperity directly or indirectly depended on a slave-trading economy with internal consequences, such as war, that were necessary to the rounding-up of slaves, who in turn were exchanged for the European military equipment that guaranteed the technical and thus the political superiority of the group. Among such states were the coastal monarchies that came into being from the sixteenth and seventeenth centuries onward (the kingdoms of the Congo, Dahomey, and Ashanti and the city-states of the Niger delta). The military theocracies of the Sahelo-Sudanese hinterland, of which the empire of Samori was one of the last examples, also fell into this category (in these, from the eighteenth century onward, the spread of Islam appeared as a possible answer to the general malaise, causing the emergence of a new political equilibrium born of internal upheavals). Finally, there were the states openly dependent on the slave trade in the second half of the nineteenth century (beginning when the Indian Ocean slave trade took over); these extended from the Nile valley to southern Africa, from

Rabah on the shores of Lake Chad to Mirambo in Tanzania (1871–1884) and Msiri in Katanga (1860–1891).

These political upheavals were accompanied by profound social changes based on a consolidation within the country of a mode of production based on slavery, reinforced by the abundance of slave labor available. This glut increased throughout the nineteenth century as the Atlantic trade became more and more problematic, hindered and then gradually eliminated as it was, following official prohibition of the slave trade; the emancipation of the slaves in the American colonies put an end to the traffic altogether.[20] It has been estimated that, on the eve of colonization, a quarter of the population of West Africa had slave status.[21] Slaves thus formed the bulk of armies that grew larger and larger, both in West and East Africa, and that had a destabilizing effect on the general situation. They also constituted a labor force that was integrated into an expanding productive economy. They worked in the palm-oil industry in Dahomey and by the "oil rivers" at the mouths of the Niger. They were also employed in the textile industries: in the Sahelo-Sudanese towns and in the Swahili cities on the coast of the Indian Ocean, such as Gumbu in Mali[22] and Kano in northern Nigeria, whose long, narrow bands of cotton cloth were sold throughout West Africa; and in Mukdisho in southern Somalia, where the textile industry, which dated from the Middle Ages, underwent unprecedented growth in the second half of the nineteenth century owing to the systematic use of slaves on the cotton plantations.[23]

We can understand, therefore, how the definitive emancipation of the slaves imposed by the colonial laws contributed to a total disintegration of the socioeconomic foundation of the African societies. Toward the end of the nineteenth century, at any rate, probably under the influence of slave-trading systems which went back several hundreds of years, the institution of slavery was not only—as we read in the somewhat mythical or idealized accounts of the first anthropologists—a largely social practice of a domestic and patriarchal character, of only marginal economic importance for the societies concerned. A precolonial "slave mode of production," making the slave into both a product and a means of production and of reproduction, had become firmly established and had an enormous influence on the organization, throughout the nineteenth century, of so-called legitimate trade.[24] The jobs of pickers, planters, and especially porters—in fact, the totality of this labor force—had generally originally been filled by slaves.[25] The abolition of slavery toward the end of the century thus caused numerous internal problems. Not only were the traditional markets and systems harmed and even often destroyed (as in the Congo Basin), but the reintegration of suddenly liberated slaves caused such serious difficulties that the colonial administration often had no option but to postpone execution of the measure.

Thus in the Gold Coast the emancipation decreed in 1874 had little effect before the 1900s, and in French West Africa the transitional solution was attempted of "freedom villages," which in fact only perpetuated slavery in another form.[26] Small political entities in the center of the continent, protected by their geographical remoteness (such as Burundi or Rwanda in the lacustrine zone) alone remained unaffected by this evolution or, at worst, only slightly affected.[27]

3

Demography and Colonization

As the influence of industrialized Europe became increasingly overt, African demography evolved in three main stages, which once again, and even more clearly than before, took a serrated form. First, the immediate precolonial period, from the 1850s to the 1880s, was probably one of demographic growth, vigorously checked, however, by the "classic" controls of premodern times—that is, by droughts and their consequent debilitating famines and epidemics. The Western presence exacerbated these effects, and, in turn, the weakened population became more vulnerable to European intervention. Second, the first phase of colonialism, 1890 to 1920 or 1930, was undoubtedly, on the whole, a period of strong demographic recession. And, finally, from the years 1925–1935, following the first sanitary measures, came a recovery and then an upsurge which after World War II became an unprecedented population explosion.

PRECOLONIAL EAST AFRICA

Scholarly opinion is divided on the difficult problem of precolonial African demography. Thus, some studies have suggested that in East Africa the population grew moderately but nevertheless significantly throughout the nineteenth century and that this growth was broken only by colonization in the final decades.[1] Others find evidence for constant demographic restraints in the form of the droughts, which gave rise to recurrent famines and epidemics, quite aside from the drain of the slave trade.[2] The debate has centered on two points: the interaction of natural demographic growth and ecological factors, the relative importance of each of which has been variously assessed; and the degree of contact of East Africa with the outside world.[3]

Those who support the hypothesis of an increase in population base their reasoning not on statistical proofs, which do not exist, but on agronomical arguments: there are undeniably signs of a process of rural development having taken place in the nineteenth century. In Tanzania emerged agricultural systems of greater productivity based on maize and rice, indicative of breaking new ground. The number of livestock increased and the pastoral economy spread out—a sign, in an area where sleeping sickness was endemic, of the efficient functioning of a control mechanism of "horticultural prophylaxis." Following the upheavals of the colonial invasion, however, depopulation led to a loss of control of the environment, vitiating this mechanism and resulting in the spread of epidemics at the end of the century.

The damage done by the Arab-Zanzibar slave trade, to which attention has sometimes been drawn, has no doubt been exaggerated. Giving credence to the explorers of the period (Livingstone claimed that Zanzibar alone handled twenty-one million slaves), historians have tended to overstress the heinousness of the "barbarities" and massacres perpetrated by the "natives"; the absence of critical studies on the transcriptions of myths and legends has done the rest. If these wars were rather spectacular, the victims were less numerous than has been said: during the whole of the nineteenth century, a maximum of two million people were taken via the Indian Ocean or reduced to slavery in Africa in the course of war. Half were transported to southern Arabia via the Gulf of Tajurra or were taken to Ethiopia or the Sudan. The rest were divided among three other routes. The Portuguese slave trade from Mozambique to Brazil and Cuba took fifteen thousand a year until about 1830, and then about ten thousand, including those taken under fictional "work contracts" to the French islands of the Indian Ocean. The Zanzibar slave trade from the Swahili coast, which was particularly intense in the period between 1830 and 1850, recorded the departure of twenty thousand slaves annually, some ten thousand were deported secretly (thus avoiding payment of dues), and an additional three or four thousand were taken directly by the sultan and his entourage. Finally, the slave trade taking the northern route, via the Persian Gulf and the Indian Ocean, involved twelve or fifteen thousand individuals a year in the 1840s. The average annual number must have been about forty thousand, most of whom came from a relatively remote inland area across the northeast desert via Nubia and Darfur.[4] Thus, the East African slave trade attracted international attention chiefly because it gathered momentum just at the moment when the Atlantic slave trade was coming to an end, but it was much smaller in scale, being an internal African concern rather than a transcontinental system.[5]

Conceivably, then, a limited demographic growth may have occurred in the nineteenth century, even if it was accompanied—and, perhaps, invalidated—by roughly parallel occurrences of drought on both sides of the continent. Thus, the great famine of the 1830s, the only one the Kerebe of Lake Victoria remember—which extended from Ethiopia and eastern Kenya to central Tanzania, and, indeed, probably affected most of the continent, since

TABLE 2. The Great Droughts of the Nineteenth Century

East Africa	Central West Africa
1833	
	1835
1835–1837	
	1837–1841
1840–1845	
	1857–1860
1865	
	1867–1869
	1879–1884
1885	1884–1888
1888–1892	
1898–1899	

SOURCES: For East Africa, G. W. Hartwig, "Demographic Considerations in East Africa during the Nineteenth Century," *International Journal of African Historical Studies* 12, no. 4 (1979): 653–72. For Central West Africa, Jill R. Dias, "Famine and Disease in the History of Angola, c. 1830–1930," *Journal of African History* 21, no. 3 (1981): 349–78.

it also struck at the heart of Angola—no doubt caused one of the main phases of the cyclical demographic recession.[6]

THE FIRST COLONIAL PHASE, 1880–1930

In contrast to the precolonial period, the first years of colonization, including the preconquest years, were a phase of marked demographic regression, not so much on account of the battles themselves (which in fact were not especially bloody) as because of the various effects of the European penetration of the continent, most important of which was the "opening up" of Africa which, through the increased circulation of people, goods, and livestock, encouraged the spread of epidemics. In this period, above all, the fatal cycle of drought–famine–epizootic disease–epidemic weakened populations unable to withstand the combined ecological and cultural shock.

East African Epidemics

The first great epidemics that we know about preceded the European intrusion into Africa, spreading, in East Africa, along the international trade routes of the Arabs. The indigenous inhabitants rarely left their own territories, but the great trade routes were used at certain specific seasons of the year by caravans whose size and number increased throughout the nineteenth century as the commerce in slaves, ivory, cotton, sisal, and cloves developed.

The first recorded epidemics were those of cholera in 1817–1823 along the east coast, in 1826–1837 (coinciding with a long period of drought), in 1842–1862, most disastrously in 1865–1875, and then, significantly, during almost the whole of the first colonial period, in 1881–1896 and 1899–1923, after which the sickness remained confined to southern Asia until it reappeared in Africa in the years 1961–1979.[7] From the pilgrimage center of Mecca it crossed the Red Sea: in 1847, sixty thousand people died of it, including thousands of slaves.[8] Epidemics ravaged the coasts of East Africa from the Persian Gulf to the south of the continent. In 1858–1859, eight thousand people died in Zanzibar and five thousand in Mozambique. Did the sickness reach the interior previous to 1862? Not to any marked extent, apparently, although it struck Buganda at least once and perhaps more. As the century advanced, the epidemic in Africa became stronger, especially from 1865 on. In May 1865, ten to fifteen thousand people died in Mecca, and in 1870, forty thousand died in Zanzibar (a third of the population) and half the inhabitants of the port of Kilwa (at a rate of two hundred a day). As we learn, "ivory was left on the road and caravans were stopped by 'the death.'"[9]

The advance of smallpox into the center of Africa along the caravan routes can be followed even more exactly. Cholera is transmitted by water, but smallpox requires personal contact, and its rather slow incubation (seven to seventeen days) allows sufficient time for it to be contracted without warning, particularly in wayside lodgings. This disease probably originally existed only on the coast: at least three major epidemics have been traced at the Cape in the eighteenth century (in 1713, 1755, and 1767). In West Africa, the merchants hardly reached the Unyamwezi to the east of Lake Tanganyika before 1830, taking the route of Tabora and Ujiji, but at the close of the eighteenth century the disease was spread by the native elephant-hunters as they penetrated further and further into the interior. In the course of the nineteenth century, major epidemics of smallpox occurred in Ethiopia, with a mortality rate of 50 percent among children and 80 percent among adults.[10] Around Ujiji in 1880–1893, endemic smallpox broke out, with a mortality rate of 50 to 70 percent. Stanley claimed that from 1876 onward fifty to seventy people died each day at Ujiji, out of an original population of three thousand.

It appears that as a rule the populations made fairly quick recoveries from the earlier epidemics, but the periods of drought, longer and more frequent in the last third of the century, together with the foreign presence, increased the incidence of sickness, while the Whites seized the opportunity provided by the weakened condition of the indigenous populations to expand and conquer. Diseases of livestock combined with a loss of pasturage were no doubt all the more injurious because they led to a deterioration of the old social and economic order. A new calamity, contagious bovine pleuro-pneumonia, which simultaneously struck various populations, most of whom lived by raising livestock, again came from Europe, with livestock intro-duced into the African continent in the years 1880–1920 via Eritrea. The disease most severely struck the stock of the pastoral Masai and Kikuyu, in the region of Mount Kenya. The country was left impoverished and empty as the first colonizers arrived; so they were able to imagine that it had been almost uninhabited.

Bovine pleuropneumonia reached Rwanda in 1891–1892. It recurred there in 1920–1921 and in 1933–1934, when livestock vaccinations, ac-cepted with difficulty by the population, finally arrested epizootic disease. Moreover, at the end of the nineteenth century, sleeping sickness ravaged the dwellers on the plains that bordered Lake Victoria. This area of swamps and elephants—and, thus, a special preserve of ivory hunters—which was for-merly populated and fertile, consequently underwent a catastrophic regres-sion in both an ecological and a demographic sense.[11]

The ill effects of sicknesses introduced by the colonizers—particularly in places where workers were concentrated, and above all in the ports—have as yet been insufficiently studied. Illnesses of this type included tubercu-losis—often very severe cases—and venereal diseases. We know that the word for *syphilis*—the *kibanda* (or *kisoga* or *kabotango*)—was probably in use before the disease appeared; it was brought to the Kenya coast by Arab merchants, and from there it spread to Uganda about 1890. Syphilis affected central Kenya little until 1914–1918, when it reached Nairobi with the soldiers of World War I. It sprang up vigorously once again during World War II.[12]

From all this, it seems likely that the population of East Africa definitely diminished toward the end of the nineteenth century, and this downward trend continued until the mid-1920s, when sanitary measures, first put into operation in 1910, began to reestablish the equilibrium that had been upset by war, famine, and disease. Moreover, the East African pattern is strikingly displayed also in Portuguese, Belgian, and French Central West Africa.

Central West Africa

The demographic situation of Central West Africa was particularly diffi-cult, as sanitary facilities for the population there were almost nonexistent until the 1920s. Apart from the Europeans, only a tiny fringe of the popula-tion, not all indigenous, enjoyed the benefits of hygiene: schoolchildren, guards, riflemen, clerks, and, occasionally, manual workers. The first schools of tropical medicine were established in Europe only at the end of the nineteenth century, and in Africa in the late 1910s (the Ecole des Médecins-Auxiliaires was set up in Dakar in 1918).

Uprooted, subjected to hard labor and an unfamiliar diet, and far from their families in a strange environment, most of the few thousand wage earners showed themselves particularly susceptible to certain new sicknesses: before the war, beri-beri in particular had affected prisoners and railway workers, whose diet consisted mostly of imported rice. Venereal diseases were becoming a serious social plague, and so were lung ailments: between 1913 and 1915, the number of cases of tuberculosis detected by mobile medical units increased from 19 percent to nearly 25 percent of the population in the Ivory Coast, and even more in Guinea. Medical examination of conscripts revealed the frightful sanitary conditions of the populations: in Lahu, Ivory Coast, in 1915, only 16 percent of the recruits were accepted. Nearly always, more than 50 percent were rejected.

These conditions made the population particularly sensitive to changes of climate and of a diet that was ill-balanced and often inadequate. The slightest accident of nature—an exceptional drought, an invasion of grasshoppers—would be aggravated by a simultaneous colonial requisitioning of food and labor, unaccompanied by any administrative measures to remedy the situation.

The recruitment of laborers for huge construction projects and the desertion of villages by their inhabitants in order to avoid being commandeered into forced cultivation projects or being gathered together in large controlled settlements (this was a systematic practice in the Central Congo, for instance) also disturbed the rhythm of life in many regions, and the resultant underpopulation rendered them henceforth incapable of maintaining the frail equilibrium of a self-subsisting economy. Local scarcities had undoubtedly occurred historically, but by World War I, which exacerbated the consequences of the great drought that began in 1913 and deepened in 1917–1921, famine reached hitherto unprecedented proportions.

Angola.   The underlying ecological weakness of the hinterland of Luanda had been accentuated by the Portuguese presence long before the nineteenth century, but by increasing the circulation of people and goods the changes that took place at that time seem to have encouraged the spread of large-scale epidemics. From 1803 onward, and especially after 1820, the Portuguese practiced immunization against smallpox—that is, the transmission of the sickness from a sick person to a healthy person, who thus might contract it only mildly—specifically to protect their cargos of slaves.[13] Despite this practice, smallpox took a huge toll in the second half of the century. In 1864–1865, probably half of the eighteen thousand inhabitants of Luanda contracted the disease, and about five thousand of them died. Official statistics give the number of deaths in the region as 11,535 out of a population of

85,000 inhabitants, or a minimum of 13.6 percent. Ten years later, in about 1872–1873, an equally terrible catastrophe took place: a third of the population perished of smallpox, and the king of Kongo in panic begged the assistance of Portugal. The combination of these calamities and the increasing pressures of international trade paved the way for military occupation.

In addition, during the same period—between 1863 and 1869, 1879 and 1881, and 1884 and 1888—through the combined effects of droughts, famines, and wars of conquest in which, from 1879 to 1926, a "scorched earth" policy was freely employed, came a series of crises of subsistence worsened by the loss of the best lands. The Africans were victims of a vicious cycle. Bad harvests bankrupted the small-scale cultivators of coffee and peanuts, and their abandoned lands were expropriated by the colonizers, who combined them into large plantations. This increased vulnerability to sicknesses, for smallpox affected densely populated areas, and sleeping sickness, probably unknown before the nineteenth century but pervasive from the 1870s onward, was spread by deforestation, increased mobility both of people and of foodstuffs, and a rising demand for manual laborers. Between 1878 and 1898, the number of White planters rose from six hundred to six thousand; the number of agricultural laborers working for them rose from one thousand to sixteen thousand in approximately the same period (1867–1887); and thousands of workers were recruited for the construction of the Luanda-Malango railway, inaugurated in 1888 and extended in 1929. From 1895 onward, this disease, which was always fatal, spread with ever-increasing rapidity, causing panic and flight until the end of the 1920s when preventive measures began to take effect.

Bovine pleuropneumonia reached Angola at the end of the 1890s, killing perhaps 90 percent of the livestock. The first decade of the twentieth century saw an almost uninterrupted series of catastrophes: drought, floods, invasions of grasshoppers. The increasing density of the population of Luanda and the forced migration of nonimmunized workers into malarial districts escalated the mortality rate from malaria between 1893 and 1904; a doctor of that period estimated the infant mortality rate at 90 percent. The distress culminated in the droughts and famines of 1911 and 1916, which weakened the Africans at a time when a reconquest became imperative to the Portuguese, in response to the revolt of Mandume in Ovamboland, ending the fiction of independence in the south. As many as 250,000 people died of hunger during this period.[14] Finally, the worldwide depression of the 1930s was here aggravated until 1933 by the most serious drought ever recorded, followed by an invasion of grasshoppers throughout the territory. By 1934 people who had flocked to the towns in the vain hope of finding work were dying in the streets.

Lack of more extensive data makes it difficult to provide figures for the decline in the population. The decline was probably greatest at the turn of the century. We must limit ourselves to a single example: the population of the Portuguese *concelhos* (land concessions) between the rivers Dande and Kivanga was halved between 1878 and 1896 (dropping from 220,000 to 115,000 inhabitants). It had risen only to 140,000 by 1928 and did not fully recover until the end of the 1930s. Although migration undoubtedly contributed to this dramatic decline, a high mortality rate was a central factor.

French Equatorial Africa.   The situation was equally disastrous in French Equatorial Africa, where colonization further reduced an already insufficient population by imposing on the country a work burden disproportionate to its capacities. The intensive recruitment of labor, low wages, and insufficient rations combined with the demographic calamities—disintegration of communities, epidemics, famines—to exhaust the population thoroughly by about 1930.[15]

The most persistent infection was venereal disease, which caused sterility. This lowered the birthrate in extensive areas of Central Africa, which had been the heart of an intensive slave trade—both the Atlantic trade in the west and the Arab in the center and toward the east. The disease was indeed introduced by the slave-traders, originally Arabs, but only reached epidemic proportions with the arrival of the Europeans and their trade in slaves, especially female slaves. The centralization of commercial trading and the exchange of women between lineages facilitated a geographical dispersal of the disease, while forced labor and other repressive measures that disorganized African societies fostered its propagation. Colonial medicine, ignorant of the pathology of infertility, was helpless in the face of the declining birthrate. Finally, the societal disruptions led the indigenous populations unwittingly to become contributors to, as well as victims of, their own demographic regression, for they responded to sterility by conjugal instability and by migration—which, of course, only spread venereal disease further.[16]

The most lethal infection for half a century, however, was sleeping sickness. In Niari, between Brazzaville and the Atlantic, in 1898, a terrible epidemic of sleeping sickness began, "caused by the continual passage of the Loango carriers. It only ceased, about 1912, when this route of porterage was given up."[17] In some fifteen years the disease more than halved the population of the plain. As trade routes became more heavily traveled, the increasing numbers of migrating people carried the infection with them. In 1904, one case was reported in Gabon, at Ndjole on the middle Ogooue, among the imported workers; from there the disease followed the stream down to the region of the lakes, where it became endemic. Traveling via the Congo River, in a dozen years the sickness reached the very heart of the country: "Here, an entire village, in a short time, paid its tribute to this infection; there, a population fled before the sickness and sowed the infection further afield, bringing with it wretches who were already sick or others who were sickening. Further on, a group was no longer to be found, but the unburied bodies of local people provided the clue to the mystery." [18] The epidemic began to abate only in 1925, after a serious attempt had been made to provide medical assistance (658,000 people were examined in 1924, and 787,000 in 1925). Nevertheless, the general impoverishment brought about by the major crisis caused a renewed outbreak of the sickness.

The sleeping sickness, whose onset had coincided with the establishment of the colonial regime, had hardly begun its first phase of subsidence when, in 1919, the influenza epidemic that had been raging in Europe in turn reached all parts of Africa. [19] It became so severe that, in order to prevent its propagation, the administration even attempted to prohibit all contact between villages. About 10 percent of the population died of influenza, [20] and many of the weakened survivors contracted smallpox, violent epidemics of which had been recorded from 1864–1865 onward, but generally localized on the major trade routes.

The population, burdened with a rising deathrate, had at the same time to satisfy the increasing demands of the colonizers for labor and, especially, for foodstuffs. From the time of World War I, famines came to reach unprecedented proportions. The most devastating, in the Fang country in the north of Gabon, began in 1918 and attained the height of its virulence from 1922 to 1926. It killed nearly half the population (which fell from 140,000 inhabitants in 1911 to 65,000 in 1933), literally emptying the south of the region. Although this was a particularly violent outbreak, it was not unique. It was due not only to accidental causes (the exceptional shortness of the dry season, the depredations of animals) but also to the disruption of the system of food supply by the colonizers' demands. The crisis of 1930, abruptly cutting short most transactions, prevented the local inhabitants from attempting to remedy the scarcity of local foods through trade, and famine once again threatened almost everywhere. Fortunately, the dangers began to be attenuated by the attention the authorities finally paid to village agriculture, but the equilibrium was not fully reestablished until 1936.

A careful examination of the few available—and sometimes highly deceptive—figures from the pre–World War I period and the more reliable administrative statistics from the period after the war once again suggests a net decrease in the population. Locally at least, within the borders of Gabon, the Congo, and Central Africa, the population fell in a few years by nearly a third, from 800,000 before the war to only 587,000 in 1921. Recently, Jan Vansina even reached the conclusion that in the first colonialist phase Gabon lost, not a third, but at least half of its population. Its underpopulation left the country with an insoluble problem: development was required after the war (work in the forests and construction work on the railways and the roads), and the labor force had to be all the larger because the lack of capital, compounding the technical backwardness, necessitated manpower to do all that could not yet be accomplished by machines. This process took place at the expense of a traditionally precariously balanced system of food supply. It was no coincidence that, a few years later, this miserably ill-used central African region was the center of the largest and longest-lasting peasant revolt in French Africa, the Kongo-Warra revolt of 1927–1932 (see Chapter 9), or that it remains one of the most deprived and politically fragile areas of the continent.

West Africa

We have examined two of the areas most injured by colonization. Elsewhere—notably in British and French West Africa—there was also an undoubted regression, but one that was less spectacular. Study of a number of cases—Sierra Leone, Ghana, northern Nigeria—suggests that even without great demographic catastrophes such as colonial repression, epidemics, or droughts, in an average year the demographic deficit was considerably increased by the colonial regime. Increased migration of the labor force (largely men) caused most of the agricultural work to fall on the women. The beginning of the rainy season, when the fields were prepared and sowed, coincided with the transitional period in the year when food became scarce. The physical effort required was thus out of all proportion to the physiological state of these undernourished women. The sickness and deathrates increased accordingly, and the period of food scarcity tended to start ever earlier. Similarly, the period of sowing corresponded to the annual peak of infant mortality: the poor nutritional value of the indigenous diet during this period required that its deficiencies be compensated for by the frequency of the meals, but in the transitional period the women had little time to cook for their children. All this suggests that these seasonal increases in the deathrate were greater than they had been in the nineteenth century, when the risks of chronic scarcity were to at least some extent mitigated by a more differentiated agriculture that could stagger harvests, owing to a greater availability of manpower.[21] This said, however, we can see that demographic recovery took place sooner in West Africa than in the other areas we have examined. The demographic decline directly imputable to colonization lasted only from 1875 to 1905, the span of one generation.

In Dahomey (Benin), one of the most densely populated colonies, the number of inhabitants apparently dropped by 9 percent between 1900 and 1921, but in the Ivory Coast after 1906, a phase of demographic decline in which the population fell below 1 million inhabitants was followed by a recovery that was sporadic and irregular in both a chronological and a geographical sense but that undoubtedly continued until 1914 (when the population numbered 1.5 million), despite the fact that Angoulvant's military "pacification" of the area occurred during that time. The rhythm slowed considerably, however, in the following years: World War I and the influenza epidemic caused a quasi-stagnation until the beginning of the 1920s and then again during the Great Depression (when the population was 1.7 million). It was only during the 1950s, when a late but violent outbreak of sleeping sickness had been checked, that the population passed the 2 million mark, reaching 2.5 million in 1960. In short, the present demographic explosion coincided with national independence.[22]

The demographic model of the Ivory Coast no doubt more or less holds for all of West Africa.[23] At any rate, the case of Ghana also seems to display this pattern.[24] Colonization here, as everywhere, by improving transportation networks and thus encouraging travel, first contributed to the spread of all kinds of epidemics: for example, with the increase in migrant labor in the mines and in the city, tuberculosis became the cause of 7 to 11.5 percent of the deaths recorded in Accra between 1930 and 1938. Venereal disease, which had existed for centuries on the Atlantic coast, made deep inroads in the cities (it was known as "Kumasi disease" in the north of the country). Generally speaking, the congestion of cities provided a fertile breeding ground for pulmonary diseases (bronchitis and pneumonia accounted for 5 percent of the deaths in Accra in 1930) and intestinal illnesses (amoebic and bacterial, accounting for 5 to 10 percent of the deaths in Accra up to 1940). The situation improved, however, once the problem of a sanitary water supply had been tackled (in Accra in 1913, in Tamale in 1932, in Kumasi in 1934).

The colonial medical services never attempted to counter certain epidemics such as influenza (which killed at least 100,000 people in 1918–1919) and infantile diseases—measles and mumps probably caused more sickness and more deaths than all the other epidemics combined. As elsewhere, the medical services concerned themselves first and foremost with the great endemic tropical diseases: smallpox, bubonic plague, and sleeping sickness. At least seven lethal outbreaks of smallpox occurred between 1908 and 1951, despite vaccination at least in the towns (more than 200,000 vaccinations were given in Accra during the epidemic of 1920, and one Ghanaian in ten was vaccinated in 1930—not always effectively, unfortunately—compared to one person out of four in French West Africa).

Bubonic plague first appeared in 1908, in Accra; a serious epidemic broke out in Dakar in 1914; the disease was reintroduced in 1924 in the ports of Accra and Secondi; and then, via the railway-line, it reached Kumasi. Systematic campaigns of rat clearance and quarantine finally succeeded in eradicating the sickness by about 1960.

Sleeping sickness was reported in 1903, mainly in Ghana, and in 1904 in the Ivory Coast. Extension of forest clearings and plantations expanded both the human and the tsetse-fly populations, and thus accelerated the spread of the disease, as did the relocations of peoples. Carried by railway construction workers, the sickness rapidly reached the north via the caravan routes. The first preventive measures (clearing the approaches to contaminated villages and isolating them) were decided on just before World War I, but it was only after the violent recurrence of the sickness in the 1920s, when from 1,000 to 7,000 people died of it in Ghana, that a serious attempt was made to fight it. A key role was played by Cameroon, itself seriously affected, which, in the 1930s, as soon as a method of prevention had been perfected, served as a kind of laboratory for governmental preventive measures. The method had first been tried out in French Equatorial Africa by the military doctor Jamot and then had been extended to all the contaminated areas of French West Africa, particularly Upper Volta and the north of the Ivory Coast, where 143,000 cases had been detected by 1939.[25]

Generally speaking, however, until 1945 sanitary measures remained very fragmentary, both for lack of money and through failure to adapt the available medical knowledge. Most of the rural areas, particularly in the Sahelo-Sudanese north, were neglected, with few or no dispensaries, nurses, or means of prevention (against mosquitoes, for instance); and, whatever the explanation, before the 1950s no effective and cheap medicines were in general use. Sanitary measures—the earliest of which appeared only after 1900 and were not seriously applied until the mid-1920s—had relatively little effect on the deathrate until after World War II. The main advances during that period were the use of D.D.T. against malarial mosquitoes; sulphamides; above all, antibiotics; yellow-fever vaccine, which came into widespread use only after the start of the war (only 1.1 percent of the population, all town-dwellers, had been vaccinated in French West Africa before 1941); and, finally, the development of an effective smallpox vaccine in the 1950s. The net result was that in Ghana, life expectancy rose from 28 years in 1921 to 39.5 in 1948 and 45.5 in 1960. One can assume that these figures are generally valid for West Africa as a whole. We ought not, however, to overlook a significant change of trend: namely, that at the beginning of the colonial era, the concentration of the population in towns, mines, and railway construction sites often resulted in a higher deathrate, while in the middle of the twentieth century, on the contrary, the town-dweller, who was the privileged beneficiary of the first sanitary measures, began to have a life expectancy far higher than that of country-dwellers.

THE GREAT CRISES OF
THE TWENTIETH CENTURY

The second colonial phase saw a slow demographic recovery. Africa had a population of 141 million in 1920 (94 million of whom lived south of the Sahara), between 145 and 164 million in 1930, between 163 and 191 million in 1940, and between 190 and 222 million in 1950 (there are 500 million today, and the projection is for one billion in the year 2000).[26] This progression (chiefly due, in the prewar period, to the vitality of the North Africans) was caused, first of all, by a drop in the deathrate, and then by advances in transport and communications that enabled famine relief to reach further and travel faster: since the 1930s, trucks have been able to penetrate almost everywhere.

This recovery, however, has continued to be countered by grave accompanying demographic crises of a premodern type—ones, that is, in which ecological calamities such as droughts and epidemics combine with the incapacity of the colonial and then the neo-colonial politico-economic system to give its attention to the deathrate.

Spanish Influenza

On 22 August 1918, Spanish influenza broke out simultaneously in three military ports: Boston, Brest, and Freetown. This epidemic, the second wave of the illness worldwide, was to be the most severe short-term demographic disaster in African history.[27] Not the slave trade, nor the European conquest, nor smallpox, nor cerebrospinal meningitis, nor even sleeping sickness killed so many Africans in such a short period. Introduced by soldiers returning from the European theater of World War I, it spread along the roads, the railway lines, and the rivers toward the towns in the interior, and then filtered more slowly into the bush, carried by travelers and traders. It penetrated into almost every region, every village, between August and November 1918 and again in March and April 1919.

The figure often cited of 1,350,000 Africans dead in less than a year undoubtedly falls far short of the real number. In West Africa, where the deathrate was particularly high among young adults and especially among pregnant women, over half the population contracted the disease and the deathrate was from 3 to 4 percent. In all, at least 1.5 to 2 million people died in sub-Saharan Africa from influenza itself or pulmonary complications—a minimum overall average of at least 1.5 percent. The enormous consequences include regroupings of population and changes in the style of life—for example, as we saw in Chapter 1, in southern Nigeria the epidemic caused an almost immediate substitution of manioc for the Indian potato crop.

Malaria

Malaria pervades Africa so universally as to have been virtually taken for granted. The disease is not necessarily fatal (although some forms, especially in Equatorial Africa, are extremely violent), but recurrent attacks are exhausting. The "underproductivity" of African workers so often decried in colonial reports was in large part simply a reflection of this fatigue. Use of the preventive nivaquine (a synthetic product that has since World War II replaced the scarce quinine, the remedy that had been in use for a century)

remains the privilege of expatriates and certain members of the more affluent classes. Any true revolution in African sanitation must include universal
access to the recently developed malaria vaccine—but the expense seems almost prohibitive.[28]

Droughts and Famines

At least three catastrophic droughts were recorded in the twentieth century
before that of 1984: in 1913–1914, 1930–1933, and 1972–1974, and a fourth
may have affected Niger and the Sahel in 1901–1903.[29] Each subsequent
drought has taken fewer lives, owing to the development of the food trade,
improvements in transportation, and, in some cases, more famine relief.

In 1913–1914 one of the worst droughts ever known in the Sahel claimed
several thousand victims in the Middle Niger alone and decimated the livestock there. The recent arrival of the French and the requirements of the war
did the rest: requisitionings of millet could not have come at a less suitable
time. The war, with its weakening of the colonial positions (the isolated outposts in the desert were evacuated), encouraged the outbreak of the rebellion
of the Tuareg of Aïr in 1916–1917. The colonizers soon realized that the
misery and distress of a population driven to despair, compounded by the
now visible risk of a demographic collapse, seriously threatened the process
of "valorization" they advocated. The Colonial Conference held in 1917 began the policy, restated in the famous plan of Albert Sarraut, minister for the
colonies in 1921, of giving priority to protecting the health of a labor force
which was increasingly in demand.[30]

In 1931 the Great Depression combined with an exceptionally severe
drought to produce a terrible famine, bitter memories of which remain with
the Zarma-Sonrai of the Niger today. The precipitating cause was an invasion of grasshoppers, but the colonial system did much to aggravate the disaster, as may be seen from the reports of the period, which are filled with
severe self-criticism. Excessive taxes (they rose from 1.25 to 7 francs) encouraged a movement of the population to the Gold Coast, to the detriment
of local food production. The colonial practice of forced labor, which had
escalated since 1927 to meet the needs of the administrative center at Niamey
and to extend the railway, ignored an agricultural calendar which the uncertainty of rain rendered particularly fragile. Storehousing millet was here not
obligatory but depended entirely on the local governors, who too often neglected this essential precaution in a land of periodic scarcity. In 1931, the
refusal to lower the poll tax, and the collective system of payment that
forced the agricultural workers to pay for deserters and the dead, resulted in
"whole villages which disappeared, and one age-grade . . . forever decimated" with, in certain areas, a deathrate of over 50 percent.[31]

The general demographic stagnation reveals the wretchedness of the
population, although spending on public welfare had increased markedly

since 1920. The case of Cameroon is instructive: a parallel increase in the number of clinics and of patients under medical care helped to allay the violence of the great epidemics (sleeping sickness, leprosy, and venereal disease), but at the same time the increased number who suffered from ordinary diseases bears witness to the profound physiological distress of the defenseless and weakened population.

The years from 1970 to the present—a period marked by the drought of 1972 and its recent recurrence—have again seen famine affecting the whole of the Sahelo-Sudanese zone from Senegal to the Horn of Africa.[32] The crisis has been so serious that the Somali government and others could find no other solution than to compel the fleeing nomads to adopt a sedentary form of life, despite the inherent difficulties of forcing such a change.

These facts require revision of the generally optimistic view of rapid demographic growth in a largely underpopulated Africa. Demographic growth began late and appeared irregularly: the "demographic explosion" is at the most one generation old. Previously, traumatic experiences repeatedly struck at the African population, and tremendous vitality was required simply for the peoples to survive. As Pierre Goubert so rightly wrote, "The true secret of a people may be how it manages to survive."[33]

Today, in Africa south of the Sahara—discounting a very small minority of privileged persons—more people die of hunger than anywhere else in the world. The rate of demographic growth in Africa as a whole is the highest in the world—with an annual average of 2.9 percent since 1970, compared to 2.7 percent in Latin America and only 2.1 percent in China—and in consequence, the per capita rate of increase of gross national product is the lowest in the world: only 0.2 percent between 1970 and 1980, compared to 1.4 percent in India and 2.7 percent in the other countries of Asia. A further effect is that the number of calories consumed per day per person is the lowest in the world (2,212 in 1977, compared to 2,233 in Asia and 2,560 in Latin America). Food production lags behind demographic growth—increasing only half as fast as the population—and thus the equilibrium is extremely delicate. Any drought can bring about a catastrophe, as happened in 1980–1981 when the Senegalese peanut crop was the smallest since World War II, and again in 1984.

The most recent famines in the Sahel nudged India and China out of the headlines in this respect, but Somalia, Uganda, and Mozambique, and Nigeria, Zaire, and the Bantustans or "Black states" of South Africa have also suffered critically. In the Karamoja region in Uganda, at least a quarter of the population died in the famine of 1980—more than a hundred thousand people. At the present time, in more than thirty-five countries of sub-Saharan Africa (out of a total of forty-five) the problem of hunger is worsening rather than improving.[34] With the important exception of Nigeria, these states cannot look to oil revenues for an amelioration of their condition.

A more pessimistic but probably more accurate view than the one frequently expressed is that of an increasing discrepancy between, on the one hand, mining, agroindustrial, and modern urban enclaves favoring the emergence of an expanding middle class, and, on the other hand, the non-mining and non—oil-producing areas—nearly the whole of West, Equatorial, and East Africa (with the notable exceptions of Guinea and Nigeria). These are regarded as nonproductive in the world economy and are thus neglected in almost all senses of the word. At best, they are used as reservoirs of cheap manual labor (the clearest example being that of the South African Bantustans); at worst, they are abandoned to famine and the consequent decimation, which in the long run can only increase, through the creation of a balkanized Fourth World, the extreme imbalance of African demographic densities.

PART II

The State

From Chiefship to Military Populism

4

Precolonial Rule:
From the Rural Community
to the State

The term *state* is generally used to refer to the Western model of a state. The term *anarchy* used to describe a stateless (or "acephalous") society, even if it is taken only in its etymological sense (Greek *anarchos,* leaderless), merely serves to underline the confusion, for an absence of state structures in the classic, hierarchical sense does not have to mean anarchy. The traditional African power structure exhibits neither disorder nor confusion, but a system of political checks and balances, sometimes very clearly defined. In approaching the question of government in Africa, then, rather than beginning with the European concept of the state, it is better to start at the basic level: that of the rural communities which once comprised almost the entire population. An analysis of the social and political relationships of these groups will at the same time reveal their way of reacting to more powerful, external entities.[1]

The economy and the society were based on rural communities that constituted agricultural units of production. Generally, these took the form of villages, that is to say, small groups of families who received nearly all their subsistence from the land, with a comparatively undifferentiated social division of labor in which even specialized or privileged individuals or groups— artisans, chiefs, priests—participated, either directly or through their relatives and dependents, in agricultural production. This describes the typical situation in West and Equatorial Africa. At the same time, much of Central Africa (Rwanda) and particularly East and southern Africa (for example, Tanzania, Mozambique) did not and often still does not live in villages, or, at any rate, the village exists only in its most rudimentary form—a single family, or part of a family, generally consisting of one of a man's wives with her children, living in scattered dwellings. The effect of this form of existence was to constrict the forces of production, confining habitual mutual assistance to certain tasks that were clearly defined and limited in time and in the agricultural calendar.

The herding peoples of the Sahel present another model of existence. These nomads or semi-nomads were occupied predominantly or exclusively with raising cattle (or, in the case of some groups in the forests, with hunting, fishing, and gathering) and settled in villages only sporadically or temporarily. Distinct units of production could readily be identified among them, however: the "tribes" or "clans" centered on a certain area and their products.

Overall, then, the expression *rural unit of production* seems preferable to *village*. Whatever the size or character of this unit, it is always possible to describe its social relationships with the outside world, for a political structure always links the rural nucleus with the exterior whether it is a village in the strict sense or not, and whether or not a state in the classical sense of the term exists.

This last point, which is an important one, was inherent in the nature of the system. The precolonial village, in Africa, was never entirely self-sufficient, even when it was not integrated into a state. It was a subsistence economy rather than a self-sufficient one. It is important to stress that we are speaking here of the past; too often anthropological-historical analysis falls into ambiguity as a result of a failure to distinguish between present-day manifestations and their prototypes in the past. Many features of precolonial African politics do survive today, more or less incorporated into the modern state and society, even if the modern versions have become twisted and deformed. This continuity under change makes it important to identify the relationship between past institutions and their modern-day counterparts.

THE PRECOLONIAL RURAL COMMUNITY:
MYTH AND REALITY

Ethnological literature has mythicized the village and the village community in all non-European societies as an untouched and untouchable entity, perfectly self-contained and living in absolute harmony. This myth, which is related to Rousseau's concept of the "noble savage," came into being in the second half of the eighteenth century and flourished in the Romantic period with its idealization of rural values, of the village as a repository of the virtues of the past, untouched by urban and industrial civilization. In the twentieth century, when the first ethnologists attempted to recreate a vision of the precolonial world, the novelty of the setting led them to extol ancestral virtues and, sometimes, gave them the illusion of a return to that mythical Eden. At the same time, the colonizers themselves fell into two camps: against those who supported the policy of drastic modernization that destroyed the village system were some who idealized that system and advocated its restoration. This point of view was adopted by the African nationalists, for whom the concept of a precolonial Golden Age became a weapon to be used against the West.

The same phenomenon occurs in nineteenth-century English descriptions of the village in India as an organized community that, although divided into castes, enjoyed an admirable internal freedom and that was studied completely out of context.[2] This, however, was a false picture, since every Indian village formed part of a kingdom and every peasant paid tribute. What existed in fact were very strong traditions of communal solidarity with a system of reciprocal exchanges of services based on what was essentially an ideology that called for such redistribution.

This is not to say that villages were egalitarian. In India, the caste system manifested the inequities; in the African rural community the stratification, perhaps less visible, was no less real. Lineages were divided into superior and inferior ones, and a single lineage would include a class of *elders*. Elder status was not necessarily conferred by birth, but could also be obtained through a varied system of exchanges, matrimonial connections, and, of course, seniority. The village council was not a democratic organ but, rather, a gerontocracy, and the village chief was not simply a coordinator but the most influential member of the dominant lineage.

Finally, the notion that the village was an ideal collective unit ignores its economic and political subordination to the outside world. The village maintained a system of exogamy, that is to say, a network of connections with the exterior that facilitated a great variety of social and economic exchanges. The misconception concerning village isolation perhaps arises from the pattern of these connections. A peasant society was a local community, enjoying undeniable relative autonomy with regard to the chief, the overlord, or the city to which it was subordinate. Most villages were largely self-supporting and therefore relatively independent, although they paid tribute (part of the crop, a levy, a contingent of soldiers) to the authority and thus had to maintain contact with external markets (especially if the tribute took the form of a monetary equivalent or a commodity currency such as gold). Moreover, the society was characterized by a certain cultural closure, a reaction of rejection of the surrounding society. A few *notables* acted both as interpreters of the wishes and needs of the community and as representatives of the superior authority; in other words, their task was to sit astride the two worlds. This model of a peasant society differs on the one hand from "savage" or "primitive" society (the food-collecting hordes) and, on the other, from the sociologists' model of an industrial society, in which the village group loses its identity. It is worthwhile to try to determine to what degree such an industrial society can be adapted to Africa south of the Sahara.

THE RURAL COMMUNITY AND
THE OUTSIDE WORLD

The assertion that the rural community was probably never a self-governing entity leads to a further claim, namely, that whether or not the village was in any obvious way subordinate, it was always connected with the outside world through three types of exchange: exchanges of products, political exchanges, and social exchanges.

Exchanges of Products

Commercial exchanges on the African continent have been recorded at all periods, in all places, and in various forms. Neighboring communities often exchanged surplus commodities. Thus, in the forests of the Congo, Bantu peasant cultivators and Pygmy hunters such as the Bapunu and the Babongo exchanged meat and agricultural products,[3] and on the fringes of the desert, nomadic herdsmen and the peasants of the oasis traded livestock for millet or dates, for example, as part of a complex set of social exchanges. In certain areas with a developed market civilization, such as precolonial Dahomey, a multiplicity of transactions formed part of everyday life, although the trading was neither economically significant nor, perhaps, truly essential for subsistence.

Regional exchanges sometimes appear to be an amplification of the local exchanges by more or less specialized professional or cultural groups such as the Dyula and Hausa in West Africa and the Nyamwezi and Yao in East Africa. These complementary regional exchanges involved and continue, in their modern forms, to involve a considerable trade: a trade formerly in iron, ivory, and slaves, and up to our own days in such commodities as kola nuts—taking them from the centers of production in the forests of Guinea to consumers in Islamic Sudan—and, throughout East and West Africa, in livestock. These regional exchanges chiefly supply foodstuffs to certain deprived populations.

Finally, long-distance exchanges have sometimes played a crucial role. They are not clearly distinguished from the regional exchanges except for the fact that they involved, at least in part, rare and thus precious commodities and were accordingly reserved for privileged holders of power such as the aristocracy, chiefs, and sultans. In this category fall the celebrated trade in Sudanese gold exchanged, ever since the Middle Ages, for the salt of the desert, and the gold, ivory, slaves, and ostrich feathers traded via the Arabs and Indians in both East and West Africa for European fabrics and guns. Even earlier, as is increasingly revealed by archeological evidence, began the trade in iron, which was also exchanged for the salt of the Sahara or of the Great Lakes of East Africa, for salt, in Africa, was a commodity as rare as it was necessary for the inhabitants, making it one of the main elements in the history of exchanges on that continent.

Political Exchanges

Centralized states and "state societies," to use the classical terminology, existed in precolonial Africa. These states, which were numerous and ancient, exhibited a wide variety of political systems. For example, from the fourteenth to the eighteenth century, Shona districts (the Monomotapa of the Portuguese) covered part of the area of present-day Zimbabwe and Mozambique;[4] in the sixteenth century, the Luba kingdom and the Lunda empire covered the province of Shaba in Zaire. These states, which controlled mining areas, were at the center of a trade in gold (exported via the port of Sofala in present-day Mozambique), copper, slaves, and ivory.

The medieval Islamic Sudanese empires of West Africa which succeeded one another from the eleventh to the sixteenth century, in Ghana, Mali, and the Songhai empire, dominated a rural mass that was still animistic and relatively little involved, except as the victims of slave-trading (from the eighteenth century on, Indian and Arab merchants of the sultanate of Zanzibar, who used the bridgehead at Kilwa and dealt in slaves, ivory, and cloves, played a similar role).

Slave-trading kingdoms, such as the kingdom of Kongo and the kingdom of Benin from the twelfth to the sixteenth century, the kingdom of Abomey, and the kingdom of Ashanti, particularly from the seventeenth to the nineteenth century, were supported or created by the economic power provided by the Atlantic trade.

Finally, warrior states flourished, particularly in the nineteenth century. These were of two types: the little national entities characteristic of the interlacustrine zone that were both military and crop-growing (for example, Buganda) or military and pastoral (Rwanda, Burundi); and the Islamized Fulbe military-religious hegemonies of West Africa.

A state comes into being when one social group—properly speaking, a class—concentrates within itself enough power and prestige to take charge of production with the assistance, and at the expense, of the other groups. In precolonial Africa this aristocracy controlled the military, religion, and commerce and thus assured its own perpetuation while sustaining its domination over the other groups—mainly peasants (free or slaves) and artisans, sometimes merchants. The state then appeared to be a necessary instrument of coercion, maintaining both social inequality and the interrelationship of the various elements. The king now became the true ruler and not merely the wealthiest individual of the leading lineage. Although these states, throughout history, took any number of forms, at the village level a superior authority was always acknowledged at least by the payment of tribute. This sum, however modest, symbolized that dominion-dependence relationship implying exchanges of goods, individuals, and rights that has largely inspired the contemporary reflections on what Samir Amin has called the "tributary mode of production."

Social Exchanges

Whether a state existed or not, there were social exchanges that in themselves implied a political relationship. A favorite kind was the exchange of women, for matrimonial alliances were chosen to strengthen the lineage of the contracting party. Emmanuel Terray's classic study of the Dida of the Ivory Coast provides an excellent example.[5] In the nineteenth century, the lakeside Alladian community sought to acquire Dida wives and other male and female captives. According to Terray, the motivation was twofold. First, the larger the lineage was in numbers—in women, and hence in descendants—the stronger it became. And, second, since matrilineage was not transmitted by slave wives, to have children by slaves reinforced the paternal lineage. Moreover, the son of a female captive or a foreigner was not granted the rights of a son or a maternal nephew, all of which was to the advantage of the receiving lineage. The wealthier Alladian trading lineages included many such captives, thus both creating and reinforcing a social hierarchy and a political hierarchy based on the relative strengths of the lineages.

THE POWER STRUCTURES

With their complex interweavings, the relationship of the village with the outside world has never been simple. It cannot be reduced to the pyramidal hierarchy that is a schematic and rudimentary definition of the state, which would consist of the territorial recognition of a superior authority attested through the payment of tribute. Three types of relationship of the village community with the exterior can, however, be found in virtually all societies: (1) lineal relationships based on kinship; (2) political relationships proper, or recognition of a hierarchic territorial state authority; and (3) relations of personal dependence, which confirm or contradict the two preceding kinds through a network of exchanges and obligations that is either horizontal—from one lineage to another or from one village to another—or vertical, from the village to the superior authority, whether or not it passes through intermediate stages such as chiefs of provinces.

Kinship Communities

A lineage is an extended family descended from a single nonmythical ancestor. In addition to relatives, both direct descendants and in-laws, it may include any domestic slaves attached to the family, at least from the second generation. This concept, dear to French-speaking ethnologists, is of limited usefulness, for individuals belonging to the same lineage can belong to different social and residential units. It is therefore interesting to consider a related concept put forward by the Anglo-Saxons: that of the household (Claude Lévi-Strauss has suggested the use of the old historical term *house,* a unit as much related to marriage as to descent). The term *household* has the advantages of indicating a co-residential unit that is at once economic (domestic), social, and political (referring to the status of land among seden-

tary cultivators of the soil), and also of minimizing the importance of con-
sanguinity in a group of which perhaps only a quarter of the members are
connected biologically and which includes elders, youngers, and their dependents; friends, adopted children, hired workers, relatives, captives, slaves,
and women—wives or otherwise. The fact of living together, of producing,
consuming, and surviving together, was the salient factor; the lineage—
more or less determined by the ethnic heritage—thus represents above all an
ideology of legitimization.

All the lineages taken together constitute the *ethnic group,* whose cultural identity is affirmed by the recognition of a common mythical ancestor
and is expressed in a linguistic unity. The synonymous term *tribe,* although
the pejorative connotation it has taken on in Africa south of the Sahara,
owing to its incorrect use in the colonial period, has made most contemporary historians avoid it, in North Africa preserves its scientific validity, especially where it is used to describe the more or less nomadic communities of
the high plains and the desert.

A great deal, in fact, could be said about the history of the concept of the
ethnic group. We shall see, later on, that although in precolonial times it
could be regarded as identifying the significant entity underlying a particular
social organization, the ethnic group is nevertheless an elusive concept, despite the fact that it has been given an excessively rigid interpretation by ethnologists. Should we, for instance, make a clear distinction between the ethnic group (supposed to be more or less consanguinous) and the professional
group (like the Dyula, and, as is increasingly thought, the Hausa) that,
having lived together for generations, shares a culture? African societies, despite their undoubtedly specific character, should not be supposed to be totally exceptional. They are both different from and analogous to those in all
other parts of the world. As Jean-François Bayart has recently so thought-
provokingly and yet judiciously said: "The realization that African societies
are societies like any others, a recognition of their banality, an understanding that their specificity is of a purely historical kind—that is something that
a century of official 'Africanism' has hardly facilitated, however great a mass
of information it has accumulated."[6]

Thus, very recent studies have questioned the relevance of this narrowly
Africanist concept of the ethnic group, which is first and foremost a historical construction, that is, one that is subject to a process of evolution. The
fact remains that kinship relationships depended on people, not on territory.
The boundaries of the territory were, rather, determined by the extensive-
ness of the lineage, so its borders were fluid, shifting in accordance with
demographic displacements and fluctuations.

To be sure, kinship primarily controlled life within the village, in which
relationships of production were determined by unequal exchanges between
elders and youngers and reciprocal exchanges between the elders—in other

words, between kin chiefs.[7] But what particularly concerns us here is that kinships could also determine intervillage relationships, if only because a prolific lineage created new villages. This becomes obvious in Mozambique and Tanzania, where the very widespread living areas often forced the lineages to set up settlements consisting of a single unit, the home of a woman and her children. It is also typical of southern Chad, where the Masa and the Taburi, who were resistant to Islam and who were farmers, fishers, and herdsmen, were characterized by a complete absence of central political authority, by a lineal subdivision encouraged by their practice of marrying exogamously, and by the size of the living area. At least three generations of the patriarchal family of a *djaf* (lineage of paternal descent) remained grouped around their progenitor in the same "concession."

Lineal preeminence also determined the political life of the Black nomadic Tubu or Agaoua herdsmen of the Chadian Sahara. A number of changing "clans" (or lineages) made their appearance, lived their day, and disappeared. Constantly split up, they created a kind of territorial mosaic characterized not only by an apparent incapacity to form a state but also by an extraordinary capacity of resistance to all central domination. The colonialists vainly attempted to divide into a chessboard of "cantons" and "tribes" an area that was really a kaleidoscope of lineal fragments, scattered and sometimes momentarily regrouped. The only recognized authority remained that of kinship, and its equilibrium, at once precarious and difficult, was regulated by complex lineal relationships, whence arises the terrible contradiction that still exists in practice between territorial and kinship requirements.[8] For this kinship system supported a political system, a network of connections between communities implying the possibility of alliances by marriage—a fact that sheds light on many anticolonial resistance movements.

In connection with precolonial times, then, we may speak of a sense of ethnicity (but not of *tribalism,* which is a recent deformation of this idea). *Ethnicity* refers to a common cultural and linguistic heritage that gains coherence and legitimacy from the kinship system. The village at that time was part of a larger whole, whether or not a state existed. There even existed, in certain cases at least, a sort of *nationalism,* a sense of belonging to a community that functions and recognizes itself as a nation.

State-created Groups

A state could exist simultaneously with communities based on kinship, creating territorial village-state relationships. Madagascar in the reign of Adrianampoinimerina is a case in point.[9] Upon highly structured communities the state imposed three obligatory forms of practical relationship: first, forced labor on the dikes, which was the mark of a free man, whereas the slave remained restricted to work within the family (contrary to the practice in Western civilizations, where forced labor was a sign of slavery); second, the obligation of going to the market even if one had nothing to sell except water, because that was the place where governmental authority was exercised as well as the only place where money was exchanged (money being a symbol of the sovereign); and, third and most important, the payment of taxes. As the state apparatus limited itself to these coercive forms, the villagers expressed their hostility only in the form of passive resistance.

In other places, resistance became violent, as in Morocco, where the militaristic Maghzen state subjugated the tribes and conquered the cities, then claimed as their legitimate—and virtually sole—responsibility the levying of taxes, which they justified by their conquest of the tribal communities that had been exhausted by the expeditions and repressions of the government.[10] As a result, the Zaouias, or maraboutic religious foundations, multiplied from the seventeenth and eighteenth centuries onward and their protection was sought by increasing numbers of individuals. This brutality also served as one cause of the Moroccan popular insurrection at the beginning of the twentieth century, which was directed both against the Maghzen and against foreign domination.

In most African states the payment of tribute is attested, but we know little about it, not even how much was asked. This very ignorance on our part suggests that it cannot have been a very heavy burden. Here probably lay the sticking point in Morocco: in Black Africa, the sovereign exploited the neighboring peoples, not his own subjects. The government surplus was not derived from tribute, the value of which was no doubt less material than symbolic, a sign of authority and a statement of allegiance to the ruler and adherence to the socio-political structures.

The sovereign did not depend for his subsistence on the agriculture of the village communities living under his dominion. He had his own lands, worked by his wives and his slaves. But there was little surplus. The soils were among the poorest in the world—tropical lateritic crusts or leached clays of the equatorial zones. The crops were threatened, moreover, by particularly frequent climatic risks, at least in the subtropical zone. And the technological system was remarkably little developed, for reasons that have been variously and, generally speaking, unconvincingly explained, so productivity was minimal. (The wheel, the swing plough, and techniques of irrigation were unknown.) The sovereign's prosperity was born of war and long-distance trade, activities which were sometimes complementary, as in the slave-trading states that each year organized raids beyond their frontiers to capture slaves, who were then sold to the Atlantic traders who in turn provided the supply of arms necessary for the raiding.

The state apparatus was at that time identified with external campaigns in search of booty—slaves, livestock, luxury articles—to be distributed to the army chiefs and the bravest warriors. It was an apparatus that remained relatively independent of village life. In fact, only two basic types of army then existed: that of peasants and that of slaves. The armies of the mighty, conquering, generally Islamic slave-trading states were undoubtedly of the latter kind. The army of the sultans of Ubangi, who in the last third of the nineteenth century dominated the local animist populations of Equatorial Africa, that of Rabah, those of the Arab-Swahili potentates of East Africa from the 1860s onwards, those from the eighteenth century onward of the warrior theocracies of the western Sudan, and, finally, that of Samori's empire until 1898 all derived much of their subsistence from the spoils of war, and the peoples they subjected and raided were able to react only diffusely, with passivity, rejection, or flight. Some autocentric states of smaller dimensions, whose sovereign represented more or less the whole ethnic group (for example, the kingdoms of Abomey [present-day Benin], Ashanti [Ghana], and Buganda), raised "national" armies. In such cases, the demands of the state on the village communities took the form, not so much of the exaction of tribute, as of the organization of an army—that is to say, of the conscription of peasants periodically required by the provincial chiefs. Since the annual raiding campaign was planned for the dry or agriculturally dead season, this recruitment was not necessarily resented. Those conscripted expected, after the operation, to receive part of the booty redistributed via the hierarchical channels of the political-military chiefs.

We have fairly exact descriptions of such governmental apparatuses, at least in the nineteenth century, revealing a definite hierarchy from the sovereign downward. All the legitimacy of the government was centered on him, and it was then transmitted by his representatives, passing through the provincial chiefs and subchiefs until the chiefs of local communities had each received their portion of authority. The role of the chiefs of provinces was ambiguous: they were at the same time dignitaries bound by personal service to the king, a function which required them to reside at court, and territorial—though not lineal—chiefs, all chosen and dismissed, in principle, by the sovereign himself from whom they received their domains. Often, as in Burundi, they were chosen from among the princes of the royal family; this system both kept heirs from the temptations of absolute power and provided a homogeneous rule over the whole country that assured national unity.[11]

The king also tended to appoint kin chiefs as territorial chiefs, depending on the amount of real authority the chief possessed, as well as on the degree of flexibility and realism displayed by the central government. In Buganda, the *kabaka* (sovereign) recognized and utilized the two overlapping forms of authority—territorial power and kin power—by pretending to be dealing with a single hierarchical system.[12] In the center of the kingdom, where most of the clan territories lay, 50 percent of the area remained under the control of the kin chiefs, whereas in the less central areas, more recently acquired, territorial chieftains strengthened their hold at the expense of the kin chiefs.

The role of both was to mobilize the peasants for three major tasks: maintenance of the roads linking the province with the seat of government, service as conscripts in the army—essential in a system of exploitation based on war—and annual payment of tribute. In the ten regions (*saza*), each divided into three or four subregions, each of which was subdivided in turn, there coexisted systems founded on different principles and yet performing the same functions, part of the same hierarchy and subject to a theoretically strict central power, at least in the reign of Mutesa (1856–1884).[13]

In another case, however, that of the kingdom of Abomey, anthropologist M. J. Herskovitz, followed by more recent scholars, probably tended to overstress the "bureaucratic perfection" of the monarchical system as exemplified in the precisely designed state apparatus and the detail in the sovereign's orders (concerning, for instance, the payment of tribute and commercial taxes or the upkeep of palm plantations).[14] Commands were rarely transmitted directly from the top to the bottom. Rather than a hierarchy of authority, there was a hierarchy of precedence: the sovereign gave orders to the chiefs of provinces, and these to their subchiefs and these again to their subordinates, but the mutual independence of the chiefs was almost total and the authority of each one laid boundaries for that of all the others, including his direct superior. The only authority that was uncontested, even if it was difficult to exert in practice, was the direct and absolute authority of the sovereign.

Relations of Personal Dependence

A relationship of personal dependence did not necessarily correspond either to kinship or to political relationships, but it could utilize either of them, and one of its major functions was to mediate between the two. Such relationships existed not only between different social groups but between those of similar status, for in these societies of low productivity the wealth and prestige of a man were measured, not by the size of his lands or the number of his possessions, but by the number of dependents whose labor was at his command. The most important chiefs were those who could assemble men and thus found villages or kingdoms; for instance, at the end of the seventeenth century Adu Pahi founded Yakasse in the Agni kingdom of Indenie (Ivory Coast) with a large number of immigrants who had come from many different areas, some under constraint, some by their own free will.[15] Runaways from village or lineage, young people in debt, or witch-doctors accused of casting evil spells were easily able to find new protectors. The most direct way of obtaining dependents, however, was by purchase, and this system was practiced by all the slave-trading societies, whose "domestic" captives became integrated into the lineage in a new kinship network.

Even apart from slavery, in this class-based society, rural life was regulated by a series of social exchanges. The term *horizontal relationship*, often

used by anthropologists, can indeed be applied to some relationships between peasants possessing identical status in the social and political hierarchy, but even there the practice of giving and giving-in-return implied a relationship of dependence between them. This can be seen in the etymology of
the terms employed. In Burundi, for example, *bugabire,* the word for institutionalized exchange, was derived from the word *bengaba,* meaning to
possess something, to give freely, to dominate, and to govern; the *mugabire,*
the client, agreed, in exchange for cows, hoes, sheep, and goats, to provide
beer and foodstuffs, and a calf born from the cow that was offered.[16]

Personal Dependence and Kinship Groups.   Within a lineage, the elders and the youngers were to some extent interdependent. The elders protected and paid the bride-price for the youngers, and the youngers supplied
food and labor to the elders and reinforced their prestige. The Alladians
serve as one example of how, within the lineage, matrimonial policy consolidated the influence of the elders, and acquisition of captives both guaranteed
the demographic growth of the kin group and provided an abundant labor
force of dependents.[17]

Lineages sometimes entered into patron-dependent relationships or even
master-slave relationships. The latter relationship existed between the Bapunu (Bantu) and Babongo (Pygmies) of the Congo within an entirely kinship (not state) society.[18] The Babongo groups were the property of the
Bapunu lineages. Each Babongo group had to pay homage to the Bapunu
(including the Bapunu youngers), to whom they offered all the game they
hunted—no doubt their most important act of fealty. The chief of the
Bapunu lineage then returned part of it for the Babongos' own consumption
and gave them a few gifts of fabric acquired through the slave trade and,
above all, salt. The Babongo role as providers of both food and various services (clearing land, building huts, and so forth), combined with their total
economic and political dependence, put them in a position approximating
that of classical slavery.

In addition, the Bantus themselves maintained patron-dependent relationships, the chief criterion of which was whether they possessed Babongos.
The Bavili and Banzati lineages were subordinate to the Bapunu, who conceded them the use of lands whose ownership remained in the hands of the
dominant lineages. These relationships of dependence affected the political
system as a whole. They tell us as much about the organization of the kingdom of Kongo as do the state structures themselves, for, in the period of the
slave trade, it was the chiefs of the patron lineages, those who possessed the
most Babongos, who could afford to travel to Loango on the coast or to
the sovereign in the capital. Their dependents' productive labor made it possible for these lineages to engage in trade and war, and these activities, in
turn, enabled the chiefs to strengthen their position still further through the

introduction of slaves or captives of war into their lineage. These patron lineages allied themselves, at the others' expense, with foreign slave-traders, thereby creating a new political equilibrium superimposed upon the kin relations of dependence. This resulted in a state structure that was both hierarchical and particularly fragile, since the territorial authority of the sovereign ultimately depended solely on the numbers and prestige of his dependent lineages.

Personal Dependence and the State.   The existence of a state implies that of a dominant aristocracy benefiting from state wealth and power. To such aristocracies, the subordinate communities would be of interest only insofar as they could be exploited. The rural communities were, however, highly self-contained and correspondingly reluctant to pay tribute. The aristocracies, thus, were only able to preserve their power because a close-knit network of personal relationships cut across all the social classes and bound them together, allowing the chiefs to extend their authority to the people, who had become their personal dependents.

The case of the Mundang in southwestern Chad, a kin group of peasant farmers and former warriors numbering about a hundred thousand people, demonstrates how this personal dependence arose.[19] Each free head of a household could offer the chief one of his sons. If the child was accepted, he worked in the chief's fields, and when he married, the chief paid his bride-price and retained full rights over the couple's children. This practice had no discernible economic purpose: the king had an abundance of wives and slaves, since all the captives of war were his by right. The aim was, rather, political: these were the elective sons of the chief who, himself situated outside and above all the clans since members of his sisters' and brothers' clans were ineligible for office, chose from among these young men his confidential advisers, about a dozen dignitaries who had access to state secrets. Thus, a personal relationship evolved in response to the problems posed by the contradiction between kin power, linked to the seniority of an individual within the lineage, and an extra-kin authority in command of a specific political apparatus.

Matrimonial ties were clearly one key to these relationships of personal dependence. Among the Amazons of the kingdom of Abomey, for instance, any village-dweller, bypassing both the kinship system and hierarchy, could connect himself directly to the sovereign by having an adolescent daughter taken to become one of the king's wives. These young women served as soldiers and in their capacity as king's wives also helped to promote the cohesion of the system. The practice goes back to the great unifying monarch Agadja at the beginning of the eighteenth century.[20]

In the classic instance of the interlacustrine states, a dual system of personal dependence developed: between the sovereign and the chief, and, in turn, between the chief and the local inhabitants. The relations toward the sovereign were usually those of personal dependence. Most of these chiefs were also servants in the king's household. In the state of Nkole, the king, Mugabe, gave preference to sons of certain dependents in appointing pages in the royal *kraal*. These pages were always chosen from among the Hima shepherds who had dominated the local population of Bantu (Iru) farmers from the sixteenth century onward. Thus, Nuwa Mbaguta, chief from 1895 to 1937, had begun to serve as a page at the age of eleven: he had been keeper of the king's milk, of the king's pipe, and of the king's beer and was then made responsible for the reception of foreign visitors. He finally obtained permission to recruit his own armed band for raids on cattle, bringing the spoils to King Ntare and so earning territorial power and a position as a favored chief.[21]

These relations of dependence existed throughout the hierarchy. In Burundi (a similar system existed in central and southern Rwanda), the Tutsi kings who, over time, seized all the land and all the livestock and then redistributed them in the form of fiefdoms, placed their political chiefs over these territorial areas. As in Nkole, the power of these chieftains was established by force, through an armed band and through the respect that was due to a representative of the royal authority. Later, however, conflict arose between the territorial chiefs and their dependents, on the one hand, and the personal dependents of the king (the *mwami*) and their retainers, on the other. Each of the chiefs, or *ganwa*, tended to make his territory into an autonomous region by creating a network of agricultural or financial dependents (*abugabire*); in other words, they established direct relationships outside both the political hierarchy and the kinship system, by redistributing the lineal territories to these dependents.

From the end of the seventeenth century, the *mwami* had been increasing his control over the center of the country, by extending his personal domains or by appointing chieftains who were directly dependent upon him. Ntare II, having conquered more distant districts (circa 1820), had to delegate authority to relatively unsupervised princes who, seizing the land and the livestock in their turn, attempted to reproduce the royal institutions for their own benefit. Thus, the king's dependents ended by establishing a chain of direct relationships outside the political hierarchy. To avoid such an outcome, a strong king tended to increase the number of his dependents and to dismiss the local chieftains and confiscate their lands and livestock. This resulted in a political process frequently encountered in Africa: that of dismissing from power princes whose lands or province had been received from a new king some generations earlier. Thus, in Burundi, the new chief had the right to take by force the hills of his predecessor at the end of four generations at the latest. (A similar practice existed among the Mundang, where the royal princes were deprived of their estates after only two generations.)[22]

Lower in the hierarchy, the subchief similarly relied on personal dependents to act as foremen when he had to supply forced labor. These foremen, acting as an unofficial para-administrative unit, enabled the subchief to divert part of the profits for his own use. Thus, there was always an unstable equilibrium: at each hierarchical level, in order to resist territorial disintegration a strong chief had the tendency to increase the number of his personal dependents, and these in turn threatened to create their own networks. In order to maintain the royal authority, a continual readjustment of power was required, which affected the system as a whole.

This relative instability of government within a system of constantly shifting interdependence characterized the precolonial period. The ties of personal dependence appeared as the means of reconciling two contradictory tendencies, the first of which was a tendency toward centralization. The exploitative relationships of a system of production based on forced labor and slaves favored a unified, hegemonic monarchy.

Opposed to this tendency toward centralization, however, was a respect for the essential kinship units. This respect grew out of the uncertain domination of man over nature, both because of the limited forces of production and the specific means of the appropriation of the soil. Territorial autonomy was expressed politically in a centrifugal dynamic of emancipation; the functioning of the Gamo society in southern Ethiopia is a good example.[23] Although wars, which provided slaves and territory, played a predominant role in the system, conscription was greatly restricted by the need to tend a precarious system of production. The hierarchy of power, then, although intact, was extremely feeble, since the king could not change the basic social structures.

The guarantor of equilibrium was the assembly: all the free men in the rural community took part in the assemblies under the auspices of dignitaries or *halaka* chosen by their fellow citizens. The eldest married male in each family was eligible to become such a dignitary. Chosen by their neighbors or the district assemblies, the *halaka*, to mark their change of status, organized very costly feasts with large quantities of food and drink. The acquisition of this title, which brought social prestige, presupposed a certain accumulation of private wealth but at the same time required its expenditure. This ideology of ostentation prevented the emergence of a rigid social stratification and thus of a true state system run by an autonomous and homogeneous ruling class. The *halaka* both symbolized the bipolar centralizing and kinship tendencies and, through the network of relationships of personal interdependence they established, resolved the conflict between them.

One factor that reveals this constant conflict and the importance of relations of personal interdependence is so common in the history of African monarchies that it seems almost an institution: that of wars of succession. It was rare that an accession to a throne took place smoothly, especially as in

general few laws of succession—such as male primogeniture—existed, and
as customs were not fixed, especially in a matrilinear society. Even when the
problem would appear to have been avoided by the practice of naming the
heir while his predecessor was still alive—as in Dahomey, where the aging
king seems to have been dethroned by the son he had chosen—the inter-
regnum was always long (lasting at least two years) and filled with strife. It
would be an oversimplification to ascribe this time lapse merely to the religious considerations surrounding the funeral; it was a matter of testing authority. In most cases, the successor was chosen from among a number of
candidates for the title, either princes of the royal lineage or elected by a
council of elders. Sometimes, the contenders' qualifications were so closely
matched that a compromise was reached, as in Fouta Djallon (Guinea),
where the supreme authority of the *almami* was given alternately to two
rival families—which did not, however, eliminate internal struggles. Dynastic histories are everywhere intersected with wars of succession (the almost
exclusive cause of civil wars), and royal genealogies are very hard to recon-
struct, owing to the numbers of false claimants retrospectively legitimized
by tradition and of the unfortunate heirs-presumptive more or less violently
prevented from assuming office (and then "forgotten" by those in authority).

The real aim, then, seems to have been to select the strongest, most capable, and most respected candidate. And that candidate's supremacy was
surely due to his capacity to gather around him the largest number of followers—in other words, the largest number of dependents.

Personal Dependence in the Village.   The peasant was not only the king's
subject, but the personal dependent of his immediate chief. In Rwanda, the
dependent (who was generally a Hutu but sometimes a Tutsi, for, whatever
has been said, the difference is not necessarily an ethnic one) offered his services to someone who was wealthier and more respected, who gave him in
return one or several head of cattle and took him under his protection. The
cow was the symbol of allegiance: the master had the overlordship, the dependent the life interest. This relationship of dependence (*ubuhake*) associated the partners at all levels.[24]

A similar system existed in the villages of Buganda: the peasant was always a dependent of either the kin chief or the territorial chief. Each peasant
had complete freedom to select his chief, although in practice elements such
as regional tradition, the presence in the village or the proximity of other
members of the kin group, or the reputation of the village chief influenced
his choice. A sort of contract was then concluded. The peasant asked the
chief to set him up with his family on a piece of land; when this was done,
the peasant fulfilled his duties toward the chief by making him periodic gifts
and providing labor, and he also followed him to war. But while the "chief's
men"—that is to say, his deputies, who, like himself, were directly account-

able to the political authorities and through whom he exerted his domination over the villages—were a relatively permanent group who followed him in all his journeys, the dependent peasants retained the right of breaking the relationship, of leaving the domain and engaging themselves elsewhere. To retain the dependent, the chief was constrained to fulfill his duties, that is, to serve as a liaison between his dependents and the king, to protect the dependent against unfair demands by the king, and to be generous in redistributing the foodstuffs or spoils of war his dependents obtained for him, assuring the chief's prosperity.

Although the peasant was free to choose his employer, he did have to choose one; he was forced, in short, to take up a concrete position within the state apparatus. The relationship of dependence thus appears to have been an excellent means of coordinating the village with the state, by incorporating the people in the political process.[25]

The complex interplay of the three variables of kinship, territorial possessions, and personal dependence suggests the flexibility of the system as a whole. The tendency has been to oversimplify this system by dividing it into a kin-ordered chiefdom and a class-divided state (contrasting, for instance, the Bameleke chiefdoms and the Bamum state in precolonial Cameroon). The chiefdom was supposed to have exhibited little or no direct exploitation and tribute was to be interpreted as a contribution to the common good, whereas the state was seen as a hierarchical system (administration, police, army) that exacted tribute from conquered groups situated at the boundaries of its territory. It would seem more accurate to recognize every shade of government in sub-Saharan Africa, from the "stateless" kin society to the most clearly structured political formation. It has been shown, for instance, that in the Bamum kingdom kinship was not only a governing ideological element in the allocation of political power, but was at the very basis of the state itself.[26]

It remains to determine the impact of these precolonial structures on contemporary African societies. Examination of all the other systems leads us back to that basic unit, the rural community. The activities of the state at the village level were almost always coercive, and thus must be seen as superimposed on the rural community, which was essentially characterized by kin structures and by the tight network of relationships of personal dependence that connected it or opposed it to the outside world. The cohesion of the village, the dogged resistance of its structures to the assaults of colonialism and even to those of modern times, has finally given rise to the idea that instead of continuing to destroy it, the attempt should be made, not only to preserve its vitality, but somehow to unite it with a new, economically sophisticated society. The question to be addressed is whether such an adaptation is feasible—or even possible.

5

State Resistance to Colonial Control

Colonialist histories have long perpetuated the myth of a sub-Saharan Africa conquered fairly easily and profiting from pacification (unlike the Algeria of Abd el-Kader, for instance). The local populations, according to these histories, were finally delivered by the "colonial peace" from the internal struggles of little local rulers forever raiding their neighbors' territories in search of slaves or livestock.

Understandably, recent African histories have tried hard to demonstrate that the resistance to the colonial conquest was in fact fierce and nearly universal and have drawn attention particularly to the last great struggles of precolonial Africa.[1] In West Africa, historians have singled out for praise the Sarakolle kingdom of Mamadou Lamine (1885–1887), the jihad of Ma Ba (1861–1867) in Senegambia, and, particularly, the Tukulor episode of Umar Tall (1852–1864) and his son Ahmadu (died 1898), whose empire stretched from Timbuktu to Fouta Djallon in Guinea and from Medina to Segu, although he never succeeded in realizing his dream of a unified Muslim state. In addition, beginning in 1804 the Fulbe people, under Usman dan Fodio, conquered the Hausa country and, under the exceptional leadership of Muhammad Bello (1807–1847), constituted a vast Islamic entity between Niger and Benue, around Sokoto. They succeeded in avoiding a violent confrontation with the British, but this was no doubt because the British, at the end of the century, agreed to preserve the area as a state under British control. We should also mention the similar episode of Samori, whose Mandingo empire resisted the colonialists from 1870 to 1898, and the stubborn resistance of the Ashanti of Ghana (1874–1900) and of Behanzin of Dahomey (1890–1894).

Elsewhere in Africa, also opposed to the colonialists were traditionalist local chieftains who embodied the ethnic nationalism of their dependents. Such were Kabarega in Bunyoro (1892–1896) and Mandume and the Ovambos in southern Angola (1911–1917). There were also recent, well-organized political formations concerned with preserving their preeminence. Thus, in central Sudan, Rabah, a slave-trading adventurer from the Nile regions, between 1893 and 1900 set up a military and commercial empire, at the expense of the Baguirmi and the Bornu, which functioned efficiently although it suffered, in comparison with the others, from its founder's reputation as a bloody, slave-trading despot.

In the east of the continent, a relatively large number of powerful entrepreneurs—more or less Islamized Nyamwezi and Yao—who created local empires that were both military and commercial and, toward the end of the century, vigorously opposed the colonial powers. Such were Mirambo (1871–1884) on the great ivory route of Tabora (Tanzania), Msiri in Katanga (1860–1891), and, until he allied with the Belgians in the Upper Congo, even Tippu-Tib in Maniema. The most famous of these far-reaching, visionary modern chieftains was also the first: Chaka (1816–1828)—celebrated by the poet Senghor—who made the Zulu people into a conquering nation that manifested its will to reject the colonial power at a late stage and was finally defeated in the last Natal revolt (1906–1908).

In the comparatively short period of the last decades of the nineteenth century, there was a crystallization of the movements of opposition to the colonialists. This is far from surprising, and is indeed a classic phenomenon in history, but its significance ought nevertheless to be studied. These instances of large-scale military resistance appear as the last burst of energy of independent Africa. It is tempting to see these leaders as African Vercingetorixes and to make them out to be the fearless and irreproachable heroes of a supremely national history. In fact, such resistance usually smacked more of politics than populism and took place within a complex interweaving of contradictory internal influences and evolving interests.

The most obvious form of this phenomenon, that of conquerors provoking military resistance, does not seem to me necessarily the most significant. There is a very simple reason for this: the best-organized precolonial wars of resistance were those in which a strongly structured political entity headed by an energetic chieftain with a well-developed political sense and well-trained army and aided by a select aristocracy extended genuine government over a relatively broad area. This situation was rare, however. Most states had been formed recently, upon shaky social and cultural foundations; had themselves gained power through conquest; and ruled over peoples who had been subjected for less than a century, some for only one or two generations. Except, perhaps, in the specific form of the jihad, the Muslim holy war whose significance we shall examine later, these wars only secondarily reflected popular sentiment. Three examples, geographically very distant from one another, illustrate this fact: the empire of Samori in West Africa, the slave-trading kingdoms of East Africa, and the Zulus under Chaka's leadership in South Africa.

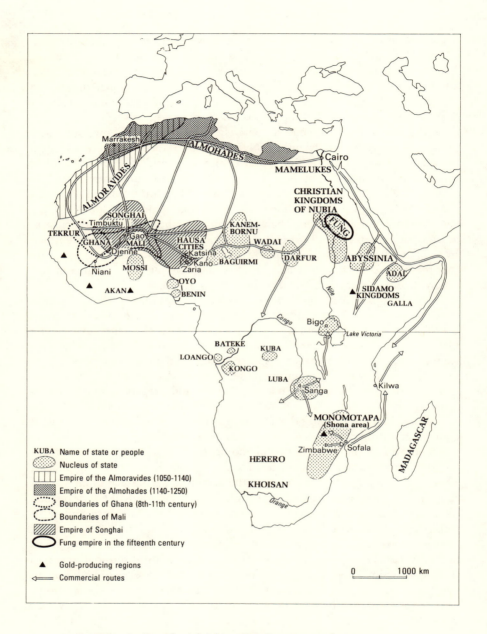

Map 2. *Precolonial Africa, Tenth to Sixteenth Century*

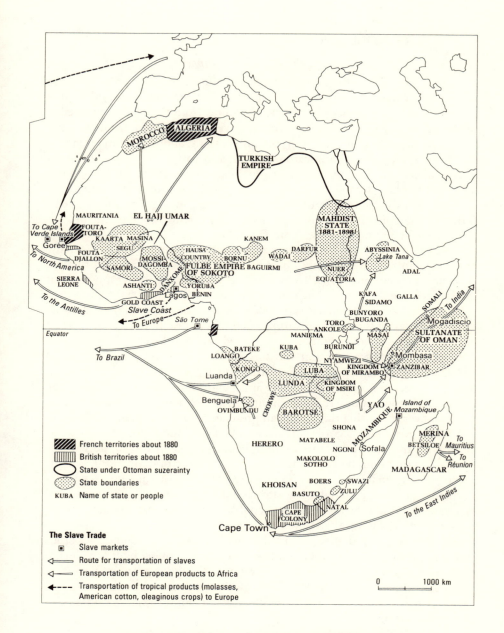

The Slave Trade

▣ Slave markets

◁══ Route for transportation of slaves

◁── Transportation of European products to Africa

◀---- Transportation of tropical products (molasses, American cotton, oleaginous crops) to Europe

French territories about 1880

British territories about 1880

State under Ottoman suzerainty

State boundaries

KUBA Name of state or people

Map 3. Precolonial Africa, Eighteenth to Nineteenth Century

CONQUERING STATES AND NATION-STATES

Samori, the Merchant Emperor

Beginning in the 1860s, Samori created an empire on the narrowest social and political base—a tiny group of more or less Islamized, wealthy merchants.[2] These merchants plied the trade routes from the Niger to the edge of the forested area of Guinea, carrying slaves, kola nuts (a product of the forests consumed in the area of the Sudan), sea salt, and European manufactured goods. A political innovator in an area in which the only centralized governments had been the very recently created state of the Marabout Sise and the little kingdom of Kankan, Samori based his authority on the effectiveness of his organization of the area, assuring, to a greater degree than hitherto, the control of regions subjugated by territorial governments administered by military chiefs. From the 1880s on, he undertook successive conquests with the aim of forming an army out of his new slaves; finally, from 1884 to 1887, he sought to base his authority on the unifying principle of Islam, proclaiming himself *almami* and declaring a theocratic form of government implying the obligatory conversion of his subjects.

Samori's economic policies received, at least at the beginning, the support of the Malinke of the south, ensuring a certain cultural unity, but his empire was above all a military edifice, constructed first and foremost for internal considerations. His initial aim was to conquer Sikasso, capital of his rival the *faama* of Kenedugu. His first clashes with the French—who were engaged in overcoming Mamadou Lamine and were advancing along the Niger River toward the Tukulor empire—were accidental. Samori, indeed, was not averse to using the European presence for his own benefit. Thus, in 1887 he made a first accord with General Gallieni, and then, when his relations with the French became more difficult, he sought the support of the English, with whom he concluded a treaty of protectorate in 1890. Finally, faced with the French advances, Samori did not hesitate to pursue a scorched-earth policy, ever demanding greater numbers of soldiers, caravans, and porters. As a result, he found himself confronted with a vast rebellion within his own empire (1888–1890).

From 1892 onward, he was forced radically to alter the boundaries of his domain, pushing them further and further east and hoping by this means to place them beyond the reach of the Whites. This was proof, if any were needed, of the artificial nature of his regime, which now extended into foreign territory. Samori was undoubtedly a major political figure and a great strategist, but he was not a nationalist hero.

The Entrepreneur-Kings of East Africa

The leaders in East Africa deserved the title of nationalist hero even less than Samori did. They were entrepreneur-kings who gained their wealth and position through trade in the Indian Ocean—including a trade in their own subjects. Thus, from 1891 to 1894, Chief Mkwawa of the Hehe of southern Tanganyika was the major native challenge to the German colonial conquest, but he had revolted primarily because he had been placed under a prohibition against levying his usual heavy dues—the source of his power—on the trade route running from the coast to Tabora. Despite all his efforts, therefore, he was unable to persuade other chiefs and tribes to unite around him. The collapse of the Hehe state structure and the resulting confusion explain why, a few years later, the Hehe were practically the only group not to participate in the Maji Maji revolt.[3]

A number of notable examples can be given of such slave-traders: half-African, half-Swahili, sometimes Islamized potentates who radically transformed the concept and forms of government in Central Africa during the last third of the nineteenth century. They destroyed the old political forms, substituting new conquering, multiethnic empires that constituted a transitory initial response to European imperialism. The pattern was nearly always the same: one individual with an exceptional background—sometimes part Arab—and degree of wealth—founded on long-distance trade—by design or necessity broke free of the traditional restraints of society and, arriving from the exterior with a small group of dependents attracted by his personality, his wealth, and his success, succeeded in establishing his authority over others among whom he finally settled. His technical and hence military superiority (based on guns from the slave trade) and political talent, reinforced by the combined advantages of wealth and power, enabled him to establish a new political entity with a new dynasty. The conqueror was thus the founder of a new social order but, swept aside in turn by the colonialist tidal wave, he came to be remembered as a great civilizer or, at any rate, as a reforming dynast, except in the cases (for example, that of Rabah) where the still-fresh grievances of his victims were only exacerbated by the new masters.[4]

One of the best examples of such individuals was Mirambo, an outstanding chief whom the explorer Stanley described successively as a "brigand" and as "the Napoleon of Black Africa," who in a few short years achieved the unification of the Anyamwezi, peoples hitherto dispersed in innumerable chiefdoms with ill-defined boundaries between Lake Nyanza and Lake Tanganyika. Muslim merchants had come from the coast to the interior to exchange gunpowder and weapons for slaves and ivory, and Mirambo understood how to take advantage of these new economic and military circumstances. Of obscure origin, he progressively built up his position as leader after 1858, making use alternately of relations of kinship and of diplomacy and force, in order to dominate the trade route between Tabora, where Arabs had settled, and Ujiji on Lake Tanganyika, exacting heavy tolls. In this way, in about two decades he set up a state whose commercial prosperity was guaranteed by a permanent army of young adventurers to whom he promised victories and booty year by year.

Although Mirambo was at first eager to maintain good relations with the European travelers, missionaries, and merchants he frequently received in his capital, which was a sort of entrenched camp housing thousands of warriors, his relations with the Belgians of the African International Association, who joined forces with his Arab competitors, became increasingly strained. Moreover, despite his search for alliances with such neighboring chieftains as the Arab Tippu-Tib or King Mukesa of Buganda, the last year of his reign, 1884, was marked by a renewal of internal divisions, and German colonization in 1895 put a definite end to the enterprise.

An original and complex personality, Mirambo was a fusion of four elements: a traditional chieftain; a military leader; the builder of a state; and a modernizer open to new developments, from the *ngoni* art of warfare to the Zanzibar trade and technological innovations, keen to reach an understanding with the foreign powers at the highest level in order to strengthen his position vis-à-vis his local competitors. To be sure, his regime amounted, at the most, to a form of subimperialism. If his attempt at unification ultimately failed, it left a legacy: the diffusion of *kirambo*, the Nyamwezi dialect of his region and his army, which was adopted by the missionaries.[5]

Chaka, the Visionary Warrior

The activities of the Zulus do not permit easy classification. In the beginning, it had the makings of a nation-state, but its influence spread far beyond its original boundaries. The Zulu nucleus was a close-knit, homogeneous group that was outstanding militarily as well as culturally. The collapse of Zulu nationalism was of course a direct result of its military defeat and physical uprooting by the colonial conquest, but, more fundamentally, it collapsed because it was based on self-destructive principles that forced it to transform itself into a conquering empire. Chaka, too, if one considers his background, can be understood as a strategist unequaled in his day, but one who worked for a political ideal that was fantastic and suicidal.

Beginning in the 1600s and accelerating its progress in the next century, the Zulu subgroup of the Nguni gradually became a nation, that is, a specific, relatively stable Bantu group with an identifiable set of institutions and a national culture. Unlike the Bantu of the south, the Xhosa ("Kaffirs"), great stockbreeders and farmers, who had entered into contact with the Europeans in 1652 and had fairly early produced a relatively developed civilization, the Zulu subgroup, protected from the Europeans by the Xhosa buffer zone, long remained rough and warlike. Its leaders showed their intelligence by finding a way of turning the basis of its socioeconomic structure to advantage, making it into a system.

In this farmers' and hunters' society of poor returns, the overriding aim was to increase labor power in order to extend the hunting areas and the areas under cultivation. In these areas, to give birth to children was both to extend one's own life and to increase productivity. For this growing population, defending and increasing its territory was a sacred duty. The property of the community, land was acquired by the use of arms. The productive process was thus dominated by war, a brutal and violent appropriation of the labor of others, reducing them to subject status and profiting from their capacity for production and for reproduction. The first to understand this principle and make it into a law was Chaka's predecessor Dingiswayo, who came to power about 1795. Education, which had previously been separate, now came to be indissociable from military training. All young people were enlisted into regiments, grouped according to age.

When Chaka came to power in 1816, conditions were ripe for a profound social revolution. Externally, the aim was to defeat the alliance of neighboring tribes and to bring them under the Zulu yoke through war; internally, in order to achieve this it was necessary to form a new man for whom war would replace all the ancient rites of initiation, those gates of entry into adult life. Chaka replaced the ritual of circumcision with a new myth: eternal youth. All the young men (*amazulu,* "sons of heaven") took as their model the victorious warrior who boasts of his brave exploits and inebriates himself with the praises of his friends. Uncircumcised and obliged to remain celibate until their fortieth year, they remained young—that is, always prepared for war—in a country that remained in a permanent state of mobilization.[6] Chaka seems to have been obsessed with the idea of youth and to have identified procreation with the process of aging. Both boys and girls were conscripted but were strictly forbidden to associate with one another. When a boy was once found scaling the wall of a girls' compound, the punishment was terrible: 5,000 other boys were massacred as well as the guilty person.

Under these conditions, the only way to reproduce the warrior community and provide for the biological renewal of the Zulus was by the Zulufication of the conquered peoples. The Zulu people and army—which were virtually identical—lived off the booty taken from conquered territories. Natal was devastated, and the south of Tukela was transformed into a no-man's-land which isolated northern Tukela from the Cape Colony. The old people and infants were killed and the young people were incorporated into the Zulu army.

The final aim was to attain the condition of *busa,* a state of blissful repose in which the people and Chaka contemplated one another. Assassinated in 1828, Chaka never achieved this dream. At the same time, the system, founded on order and discipline, proved to be demographically disastrous: simultaneously with forming a Zulu nation, Chaka assured its ruin.

Could the Zulu empire be interpreted as a symbol of African national resistance? The answer is both yes and no, insofar as the cohesion of the group did not prevent the sovereigns from making a number of compromises that led to the loss of their independence. Under Dingirane, Chaka's successor (1828–1840), Durban became a trading port with increasing importance in the internal politics of the country as a place of refuge from Zulu domination. Under Mpande (1840–1856), who entered into an alliance with the Boers in order to overcome his predecessor, the British, after an admittedly very difficult campaign, founded the colony of Natal (1843); and under Cetshwayo (1856–1873), who had been crowned by the British commissioner, the British invaded and devastated the country.

To be sure, to conquer the area the British needed four years of campaigning, two major engagements, reinforcements from the army in India, and the introduction of the fire-lock gun. And although the Zulu empire crumbled, Zulu nationalism survived the Protectorate of 1887 and had a late, spasmodic flowering in the desperate revolt of Bambata in 1906–1908. It could, however, also be said that the Zulu conquests encouraged, or, at any rate, prepared the ground for, the colonialist intervention. The process of Zulufication had upset the preceding structures. The Boers, on their 1836 Great Trek, or exodus toward the interior, were able to settle without difficulty on the high plateaus of the Orange and the Transvaal partly because the Zulu raids had emptied the land of its defenders, for Chaka's rigid autocracy had caused the more active and ambitious chiefs to move on to conquer and transform neighboring regions on the Zulu model for their own benefit. Thus Mzilikazi, from 1821 to 1823, created an empire in Southern Rhodesia, making an entirely new nation around his capital, Bulawayo, out of people of very varied ethnic origins. These were the Ndebele (or Matabele), who first fought the Shona and then, at the end of the century, fiercely opposed the European intrusion. Another example was Shoshangane, who, before crossing the Zambezi in 1835 to found the Ngoni kingdom on the western bank of Lake Malawi, created the kingdom of Gaza in southern Mozambique, which was destroyed only at the very end of the century, by the Portuguese. Finally, Zwangendaba—who in 1821–1825 took flight in the direction of Lake Victoria—completed the destruction of the old Shona civilization of Monomotapa (Zimbabwe) and, continuing as far as Nyasaland, Zulufied Burundi and Rwanda.

Migrant groups in turn left these Zulufied kingdoms, spreading out, in a single generation, over more than three thousand kilometers and effecting profound internal changes through the diffusion of a military concept of the state radically different from that of the old patriarchal and commercial empires. The consequences were that the White invaders found themselves confronted with new and in some respects progressive African forces, but also that the traditional ways of life were disorganized and their capacities of resistance weakened.

Ashanti and Abomey: The First National Resistance

In the course of its history the Zulu empire illustrated two possible main types of precolonial resistance: that of recently created military states which, with a few exceptions, lacked a nationalist foundation, and that of sociopolitical entities, forerunners of true nation-states, whose members were bound together by a common history and cultural heritage. The Ashanti kingdom and the kingdom of Abomey were good examples of this latter type.

Ashanti was one of the most stubborn defenders of independence throughout the nineteenth century. The first encounter with the British took place in 1823. Although the capital, Kumasi, was sacked in 1874, the Ashanti continued to resist until 1896, when the British, who had long been settled on the coast in the Fanti country, instituted the Protectorate.

The struggle had been organized by the sovereign (*Asantehene*) Prempeh the First, aided by his provincial chiefs, but the resistance movement outlasted him. When he was deported despite his submission, the conquest was not yet accepted in the country: as late as 1900 Ashanti rose up under the Queen Mother and fought a memorable battle, and the colonialists had to assemble nearly two thousand men for a real war of conquest.

Ashanti had emerged as a political formation in the second half of the seventeenth century. The first architect to unite under a single authority the peoples speaking the Akan language was the celebrated Osei-Tutu, who reigned about 1680 to 1712 or 1717. His role was similar to that of King Agadja among the Fon in neighboring Dahomey, who ruled from 1708 to 1740. The state was based on a military regime financed by the commercial expansion of a homogeneous cultural group.[7] The central political nucleus was relatively small. The more distant provinces were ill-controlled, and Ashanti rule was extended with difficulty to the Fanti states on the coast, which, throughout the century, pursued a concurrent policy of alliance with the British that was clearly incompatible with Ashanti hegemony. Their attitude was rather similar to that of the little coastal kingdom of Porto-Novo toward the kingdom of Abomey, which in the same way claimed to rule it. The difference between the two kingdoms was that whereas Ashanti was situated inland at the junction of the southern Atlantic trade routes with the northern ones through its great kola-marketing centers such as Buna and Daloa, from the beginning of the eighteenth century, when it acquired the trading port of Whydah, the kingdom of Abomey had an outlet to the sea.

The struggle against the West was part of the very life of the territory and its socioeconomic structures, and this long-drawn-out resistance demanded improved weapons. Before the beginning of the nineteenth century the Ashanti had abandoned their bows and arrows for the gun, which their merchants acquired in large numbers on the coast. In 1728, the Danish of Christianborg, Accra, reported that two thousand Ashanti merchants had bought guns and powder in exchange for slaves and ivory. At that period, the Asantehene was able to demand payment of rent in the form of armaments from the Europeans of various nationalities, for their forts at Accra and Elmina on the coast.[8]

Like Samori's empire, Ashanti was a political entity based on a military tradition at the service of commercial activities, the source of the wealth of the aristocracy. In Ashanti, however, the oligarchy was not a superimposed minority that sought to establish itself by an ideology of legitimization; it was a real linguistic and cultural community of which the Asantehene was the national representative. Moreover, the commercial activities were subordinated to the government: the minority of Muslim or Dyula merchants remained a foreign community controlled or even exploited by the state, rather than that community ruling the local populations. The Ashanti population itself was forbidden to engage in trade, that is, to attempt to acquire a degree of wealth, and hence power, that might threaten the royal supremacy.

It should be pointed out that when the British advocated the abolition of the slave trade and of human sacrifices in Ashanti in the name of what they called humanitarian Western values, they encountered a collective hostility for these rites were central expressions of the national culture. Similarly, once again, in Dahomey the great feasts known as "the Customs," in which human sacrifices were offered, were not an independent phenomenon but were a basis for the entire civilization. The European witnesses themselves realized that to suppress these practices would deal a fatal blow to the institutions and social relationships and to the very foundations of the kingdom of Abomey. These yearly feasts in which a few dozen slaves were sacrificed, or, at the funeral of the reigning monarch, a few hundred, represented first of all a critical moment in the military life of the kingdom—just after the annual raiding expedition. The victims were consecrated by an unchanging and exact ritual that expressed the religious beliefs and political system of Dahomey. The rituals celebrated the transmission of the royal authority and, by their ostentation, symbolized the transmission of the royal wealth. The king was quite sincere when he replied to the Western envoys that the sacrifices were such a sacred duty that nothing could make him decide to dispense with them even if he were offered the greatest possible remuneration for the slaves who were used for them.[9]

The Ashanti struggle against the Europeans was therefore long-drawn-out, persistent, and, finally, partly victorious: in 1924 the exiled King Prempeh and his companions were repatriated, in Ashanti, and in 1926 Prempeh became *Kumasihene* (head of the town of Kumasi). For the people of Ashanti, however, he remained the king, and in 1935, when the Ashanti Confederation was officially reestablished, his successor, Nana Sir Osei

Prempeh II, regained both the title of Asantehene and its symbol, the golden stool.

A recent event illustrates the continuing important symbolic role of the Asantehene (and the use that can be made of it, seeing that it concerns a notorious opponent of the "socialist" regime of the time): the pomp and ceremony which accompanied the visit of His Majesty the Asantehene in 1983 to New York, on the occasion of the opening of the exhibition of Ashanti treasures.

The precolonial history of the kingdom of Abomey has, as we have seen, strong points of resemblance with that of Ashanti. There, too, the people shared language, traditions and myths of origin, and economic and cultural activities. For the Fon, the state was not simply a territorial unit but, above all, a spiritual entity. The preservation, expansion, and glorification of the group had become a national purpose, embracing all the members of the community—the living, the dead, and future generations, whose membership in the group was guaranteed by the fact of being born on the soil of Dahomey (the son of a slave was thus automatically free). This outlook caused the Fon to resist as a single man any assault on their territorial or cultural integrity.

Until the 1870s, contacts between France and Dahomey, mainly of a commercial nature, were fairly friendly (largely due to the diplomatic skill of a great sovereign, King Ghezo, 1818–1858), but tension mounted when the French claimed the port of Cotonou and made an alliance with Porto-Novo, which in 1878 and 1883 concluded two treaties of protectorate with France and in 1888 rejected the sovereignty of Dahomey.

The determined expansionism of the French met with fierce opposition from the crown prince, Kondo. Accordingly, in 1889, the French decided to take Cotonou by force, and the new king, who had taken the name of Behanzin, responded by mobilizing all his followers. Such an operation was feasible, but it did not happen often: the annual raiding campaign generally mobilized only the two or three thousand people on the plateau of Abomey who depended directly on the sovereign or the highest dignitaries. An armistice was declared, but hostilities broke out again two years later. The French then decided upon conquest, invading Abomey at the end of 1892. Although General Dodds proclaimed the deposition of Behanzin, the people of Dahomey showed no disposition to replace him, while the king, who had fled to the north, attempted to regroup his army. The French, realizing that the person of the king symbolized the state for his subjects, undertook a new expedition at the end of 1893 to capture Behanzin, but the fleeing king was sheltered and protected by his people. It was not the people, but the Fon chiefs who were taken prisoner, who decided in favor of what they saw as a more profitable policy of collaboration. They appointed a new king who was willing to recognize the treaty of protectorate, which would provisionally allow a semblance of autonomy. Throughout this whole period, however, the popular resistance seems to represent a kind of national legitimacy.

Nevertheless, this popular resistance could not stand up to the class collaboration on the part of the chiefs. Very few rulers, in fact, chose to fight to the finish like Behanzin in Dahomey and Kabarega in Bunyoro, whose obstinacy only had the effect of delivering up his little kingdom to his neighbor and traditional enemy Buganda, which had resigned itself much earlier to the British Protectorate.[10] Chief Mandume of the Ovambo, too, put up a fierce resistance to the Portuguese in the four years of his reign, 1911 to 1915, on the borders of Angola and Southwest Africa (Namibia). Mandume was the prototype of the survivor of an independent ethnic society who exploited the ambiguity of the frontiers established by the Europeans in order to assert his intention of preserving intact the precolonial status quo. This nationalist, who never abandoned his fight against colonization, commanded an army of thirty-five to forty thousand men, most of whom were armed with military rifles (not rifles from the slave trade). In the final battle, a supreme struggle where an entire people combined forces in an attempt to expel the foreigners, he mustered some fifty thousand men armed with some ten to twelve thousand late-model rifles, and five Boer tanks filled with munitions. Except in Ethiopia, nowhere else in the history of the conquest of Black Africa was there a pitched battle involving such a large number of Africans.[11]

Conclusions

It seems, then, that the effect these precolonial uprisings had on the later evolution of resistance movements was on the whole less powerful than one might imagine. It was only much later, on the eve of independence, that the great chiefs we have described, such as Chaka and Samori, began to be invoked as precursors and symbols—as they were to a certain extent, at least in the long run, but in the short run their effect was generally the opposite. In this respect, the collapse of the little nation-states was instructive: sooner or later the precolonial power submitted to European domination, as did the local sovereigns of the Wolof kingdoms, the royal families of Abomey, and the Asantehene. It had become obvious that only passivity would guarantee even a few prerogatives such as concessions of land and the right to cross borders. A definite class alliance sealed the collaboration between the colonialists, interested in using the former authorities' useful and effective powers of mediation for their own benefit, and those authorities themselves.

One example was that of the Hehe. Another was the violent revolt of the Shona and the Ndebele in Rhodesia in 1896–1897. Confronted with the expansion of the British South Africa Company, which, at the end of 1893, overran the Matabele country, these two historically rival peoples united against Cecil Rhodes' white colonizers. Very soon, however, the Ndebele found that a policy of collaboration proved more advantageous: they were the first to be "pacified," agreeing to accept important positions. At the same time, the massacre of the Shona achieved the same result by opposite means, and this clear demonstration of the power of the Whites contributed in the following years to the obvious passivity of the Zimbabwe people.

In short, the majority of the population, traditionally attached to the chief, who was the symbol of their permanence and the guarantor of their prosperity, continued to follow his orders even when he submitted to the colonizers. Thus, in the precolonial nation-states, paradoxically, collaboration became popular soon after the conquest. One result of this, perhaps, was relatively rapid cultural assimilation, and this in turn may, a few decades later, have encouraged by way of reaction a comparatively early awakening of nationalist sentiment. One example of this process is Ghana, which by 1911 had already become the world's leading producer of cocoa, and in 1957 became the first country in sub-Saharan Africa to gain independence. Another example is Dahomey (Benin), considered in the interwar period the "Latin Quarter" of French-speaking Africa because of the number of African elite who had attended colonial upper-level schools.

As for the great empires of conquest that were overthrown, they also, for different reasons, had little lasting effect. Each of the conquered peoples reacted in their own way, in accordance with their history, environment, and culture. On the one hand were those who were grateful at being delivered from an almost unbearable constraint, especially if that repression had been accompanied by a reinforcement of the slave-trading system (as was the case for the Bantu peoples enslaved by the emirates and sultanates of the Upper Ubangi or the Chad Basin, or the peoples exploited by Samori). These tended to throw themselves into the arms of the colonizer, whom they briefly considered an ally—for disillusionment was not slow to set in. On the other hand, groups traditionally hostile to the imposition of any superior authority retained that attitude after the coming of the Europeans: the Baule on the Ivory Coast and the Hollidje in Benin, for example, required a slow and painful "pacification." In other words, when state resistance came to an end, popular movements regained their strength and validity.

PRECOLONIAL ISLAM

The Muslim countries of sub-Saharan Africa take in the whole Sudanese area, which stretches from Senegal in the West to the Horn of Africa in the east and includes most of the east coast and a continually increasing percentage of the Guinean forested area. These countries confront the West with a structured ideology which is not easily shaken, for it combines religion, politics, and culture into one integrated whole. Islam colored the forms of resistance these nations made against colonization; they were often the product of institutionally hierarchical systems in which there was a relatively clear manifestation of the contradictions between popular pressures and the interests of the ruling aristocracies.

The contradiction goes back to the precolonial period. For a number of centuries, Islam had appeared as a system of the ruling classes, for in the eleventh century, two imperial centers became Islamized, at least nominally. One lay in the west—located successively in Ghana (eleventh century), Mali (thirteenth to fifteenth century),[12] and the Songhai empire (until the Moroccan conquest in 1591)—and the other in the east, around Kanem (from the ninth century) and Bornu (from the fourteenth century). Only the court— the sovereigns and dignitaries—and those in commercial circles connected by political and economic interests to the Mediterranean Muslim world, however, adhered to Islam. These shifting empires with imprecise frontiers, which developed at the outlets of the trans-Saharan trade routes, took advantage of their special position to set up aristocratic warrior-states, trading the gold and slaves they had pillaged for horses and luxury goods. The gold, shipped via the Mediterranean, formed the beginnings of Western wealth, and between the tenth and the fourteenth century, four million slaves were carried along the trade routes across the Sahara. The status of Islam here was ambiguous, the leading clans seeing it primarily as an additional source of power complementary to the traditional forms of authority.[13]

Beginning in the seventeenth century, when the unceasing demand for slaves pushed the evil effects of the slave trade further and further into the interior, Muslim holy men, or marabouts, became prominent. They set themselves up as defenders of maltreated populations whose wicked sovereigns delivered up their subjects to the slave-traders.

In the south, particularly in the Malinke country from Senegambia to the edge of the Ivory Coast, Islamic penetration took place at a late date and in a peaceful manner, spread by Diakhanke or Dyula learned or trading communities, while the Sahel was the special preserve of the jihad.

For instance, Saint-Louis in Senegal had been a French colonial trading post since 1638. In about 1675, under the leadership of a Moorish shaykh who mobilized the Berber populations, the movement of jihad spread to the left side of the river there, traditionally a source of food for the nomads of the desert, and it eventually conquered the principal Wolof states and Fouta-Toro, where the rebellious Tukulor Muslims even succeeded in temporarily pushing back the animist Denianke kings. When the movement collapsed, in reaction the warrior aristocracies hostile to Islam were returned to power. The people, meanwhile, increasingly despoiled, came to look with favor on the new religion, for the marabouts now abandoned politics to return to commercial and religious activities. Communities of Islamized traders thus organized outside the state structure: the "merchant power" to which the urban development on the bend of the Niger in particular bore witness grew up "everywhere as a secondary motif behind the power of the military aristocracies, ready eventually to take its place." [14]

This division of society into a military and a merchant power marked a new stage of development. Both the merchants and the people had been influenced by Islam, in different ways but with the capacity to converge, and herein lay the revolutionary potential of the Muslim ideology. Islam became largely the expression of what we, risking an anachronism, might call the opposing "intelligentsia," capable, when conditions became unendurable, of gaining the support of the masses. Thus, among the Soninke and the Malinke in the fifteenth century and later in the Hausa cities, special oligarchic Muslim groups emerged whose membership included the scholars. Islamic studies developed rapidly. The main centers were southern Mauritania and northern Niger, where the learned lineages, the Zawaya, disseminated their knowledge and taught a large part of the West African literate classes, spreading an ideal of study in the form of reading of the sacred texts and journeying to imbibe learning from new masters.

Beginning in the eighteenth century, the Fulani-speaking scholars, the Torodbe, who originated in Fouta-Toro—one of the oldest Muslim regions of West Africa (Al-Bakri's Tekrur)—activated the wave of Islamization that progressively submerged the Sahel. The movement was connected to the local traditions of Islamic learning, which until then had been the preserve of a minority but which were rich and ancient, passed on over the centuries via the Sahelian urban centers of Mauritania, Agadès, and Timbuktu. It was a conservative ideological movement, whose religious ideal was a return to the pure faith of the "righteous men" of the early days of Islam and whose political ideal was an orthodox state ruled in accordance with the dynastic principles laid down at the time of the Prophet.

But Islam also became, through the jihad, a force making for renovation of the social order and providing a clear answer to the challenge the West extended—though only in a vague and indirect manner—from the coast. The slave trade had reached its height in the eighteenth century, the great century of the sugar plantation. We have seen that in West Africa its effects certainly sufficed to give rise to strong social and political reactions, for example, the revolution of the Fouta Djallon (Guinea) in 1720–1730, partly in response to the opening up of the "Rivers of the South," and that of the Fouta-Toro (Upper Senegal) in about 1776, which overthrew the Denianke dynasty.

Throughout the nineteenth century Islam accentuated its politically revolutionary aspects. The urban elite joined forces with the newly Islamicized Fulbe herdsmen in order to take advantage of the explosive social situation that had come about because of the slave trade. The populations had been whittled down by the Atlantic trade, which had restructured the internal economies so as, for instance, to create local slave markets and transport routes.[15] Within the Sudanese area, the additional slave labor led to an increase in mining and in agricultural and artisanal production, but also to an increase in wars for the capture of slaves and in slave-trading for internal purposes. The number of slaves had climbed in relation to that of free men: in certain areas, slaves constituted at least half the population. (This state of affairs was to become the economic foundation of new imperial regimes.) The slave-trading peoples nearer the coast could not resist the demands of the expatriate European import-export firms. As the local chiefs attempted, at their neighbors' expense, to regain the manpower they had lost in the commerce with the Whites, war for booty became the main occupation of the political classes, increasing insecurity, ruining the weak, and diminishing the productive capacity of the society as a whole. The Yoruba wars which continued throughout the century in southern Nigeria serve as a prime example of this climate of instability.[16]

The appeal of Islam as a way of salvation from this situation raced through a good part of the traditional animist peasantry, preparing the ground for the emergence of populist-based military theocracies. Beginning in 1804, Usman dan Fodio's conquests reunified the city-states of the Hausa country. This campaign, fought in the name of Islam, led to the creation of the great emirates of northern Nigeria. It was thus that the hegemony of the Masina at the bend of the Niger (1817–1819) and of Musa Molo among the Mandingo of Gambia came into existence.[17]

One of the best examples of the Muslim response—at once political, religious and military—to the European challenge is the career of El Hajj Umar. Umar Tall was first and foremost a fighter for the Faith. An eminent scholar from Fouta-Toro, after his pilgrimage to Mecca in 1827 and prolonged sojourns in the principal Islamic centers of West Africa (Sokoto, Segu, Fouta Djallon), he set up his religious and military base at Dinguéraye. His aim was to create an ideal, traditionally orthodox society based on a theocratic state. This concept implied the necessity for submission by or destruction of non-Muslim states and even of some Muslim states whose religious practice was, rightly or wrongly, considered insufficiently orthodox. His tool was the jihad, declared in 1854.[18]

The avowed enemy of El Hajj Umar and his Tukulor followers at first was not the French colonial power, but as he came into possession of the gold mines of Buré and Bambuk, he found the French on his path. After a violent encounter at Medina in 1857, however, he tended to avoid such unequal confrontations. His policy aimed—although cautiously, with due respect for treaties that had been concluded—at limiting the activities of the Whites to commerce and requiring them to pay a tribute that would prevent them from slipping out of the control of the Muslim state. However, the French advance, which forced the shaykh to push his conquests ever further to the east, as Samori was to do a quarter of a century later, upset his plans. In

Upper Senegal, especially in the Kaarta empire on the right bank of the river, the Bambara animist peoples resisted him fiercely but unsuccessfully. Beyond this point, he conquered the kingdom of Segu at the heart of the Middle Niger and the empire of the Masina, although the latter was already Muslim.

El Hajj Umar was now master of Sudanese West Africa, but his domination was transient. When he died in 1864, his son Ahmadu, trying to grapple with a situation that was beyond him, found himself facing the French alone, for the Tukulor ambitions had at last encouraged the advance of the French, who were adept at gaining and utilizing the confidence of rebellious sovereigns.

Even if it did not represent a militant resistance to European conquest, Umar's endeavor did represent a coherent African response to a social and political crisis, and that is why his dissemination of the Tijaniyya doctrines from the north instead of the former Qadiriyya gained the wholehearted support of all classes of the Fouta. Hence, there was a certain egalitarian character to the new confraternity that might explain its success, although it nevertheless remained strongly aristocratic, requiring total submission by the *talibe* to the shaykh. The total dedication of Umar's disciples to the wars of conquest of their spiritual leader demonstrates the depth of the grievances felt against the desiccated former regime after the first Muslim "revolutions" of the eighteenth century. In reality, however, this response was less novel than it appeared: in seeking to unify the purified Muslim communities within a multinational framework, it followed a Muslim political tradition that went back to the Middle Ages.

Muslim Reformism in Central and Eastern Africa

In a different way, Islam had a somewhat similar effect in Central Africa. In the south of this area lived sedentary animist peasants, and the north and west contained Arab herdsmen, who had had little to do with Islam until the mid-seventeenth century. Islam had been institutionalized in that region and given its usual form, at once religious and political, by Abd-el-Karim, a conqueror probably of Arab descent, founder of the kingdom of Wadai.[19] In 1820–1830, this first wave was submerged by the political reformism of Shaykh Senusi, founder of a sect, the Sanusiyya, which preached a positivist conception of the world, the believer being expected to provide himself with a sound economic foundation. The confraternity showed an awareness of social changes by accepting slaves, hitherto rejected by Islam, into its ranks. The slaves, who were becoming ever more numerous, became Islam's most loyal adherents at the same time as they supplied labor, thus assuring the economic viability of the whole. The Sanusiyya seized control of the pilgrimage route between Chad and the Sudan, thus becoming the principal intermediary between the Wadai and the Mediterranean for the exchange of gold, slaves, tea, sugar, and other commodities. In this area ravaged by the brigandage of slave-traders, the Sanusiyya established a certain peace through its vigorous missionary proselytism and its political and financial state organization.[20]

Even more revolutionary was the career, in the Horn of Africa, of Muhammad Abdul Hassan, whom the British mockingly nicknamed "The Mad Mullah" but whom his warriors regarded as a new Mahdi. He too was simultaneously a preacher of a militant Islam, a poet of epic inspiration, an inventive strategist, and a modern political leader. From 1899 to 1920 he preached jihad against the foreign invader and carried with him the populations of the Ogaden; he even succeeded for a time, before aerial bombardment forced him to flee, in holding his own against a coalition of English, Italian, and Ethiopian armies, a feat that has won him his present-day reputation as the founder of the pan-Somalian movement.[21]

Conclusions

In spite of the partial or temporary success of these resistance movements everywhere colonialism appeared and triumphed, once the state had collapsed it left no political traces. Nevertheless, the work of these great thinkers and vigorous men of action remained in the popular consciousness. The Muslim revolution they had helped to promote was to a certain extent to provide in the future a foundation for resistance to colonization.

The structures they had created, however, which were based on submission to a clearly defined religious aristocracy, later lent themselves to "recuperation," that is, manipulation, by the colonial powers. Once they had been defeated, these former aristocracies, which had often tried to find an intelligent and vigorous answer to colonialism, aimed above all at salvaging whatever prestige and privileges could be passed on to them and guaranteed by the new masters. To armed struggle there succeeded—despite the obvious inequality of forces—a strategy of sharing authority and an alliance of classes. Thus was consecrated, and sometimes proclaimed, that principle of "indirect rule" made into political dogma by the British colonialists: the collaboration of the "old" and "modern" ruling classes for the exploitation of those who had always been dominated.

6

From Chiefdom to Tribalism:
The Contradictions of
Government

In the process of decolonization, the contemporary African demand for statehood has played the role both of a defense and of a necessity for survival. In one sense, it is the weapon that has permitted peoples to rid themselves of the restrictive colonial yoke, even if it later became the instrument of new forms of oppression that have more or less openly flouted human rights. The modern African state thus represents, to a certain degree, a transcendence, actual or theoretical, of the contradiction between traditional societies and the Western model.[1]

Attainment of this goal, however, is a painful process, and, as one sees every day, far from complete. In the West, the model of the state came into existence over a period extending back at least to the beginning of modern times, primarily by means of a gradual conceptualization which in slow stages elaborated a theory of state government. Throughout the African colonialist phase—itself a particular coercive model—and especially since the African countries gained their independence, the Western model has been grafted, more or less forcibly, onto the preexisting autochthonous societies. This grafting was done from without, either internationally (by consuls and diplomats) or nationally (by constitutional, administrative, and judicial means). Imported concepts, such as "sovereignty," "moral personality," and the "sovereign equality of states," and institutions such as a "normal" constitution and centralized administration were thrust upon the existing system.

It is not clear that such grafting succeeded, or, considering the circumstances, that success was even possible. The transference took place in an uneven and partial manner, since the essential underlying ideology was missing. The Western cultural heritage, which integrates, assimilates, and, by definition, internalizes the modern European state, was transferred only in an incomplete and distorted form by the colonialist and postcolonialist school and to this day has affected only a privileged minority of individuals. In Africa, another tradition of government exists, derived from a different heritage and different founding myths.[2] The founding myths of the Western state and the African precolonial system of rule contain almost contrary logics. Study of this phenomenon may, then, give us insights into the reasons for the difficulties in the encounter between Africa and the West.

AFRICAN PLURALISM VERSUS WESTERN NATION-STATE

The Western model of the state is based on the three main principles of *unity, accountancy,* and *bureaucracy*. The unity of governmental authority corresponds, in the divine sphere, to the idea of the unity of God in Judeo-Christian monotheism, and, in the human sphere, to the idea of the individual that underlies Western individualism. The idea of accountancy is the basis of both public and private economics, while the bureaucratic principle is connected with the art of writing and with management.

This model leads to an evolutionary concept of time and a cartographic and hence territorial concept of space that make the written word in the form of constitutional law, institutions based on belief in the twin concepts of the separation of powers and the general interest, and the identification of the individual with society as a whole the basic instruments of state government.

Precolonial Africa, by contrast, preferred plurality to unity. In place of accountancy was adopted a system of classification through naming. To name someone causes him to exist, whereas to pass him over in silence is to ignore his existence—hence the importance of speech, symbolized in the role of the *griot,* the traditional court historian. Finally, the individual was replaced by the family community, which was both a social and a political unit.

Time had three dimensions: the time of the beginning, the time of political action, and the time of becoming, or production. Space was pluralistic, since each wielder of authority possessed a certain area of jurisdiction superimposed on those of others but not necessarily coinciding with them. Examples of such areas are that of the political chief, that of the chief of the land, that of the master of rain, and that of the family kin groups. All this explains the preeminent role of the spoken as against the written word, the importance attributed to ancestors as guarantors of the ideology of descent, and the complexity of the concept of reality, which existed on the two planes of the visible and the invisible. This multiplicity was completely opposed to Western unitarism or even totalitarianism.

The great difficulty of making the contemporary model of the African state work harmoniously therefore becomes understandable. Officially, of course, governments are fully centralized, on the Western model, in conse-

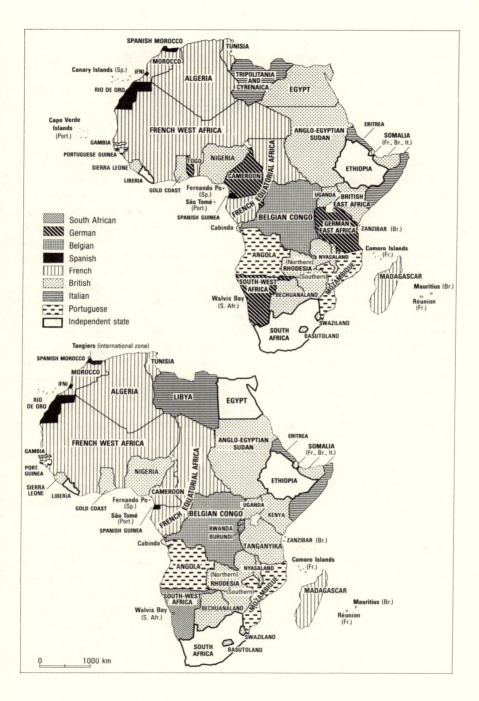

Map 4. Colonial Africa: 1913 (above); *division of the German colonies after World War I* (below)

quence of the fact that the "right of peoples to self-determination" has amounted in practice to the "right of peoples to establish a state."[3] The principle of unity appears to have triumphed: a single man exercises power (in the presidential system) and a single authority mobilizes the citizens (in the single-party system). However, it is well known that social relationships continue to be governed by "traditional"—that is to say, pluralistic—cultural principles. Even the most authoritarian head of state cannot escape the bonds of family connections, and the most technically elaborate plans of development come down to a formal manipulation of figures, since the very fact of naming a project (mentioning it in the plan) is sufficient to guarantee its existence. The bureaucratic principle has come down to the myth of the government official: to "get on" in life is to go to town and enter an office.

In short, the political concept has malfunctioned: on images proper to the Western system it superimposes earlier autochthonous images, leading to a linguistic and ideological mixture, a contraption that may sometimes be a thing of genius (as in Félix Houphouët-Boigny's successful combination of clientelism, paternalism, and modernism, for example) but is almost impossible to disentangle, so much does it result from the impossible assimilation of a unitary model antithetical to the preexisting culture. Hence it risks stifling all capacity of innovation and paralyzing any independent attempt at confronting the challenge. Obviously connected with this marked fragility of the contemporary African state is the phenomenon of military dictatorship, which only serves to demonstrate the impasse produced by the extreme difficulty of combining the African and the Western concepts of government.

Does a "genuine" process of decolonization involve—or ought it to have involved—a pure and simple rejection of the European type of state? This seems to be the opinion of E. Le Roy, but I think that in view of the historical development of integration and foreign dominion, this conclusion, however correct it may be as theory, must give way to practical considerations. Whatever the difficulties, the present contradictions will in one way or another eventually be overcome, and the future African form of government will no longer have much in common with the traditional heritage. Common sense requires us to avoid falling into the pitfall of earlier ethnographers who often concentrated solely on the precolonial era. The colonial episode, though it may have been short, was profoundly traumatic; it permanently transformed first the institutions and then the structures of the old Africa. It is thus wrongly that the former African tradition is often blamed for two of the present scourges of the continent: the totalitarian cult of the charismatic leader, and the ravages of tribalism. As we shall see, both were artificial results of the disfiguration by colonialism of two elements of the traditional political scene: the chiefdom and what we have already called ethnic nationalism.

THE CHIEFDOM CO-OPTED

The traditional chief was the center and symbol of a complex interweaving of a number of systems of authority—lineal, territorial, and personal. The European conquest brought about the establishment of an administrative system whose political, social, and economic objectives appeared irreconcilable with this regime. However, because they lacked manpower and financial and technical means and could not bring enough pressure to bear on the natives, the Europeans first sought to transmit their demands through carefully chosen political allies. This technique was known as "native policy," and its purpose, in the final analysis, was to find subservient chiefs who could be used to change their people's ways of thinking.

EARLY EVOLUTION

The "native policy" only carried on an evolution that had begun as soon as the aristocracies then in power were able to benefit from the privilege of acquiring European goods. The colonial powers intensified and systematized the process, which proved particularly effective when the administration was able to co-opt a strong authority already used to imposing regular demands on a population largely reduced to slavery, although petty chiefs and kings showed themselves equally skilled at finding new ways of exploiting their former dependents.

Southern Angola at the end of the nineteenth century provides an excellent example of the transitional phase in which the local rulers themselves gave rise to the social changes that encouraged this process of transference. In the 1860s, the chiefs had taken advantage of their monopoly on commerce to benefit from the technological revolution of the period: instead of issuing cheap but ineffective slave-trade muskets to the whole population, they began to form a kind of praetorian guard of picked and trained young men (the Lunga) armed with modern repeating rifles. This new group—sons of chiefs traditionally excluded from power by the rules of matrilinear succession and ambitious young people of common stock or those who had fled from other groups—helped the chiefs to organize exploitation. At that period, the slump in profits from the widespread elephant-hunting forced them to increase their exploitation of slaves and cattle. Requiring additional forces of production and of reproduction, the chiefs intensified the practice of raiding. Above all, direct extortion in the form of taxation became more and more attractive to them. This practice grew to terrifying proportions in Ovamboland in the 1900s; the chief of the Kwambi even forced his young men to work for the Whites in order to acquire the means to pay him his tribute in heads of cattle, and other chiefs did not hesitate to exploit the prevailing credulity by spreading accusations of witchcraft that would enable them to appropriate the possessions of the accused.[4]

The Portuguese conquest ended this social differentiation and pillage, but the chiefs and their Lunga nevertheless retained numerous advantages in the new system. They were increasingly threatened, it is true, by a new rising class, the first literate groups who were used as interpreters, but despite this, in the 1930s the status of the chiefs in their vast kraals, surrounded by numerous dependents (descendants of their slaves) and huge flocks, remained far above that of the miserable mass of peasants.

Thus, contrary to the stereotype that contrasts British indirect rule with Portuguese authoritarianism and French assimilatory centralization, all the colonialists, of whatever nationality, desired effective collaboration with the local chiefs. This policy aimed at breaking the group spirit of the local community by encouraging an individualistic spirit through the judicious use of rewards.

The French Model

The example of France, which is often regarded as the colonial power most given to assimilation of the Africans, is typical. Its colonial policy was, in fact, pragmatic, if only because of a chronic shortage of staff (in 1921 Dahomey had only one administrator for each 19,000 inhabitants, and it was regarded as particularly well supplied; Upper Volta had one for each 66,000). The guiding principle was to make the administration's wishes known and to assert colonial authority while taking maximum advantage of the local situation. Many chiefs, in both the Muslim and the animist areas, collaborated with the administration to the disadvantage of their dependents. This process constituted a distortion of their office at all levels and in all situations—whether it was that of an emir ruling over vast areas and many peoples, or the local chief of a village or of a larger kin-group.

The colonial powers, however, even if they felt a strong desire to abolish the chiefdoms, knew very well that the great families assured of their authority owing to their rank were more willing to serve the colonialists than anyone else was. Thus, in eastern Ubangi-Chari, where Islam first appeared as an instrument of political rule over subject animist populations, the French indirect policy long had no grounds for envy of its British counterpart. The sultans of the right bank of the Ubangi were large-scale slave-traders who had come from the northeast and settled there in the last third of the nineteenth century, lured by the trade in guns, which was then very vigorous in the Sudan, and by the tacit protection of the king of Belgium, who made use of their services in his penetration into the northeastern Congo. The French colonialists transformed the sultans from robber-warriors into agents of repression, administrative representatives and commercial entrepreneurs working with the agents of the Company of the Sultanates of the Upper

Ubangi, who, in 1900, received the monopoly on the commercial exploitation of the area. Thus, the "French peace" was maintained cheaply: the administration, short of staff, as long as possible pursued a policy close to a protectorate by employing these useful intermediaries throughout their lifetimes (Semio until 1912, Sultan Labasso, successor of Bangassu, until 1917, and Sultan Hatman of Rafai until 1940).[5]

This policy was followed with every strong local authority, as in Fouta Djallon. There the post of *almami* was abolished in 1912 but the supremacy of the great ruling families was maintained for the benefit of the administration—including officially disallowed privileges such as internal slavery, which was the source of their agricultural wealth and traditional prestige, as well as a means of satisfying colonialist demands for forced labor and conscription.[6] And in the Murid area of Senegal, the marabouts, who cooperated with the colonialists in the scientific cultivation of peanuts, instituted a form of serfdom that profitably replaced the administration's former system of forced labor. This political role the marabouts retained even after independence.

Elsewhere, the attitude of the administration varied in accordance with the docility of the chief. Thus, in Senegal, two similar neighboring kingdoms received opposite treatments: in Salum, the title and position of chief (Bur) soon lost their value, and the country was divided into purely administrative cantons, while in nearby Sine, Combo Ndoffene Diuf, Bur from 1898 to 1924, succeeded in avoiding administrative division until 1924, and the title of Bur persisted as late as 1963.

Elsewhere again, a chiefdom that had not hitherto existed or one that had been largely destroyed at the time of the conquest was actually created. In southern Nigeria, where the British wished to implant the system of indirect government they had used in the north, kin-based groups controlled only small areas. Therefore the British invested "warrant chiefs" with authority over a reasonably extensive expanse of territory. The first task of the colonial administrator was, then, to decide which internal mechanism to use—a choice made particularly difficult where the administration had traditionally been decentralized.

In Gurunsi, Upper Volta, the administrators, carefully choosing "loyal" chiefs, divided the country into entities more or less corresponding to the precolonial divisions.[7] The same was true in the Congo, where Governor-general Merlin acknowledged in 1909: "In the colonies it is impossible to practice direct administration, that is, one that dispenses with any indigenous intermediary. . . . Everywhere, therefore, one must pursue a policy of cooperation and collaboration with the indigenous chiefs."[8] He recommended seeking the most influential families, to whom, he said, it "will be enough to grant . . . a scrap of authority." Beginning in 1916, the colonial administration tried to institutionalize a complete hierarchy of chiefdoms—

first in the area of the Kongo and then progressively extended, from 1922, to the rest of the colony—from the village chief, who could delegate some of his powers to the *capitas* of a smaller village, to the chief of a subdivision (who was at the base of the White hierarchy), by way of the territorial chief and the tribal chief. The latter, the only one to receive a salary, had the task of transmitting orders and supervising their application; the territorial chief, who received a rebate on the payment of taxes (on condition that the village chiefs paid the required amounts), was in charge of collecting dues and requisitioning labor, inspecting markets and agriculture, and so forth. The village chief was responsible for the execution of the prescribed tasks at the local level.

A somewhat similar system was adopted in Cameroon, modeled on the German colonial pattern but without much relationship to the precolonial social divisions, if only because of the size of the new chiefdoms. In the Yaoundé area, for instance, seven senior chiefs were in charge of some thirty chiefs of cantons which were created in 1925. Each of these thirty was in turn responsible for between five thousand and twenty thousand individuals who were under the authority of a thousand subchiefs altogether.[9]

The chiefdom thus progressively turned into a form of administrative machinery. It is true that even if not all cantonal chiefs had belonged to the traditional political hierarchy, the basis of their authority, at least until 1914, tended to be traditional. But their people no longer paid them dues or tribute for their administration of justice; instead, the colonial government paid them salaries or rebated their taxes. These sums were generally insufficient either to satisfy the chiefs' traditional dependents (followers, court historians) or to meet the expenses of their new responsibilities, such as accommodating visiting administrators, paying middlemen or scribes, and maintaining a small militia. Assisted by strongmen who, knowing the region, did not hesitate to exploit the villagers, the chiefs continued to exact a kind of forced tribute, aided in this by colonial protection, even though the least-founded accusation by some needy commercial traveler could cost a chief his position or even subject him to prison or deportation in a society in which malpractices—misappropriation of taxes or of crops—were quite common.

The Chief: An Ambiguous Figure

It would be mistaken to describe the chief simply as a traitor, a collaborator in the misdeeds of colonialism. The village chief, particularly, on whom the whole weight of the system fell, who, standing at the foot of the ladder, had to satisfy all requirements, had little freedom of choice.

However given to centralization the colonial powers may have been, the village chief never became redundant. He constituted the sole constant link between the rural masses and the new masters, for the only other means of contact was traveling officials, who of necessity appeared infrequently at best and whose visits were prohibited during the rainy season, due to the bad state of the roads. Even in the Portuguese colonies, the village chief was the lowest but indispensable rung of an administrative hierarchy that, apart from him, was entirely White and as much bureaucratic as authoritarian.

A necessary channel of communication between the administration and the administered, the village chief was not, however, always docile. Acts of rebellion such as a refusal to pay taxes or to recruit forced labor were by no means unusual, but then the rules of the alliance inevitably exacted their due. The chief had to cooperate with his superiors, whatever the cost, or take the consequences. A certain number paid for their audacity or their weakness with their lives.

The chief did, however, have some support in his dealings with his inferiors. Since the administrator depended on the chiefs, who were his main executive tools and sources of information, he tended to support them by interpreting the official Code de l'Indigénat in their favor or even by sending a repressive police force to protect them.

The condition of the village chief suffered a basic ambiguity: on the one hand, he was extolled by the administration as the representative of African "tradition" and, on the other, he held his position only by the consent of the colonialists. This was undoubtedly the significance of the famous memorandum from Governor-General Van Vollenhoven, who, while insisting on the necessity for restoring the status of the chiefs, stated that "they do not have any power of their own of any kind, for there cannot be two authorities, the French authority and the indigenous authority; there can be only one. Only the governor gives orders; he alone is responsible. The indigenous chief is only an instrument, an auxiliary." [10] This loss of power became more marked with the passage of time. The "traditional" chief was soon bereft of his functions, but this came about so insidiously that even those who were administered by him were not always conscious of the fact.

In some cases, of course, brutal means were adopted: for instance, the administration sometimes made use of veterans of World War I as a means of speeding up social change, appointing them as agents or even as chiefs of villages or cantons. This served to reduce the prestige of the great traditional families or to lessen their rivalries, as happened in Fouta Djallon. [11] As the conscripts had been chosen by the chiefs from among the slaves, this procedure contributed to the collapse of the traditional hierarchies: having left as dependents, they returned as superiors.

Examples have been recorded of peasant resistance, of cases in which there was a "counter-establishment"—a traditional and recognized, though unofficial, chieftain—while the responsible official was merely a puppet, but such a situation was difficult to maintain. To have lasted, it would have required the consent of the villagers, and, above all, the mutual agreement of the two rival dignitaries, which clearly was rarely the case. Sooner or later the administrative chief, who held the only real power, gained the upper hand. He had, moreover—and this is the point—every interest in doing so. The alliance with the colonial power was advantageous for him both materially and ideologically.

The Belgian experience is particularly instructive in this context. The Belgian authorities early stressed the importance of a profound knowledge of the local political-juridical organization. "Tradition," for them, was summed up in two main points: the rights of the chief with regard to the subchiefs or other notables in the region, and the conditions of the exercise of his authority over his subordinates. The aim was not suppression but, on the contrary, utilization.[12] And at the same time, lineal heads, elders, and notables could benefit from the effective support of the colonial system, which was expressed, for example, by the police force, which was placed at the chiefs' disposal. The chiefs also reaped material benefits from the alliance. The indigenous chief represented the state, and as a functionary of the government he enjoyed a double remuneration: on the one hand, his administrative salary, and, on the other, his customary tribute—all under the shelter of the colonial administration.

The salary was paid annually and retroactively, which allowed the administration to use it both as a disciplinary sanction and as a guarantee that the chief would carry out his obligations. The payment was calculated on the basis of a census of "*hommes adultes valides*" (H.A.V.) (able-bodied adult males); and it depended on the productivity of the territory in question, so conflicts arose between neighboring chiefs concerning various border villages. The collection of taxes was the third criterion taken into account in the fixing of salaries; what is more, the rate, proportional to the tax, varied in accordance with the degree of development of the area—that is to say, with the penetration of the Western economy. This policy must have not only encouraged the chiefs to support the colonial system but aggravated the opposition between the chiefs and their dependents. The role of the colonizers was veiled from the Africans, for the administration did not directly intervene in the work of collection, which was carried out within the framework of the various native kin systems. Moreover, if the chiefdom had subdivisions, the main chief collected two-fifths of the taxes from each subdivision.

By 1928, the hierarchy of chiefs and subchiefs had begun to include area chiefs, "great chiefs," and chiefs "commissioned to collect taxes" as well. In addition to the basic salary—fixed at that time at 0.30, 0.45, and 0.60 francs per H.A.V., depending on whether the beneficiary's share was "mediocre," "good," or "very good"—fiscal payments were rebated by an amount that ranged from 0.45 francs (if the tax was less than 6 francs) to 1.50 francs (if it was more than 48 francs). In addition, the "great chiefs" received 5 percent of the payments of the preceding year. This explains the role played in political struggles by the payment of the chiefs: a subchief naturally wished to see his territory transformed into an independent entity so as to enjoy the full rebate, while the chief wanted to defend the territorial integrity of his chiefdom. These economically inspired antagonisms were generally expressed in ideological terms: the chief spoke of clan unity, or ethnic and cultural unity, supporting his claims, on occasion, with historical arguments, while the subchiefs rejected this kinship for similar reasons. Much "tribalistic" mystification came into being in just this way.

Today, with a few changes, similar policies are followed by the South African government in order to dominate the "traditional" chiefs placed at the head of the "Black states" or Bantustans. The 1971 law creating four Bantustans which are economically nonviable and politically controlled by the Pretoria government not only has an economic purpose, but expresses a wish to respond to a nationalist desire for unification with a definition of *Bantu nations* that divides Africans on linguistic and tribal lines. Four "Black states" have so far gained "independence." This "independence," which really aims at making the Africans strangers in their own country, is likely to give rise in the coming years to fratricidal struggles, with the Bantu militants who truly aim at regaining the right of self-determination coming into conflict with the traditional pseudo-aristocracy allied with the White authorities. This phenomenon is far from new. From the very beginnings of colonization, when traditional chiefs were subjected to new rules and frequent inspections they came to have very little in common with the former chiefs of tribes or lineages, owing to the fact that they had become associates of the Whites—even if they "ruled" in a neo-traditional manner within protected reserves.

This was a general phenomenon: everywhere the chief became more or less absorbed into the public administration, and his territory tended to be transformed into a simple administrative subdivision. Here, the French example has something to teach us. The chief, in French Africa, was in principle chosen from among the families traditionally entitled to rule the country, but a 1927 decree ordered a reorganization of the School for the Sons of Chiefs, in which the candidates were selected by competition from the members of the families of notables who had received an elementary education. Then, in 1930, a memorandum insisted "on the necessity, in certain circumstances, of obliterating the traditional framework . . . and substituting, if necessary, a newly created framework."[13]

After 1937, the cantonal chief, who had always been nominated by the governor, held his post on the recommendation of the council of notables of the colony. Thus, a veritable chiefly caste came into being through a system which was very remote from the precolonial tradition. An allowance, recommended in 1917 and specified in 1922, went into effect in 1934. The following year a form of retirement pension was instituted, with honorary membership of the council. In 1935, the chief's functions were defined: his judicial powers were curtailed and were replaced by a modern form of justice. He remained both the agent of the colonial administration and the representative of ethnic groups. This ambiguous situation was heightened by the establishment of colonial commissions that were intended as a revival of the former royal councils. Their composition was fixed by custom or, failing that, by rules laid down by the leader of the group, and their role was simply to ratify the decisions of the administration. The logical outcome of this process was the ultimate elimination of the chiefdom and its replacement by a petty official who would at last be constrained in using traditional privileges to exploit those he administered. This happened, for example, in Guinea and the Ivory Coast in the 1950s.

The ambiguity of functions proved to be long-lasting. It was carefully preserved by colonial practices and by confusion of terminology: in the Belgian Congo, the "tribute" was defined as a remuneration "customarily granted to the chiefs for the services they rendered as a traditional and customary authority." This practice was maintained until independence, despite a few attempts to change some of its more conspicuous features, such as employing forced labor in the cultivation of the chief's land or the construction or repair of his house. Its most classical forms were the dues on game and the right to free conveyance for up to fifteen people, claimed by the chief of a group, the chief of a clan, or the chief of a district. Yet what had survived of the chiefs' "traditional" services and at what point did these become "modern"? In reality the idea of any traditional purpose had long since disappeared. The role of tribute was twofold: on the one hand, it constituted a kind of salary, derived from the kin system, that guaranteed the advantageousness of the position; on the other hand, it played an essential ideological role by emphasizing a respect for hierarchies that were not restored but refurbished and "recuperated."

No less significantly, however, the district governor, formerly White and today African, in Togo is still called the "*chef-cir*" (chief of the *circonscription,* or district). There is hardly a village in Africa where one cannot meet the "traditional chief," whether or not he still retains a trace of administrative authority, usually as a sort of Justice of the Peace. But what does this mean exactly? Through what connections, through what accidents, through what changes of incumbent on the part of the colonial regime, through what accommodations of his predecessors with the ruling authority does the so-called traditional chief hold his position today? He is recognized as such both by those under him and by foreign visitors who expect an audience and hospitality, to learn from him the local dynastic tradition, and to bestow on him the gift which continues to provide a material basis for his relative authority. He has indeed often used his special position at the convergence of two systems to acquire, in the name of a somewhat factitious tradition, a quite modern degree of comfort as a planter or shipper—in short, as a small-scale regional capitalist.

Today the tendency is to explain the passivity of people bearing the verbal attacks, abuse, and destructive folly of certain public figures in Africa—local chiefs or unpopular heads of state—by the absolute charismatic religious respect accorded to the precolonial chief, but it may well be, rather, a legacy of the terror inspired by the White governor, who in his area enjoyed discretionary control over thousands of individuals. He enjoyed every sort of power, reinforced by distance from the center and the difficulties of communication. He was administrative chief, tax collector, recruiter of manpower, head of police, judge and head of the law courts, special agent, director of prisons, meteorological observer, and head of customs. Until 1968, in the former Independent State of the Congo he was also head of a business and the sole person responsible for local trade and production, an official all the more awe-inspiring in that his administrative and legal prerogatives gave him the ability to limit or increase the production of rubber or the collection of taxes. In the areas of French colonization, this absolute power was confirmed by the Code de l'Indigénat, which allowed the administrator, beginning in 1907 in French West Africa and in 1909 in French Equatorial Africa, to inflict on the peasants, directly and without scrutiny, disciplinary penalties of up to 100 francs fine or fifteen days in prison. The range of offenses ran to more than twenty articles, including refusal to pay taxes or to participate in forced labor or requisitions, "acts of disorder," and "seditious statements"—in short, any attempt to impede colonial authority.

After World War I, certain categories of people—war veterans, important chiefs, people considered to be "advanced"—were exempted from this jurisdiction; nevertheless, until 1946, it made the local administrator an almost absolute ruler who tended to make his territory into his fiefdom, with "his" natives, "his" guards, "his" cultural agent.[14] To the local population there was no doubt whatsoever: the heir to the former warrior chief was the White chief or governor.

He was regarded as a model—an object of envy as well as fear. The system, which inevitably gave rise to abuses, spread the idea of the absolute power of the chiefs and the uselessness of resistance. Both of these notions were foreign to the traditional concept of authority, for, if the precolonial chief had been respected, he had symbolized the power and the equilibrium of the group on condition that he recognize its internal control mechanisms and refrain from despotic interference.

The Duala of Cameroon provide a good example of people of this category. Intermediate both in time and place and having held authority over trading populations for a long period, they were well aware of the advantages they could reap if they were to regain their power. Not just forerunners of a heroic nationalism (which they were as well, even if they were not particularly conscious of the fact), throughout the colonial period the Duala chiefs aimed above all at preserving their authority and adapting it to circumstances—which only underlines the ambiguity of their historic role. The same could be said of the Beti chiefs of the Yaoundé region, the most famous of whom was the "superior" chief Karl Atangana, a splendid example of the transition between the "old" elite and the "modern" one. He was a product of missionary schools and a pillar of the German colonization who—after some years of exile and prison, it is true—regained his post in 1921 under the French administration and retained it until his death in 1943.

The chief of today—both the so-called traditional chief and the modern official—is a sort of monstrous hybrid. That is to say, his position is a misbegotten combination of two systems of rule that originally had not a single feature in common. At the same time, that position testifies at any rate to an attempt at mutual assimilation between the former dominant groups and the elites created by colonization and decolonization. This attempt has had two results. First, the social hierarchy bequeathed from the past to the present was never really questioned. The "contemporary forms of inequality and domination are a direct prolongation of the colonial social structures," since "the dominated of yesterday" still remain "the mass of the dominated of today."[15] The second result is due to the fact that only a strong government was able to impose a relatively stable balance of forces upon the different dominant groups, old and new, and upon the various regional and ethnic groups, with all their differences, which the colonizer had forced to coexist within a single national framework. Hence, in most areas, a hegemonic system now exists, based on a presidential single-party regime more or less dependent on the support of the army.

FROM PRECOLONIAL ETHNICITY TO CONTEMPORARY TRIBALISM

"Tribalism" today is the final manifestation, debased by colonialism, of precolonial "ethnic sentiment." Three main stages of this development may be distinguished.

Precolonial Equilibrium

In the first stage, the precolonial situation, political, social, and lineal structures were closely interconnected. The social organization represented a certain level of productive force that encompassed a number of family units or units of production within a historically situated cultural whole that recognized itself as such—what specialists call an *ethnic group*.

The ethnic group was the outcome of complex historical demographic processes that were generally very extended in time. Myths of origin bound and unified the village traditions, with a tendency to minimize or even to obliterate discrepancies. A series of adjustments signifying a change from open conflict to alliance or to associations between successive layers of population thus gradually created the specificity of the group.[16] From the time that this process reached its conclusion (which did not always happen), the sense of a common heritage and the feeling of interdependence that linked together those basic units merited the term *ethnic nationalism,* for the kinship structures then played their full role, both assuring and representing an equilibrium between the social and the political system, between the organization of production and commerce and the ideology and culture of the group.

The "Ethnic" Revival under Colonialism

The concept of ethnicity, although accepted (for reasons that will be discussed below) by the Africans themselves, was in many cases imposed by the colonizers upon hitherto undifferentiated groups. During the colonial period, the administrator and the ethnologist combined their efforts in order to settle various migratory peoples. It was at that time that the ethnic groups were, to a great extent, fabricated, both to facilitate political and administrative control and for religious purposes.

In its attempt to create order out of the mosaic of peoples under its rule, the French administration was understandably traditionalistic. Thus, in the maritime areas of the Ivory Coast it took the authoritarian route. The lagoon-dwelling peoples, characterized till then by the similarity of their origins, of shared activities centered on fishing, and of their way of life, were organized into "chiefdoms," in increasingly well-defined areas, that became identified as "ethnic groups" (the Aïzi, the Dida, the Ebrié, the Alladians). Similarly, in the Bete country, the ethnic group, an "effect of authority" defined "as an administered area, as a dependency, and as a civil society," was formed "in the wake of colonization."[17] And, as we saw, in the Belgian Congo the "superior" chief had a clear financial interest in dominating as much territory and thus as many chiefs as possible, while each petty king clung to his scrap of colonial power and its associated revenue. The resultant strong centrifugal forces tended to accentuate and rigidify "ethnic" diversities that until then had been perfectly compatible with an integrated political organization and social coexistence.

The missionaries, too, played a cultural and, above all, linguistic role in the history of Africa that has not been sufficiently considered. All the Protestant missionaries, and the earliest Catholic ones, based their hopes of success on communicating with the Africans in their own language. Hence they endeavored to understand, translate, transcribe, and teach—in other words, to standardize—the local languages, using as their starting point the specific dialect of the place where they first happened to settle. Thus came into being the "ethnic" frontiers of linguistic groups determined and fixed through the efforts of the missionaries. Even in traditionally Catholic countries such as Angola, this sense of identity was formed in those areas where Protestant missions were set up. The backgrounds—too readily supposed to be "ethnic"—of the three national liberation movements, MPLA, FNLA, and UNITA, were in fact, at least in part, three areas of Protestant influence: Methodist in the case of the first, Baptist for the second, and the Protestant missions of central Africa for the third.

The ethnic group, although created and fostered by the colonizers, was subsequently appropriated as an expression of resistance to colonization by the social groups that had existed before the European conquest and were forced to recognize themselves and to decide on a course of action within this framework provided by the territorial state. The colonial administration in turn sought to exploit this vague neo-traditionalism by maintaining localized, subdivided ethnic chiefdoms and by encouraging rivalries, bestowing gifts, and granting rebates on taxes.

The African claim to ethnic particularity, which is especially strong in such countries as Zaire, the Congo, and Gabon, is thus more readily explicable by local colonial history than by a precolonial tendency to subdivision more marked in some areas than elsewhere—a dubious distinction (the tendency toward subdivision appears to have been at least equal in Upper Volta, Niger, and the Ivory Coast). The truth is that the force of the reaction corresponded to the nature of the aggression and that colonization was more rapid and violent in central and eastern Africa. West Africa displayed a continuity in "native policy": colonization followed a long period of incubation and interpenetration. By about 1850, precolonial European penetration had had a profound and ineffaceable effect: trade with Europe was solidly established in the form of export of agricultural raw materials within the framework of a commercial economy, and on the fringes of this economy there had grown up, along the coast, a so-called creole civilization and, in the hinterland, a commercial petty bourgeoisie of intermediaries closely bound to Western interests. In areas such as the Gold Coast, these Europeanized groups began from that period to encourage the beginnings of nationalist movements whose aspirations were modeled on the Western democracies. In Equatorial Africa, nothing of this kind existed: the colonizers conquered a land whose experience of the West had been limited to the particularly destructive and negative form of the slave trade, which belonged to the mercantilist era. The transition to capitalism was abrupt, and it appeared in the relatively developed form, for that period, of colonial capitalism. The colonizers made no attempt to raise up, in the years 1885–1910, a local middle class that would adopt Western views. Quite the contrary: they destroyed or tried to destroy such precolonial economic structures as the traditional and well-organized, large-scale Congolese riverborne trade.

In the independent state of the Congo (the autocracy of the king of Belgium) and in the French Congo, in German Tanganyika, and in the Portuguese colonies, monopolistic commercial companies created an economy based on pillage, paying rubber producers and ivory hunters incredibly low sums. This practice was tolerated by the authorities, who acquiesced in the companies' assertion that they owned the product and need only pay the local people for the work involved in gathering it, regardless of the product's value.

After a first phase of desperate revolts against this maltreatment, the local people turned inward, emphasizing ancestral values and in general rejecting Westernization. At that period emerged no more-or-less acculturated petty bourgeoisie, willing to ally itself to the colonial power, but, at most, a class of particularly badly paid salaried workers—administrative clerks, militiamen, railroad workers—who constituted the embryo of a very quickly urbanized proletariat.

To a greater or lesser extent, ethnic sentiment came to the fore everywhere in Africa at the same time, around World War I. Its greatest period of growth was between the two world wars, that is to say, when armed resistance had become impossible. This ethnicity rejected cultural alienation in the name of an exalted and idealized native past, repudiating the colonialist order by contrasting it with a mythical Golden Age of Africa. It was a refuge in the imaginary, a school of thought that was perfectly expressed by Messianic-type religious movements. The point here is that this sense of a native past and this differentiation of ethnic groups resulted not only from genuine African history but also from the imagination of the colonizers, "who made the ethnic idea into the dominating element in their conception of social realities to administer,"[18] at least in those African societies that had not yet begun to evolve toward statehood. There, ethnicity was the consequence of a late realization, not of traditional values, but, rather, of the usefulness of ethnicity as a mode of political organization.

The Neo-colonial Reality

Ethnicity, created by the colonizers, then adopted by local peoples as a form of resistance, ultimately developed into a political factor. This development was encouraged by the creation of "administrative chiefdoms" selectively legitimized by "colonial ethnology." At this point appeared the third stage, *neo-colonialism*. Tribalism—that is to say, the conscious manipulation of an ethnic sentiment that had been reinforced and distorted by half a century of colonial rule—came into being. This neo-colonialism can be seen in the choices and behavior of the first leaders of the new independent African states. For example, Abbé Fulbert Youlou used the Lari ethnic origin of André Matswa for his own tribalist purposes based on Matswanism in the Congo, as he could easily do, because the links between the town and the rural areas had remained strong. Examples of clear distortion of ethnicity multiplied at all levels, from local affairs to the election of heads of state. The tripartite system instituted in Dahomey in 1970 carried this idea to the point of absurdity. Apithy, Ahomadegbé, and Maga were descendants of the ancient reigning families in their respective regions: Apithy from the southeast, seat of the ancient kingdom of Porto-Novo (represented by the Republican Party of Dahomey); Ahomadegbé from the southwest, the Fon kingdom of Abomey (represented by the Dahomean Democratic Union); and Maga from the north, the Borgu kingdom with its Bariba majority. In an attempt to circumvent the rivalries—personal as well as tribal—among these three men, a presidential council was formed, with each of the three to direct the state in his turn.

The history of electoral manipulation in Nigeria since independence, although more complicated, does not differ in essentials from the previous example. Until the putsch of 1966, the various factions of the Nigerian intelligentsia waged a fierce struggle for control of the government and hence of the economy. Although they were agreed on the main issues, they nevertheless wished to distinguish themselves from each other by other criteria, primary among which were ethnicity and region.[19] The apparently simple system was largely unrepresentative in detail, for the mosaic of peoples overlapped in complex ways. This system identified three regions, three dominant ethnic groups, and three political parties, setting up a game of shifting alliances of two against one that was compounded by rigged elections. Thus, in 1965, thousands of rigged votes assured the success of the NNDP (the Nigerian National Democratic Party, which had grown out of the Action Group or Yoruba Party of the west), with the result that for several years the figure for the total population of Nigeria became hypothetical, varying according to convenience between fifty and eighty million.

The problem cannot be defined simply as a division between rulers and ruled, with more or less honest leaders who are clever at manipulating popular feeling in their favor. Rather, the traditional idea of government and the "tribal consciousness" of the masses include political practices that are frowned upon by the Western democracies. An "advanced" person in a village or a region who, by virtue of his diplomas, has succeeded in obtaining an envied post in town must bestow upon his relatives and those who assisted him—in short, his dependents in the old sense of the word—part of the bounty to which he is supposed to have access: financial benefits, of course, and also privileges that are incompatible with the rules of public office. A person responsible for a given service will be expected to use his influence—whether legally or otherwise—to obtain positions for his dependents. For example, the primary-school inspector will be expected to find a place in the regional school for a nephew who has failed his examinations. At the very center of the administrative hierarchy, "tribal affiliation" is regarded as such an important factor that, from top to bottom, orders will be accepted and executed only if they proceed from a "compatriot." In the People's Republic of the Congo, for instance, the division of portfolios reveals a studied concern for allocation according to tribes; moreover, when a new official takes office, his entire staff, from the messenger to the director of his bureau, must be replaced in the interests of ethnic homogeneity. Still more frequently, of course, the president's ethnic group acquires preeminence over all the others.

"Tribalism" has, then, become a social and political fact that must be accepted. It was rooted in the minds of the people by the precolonial and colonial heritage and through the state apparatus, which encouraged it and protracted its existence. It would be an oversimplification to explain the phenomenon as mere ethnic or linguistic differences; on the one hand, groups may speak different languages, yet coexist in harmony, while, on the other, populations with a common culture may fiercely claim autonomy from one another. Thus, the peoples of Tanzania have all adopted the Swahili language, which was originally that of the group that was culturally (if not demographically) dominant, but in Zaire the Luba and the Lulua, who had a common origin and language but different reactions to colonization, strongly affirm their separation, which is in fact of quite recent origin. The Luba, a traditionally migrant group accustomed to playing the role of a minority in a foreign land and to pursuing professions, such as trade, with connections outside the country, have been very open to Western influence. They have achieved an important economic and cultural position throughout Zaire and today constitute an elite of the country. The closely related but sedentary Lulua, on the other hand, have been averse to all innovation—even, formerly, that of having a railway crossing their territory—adopting an attitude of hostility to the colonialist contamination, which has resulted in a vehement tribalism.

It is useless to deny or even to condemn the phenomenon, for it is inescapable. It demonstrates, among other things, the interconnection and, sometimes, confusion between the two contrary factors of ethnic affiliation and class affiliation. In the blatantly divisive state of South Africa, for example, the policy of apartheid helps to obscure the problem by causing the Africans, nearly all of whom are actual or potential proletarians, to identify their social awareness with their racial demands: hence the confusions and the difficulties encountered by protest movements such as Black Consciousness, which are often manipulated and "recuperated" by the White authorities.

Tribalism should not be seen as an end in itself, even if in certain notable cases it became one, as at one time in Benin. And in Burundi, confronting the formerly dominant Tutsi, the Hutu were massacred, while in Rwanda they were carried to the heights of power. In both these last cases, the responsibility of Belgian colonization was considerable, for it accentuated and distorted relatively small traditional differences, especially in Burundi, where social and cultural osmosis was encouraged by the frequency of interethnic marriages and the mutual dependence on agriculture. The minority of "noble" Tutsi shepherds (15 percent of the population in Rwanda, less than 20 percent in Burundi), judged a priori as more capable of adjusting to modernity, was systematically favored by both the administration and the Catholic missions. As we read in one study: "A cumulative process has been set in motion, the dominant ethnic group gradually adding the advantages gained from education to those it already possessed." [20]

Prince Ruagosore, the eldest son of the former *mwami* (sovereign), in the early days of independence attempted an experiment in interethnic collaboration in Burundi which was thwarted by precisely this process. The Tutsi responded to three successive attempts on the part of the Hutu to seize power (in 1965, 1969, and 1972) by a savage massacre of the Hutu elites. Thus Tutsi supremacy was at least provisionally assured, as was a continuation of the bloody hostility between the two groups. The responsibility of colonialism was even more obvious in Rwanda. There the Tutsi supremacy, which was traditionally more directly authoritarian than in Burundi, was invested by the colonialists with a despotic power that was well-nigh intolerable, especially in the northwest of the country where the Tutsi, before the colonial era, had been a small, powerless minority. Forced labor was imposed on the Hutu peasants, who were economically exploited without the traditional reciprocal arrangement being made for social exchange or for an exchange of manpower. When decolonization came, the Tutsi notables' absolute control of the state apparatus rendered the situation explosive. The Hutu acted first: even before independence (1949–1960), Hutu massacres of the Tutsi assured the elimination or the flight of their social, political, and "tribal" adversaries.

Nowadays, tribalism is the expression of the political problem, which is itself the consequence of a still unresolved economic and social contradiction, the clash of two outlooks and ways of life—a "wild" capitalism of the Western kind, and an unchecked "corrupt" clientelism or patronage system. Taking up the idea, put forward by Fred Riggs, of a "prismatic" society filling the inevitable gap between a traditional society and a modern "rational" society on the Western model, R. Lemarchand suggests the concept of *factions*, embracing both ethnic factors and those of class, which take the place of the declining state (as in Chad, Zaire, Rwanda, Burundi).[21] B. Verhaegen more strikingly speaks, in connection with Zaire, of a "presidential clique" and a "reigning confraternity" that developed in the absence of a bourgeoisie, which is just now beginning to gain power.[22]

At its worst, the phenomenon of tribalism can throw the state mechanism out of gear, causing an escalation of corruption that results in situations of acute crisis today (as in Nigeria and especially in Zaire). At their best, however, "tribalism" and patronage appear as typical manifestations of a transitional phase. Contrary to appearances, even the most capitalistic phenomena in Africa have little in common with the economic conceptions that prevail in the West. In the Ivory Coast, for example, patronage and corruption (the inevitable consequence as soon as the patron becomes a manager of money in the modern sense) play a complex role as a form of social adjustment whose effect, in the final analysis, is to attenuate contrasts that would otherwise be unbearable. A number of the higher functionaries of the regime and a great body of petty officials are, in truth, paid for doing nothing. The better-positioned among them of course accumulate relatively vast fortunes but, at the same time, the system ensures a significant redistribution of wealth.

The *economic* profitability of such a system according to Western norms is obviously nil; it is even regarded as negative by the international financial experts (quite apart from the fact that the waste and corruption are to be condemned from the point of view of the Judeo-Christian moral tradition). But its *social* profitability is another matter. For the government and the well-to-do, through the patronage system, to take charge of a goodly number of dependents is less costly than the legal, honestly run social assistance departments for the indigent one finds in such industrialized countries as the United States and France. Later we shall see how far this patronage system extends, most strikingly in those sectors that are regarded as "modern" and "informal."

Some underdeveloped countries with limited resources, then, long accepted a conspicuous economic "waste," which even the most prosperous Western state could scarcely tolerate, precisely because the waste was more apparent than real. It amounted to a system of social compensation in a delicately balanced situation which was very unstable, yet at the same time relatively constant. Such a situation could not, however, last indefinitely, but must lead either to disaster or to a final resolution within the framework of a political evolution. The outcome will depend on the general level of education and on the directions taken by successive generations.

THE ROLE OF ISLAM

The question often arises of whether Islam will be able to take on a national political role. It is both a very old presence in Africa, dating back to the tenth century within the limits of the Sahara and on the east coast, and in another sense quite a new one, since its main period of expansion was the nineteenth century.[23] The forest areas of Casamance and the Ivory Coast are only today becoming Islamized, more as a result of immigration than through a process of massive conversion. At the present time, Islam appears mainly as an international phenomenon that has little effect on internal politics.

People fantasize a great deal about the role of al-Qaddafi. On the international scene, his actions create some real and dangerous problems: the OAU (Organization of African Unity) nearly split up because of him. It must also be remembered that al-Qaddafi is seen by many Muslims as a religious heretic, since he does not accept the Sunna (the ancient sacred tradition) but recognizes only the Koran, and he dates the beginning of the Muslim era from the death of the Prophet and not from the Hegira.

What is happening is that the North African countries wish to regain their influence in the Sahara, which would then become, as in the great days of the Arabs in the Middle Ages, a link between the two parts of the continent. The Chad war and the Moroccan Saharan conflict have refocused attention on the old desert routes. Al-Qaddafi has undeniably succeeded in gaining influence over some disturbing African potentates, including Idi Amin and Bokassa. Around 1975, provoked by the Yom Kippur War and the raid on Entebbe, Libya broke off relations with Israel, and in those days of high oil prices, the Bongo, among others, converted to Islam amid much clamor. Most African leaders, however, regarded the Libyan ambitions with concern (which explains their indulgence toward external interventions such as that of Tanzania in Uganda and of France in Chad).

Al-Qaddafi's method is always the same: he begins by offering a great deal, but, whether through disorganization or inability, he rarely keeps his promises, except for supplying prayerbooks and building mosques, sometimes without any real justification. The great mosque at Niamey, Nigeria, is a masterpiece of Libyan financial and Moroccan artistic collaboration, but the one at Lusaka, Zambia, can boast at most a few thousand worshippers, most of whom are foreigners. And al-Qaddafi's political propositions are generally rejected. The Nigerians were incensed when he suggested that he address the entire army and the students in a stadium, and gave him instead an audience from the officer training school.

The Libyan threat is real enough, but it has been blown up somewhat out of proportion. Hissen Habre, for example, was able to use it to obtain American and French financial aid, more dependable than al-Qaddafi's. In Niger, too, the announcement of a "Libyan plot" helped to deflect anti-government tendencies and to capture the attention of the French.

In Chad, al-Qaddafi's strategy is to annex the north, basing his claim on the "historical" Chad-Libyan frontier, the celebrated Auzu Strip, the area of influence secretly granted in 1885 to the Ottoman Empire, which at that period was Suzerain of Tripolitania and signatory of the Berlin Conference. (The agreement was taken up again by Mussolini but was not ratified.) Al-Qaddafi likes, in support of his claim, to stress the "Arab character" of Chad.

That is precisely what frightens the Africans. It is important to understand that, with the exception of the Sahelian border areas, the Muslims in sub-Saharan Africa are *not* Arabs. The Arab influence there is strongly counter-balanced by the effects of the millennial contempt of the whites for their former Black slaves. To the Arabs' way of thinking, a Muslim can be a proper Muslim only if he speaks Arabic, the language of the Koran. In Africa, however, even in Chad, this criterion is rarely met. Moreover, African tonal languages are very difficult to transcribe into Arabic, in which there are no vowels. Fulani, Hausa, and even Swahili (a one-third Arabized Bantu language) and Somali (the language of a state belonging to the Arab League) have adopted Latin characters, and in Burkina-Faso, Upper Volta, al-Qaddafi's "little green book" is disseminated in a French version. Even in Chad, where there is a true Arab presence, the Libyan claims disrupt internal politics by placing the southerners—the part of the Chadean population that is most productive and most closely connected to the world economy—in an uncertain position. The non-Arab and Christian part of the country can assert itself only if the Libyan peril is eliminated.

Sudan, like Chad, is a country divided into a Muslim north (forty thousand Egyptian soldiers are billeted at Khartoum), and a south in which only 3 percent of the population are Muslim, and the 25 percent who are Christians form the majority of the elite. The strongest sign of any Muslim influence over the country is the extremely bastardized form of Arabic dialect used to communicate between diversified and diffused ethnic groups. Islamization (first advocated by the Muslim Brotherhood) has not become evident or capable of arousing the people to action. Muslim law (the Sharia) has been imposed, but purely as a matter of government policy; indeed, the Muslims themselves object to it.

The southern Sahara (with the exception of Mauritania) claims no state religion nor even a Muslim party. At the most, the state sometimes takes an interest in concluding agreements with Islamized economic groups, in much the same way as American presidents concern themselves with powerful minority groups. To obtain petrodollars from Arab nations, the government will make a show of favoring Muslim elements within the country, as, for example, the Senegalese government does with the Murid confraternity who run the peanut industry and have been increasing their business holdings. The Tanzanian government, though based on *ujamaa,* has been forced to come to terms with the Islam-Pakistani trade.

As a rule, however, the state is careful not to brandish the weapon of religion. The religion of the head of state does not take precedence in multi-faith nations (in Burkina-Faso, for example, animists remain in the majority whereas Sankara is a former Catholic choirboy). Even where Islam is dominant, as in Niger, it is characterized by extreme discretion.

Outside of Chad and the Horn of Africa, Islam forms a significant presence only in West Africa, where it is centered in three areas: in Senegal, where the brotherhoods (followers of a charismatic family) have been dominant since the beginnings of colonization, a phenomenon echoed in Tanzania; in the Mandingo region, especially around Kankan, Guinea, in the old commercial networks of the Dyula; and in northern Nigeria, home of the great Islamic revolution of the nineteenth century, where fury against the prevailing corruption still sporadically breaks out.

Although Islam has existed in East Africa for centuries, its reputation is tarnished by its history of the great slave-merchants and the sultanate of Zanzibar. Apart from coastal Swahili communities, moreover, the Islamic community, although influential, comprises only a foreign minority and therefore has little chance of becoming dominant. Finally, only a few isolated foreign Muslims live in central and southern Africa; Christians form an overwhelming majority there.

Quite clearly, Islam in Africa has little in common with the Arab-Mediterranean world. According to an old joke, Africa south of the Sahara contains only "Muslim animists," "Christian animists," and "animist animists." Is Black Islam a "false" Islam? Whatever the case may be, it has taken an original form, as can be seen in its social customs and the freedom allowed to women, who are neither veiled nor kept in purdah (except in upper-middle-class Hausa families in Kano—and even these women can still engage in such income-earning activities as cooking food for sale, spinning, or weaving).[24]

Islam in Africa must above all be seen as an established cultural fact. The pilgrimage to Mecca is an ancient custom, creating a vast common experience. That great voyage gave rise to a flux of ideas, merchandise, and people, embracing the whole of northern Africa from Senegal, Mali, and Burkina-Faso to Mecca. The great trade centers were Fort-Lamy (now N'Djamena) and Khartoum. The hazardous journey, which could take months or years, served as a rite of passage to adult life and marked subsequent epochs in a life history. I met an old El Hajj from Burkina-Faso who had made his first pilgrimage on foot, immediately after World War I, the second in a truck just before World War II, and the third by airplane, not long ago.

By the time of independence, Islam was generally regarded as a somewhat old-fashioned family cult compared to the new ideas of nationalism, trade unionism, and modernization. Very recently, the tide has begun to turn somewhat. More students undergo Arabization at El-Azar University in Cairo, as well as in Kuwait, Saudi Arabia, and, of course, Libya (but the number is far smaller than that of those who go to the West). The youths thus laid open to Arab slogans have started a vogue for a possible alternate to the Western model. Thus, the Young Muslim party had some success in

Senegal at the beginning of the Khomeinist revolution, and some integrationist tendencies appeared, although Muslim pressures have so far been counteracted by the rivalries between Sunni and Shiite brotherhoods (especially between the Murids, who are the most enterprising, and the Tijani, who are the most numerous). But with the rapid progress of Islam visible in the construction of numerous mosques (the first collective act of the inhabitants of any new district) and the accession to office of a Muslim president who, contrary to precedent, is tempted to utilize the political power of Islam, Arab influence could predominate.

Elsewhere, only the "Kano affair" could be seen as a possible sign of Arab strength. It concerned a recent convert, the founder of a heretical sect, and it was put down in a pitched battle in the city in December 1980 that left nearly four thousand dead. A few repercussions were felt in 1982 in certain towns in the north. Whether it was a "Libyan plot," only the future will show.

THE SEARCH FOR NATIONAL IDENTITY

The search for a national identity has two main facets. First, an integrated system of education that is as different as possible from the colonial cultural heritage is needed. The second aspect of the search requires that the groups thus freed from the constraints of a Western model superimposed on an ill understood and unwillingly accepted African situation come to question the classical political and economic conceptions. They must in addition insist that government and development not only involve a takeover, with the "available means," the direction of a transplanted system, but include a reinterrogation and a redefinition of the underlying concepts.

To a certain degree this process has already begun. In politics, the results are not very impressive, but in the sphere of culture a critique of the existing system is being successfully combined with an elaboration of new values. In the Congo a lively French-language literature has appeared, and the percentage of poets and novelists writing in French there is undoubtedly higher than in France itself, with its "old" Western civilization.[25] Upon their rough and checkered past, upon inherited excesses and the travesties created by the local elites, the African writers cast a lucid and critical gaze that is remarkably conscious both of the value of the Western model and of the danger of its emasculating the precolonial heritage. Take, for example, the exuberant, superb, cruel, and inventive language of the young Congolese novelist Sony Labou Tansi.[26] In a more classical vein, the fine recent political novel of Henri Lopes, in a poetic style rich in coinages, mocks the dictatorial potentate of a semi-imaginary country that combines "tradition" with a modern military dictatorship.[27] For a pitiless indictment of the society of violence coming into being in Africa today, where people's value lies in their obedience—yesterday, to chiefs, elders, and customary practices, today to the new politicians and the *nouveaux riches*—one must look to Ibrahima Ly's *Toiles d'araignées*.[28] He tells the tragic story of a young peasant woman who falls victim to her desire to assert herself and to live in a free, straightforward, "modern" manner in the face of a social traditionalism merciless to women. There again, the traditional society, seen from within, is understood and loved, while its inegalities and its obsolescent social restrictions, appropriated by the new privileged classes, are lucidly and implacably condemned. The English-speaking novelists (perhaps particularly the Black writers of South Africa) began even earlier to cast a penetrating gaze upon an Africa torn between the past and the present, between hope and despair. The recent news that Wole Soyinka, a splendid, militant Nigerian writer, was awarded a Nobel prize proves that these voices have at last begun to reach an international audience. This vitriolic literature shows up the pleas, full of goodwill and bad conscience, of the "generous and liberal" left of the Western world as clumsy, simplistic, and erroneous.[29]

This new culture embraces modern society in all its dimensions—political, economic, literary, poetic—at the same time as it encompasses the Western heritage, including the Greco-Latin (at one point Ly addresses himself to the sun, invoking Phoebus—and the device works). The struggles of daily life, which are at a certain remove from both the attractions of the West and the ancestral heritage, have given rise to an awareness, not social but literary, that embodies the tenderness and the ferocity, tinged with humor, with which certain intellectuals live and feel their history and thus reveal themselves, even if they remain in the minority, as the seers and historians of these newly forming societies.

The vigorous new literature in French and English should not be allowed to obscure the value of the popular culture, expressed almost entirely in local languages, that is just now springing up. In most rural areas and also often in the towns, the colonizer's language, although it is generally the official language of the state, is not understood, much less spoken. A popular written literature develops only in those cases, still exceptional, in which a true national language is in use. Tanzania is developing a Swahili "literature of the market" that somewhat resembles the seventeenth- and eighteenth-century French *littérature bleue* (popular tales of adventure).

Similarly, the areas of use of the Kinyarwanda language in Rwanda and of Kirundi in Burundi correspond almost exactly to the boundaries of these two little states and have long been transcribed and taught by the missionaries (they are today the languages of primary education).[30] Even when the language is of foreign origin, however, an original voice proclaiming the realities of group life makes a vital contribution toward the reconquest of identity.

This new culture, then, has begun the process, but a last element is necessary to create a true group identity, one that is not only intellectual but popular. The growing, heterogeneous mass of migrant workers, who are rapidly becoming a proletariat in the urban melting-pot, must learn to live together in the cities and to formulate common social demands (see Chapter 13).

PART III

The Land

From Subsistence to Scarcity

7

Peasant Societies: Endurance and Change

We will not spell out at length the traditional way of life of the African peasant, for a great deal has already been written about it.[1] A vast anthropological literature, much of it of great value, examines in detail, often microregion by micro-region, the mechanisms of peasant life, whose dominant features were the rhythms of the agricultural calendar and the self-regulation imposed by clan structures that aimed at preserving the rural family or unit of production. These mechanisms have been said to have been increasingly disturbed and eventually in large part shattered by the "modernizing" intrusion of the West with its system based on money, a market economy, and private property. The peasantry has become increasingly incorporated into a system of international exploitation that has been explained in terms of dominant/dependent modes of production. About this incorporation much has also been written[2]—so much, in fact, that there are now many who claim that this process has been exaggerated. These scholars seek to demonstrate that peasant societies and ways of thinking, thanks to their enormous powers of resistance, have not been destroyed by the capitalist system but can be utilized just as they are, at minimal cost. The constraining milieu of the family-based society and the rhythms of agriculture have a combination of immutability and adaptation to change against which the forces of the dominant "modern" state, whether they are schemes for modernization in the Western manner or attempts at socialistic reform, are helpless.

Colonialism seems only to have encumbered but not to have fundamentally altered the rural way of life. The traditional life of subsistence sometimes seems to have survived intact. Quite typical is the case of the Dagara of Burkina-Faso, who have continued to subsist on the cultivation of millet and the fabrication of *dolo* (millet beer) in scattered villages built in the traditional style, in which the only tangible sign of Western industry is the gas lamp. They have no cooking utensils, no furniture, no radio; straw mats, traditional pottery forms, and calabashes still supply all the housewife's needs. The only change, though it is almost invisible, is a fundamental one: these traditional social structures can be maintained only because one young man in each family goes away to work as an agricultural laborer in the Ivory Coast for at least one or two years, bringing back the cash that has become indispensable. Thus, in this case, the cohesion of rural society has remained sufficiently strong to utilize the new economic situation to facilitate its own survival. The "failure" of the Tanzanian agrarian policy also shows the power of the peasantry. Even though the policy was based on respect for the *ujamaa*, the traditional community, it may have failed just because the peasants absolutely rejected state manipulation.[3]

As a rule, differences between African precolonial and colonial or contemporary society appear less obvious at the level of village life than at that of government, where the indigenous aristocracy was replaced first by the European administrative authority and then, after independence, by the apparatus of a modern state. A number of rural society's social and ideological characteristics have survived unchanged, even though the political and economic foundations of the system have disappeared. An analysis of the situation is required in order to gain an understanding of how a transition from the peasant way of life to an integrated modern society may be achieved and how these forces can be harnessed, for it is useless and no doubt destructive to regard them merely as "obstacles to development."

THE RURAL SYSTEM: SUBSISTENCE
AND SELF-REGULATION

The rural way of life and form of land use in Africa rest on two fundamental principles: the perpetuation of certain agricultural techniques, and a system of self-regulation with regard to private property.

Agricultural Techniques

Traditional agricultural techniques appear to the modern agronomist to constitute a complex system of religious rituals that strictly determine what must be planted and when to prepare the soil, weed, or harvest. All these operations are generally presided over by the land chief and are accompanied by a specific ceremonial which also guides the alternation, order, and degree of proximity of the plants that are being cultivated.[4]

Each operation, however—clearing by hand, fallowing land, burning areas of soil (only effective in a system of long strips of fallow land)—serves a very precise function in an economic system that is balanced, but in which production is limited. Western technicians have insufficiently recognized both that the agricultural techniques evolved gradually over millennia by generations of Africans must achieve maximal use of the ecosystem and that the ecosystem itself is very fragile. In consequence they have encountered enormous difficulties and have sometimes sparked real agrarian disasters. The solutions they have proposed have tended to modify the traditional agricultural cycle or techniques of cultivation, for instance by substituting a salable cereal crop for the yam. These "improved" systems upset the equilibrium of the soil and thus ultimately yield fewer consumable calories for each working day; this fact, rather than simple resistance to change, explains their rejection by the peasants. For example, in Nigeria the refusal to consider the peasants' needs resulted in the failure of an apparent technical improvement: doubling of the density in the sowing of peanuts, which increases yield 20–50 percent. The Nigerian peasant, however, is limited in the amount of money at his disposal, and thus in the quantity of seed he is able to plant; he must reject a system that increases production only on condition that he invest at least twice as much money at the beginning.[5]

The greatest disappointments have been and remain due to ill-considered attempts to intensify the means of production. The 1950s saw many resounding failures, the most famous of which was the British Tanganyika scheme for the intensive production of peanuts, intended to remedy the postwar world scarcity.[6] The introduction of modern machinery to work the soil over vast areas assured exemplary yields in the first year, but they declined to zero after a short period. To be sure, to work with the *daba* (hoe) is exhausting and unsatisfying, for a worker's productivity is restricted to what can be cultivated by hand in a day, but the tractor and even the cow and plow cannot be applied as universal panaceas. If introduced unintelligently, they are likely to prove unassimilable because of the high cost (the upkeep of the tractor, especially, is generally a hazardous proposition) or, at best, because they overthrow the precarious balance of social and ecological conditions required to maintain a fragile system at its original, optimal level.

The traditional agrarian system represented a relatively stable interrelationship among poor soil, a comparatively low population, and a kin-based social order. This equilibrium should certainly not be idealized, for it did not exclude cases of inadequacy and demographic catastrophe. For instance, the fluctuations in food supply in the Sahel go back to the beginning of human history there, for the poor resources limit the flexibility of the system and thus the slightest disturbance—excessive drought, a wet year, war, population, increase—can destroy it. Under such conditions, the colonial conquest must have caused tremendous upheavals, considering that even the best-intentioned contemporary technicians of agricultural services are unable to prevent them.

Social Self-Regulation

The second main element in the internal stability of the rural system is its social self-regulation. Land distribution seems to aim—or, rather, have aimed—at protecting the group against an artificial scarcity of land by preventing its accumulation in the hands of a few privileged individuals. First, private ownership of land did not exist. The rights over the soil, which was collective property, were jealously protected in the institutions under the control of the land chief. Partly, this resulted from the fact that the traditional agricultural cycle barely sufficed for subsistence and reproduction of the social body; an idle social stratum that "lived off the land" could not have emerged without weakening or destroying the system.

This agricultural frailty explains the gravity of the disruptions of equilibrium caused by colonialism: either the communities lost part of their land through the blind colonialist policy of granting large European concessions, as happened in the Belgian and French Congo at the turn of the twentieth century, or else the recruitment of labor caused a vast exodus of able-bodied rural workers, leaving behind the elderly, women, and children, who were unable to do all the work necessary for their own subsistence, let alone that required by these new workers' agglomerates. A particularly dramatic example of this phenomenon occurred in northern Gabon, where the commandeering of the Fang peasants as porters and, especially, as lumberjacks during the military operations against the German Cameroon began a long and deadly famine that lasted from 1918 to 1925.[7] Alternatively, a great upsurge in demographic growth, such as happened from the 1930s onward, and particularly after World War II, enormously increased the ratio of children to productive adults. Finally, a disproportionate development of commercial crops could divert too great a number of laborers from subsistence food production.

Faced with the disturbances of the African system that the European presence had made unavoidable, the traditional society learned to protect itself as much as was possible with the modest means at its disposal. The social system provided, and still provides, its own means of stabilization. Its underlying principles differ from those of capitalist society. In the peasant economy, the fundamental motivation is not profit but the maintenance of the family as a productive unit. The attempt to keep the delicate equilibrium between the family labor-force, production, and consumption can cause an alternation between expansion and regression. If, for example, the younger generation shrinks in number, the area of land under cultivation will be to that degree restricted.

This classic model, made familiar by anthropological research, ought nevertheless not to be accepted simplistically. The concept of a "village community" does not negate the possibility of social inequities in the form of some members exploiting the labor of others. We know that the Sahelo-Sudanese societies were much given to slave-trading; in the nineteenth century at least, slaves did most of the productive work. We even have an example, in the great slave-worked Songhai state in the sixteenth and seventeenth centuries, of the emergence of a great landed estate in the bend of the Niger whose growth, aided by the flooding of the river and the availability of transportation, was solely to supply the needs of the administration and the army.[8] The descriptions of "domestic captives" more or less integrated into the family are probably at least to some extent idealizations for which foreign ethnologists are primarily responsible.

The concept of superior and subordinate age-groups also embraced a complex system of legal and social inequities that corresponded to an equally inegalitarian distribution of tasks within the family group. Moreover, at all levels, everywhere—particularly in central and eastern Africa—women performed the lowest and most laborious tasks. It is too often forgotten that any unmarried man who was recruited by the colonizers for statutory labor and forced cultivation (the H.A.V., able-bodied adult men, of the statistics of the Belgian Congo) sought to find a wife, however young, who could take his place in working for the Europeans, or, failing that, to send a slave, preferably female, to do so. Similarly, in the French Congo (for instance, on the Batéké plateau on the traditional lands of the *makoko* or chief of Mbe) the police adopted the practice of direct recruitment of women from the local villages to maintain the roads. Finally, the productive slavery of women was for a very long period, most emphatically in the nineteenth century, the main source of labor in Tanzania and Zambia. This caused problems for agricultural agents and experts who (even today we know of one case in Cameroon) sometimes insisted on bestowing their instruction and technical guidance on the men of the village, whereas it is the women who work in the fields.[9] Only in West Africa, for reasons that are unclear—perhaps partly attributable, at least in the Sahelo-Sudanese zone, to the influence of Islam—has the stress been laid on women's reproductive role rather than on their productive capacities. That emphasis on reproduction explains how women have sometimes achieved high status within the family circle or in the state: for example, the king's mother may play a religious and sometimes even a political role, and women have been known to act as heads of commercial enterprises ever since precolonial times. (Although we have not been able to include in this volume much discussion of the specific role of women, the topic is a vital one. The system of production, like the system of kinship, places women at the center of economic and social life, despite the great exploitation to which they were and still are subjected and even though the men hold the power both in appearance and in reality.)

A similar misunderstanding has arisen about land use. It is quite true that the soil was neither appropriable nor appropriated, but it has wrongly been inferred from this that land use was unchangeable. The use of land circulated in at least two ways. The ancient, classic method was by abandoning old lands and moving on to new ones, a development dictated by the needs of bush-fallow agriculture. A less well known but nevertheless basic form of land circulation was the use of land as a pledge: this practice, which seems to have been overlooked by the French colonizers,[10] appears to have been in effect a transference of rights over the land, directly connected with interpersonal or interlineal relations of dependency. A major difference between this pledging of land and a Western sale, mortgage, or rent was the absence of any finality to the bargain. A person who pledged his land retained, at least in principle, his right and that of his descendents to reoccupy it. Thus, unlike the very temporary relationship between seller and buyer, that between the pledger and the pledged lasted as long as the land was held, which could be for generations.

Here, once again, we see the complexity and durability of relationships of personal interdependence but, at the same time, some permanent features of rural society: squabbling and wrangling over land, usury and accumulation. Bitter disputes might arise when, after three or four generations, someone tried to redeem a pledge. The pledge generally nearly equaled the value of the crop, and the lender kept his rights to cultivate the land until the debt had been entirely paid. Of course, if the borrower received, for instance, a cow in exchange for the land use, its progeny would belong to him, but each annual harvest counted, in European terms, as simply the interest on the debt: 100 percent a year. If the pledge lasted a generation, the rates became wildly exorbitant. Powerful men, men rich in prestige, in cattle, in wives, in slaves, and, later, in revenues, could thus be the beneficiaries of many lands taken in pledge which were cultivated first by their own dependents and ultimately by paid agricultural laborers (like the rice growers of Casamance) or even by the borrower, who had to hand over all or part of his crop (this happened quite often among the cocoa-planters of the Gold Coast). The flexible conditions of land tenure thus permitted the emergence, not, properly speaking, of landowners, but of exploiters who accumulated wealth and political power, for a rich man naturally took advantage of this method of increasing the number of dependents indebted to him.

"Plantations" on a large scale thus came into existence here and there (in the kingdom of Abomey, for instance, they were run by the king and a number of his dignitaries). A dominant class created by speculative agriculture may even have come into being: the planters of the Gold Coast (present-day Ghana), which in 1911 became the world's leading producer and exporter of cocoa, could be an example. The pledge system of course changed with monetarization, being used for purposes of small-scale agrarian capitalism. In the colonial era, it was much employed during the clearing of lands for cocoa plantations, as a means of circumventing, in the name of respect for "traditional" practices, any legislation opposed to native appropriation and sale of lands on a private basis. These disguised cessions took place on such a scale that in some cases (for example, in Kenya) the British put the matter under the control of the administration, which demanded, in addition to the permission of the "native authorities," firm proof that the land thus pledged was not indispensable to the dependents of the person who was offering it.

The success of this small-scale capitalism remained largely illusory, however, at least until recent years, because of the relatively very low profits from cocoa production and, above all, the way this revenue was spent. Small dwellings, marriage portions, and manufactured consumer goods have certainly left their traces in the cocoa belt, where beautiful but rundown homes dot the landscape, but they have hardly given rise to productive investment.

THE BREAK-UP OF THE SYSTEM

Production of crops for export has altered both the life of the rural peasant and precolonial patterns of land use. Both have shown a perhaps surprising ability to adapt, within certain limits.

The Peasant in the World Economy

The cocoa, coffee, palm oil, peanuts, and cashews of Africa are all destined for export to Europe. Whether they like it or not, the most "traditional" African peasants—that is, those who are truest to their ancestral heritage—are integrated into the world economy through cash crops and are subject to that market. They purchase basic commodities, thus undermining local craftsmanship, and, to an increasing degree, they must also buy essential foods that are unprofitable for them to produce themselves. One of the most absurd examples is no doubt that of the Murid producer in Senegal, who is subject to a pseudo-feudal system of peanut exploitation controlled by the great marabouts within a framework that was created, maintained, and fostered by colonization and then by an independent state.

Rural society need not depend directly on world capitalism, as in large plantations, for instance, where capital is involved at the production level through a concentration of land and intensive mechanization. It is enough that commercial and industrial demand should dictate requirements (for the cultivation of cocoa, oil-yielding crops, and so forth). As small independent producers, peasants may have a different self-image from that of rural wage earners, but they are nevertheless reduced to a similar status, as market conditions make ever more clear.

Reduced in practice to an exclusive reliance on their capacity for work, they base economic calculations not on profits but on individual efforts alone. Peasant rejection of modernization is far from a simple manifestation of ignorance and ill will. In southern Cameroon, for instance, the educational level in the cocoa-producing areas is high. All the peasants have been to school, and they know, understand, and discuss the ideas of the agricultural agents. But the economics of the field triumphs, for peasant judgments continue to be based on the best work/production ratio, and this is better assured by extensive cultivation of a traditional kind than by improvement of yield through modernization. The passivity encountered by attempts to improve cultivation is in fact to be interpreted as resistance to the exploitation made obvious by comparing the prices paid for the basic products for export and the prices paid in Western countries. In Senegal, for example, whenever prices drop below a certain level the peasants return to subsistence farming, cultivating millet instead of peanuts. Thus, to be adopted, a new commercial crop must be integrable to the rural system without major changes. The production of Tanzanian coffee increased from 235 tons in 1905 to more than 10,000 in the mid-1930s, by which time it had achieved the maximum results possible in the rural structure through utilization of the land and manpower. Since then, production has stagnated at that level. Today, under the same restrictions, two hectares is estimated as the maximum area that can be worked by a coffee- or cocoa-planter of the Ivory Coast. To go beyond that limit, external intervention is required: a forced colonization of new lands as in eastern Senegal, or the development of large capitalist plantations of foreign origin as in Zaire and, to some extent, in the Ivory Coast.

Changes in Land Use

The precolonial agricultural system required very large areas of land. In Cameroon, where the soil has to rest for twenty to twenty-five years in order to reconstitute the humus, twenty-five hectares of fallow lands at various stages were needed for every three hectares of effective cultivation. This requirement forced groups to migrate after a period ranging between ten years and two generations. Similarly, in the Baule country (Ivory Coast), the fallow period lasted eighteen years on an average, while only 10 percent of the land was under cultivation.[11] Thus, several decades were needed, or several generations, before the population doubled. Only once in every three or four generations, or about once in a century, an overpopulated lineage, in order to deal with the fallow land (which it had become necessary to cultivate after no more than ten years), was obliged to divide up and send some of its people to found a new habitation in the virgin forest areas of the south. In other words, in any given year, a lineage had only about one chance in a hundred of expanding. This slow, undramatic progression was suddenly upset by a series of new developments: the growth of speculative cultivation, a strong acceleration of demographic growth, and hence an exodus from the rural areas and disorganization of lineal relationships. In Ghana between the two world wars, the traditional authorities themselves officially sanctioned the patrilinear line of inheritance rather than the matrilinear tradition, since a father preferred to leave a plantation in which he had invested to a son rather than allow him to lose it to his sister's descendants. The new conditions created by the capitalist plantation economy, then, necessitated a basic reform in the system of succession.[12]

Of course, we must not overdramatize the situation. In a certain number of cases, especially in forested country where extensive regions remain relatively underpopulated, the spatial elasticity of the rural areas is still great. Food production can grow rapidly because it is roughly proportionate to the growth of the local population. The low demographic density of the Ivory Coast allows that country to extend the areas cultivated by traditional methods while absorbing a large influx of foreigners.[13] A minimum of technical progress—the use of the cow plow, selected seeds, and, above all, in the last four or five years at the most, the introduction of high-yield crops, especially rice—has apparently had spectacular results, since today in Africa only the Ivory Coast and Zimbabwe are self-supporting in foodstuffs.

The traditional agricultural system thus demonstrates its capacity for profitable expansion today, as it did in several cases during the colonial period. At the turn of the century the peasants of Sine-Salum in Senegal, who produced peanuts, were able to satisfy a rapid increase in the European demand (5,000 tons were exported by the region in 1898 and 58,000 in 1911, one-third of Senegalese production from that date onward) without neglecting—at least not until the 1920s—the cultivation of millet, which, in an average year, occupied 50 percent of the fields.[14] Similarly, between the world wars the Beti of Yaoundé, Cameroon, readily supplied food for the surrounding work sites.[15]

Today, however, this elasticity appears increasingly threatened. It is often obliterated by a level of population growth that necessitates an intensification of cultivation dangerous for the soil. In the eastern Ivory Coast (which for a longer period than the rest of the country has been used for speculative agriculture), the maximum of 2 to 2.5 hectares per active person is said to have been reached, as it has even in the "new" areas of the west, for instance around Man, because of the present density of the population. This is also the case in the hinterland of San Pedro, in the Bakwe country, formerly almost uninhabited (0.5 inhabitants per square kilometer), where a spontaneous influx of migrants that has been taking place since the beginning of the 1970s now appears uncontrollable. An annual growth rate of about 55 percent between 1971 and 1975 (from 1,480 to nearly 10,000 people) has given rise to much contentiousness and many palavers.[16]

This overexpansion is particularly noticeable in the southeast of Togo, where the average population density is about 150 inhabitants per square kilometer but can exceed 300 per kilometer. The Watche country, as a result, is an extreme example of almost total utilization of the soil, of excessive subdivision, and of a consequent dramatic collapse in the productivity of the soil, owing to the sterilization of the land. Here we have an example of the impasse to which demographic pressure can drive the precapitalist mode of production, to which the peasants are attached. These areas began with an agriculture closely associated with hunting and gathering. It was based on planting and propagation through cuttings, within the framework of an egalitarian social organization. Now, however, they are called upon to supply the coastal urban markets with cheap food through channels over which they have no control. Over only a few decades they have made the transition to continuous cultivation, but with no increase in productivity. The habitual practice of subdividing the land and the kinship system are incompatible with the development of a genuine profit-based economy. Techniques have instead consistently remained at the lowest level, for the peasants have been content to seek a monetary surplus by means of a predatory exploitation of the gathering economy (exemplified in such practices as overcutting young palm trees to make wine). The exodus from the rural areas, which assures the city of a cheap supply of unskilled labor, seems to offer a solution to the overcrowding. The apparently traditional life that results is an artificial one, however. Migration strips the area of the younger generations who would be expected to maintain the system, merely permitting the elderly, whose numbers continually increase, to retain their customary form of land tenure and agriculture.[17]

Once again, the rhythm and the scale of demographic growth appear to have been the determining factors in the destruction of the previous land system and subsistence economy.

The Cycle of Peasant Debts

The requirements of the peasants, who need more and more money, oblige the rural areas to enter the monetary economy under the worst possible circumstances. In the colonial era, the necessity of having to pay tax and, even in those days, to purchase basic commodities forced the peasants to give up immediately, and thus at the lowest price, part of their crop. Since this forfeited crop rarely constituted a surplus, during the annual period of scarcity just before or at the beginning of the rainy season they had to buy back, at a higher price, whatever was required for their needs. This process, characteristic of the colonial period, was still current after World War II, prevailed in Mozambique up to independence (1975), and has not disappeared or even diminished in sub-Saharan Africa today. It is true that the peasants need money less and less to pay taxes, but they feel the need for it increasingly in order to acquire consumer goods such as clothes, foodstuffs they no longer produce, or at least not in sufficient quantities, and the means of production required for the modern agriculture they are urged to practice (tools, fertilizers, insecticides). The prices of these products have, moreover, increased yearly. A case study of the peasants of Maradi in Niger since the great famine of 1972–1974 showed "an increasing gap between the weight of the financial burdens carried by the family unit and its head in particular, and the quantity of agricultural products it has to sacrifice in order to meet these commitments."[18] A process that has been in existence since the beginnings of the colonial era is today accelerating: it was this spiral of debt and not any form of direct constraint that caused the peasants of Sine-Salum to devote themselves, as we said above, to the cultivation of peanuts for European consumption. The effort was apparently voluntary, but it was inspired by needs that had been in large part created, or at least increased and diversified, by colonization.

As we suggested above, cultivators cannot be seen as simply marketing a "surplus" over and above what is required for the survival of the group. It is not a matter of disposing of the remainder of the crop after family consumption and the needs of exploitation have been provided for and a deduction has been made for levies in kind (rents, various obligations) and losses due to storage. The quantity of produce sold has little relationship to family needs and can indeed exceed the reserves available, especially if a cultivator sells in order to meet some immediate expense. Later, when their stocks are exhausted, they may be obliged to buy back at market rates part of the product that they had sold. They may indeed need to draw on resources such as jewels accumulated toward a bride-price. More often, the family instead decides to reduce its consumption of food. It is the group's physical resistance to undernutrition or malnutrition that provides the elasticity of the system. This is proven by the fact that an increase in the small producer's revenue or production does not generally lead to increased commercialization or to accumulation of capital, but to an increase in the portion set aside for subsistence, either directly or through a change to the consumption of more nutritious cereals (wheat or rice instead of millet). We must therefore abandon the idea that the market is created through the existence of a variable and accidental "surplus"; it is due, rather, to a diversification of money requirements.[19]

In this situation of permanent scarcity, the only hope that offers itself is accelerated peasant migration, which both lightens the demographic burden in the rural areas and provides the extra money that is necessary, but unobtainable on the spot, for the perpetuation of the rural cycle of agricultural subsistence. This instability appears permanent, inevitable, and irremediable, and results in flight to the city and unemployment.

MIGRATION TO THE CITIES

Confronted with the dismal situation in the rural areas, young peasants have understandably been attracted by the prospects offered in the cities, on the work sites, or in the mines, and by the wages in some neighboring countries where opportunities for work are continually increasing. An exodus has been going on since the beginning of the century. Thousands of Mossi peasants have left Burkina-Faso for the plantations of the Gold Coast (or, since 1957, for Ghana) or for the great city of Abidjan. From Nyasaland (Malawi) and from Mozambique so many workers fled to the mines of South Africa and the plantations of Rhodesia that the control of this migrant labor became one of the financial mainstays of the colonial administration: the purchase of emigration permits accounted for nearly 12 percent of the budgetary revenues of Mozambique in 1930.[20] This development dates from the middle of the colonial period, as peasants showed a desire to escape from the prevailing conditions of rural poverty, forced labor, and compulsory cultivation. Mozambique saw an average of 50,000 annual departures between 1910 and 1930 and 70,000 between 1960 and 1970, with a peak of 115,000 in 1975, the last year of colonization.[21] Today the restrictions placed by the South Africans on the recruitment of Mozambican miners, due both to the world recession and to political differences, have brought chronic unemployment to southern Mozambique, presenting the government with the problem of reintroducing an urbanized labor force into a setting of rudimentary rural subsistence.

In the plantation areas of the Ivory Coast, immigrant labor rose from 15 percent of the labor force in 1950 to 45 percent in 1965, and it is today becoming the dominant form of labor in certain industries, permitting a rapid expansion of some industrial sectors. The exodus of laborers, a condition of rural survival, has thus become a customary feature of life. It is now regarded as a necessary initiation into adulthood. The acceleration of migration to the cities, where—as in many underdeveloped countries—a mass of underemployed or unemployed workers is accumulating, can be taken as a symptom of the disintegration of the system. To be sure, the traditional social and ideological structures of the villages often seem to persist, but they are divested of their economic substance, for the peasants cannot provide for their own needs.

The paradox emerges of a form of society which, although it still clearly represents the majority, is nevertheless a residual element within a system dominated by a nonagricultural urban sector. An extreme example is that of Gabon, which, it is true, is an underpopulated country where the young people are pulled rather than pushed into leaving—that is, industry offers high salaries because of the acute shortage of manpower. In Gabon the migrant wage-earner receives two or three times more than in neighboring countries. As a result, the women are left to maintain villages populated only by elderly people and children. Farmers of twenty to thirty years of age represented only 3.4 percent of the total rural population in 1974, as compared to 10.2 percent in 1960, according to the FAO, and the agricultural production is dwindling. The government fully approves of this state of affairs, for this predominantly forested and mining country has developed chiefly—apart from Port Gentil—around two urban concentrations newly

linked by a railroad: the economic capital, Libreville; and the birthplace of
the president, Franceville, which is underpopulated but at least possesses an
urban infrastructure. The rural areas have been deliberately sacrificed, and
the monetary remuneration of the peasants is pitiful. The government has
habitually devoted less than 2 percent of the development budget to agriculture, and the countryside, with its isolated, elderly population, is in an
alarming state of decay.[22]

THE ROLE OF THE MIDDLEMAN

From the nineteenth century onward in West Africa (indeed, from the days
of the slave trade) and since then in the continent as a whole, between
producer and consumer a service sector has stepped in, offering collection
and distribution, wholesaling and retailing, and transportation of products.
At the top of this sector were the great foreign import-export companies;
below them, from the tax collector to the itinerant salesman, "chest-man"
(who carries his goods in a portable chest), or "table-man" (who spreads
them out on a makeshift table), to the Greek, Portuguese, Indian, or Lebanese
entrepreneurs (depending on the area), many different activities were performed by middlemen, a nonagricultural sector that is perfectly integrated
into the economic system. Providing the necessary link between the rural
producers and the world market, these people were directly involved in the
financial operations, administration, and public services of countries in
which, as a rule, from 70 to 90 percent of the income derives from international trade.

After achieving independence, most African countries have nationalized
the upper levels of this sector. The former import-export companies have
been transformed into vast enterprises for the distribution of imported
goods (wholesale, and in the great urban areas), abandoning small-scale
retail trade and rural distribution. Exports have been left to a National
Marketing Board (Office de Commercialisation des Arachides du Sénégal
[OCAS] for Senegalese peanuts; Société Malienne d'Importation et d'Exportation [SOMIEX] in Mali; Société Nigérienne de Commercialisation de
l'Arachide [SONARA] in Niger; Office National de Commercialisation des
Produits Agricoles [ONCPA] in the Congo) or taken in hand by a marketing
cooperative (as in Tanzania). Within the countries, the privileges of foreign
minorities (Indians, Lebano-Syrians) have been greatly reduced, and it is
generally Africans who now dominate this nonagricultural sector. This
means that a restricted but powerful group controls all the inner workings of
the economic and social system, such as access to the revenues from commerce and employment, the administrative and financial positions, and the
mass media, and makes large inroads upon rural finances. To take one example, in the Tanzanian coffee-growing area of the region west of the lake,

TABLE 3.   Distribution of the Profits from the Sale of Coffee

	1955–1957 (N = 44 million shillings)	1961–1963 (N = 24 million shillings)	1967–1969 (N = 54 million shillings)
Nonagricultural sector:			
Cost of transportation	8%	17%	38%
Taxes	5	7	14
Cooperative union and societies	6	11	12
Total	19	35	64
Payment to planters	81%	65%	36%

SOURCE: Jannik Boesen, "Les Paysans et l'exportation du café en Tanzanie," in Samir Amin et al., *L'Agriculture Africaine et le capitalisme* (Paris, 1975), p. 136.

within twelve years the portion of the revenue from coffee earmarked for the producers fell from 81 percent to 36 percent (see Table 3). A similar development has taken place in the tea and banana industries.

In theory, these organizations are designed to defend the producer from the vagaries of the markets. Surplus profits from favorable periods go into a fund to be used as a cushion against a collapse in the world market prices. In practice, however, the benefits to the producer are low or nonexistent, for the price the cultivator receives always falls appreciably below the world price. This was obvious in the case of peanuts in West Africa, whose price constantly rose during the 1960s, enabling SONARA to make larger and larger profits (600 million CFA francs in 1968 and 2,570 million in 1970), precisely because the producers' price had risen only from 19,000 to 21,000 francs per ton. And in Mali it was SOMIEX, not the producers, who profited from the 1974 tripling in the world price of cotton.

SOMIEX indeed serves as the prototype of the organization whose activities lie somewhere between the laudable and the questionable: at the impoverished peasants' expense, the surplus profit is returned to the state treasury, which uses it to meet the ever-growing deficit resulting from the increasingly high costs of imports and the heavy burden of the public-service sector. The boards that deal with food products, such as Office des Produits Vivriers (OPVN) in Niger and Office des Produits Agricoles (OPAM) in Mali, force the peasants to sell them their cereals (millet, sorghum, rice) at prices from three to five times lower than those on the free market so as to prevent a price rise prejudicial to the supply to the cities—or, in other words, prejudicial to the officials.[23]

Thus a larger and larger part of the revenue from agriculture finances the high costs of administration, commerce, and transport. This observation, however, should be qualified in view of the increasingly marked social differentiation in the rural areas. Most of the more well-to-do planters participate to some degree in the "modern" activities associated with urbanization and for that reason earn three or four times more than simple peasants. These producers, then, can be said to have a favorable financial relationship with the cities,[24] but they use most of this additional revenue for the traditional purpose of extending their family or their lands. The portion set apart for directly productive investment is very small: the amount spent on the means of production (agricultural equipment, fertilizers, etc.) does not exceed about 4 percent of the value of exports as a whole. In other words, the introduction of small-scale agrarian capitalism has hardly altered the face of traditional agriculture, except in giving, at its expense, support to the financing of a rural petty bourgeoisie in the making, and above all to the urban and administrative economy.

Small-scale peasants are exposed to the highest possible rate of taxation on the value of their crops and, in some areas, to a land-tax, as well as to a constant rise in the price of imported goods exacerbated by import taxes, which, as in the days of colonization, often serve as the principal source of government revenues. They are therefore made extremely aware of being exploited by the "city people."

It is a matter of common sense: agriculture in sub-Saharan Africa at best permits family survival. Despite all professions of respect for the traditional ideology, we must recognize that any attempt to promote economic—and thus social—development must inevitably lead beyond the agricultural sphere. In consequence, an agrarian capitalism is unlikely to develop spontaneously, "not because the cultivators are obstinately traditionalistic peasants, but because capitalist agriculture, according to the norms of capitalism itself, cannot bear competition."[25] Even if a strong sociological resistance still persists, then, the "modernization" of the rural sector seems unavoidable—but what form should it take? At least two possibilities exist, whose patterns and significance we shall examine: agrarian capitalism, and the socialization of agriculture.

8

Capitalism or Socialism? Recent Developments in the Rural Sector

An examination of the permanent characteristics of African rural history will make it clear to us why official ideologies, whether capitalist or socialist, so often fail. Opposite schools of thought end at the same impasse, because, at all times and places, the problem remains the same: when the state seeks to act on behalf of the peasants it attempts to impose its dictates upon them, that is, to precede the peasants rather than to follow or to accompany them.

AGRARIAN CAPITALISM

Small-scale Rural Capitalism

Agrarian capitalism has sometimes developed on a small scale. The case of the cocoa-tree planters of Ghana has given rise to the debatable but instructive concept of "penny capitalism," that is to say, the principle that peasants with even a little capital can increase it if they apply themselves properly. The small-scale planter is a capitalist because he has bought his land in order to plant trees, and because he invests part of his profits in the purchase or pledging of other lands which he will plant in turn; a well-to-do farmer sometimes possesses as many as several dozen separate plots.[1]

Although it is unpopular with Marxists because it treats capitalism as an obviously progressive model and ignores the implications of dependency, this concept nevertheless has the virtue of taking into account the often-overlooked fact that the African peasants are not entirely bound by their "traditional economy of self-subsistence": they are as capable as anyone else of seizing opportunities as they arise. After all, that was precisely what the peasants of Dahomey and Senegal did in the nineteenth century when they took up gathering palm nuts and cultivating peanuts because they yielded greater profits than the declining slave trade.[2]

In recent years, agrarian capitalism has grown markedly in certain regions of Africa. After World War II the forested eastern part of the Ivory
Coast was broken up into small coffee plantations cultivated by traditional
methods, of approximately 2 to 2.5 hectares per worker. And in less than a
generation, almost all of the Baule savannah and a large part of the western
forested zone were converted into plantations. In 1950, only half of the
Baule peasants cultivated the coffee and cocoa plantations that covered
330,000 hectares, 20,000 of which belonged to Europeans. Fifteen years
later, the areas had more than doubled, while European-owned plantations
had virtually disappeared (accounting for 0.7 percent of the yield, compared
to 9 percent in 1950).[3] By 1978 it was estimated that there were 280,000
coffee plantations covering about 1,200,000 hectares (an average of a little
over 4 hectares each). The effects of the agrarian revolution today are probably still more impressive, but the census of 1977 has long remained confidential, because of the explosive information it contains on the influx of foreign
labor.

The plantations are generally small—2 to 10 hectares—and are worked by
family communities of about a dozen subordinates and dependents grouped
around the planter/head of family. Among these, approximately a tenth, or
20,000 to 30,000 planters, make up a well-to-do rural bourgeoisie that controls approximately a third of the land. The wealthiest—a few hundred—
have plantations of 50 to 100 hectares and each employs 10 or more agricultural workers (totaling at least two-thirds of the immigrant labor), but even
these extensive plantations find a place within the traditional agricultural
system, owing to the sparse population. Thus, in the Bakwe country, in the
vast perimeter of development of San Pedro, although the attempt at an organized and deliberate transfer of 60,000 Baule displaced by construction of
the Kossu dam ended in almost total failure, spontaneous immigration did
develop, at least in the early years, in an atmosphere of optimism on all
sides. The Bakwe, who had long been isolated in the forest and were few in
number, welcomed these immigrants, offering them extensive space. A request for land was passed by the representatives of the local community to
the notables for examination and was confirmed by a gift, which was generally restricted to a bottle of gin, whiskey, or rum and a case of wine or beer.
The drinks were consumed collectively in the course of a ceremony in which
the ancestors, invoked in a ritual libation, were invited to give their approval
to the transaction.

This phase continued as long as the Bakwe retained their numerical superiority, but in the mid-1970s the Baule and other immigrants began to be-
have as though they owned the territories of which they were supposed only
to have received the tenancy. Today, some of them, exploiting a traditional
tendency to avoid precise terminology, say that a payment they made in cash

(as opposed to the symbolic gift) gave them possession of considerable territory. One of them claims rights of ownership over as much as 12 square kilometers, that is, most of the soil of the locality.[4]

This development is today reaching its limit. The politically and economically powerful rural bourgeoisie spends much of its income, not on production, but on consumer or luxury goods or in urban speculations that offer easy and quick returns (property, taxis or other transportation, trade). Meanwhile investment in agriculture remains insufficient. An increase in production depends above all on extending cultivation to lands that until recently had been unclaimed forests, with the assistance of the immigrant labor force, which is becoming ever cheaper and more numerous. Half of the seven million residents of the Ivory Coast are foreigners (Burkinabe, Guineans, Senegalese, Nigerians) and 90 percent of the agricultural workers are immigrants, always ready to leave for other reserves or for the city.

Elsewhere, this small-scale rural capitalism already seems doomed, either because, although long established at the traditional level, it has been unable to make the necessary technological advances (as in Ghana, where the process began much earlier than in the Ivory Coast), or else because great demographic pressures have required the land to be divided and subdivided until the holdings are too small to provide for even the subsistence of their cultivators (as in southeastern Togo or the rice plantations of lower Casamance). Sooner or later, this micro-capitalism is bound to give way to a far more pronounced "kulakization," whether or not accompanied by large-scale state capitalism.

The trend toward private appropriation of lands on an ever-larger scale has accelerated the disorganization of rural society. The peasants, driven from their lands by demographic pressures combined with the innovations of an enterprising minority of well-to-do planters who are encouraged by an interventionist state policy, have been transformed into an urban proletariat. Ironically, in 1976, the head of state of the Ivory Coast expressed satisfaction at "having been able to interest the cadres in agriculture. On my advice, they all created plantations in their villages. The deputies and notables of the north developed rice plantations and cotton fields. Those of my own region created coffee and cocoa plantations."[5] From this point of view, the agriculture of the Ivory Coast may be considered a success.[6] The country—and this is unusual in Africa—in the late 1970s enjoyed a few years of quasi self-sufficiency in foodstuffs, particularly rice, the annual production of which is about 500,000 tons. The annual per capita income has doubled in under twenty years, from 1960 to 1978 (but at the cost of creating grave social inequities), even though the population has also doubled. Since 1978, the Ivory Coast, overtaking Ghana and Nigeria, has become the world's leading producer of cocoa and Africa's greatest producer of coffee (but the data may include some contraband). The list of other agricultural produce for export—palm, copra, cotton, sugarcane, citrus fruit—is expanding. But this is precisely because small-scale capitalism is being superseded. For the last twenty years, the government has systematically promoted liberal Western methods of development and has energetically practiced the techniques of state capitalism. Generally acting through semi-public corporations by agreement with Renault, Bata, and Nestlé, the state has become the largest landowner, the largest trader, and the largest owner of industry. It has total or partial control of most of the great new agricultural projects (oil-yielding plants, sugarcane) while at the same time it has strongly encouraged private initiative.

The future of Africa does not lie with small-scale capitalism to benefit the peasantry, but with medium- if not large-scale capitalism, promoted partly by the property-owning urban bourgeoisie, partly by the state, and partly by international capital. If the aim of this process and sometimes its general result are to increase production, another result—as since the eighteenth century has always been the case, at least in the rural areas, in all countries in the course of industrialization—has been to make a proletariat out of the country-dwellers and to encourage their flight to the cities. The extreme poverty of the majority of the inhabitants of Abidjan—which in a few years has become a vast metropolis of more than a million inhabitants where extensive areas, constantly subject to "squatterization" and inhabited by the un- or under-employed, lack elementary amenities such as water supply, sewers, or transportation—denies the existence of that "miracle of the Ivory Coast" which is announced on the basis of total-production figures alone. It is an agricultural miracle, perhaps, but certainly not an agrarian one, and it is one that is constantly threatened since, according to the World Bank, the Ivory Coast coffee and cocoa, which in an average year represents half its exports, after having attained record prices in 1977 was likely to lose half its value by 1985 (a prediction that has been borne out). And the even more pessimistic predictions of agronomist R. Dumont seem to be supported by the economic failure of the agroindustrial programs (Soderiz for rice, Sodesucre for irrigated sugar).[7]

Large-scale Landed Capitalism

Other countries are attempting to follow the example of large-scale capitalism set by the Ivory Coast. In Zaire, the land law of 1973 institutionalized the appropriation of private property. In stating (article 53) that "the soil is the inalienable and indefeasible, exclusive property of the state," it voided any recognition of ancestral lineal territories. A public domain and a private domain were then formed. Land can be conceded to private owners in the "ordinary" way (that is, by leases of limited duration) or "perpetually," through "the right which the state acknowledges to a person of Zairian nationality of enjoying his land indefinitely" (article 80). In other words, the state can grant all or part of the territories of a lineage to the most dynamic members of the family community on an individual basis.

Since, however, tradition is still powerful and the small-scale planters lack capital, semi-nationalized or foreign companies are best able to set up and develop a modern agriculture that produces for export. No systematic study has been made in this area, apart from the 1978 inquiry by the Société d'Etude de Développement Economique et Sociale (SEDES) on the results of the 1963–1971 projects around Tahua in Niger, but it appears that the major developments, especially in the Sahel, are the vast hydraulic projects in regions where evapotranspiration exceeds precipitation, but where with drainage, irrigation, and road-building, the extremely low cost of land and labor nevertheless promises good prospects for exploitation.

Failed Attempts for the Sahel.   After the great drought of 1973–1975, which ravaged the traditionally raised livestock in the western Sudan, stock-breeding ventures were begun. Hopes for success were based on the water reserves in extensive geological sheets at great depths (about 1,500 meters) in Mali at the bend of the Niger River, to the south of the Senegal River, in the northwest of Niger, in the south of Aïr, and in the north of Nigeria. Although a certain number of watering-places were constructed, however, drainage of these natural reserves proved not only costly but temporary and destructive. The water did not renew itself in the sheets, and the ecological imbalance created by the introduction of dense concentrations of people and cattle caused deterioration of the vegetation and the soil and thus led to desertification.[8] Ranches for intensive stockbreeding of specially fattened cattle, to be exported to the Western countries, achieved little success. These great projects have been abandoned, at least for the moment.

The Sahel Development Program, published by the OECD in 1977, suggested a three-stage plan (1977–1982, 1982–1990, 1990–2000) that was greatly influenced by the Food and Agriculture Organization's five-year plan for the Sahel. The plan, which aimed for self-sufficiency for the area by the year 2000, was approved by the Interstate Committee to Combat Drought in the Sahel and by the Club du Sahel. The Interstate Committee brought together the seven Sahelian states in Ouagadougou in 1973, and the Club du Sahel convened the states of the OECD in the United States. Lack of funds, however, prevented implementation of the plan.[9]

Irrigation Dams and Food-growing Projects.   Much attention is being given—and not only in the Sahel—to plans for hydroagricultural complexes for food production and truck gardening. These projects, while providing food for subsistence, would be primarily directed to the export market and thus are of interest both to the Western investment markets and to the local states in search of foreign exchange.

This is the latest version, oriented toward agriculture, of the great hydraulic works which had previously been constructed chiefly for the production of energy. The Akosombo dam over the river Volta in Ghana in 1964 and the Kossu dam in the Ivory Coast built in 1970 were both intended for hydroelectrical purposes, but a secondary concern was to provide a solution to the problem of the tens of thousands of peasants (70,000 and 80,000, respectively) displaced by the flooding of their lands. The tentative efforts and the setbacks encountered by the state authorities—the Volta River Authority (VRA) and the Société pour l'Aménagement de la Vallée de Bandama (AVB)—at least demonstrate the great difficulty of putting such plans into practice. The VRA in Ghana first conceived a program of self-managed family farms grouped in cooperatives, using highly mechanized agricultural techniques on land cleared entirely by machine. This scheme aroused the hostility of the tribal chiefs, however, and the VRA took advantage of the disruptions caused by the fall of Nkrumah's regime to adopt a more modest and pragmatic program based on a legalized expropriation of land and its redistribution in small lots (one to two hectares) so as to foster a spirit of individual enterprise. The beneficiaries of this plan rented their land to newcomers (60,000 Ewe fishermen attracted by the new lake), while they themselves went to live elsewhere. The AVB preferred to persist in its original policy of voluntary negotiation, based on Baule ethnic solidarity, in order selectively to acquire the best lands and the most technically developed holdings, covering an area of 150 hectares. It then distributed these lands to some thirty volunteer families. After a certain period of infatuation with the project, disappointment in the results turned most of these families back to traditional methods of cultivation. More than half of the original occupants were reduced from the start to the condition of a landless peasantry. Their only choices were to emigrate, or to beg the local chiefs on personal grounds for their traditional land rights. Since 1978–1979, the AVB has adopted a policy of strong encouragement for the agroindustry of oil-yielding crops (peanuts, castor-oil beans, cotton), placing its lands under the management of an Israeli firm, Universal Seeds and Oil Products.[10]

In recent years, the failure of such programs has combined with the increasing food shortage in Africa to give rise to hydraulic projects for primarily agricultural purposes. Thus, the Organisation pour la Modernisation de la Vallée du Fleuve Sénégal (OMVS), financed by international funds under the auspices of the states of Senegal, Mali, and Mauritania (two hundred million CFA francs), proposed, by constructing two dams—one, at Diama, for desalination at the level of the delta, and the other, at Manantali, to regularize the flow of the Bakhoye (Mali) further upstream—to put 375,000 hectares of irrigated land into cultivation by 1989, where only 23,000 are cultivated today.[11] How the project is to be operated now that the dams have been completed and how the farmers will be trained has not yet been explained. Similarly, the dam at Kendaji on the Niger is intended to complement the work of the Office du Niger by irrigating 150,000 hectares. This dam, which will probably cost 150 billion CFA francs, was due to come into operation in 1983, but the collapse of Nigerian uranium prices has made its financing uncertain. Such projects or developments have become almost ubiquitous, although some are more localized in character: for instance, the huge sugarcane plantations in the plain of Banfora south of Bobo-Dioulasso in Burkina-Faso; the mills established by the Grands Moulins de Dakar around Richard Toll on the lower Sénégal (Mimran, a Moroccan mill, has been operating in Dakar since 1956); the Italian venture of introducing tomato crops into eastern Togo at Tokpli in the north of the Watche country; and the Cumere complex planned in Guinea-Bissau not far from the Senegalese frontier, a huge agropastoral project financed by Sweden for the production of peanuts, cotton, truck-garden produce, and fodder to improve stockbreeding. In the Ivory Coast, a sixth dam is now being constructed, less grandiose than that of Kossu but, because the planners benefited from the previous experiences, more effective.

THE LIMITS OF AN ECONOMIC SOLUTION

Despite appearances, the current economic policy continues that of the preceding period and of the colonial era, namely, intensive modernization of agriculture by means of massive injection of capital for the purpose of developing a large, speculative export trade. The process began in the colonial period with Unilever's oil-palm plantations in the Belgian Congo and with the grandiose projects of the Office du Niger. This institution, founded in Sudan in 1932 on the bend of the river Niger and revived and enlarged by Fonds d'Investissement pour le Développement Economique et Social (FIDES) after 1946, throughout its long history swallowed a great deal of capital (more than half of the FIDES funds went for agricultural equipment) with very poor results. In the 1950s, at the beginning of the era of decolonization, many other great projects of the same type, aiming chiefly at export, had the same disappointing results: for example, the Tanganyika Groundnut Scheme;[12] the experiments of the Compagnie Générale des Oléagineux Tropicaux (CGOT) in Senegal; and the cotton plantations in northern Cameroon and those of sugarcane or fruit trees on the Niari plain in the Congo. Of course, the objectives have changed. The emphasis today is less on the exclusive production of raw materials necessary to industry, such as oil-yielding products or cotton, than on foodstuffs which, with a few exceptions such as sugarcane, are new crops raised for the White, bourgeois, or export markets (e.g., tomatoes, strawberries). And if most of the produce goes to the export market, we cannot always blame the enterprise in question. The Senegalese urban consumer, for instance, prefers imported broken rice to the rice of Casamance (which, however, is mainly consumed within the country) and rejects the local tomato sauce in favor of the more highly colored Italian product.

Unprofitable "Giants"

Until now, most large-scale modernization schemes have been somewhat unstable, and if some of them now seem to be gaining strength—assuring, for instance, national self-sufficiency in sugar—these successes are a very recent and still rare phenomenon. We should not forget the enthusiasm aroused in 1974 by the vast sugar-producing scheme for the northern Ivory Coast—a region hitherto neglected by investments, where the per capita annual income in 1965 was less than a quarter of the national average—involving a projected ten complexes (six were carried out) with a production capacity of 500,000 to 600,000 tons. This import-replacing scheme was considered by the experts to offer the triple advantages of reducing imports, satisfying local requirements, and developing exports. In 1975–1976 the plan led to the signature of contracts for irrigated cane-fields and ultra-modern sugar refineries that were to enter into production in 1978–1979. But world sugar prices dropped from 300 to 50 CFA francs.

Either overambitious or ill conceived, the plan remains today an almost total and very costly failure. The sugar is produced and sold at a loss on the international market, thanks to the subsidies of the Caisse de Stabilisation et de Soutien aux Prix des Produits Agricoles (CSSPPA, a kind of marketing board), while the Ivory Coast consumers make their contribution by paying three times the world price for sugar. Finally, from a strictly economic point of view the effects of the sugar-producing scheme are marginal. The addition to the GNP is almost negligible, no towns have grown up around the complexes, and no activities have been developed that can readily be identified in the national accounts. Of course, Western economics cannot provide a complete understanding of the local situation; the sociological results of the program must be considered as well. These include young people out of school migrating to the north in search of good jobs; families abandoning their holdings, with their "traditional" constraints, for wage-earning agricultural employment; and the Sodesucre social program of schools, roads, and hospitals. Similarly, what appears to be wasteful (the proliferation of personnel, minimal productivity) can be interpreted as a form of redistribution necessary to the social equilibrium of the country, guaranteed by the support given to the government by the notables of the north and by a section of the young cadres employed in the state-owned companies.[13] R. Dumont, however, considers it fortunate that a similar project for a giant sugar-manufacturing plant in Gambiel in Guinea-Bissau has recently been abandoned.[14]

The responsibility is said to lie with the inefficiency of the governments of the newly independent African states. The state-owned companies are heavy apparatuses and their numerous employees absorb a large part of the available funds; moreover, the bureaucracy thus placed in a position of command may fraudulently appropriate much of the money. Thus, the Caisse de Stabilisation in the Ivory Coast, which guaranteed the producers a relatively stable price for their cocoa and coffee and took charge of selling the products on the world market, accumulated a surplus of funds in the peak years 1975–1977. These served to finance a wide range of projects (what has been called the Ivory Coast "oil syndrome"), but nobody can say where nearly 30 percent of the money disappeared. "The Stabilisation Fund is a little too independent," the report of the World Bank published in August 1979 observed drily. Similarly, the Société d'Aménagement et d'Exploitation des Terres du Delta (SAED), constantly refloated, has gained a most undesirable reputation in Senegal, at least where finances are concerned.

In fact, the programs have often proven to be unprofitable in the capitalist sense of the term, for three reasons. Obvious technical errors may be introduced (as in the Tanganyika Scheme). Bad judgments about the ecology and social and human factors may be made (as can be seen in the history of the Office du Niger and the construction of dams and reservoirs; apart from those already mentioned, Cabora-Bassa in Mozambique and the Aswan dam in Egypt are vivid examples). Finally, installation and running costs far outstrip profits. This lack of profitability increases as export costs such as fuel prices rise. The process is unlikely to reverse even if more internal urban markets begin to utilize the produce—which in turn can happen only if the internal transportation networks improve, which is rarely the case.

The Importance of Scale

The tragic paradox is that it usually appears to be unremunerative to try to acquire foreign currency through the export of foodstuffs. It is actually more cost-effective to feed the local populations through the massive import of wheat and rice from more developed food-producing countries such as the United States and the European Community. In the decade from 1974 to 1984, food production in Africa declined by 10 percent, while food imports more than doubled.[15] Senegalese rice costs 150 CFA francs per kilo, while imported rice costs 95 francs. The situation is especially profitable for multinational firms; in Nigeria, 85 percent of the imported wheat is processed in the Flour Mills of Nigeria, a multinational company that possesses the only silos in the country. It thus is able to set bread prices. This monopoly is made more profitable by the help of the Nigerian state, which lowers customs tariffs so that the company can acquire American wheat on the international market at much lower prices than those prevailing on the home market.

Bread indeed serves as an index to the situation regarding foodstuffs in Africa. In the last few years this commodity, which requires imported wheat, has come into demand not only in cities and in oil-producing countries relatively rich in foreign currency (such as Nigeria, which imported 380,000 tons of wheat in 1975 and 1,000,000 tons in 1978), but also in countries that are relatively poor but open to the exterior (such as Senegal, where village bakers can be found as far inland as the island of Morfill on the upper Sénégal, and Togo, where the consumption of bread has spread like wildfire since the poor harvest of 1975). As well as so far having been unprofitable in economic terms, then, agribusiness fails to engage the peasant producers, who are left to suffer the effects of their low productivity.

Two examples from Senegal illustrate the innate conflict between peasants and large-scale industry. In the "tomato war" on the 1,000 hectares (yielding 20 tons of tomatoes per hectare) allocated by the SAED on the river at Dagana the authorities have ranged themselves against the peasant producers. The peasants had been intended to give their produce to the state cooperative for purposes of industrial conservation, but they have refused to comply with this requirement. Rather than send their goods by the official trucks whose destination is checked on the roads by the police, they load them on the many unauthorized vehicles that travel by side roads to the open market at Louga, where the tomatoes, bought to be resold in the urban centers, bring relatively high prices.

Even more striking is the contrast between the OMVS's large-scale projects and the local division of land into small areas in the village communities on the upper river. From Bakel to Podor, the riverside villages show themselves to be quite capable of assimilating technical innovations on an appropriate scale, under the direction of SAED in Senegal and the Société Nationale pour le Développement Rural (SONADER) in Mauritania, within the framework of the preliminary studies of the OMVS. The exploitation of the large areas (irrigation units of thousands of hectares in the Oualo and on the floodplain, the lowest land with the heaviest soils, necessitating the use of expensive machinery) has been a failure, while that of the small irrigated areas in the higher Fonde lands (which are situated along the riverbank next to the floodplain and are therefore more accessible to the local inhabitants) is a decided success.

In the Fonde land, one-half-acre plots have been granted to volunteer families who perform all the agricultural operations. They maintain and supply fuel for the hydraulic irrigation pumps, the first of which were provided free. The villagers save money sent by migrant workers (this valley has one of the highest rates of emigration in West Africa—about 50 percent of the male villagers of working age are earning wages elsewhere) to group together to buy a pump cash down (the peasants object to paying interest) or to acquire other machinery or pay for needed social services (wells, schools,

a clinic). All this enables them to transform the landscape: through irrigation, their tiny plots become verdant ricefields surrounded by maize.

The recent adoption of varieties of rice, developed by the Chinese, that
yield as much as six to seven tons per hectare, in two and sometimes three
crops a year, today provides for about 60 percent of the villagers' subsistence needs, but these present transformations of the agricultural scene are
incompatible with the mid-term large-scale plans of OMVS, for several reasons. First, the small holdings, although they are the best adapted to the
peasants, are the least profitable in the Western sense (they only suffice for
subsistence and the peasants must rely on the migrant workers' wages to
cover cash expenses and improvements). Second, the peasants themselves
often prefer an intensified cultivation of millet over rice, for although millet's
total yield is less, it is far less labor-intensive (this is an important point, for
their labor is the villagers' principal, if not exclusive, contribution to the
projects, and emigration leaves them perpetually short of manpower). Finally, control of the river would eliminate the subsidence soils which at the
present time assure a third of the valley's food production (traditional low-
yield millet, 500 kg to the hectare, and vegetables).[16] For these reasons the
confidential interim report of OMVS, despite the experience of these recent
years, announced the necessity of rejecting this "transitional" solution in
favor of "great natural units" in which mechanical equipment would be
used to extract a yield of several tons of millet per hectare from the heavier
clay soils. But this plan threatens not only the historical and sociological
heritage of the valley but, above all, the present-day economic achievements
of its inhabitants.

Wealth and Famine: The Case of Zaire

The most dramatic contrasts are to be found in Zaire. There, a capitalist
economy of plantations for export somehow succeeds in surviving in uneasy
coexistence with a traditional form of subsistence agriculture. The state is
suffering from endemic famine, even though—in certain cases, precisely because—an increase in urban unemployment has caused a return to the rural
areas. Of course, the situation is not uniformly dismal. In some areas it
seems stable or even improving, as is demonstrated in the history of Makuta,
a village of the Manyanga in lower Zaire. Makuta, which is situated not far
from the railroad, supplies food to Kinshasa, which is over two hundred
kilometers away. The ancestral ideological and family system exists in full
force, making use of the opportunities provided by the large-scale neighboring modern agricultural enterprises while at the same time succeeding in
slowing the development of small-scale agrarian capitalism.[17] In general, the
village continues to practice a subsistence agriculture based on tubers, small
livestock, and gathering and hunting. It respects the traditional framework
of the lineage, which possesses the whole of the family lands and manages

them in accordance with a variety of customs based on interlineal marriage and transmission by inheritance. At the same time, nearly all the peasants participate in the two mechanized agricultural enterprises of the region: they rent the machinery of the Groupement Economique Rural (GER) when they have the money to pay for it, they receive cattle from this organization as "share-croppers and stockbreeders," and they work half-time as agricultural laborers on the rice plantations of the Mission Agricole Chinoise (MAC). Although most of the employees of these two enterprises are migrant workers, the villagers have decided that it is worth their while to give up at any rate part of their land to speculative cultivation and to earn supplementary income through part-time employment.

The traditional system in the village seems to be sufficiently strong to resist any internal transformation of the present methods of soil utilization in the interests of technical progress. When an important local bourgeois, a professor at Lovanium University, returned from the city, he attempted to take advantage of the land law of 1973 to appropriate a relatively large area on which he kept improved breeds of livestock housed in modern buildings. All the occult forces in the village then went into action: he met with a car accident; his sheepfold went up in flames. This prospective agrarian capitalist finally recognized that he had been beaten by the village witch doctor. He gave up his plans.

Admittedly, this rural community has a number of advantages: it is well situated, possesses relatively fertile lands, and the population is able to work both on the traditional village level and on the modern urban level. Elsewhere, the situation is generally catastrophic. The eastern province has been suffering from famine for several years, and the rural areas are unable to feed either themselves or Kinshasa, where people are dying of starvation because they cannot pay black-market prices for rice. The famine in Kinshasa stems in large part from the disorganization of the internal transport network and parallel circulation channels, but it is also due to the incapacity of traditional agriculture to supply both the relatively overpopulated rural areas and the urban masses as well. The ruling national bourgeoisie seems unable to act. In this desperate situation the International Monetary Fund and the World Bank are likely to join with the government to extend to the agricultural sector the financial and technical controls they imposed on Mobutu at the end of 1978 in the speculative import-export sector—a modernized form of authoritarian economic colonization.

The Colonial Heritage

Travelers through the rural areas of Africa are forced to ask a question that is elementary and yet apparently rarely considered by the international institutions of development: why, over several decades, have billions of dollars been poured into grandiose schemes which are constantly planned and sometimes carried out, but all too often disappointing, when small-scale rural development appears to be not only far cheaper but far more effective? The digging of a well for each village, as a handful of volunteers are doing in the north of Burkina-Faso; the construction of small dams that create little local reservoirs, as is being done in the same area in a program financed by the Swedes; or the systematic installation of public fountains, as the Togo government has done in the Kabye country, delivers women from a millennial drudgery made visible in their endless lines along the roads. Such undertakings do more to help the rural areas than the construction of large dams which, even if they are not left unfinished (as often happens), operate at far below capacity (beginning with the Cabora-Bassa dam in Mozambique, constructed by the South Africans for the colonialists, or that of Inga in Lower Zaire, which would need additional construction even to supply the neighboring Congo with electricity).

This banal observation is not new. The economic report written in the early 1930s on French West Africa by ex-Inspector of Finances Edmond Giscard d'Estaing pointed out the dangers of the Office du Niger: "Everything has to be done, or to be done again, in the bend of the Niger: to bring in water, to bring in people or to bring them back, to plant crops and to organize transport for the products when they exist. . . . It epitomizes the vast organization of the future, a very burdensome effort in the early years, but capable of later bringing in a wave of prosperity that will reward the true boldness shown now." [18]

In 1936 the Conference of Governors-General organized by the Popular Front government offered similar advice: "For fear of aiming too low, we have aimed too high. . . . It is better to use a given sum of money for the execution of several modest works yielding immediate advantages in a number of regions than to concentrate it on a single major work that benefits only one region, and whose capacities will long exceed the requirements. . . . [We should therefore give preference to] concrete silos [to protect crops] against fires and insects, to cement wells, to local roads and permanent bridges to eliminate the odious imposition of forced labor, to trade schools and rural schools." [19]

And in 1944, an internal report of the Brazzaville Conference (ironically, the creator of FIDES, which was deeply involved in plans for spectacular projects) stated plainly that what was needed were irrigation projects planned on a scale appropriate for use by the indigenous peoples. Instead of impressively huge but unprofitable works, a multitude of small installations should be built, anywhere a water source and a sufficient incline could be found: "[We should envisage] the immediate, large-scale, limitless development of food crops. We should never again see these periodic famines. . . . We do not wish to play the troublesome prophet, but it seems that Africa and its satellites are subject to a terrible scourge which has been prevalent for several consecutive years in the eastern part of the continent. We are referring to droughts." [20]

The Neo-colonial Heritage

The same errors have been constantly repeated, and the reason given is always the same: basic small-scale investments may be essential for the maintenance of the food supply and improvement in local conditions, but their obvious contributions to the struggle against malnutrition and pauperization do not outweigh the fact that they are not profitable in the economic sense. Their results can scarcely be judged in terms of financial profits, since even when food surpluses are produced they cannot be utilized for lack of a transportation network. In the Congo, for example, the varied produce (greens, potatoes, and so forth) of the small and isolated Kukuya plateau in the Batéké region rots on the spot because the road is not suitable for motor vehicles.

The international financial experts cannot regard schemes of rural "social assistance" as economic, for the very definition of capitalist economics is that the lenders should obtain a profit on their capital. All the great banks—and the World Bank is no exception, even if competition highlights the eagerness of private financial groups—have as their first concern the acquisition of markets that yield a high profit. The larger the loan, the higher the interest will be. Contrary to the common belief, the banks are hardly concerned about the amount of capital invested—quite the contrary, in fact, for they have no expectation of getting it back (the underdeveloped countries are clearly incapable of paying such sums), but simply of ensuring regular profits through the guaranteed repayment of the interest, even if that necessitates contracting new loans. Thus, in Senegal in 1980, the sum of 30 billion francs required for the repayment of the foreign debt (out of a total amount of about 275 billion CFA francs) could only be covered, if the original terms were not extended, by contracting new loans. [21]

This method works as long as a country has credit. Senegal has been able to survive by taking advantage of the political support the West gives it because of its strategic position at the extreme west of the continent. The Congo was able to borrow 60 billion CFA francs (within the framework of a project later calculated to cost 90 billion, but which in fact easily reached the sum of 110 billion CFA francs) to realign a section of the Congo-Ocean railroad a few dozen kilometers long, because it is needed to transport Gabon manganese and Central African wood to the international market. The banks would look askance at being asked for one-tenth that sum, however, to alleviate the degradation, so fatal to the circulation of foodstuffs, of the internal road network.

Here, for the sake of convenience, we have taken a few examples from French-speaking Africa, but it is quite clear that it is a general rule that philanthropy is unacceptable both in economics and in politics. The logic of the capitalist system demands this conclusion, but the great socialist powers use essentially the same criterion. Even if they give their support to projects of a socialist nature, the primary motivation remains world imperialistic rivalry. In a number of cases, not only are the capitalist and socialist blocs in competition, but so are the two great socialist forces, the Soviet Union and China. Thus in the postcolonial wars in Angola, China gave aid to the southern party of UNITA, although it is supported by the South Africans, because UNITA has opposed the pro-Soviet MPLA, whose rule is supported by the Cubans. Another example is the Soviet aid given to the moderate party of Nkomo during the struggles leading up to the Rhodesian elections of 1980, against the radical party of Mugabe, the present political leader of Zimbabwe, who was supported by China. Certainly, it would be an oversimplification to take Chinese cooperation in Africa as nothing more than a manifestation of the Sino-Soviet conflict. The Chinese are carrying out a specified and original strategy; it may have changed over the years but, originating as it does in a Third World country, it often seems better adapted to African realities than those of the other powers. It is nevertheless true that the high stakes involved in aid to Africa lead inevitably to one-upmanship.

The markets captured never seem large enough, the schemes grandiose enough, the funds substantial enough to satisfy those concerned. Apart from the fact that mining and industry appear far more profitable than agriculture, it is well known that large firms must progress in order to survive, that is to say, must capture their markets whatever the cost. To the firm that is constructing a dam (or an airport) or providing sophisticated agricultural equipment, it matters little whether or not the product will be effective; a data-processing firm providing extremely costly technological material— such as the one equipping the World Center of Commerce at Kinshasa— need not consider whether in two years' time the system will be dysfunctional because of the inexperience of the local personnel or the humidity of the environment. The two sole guarantors of the suitability of an economic program remain, in principle, the government of the country concerned and the international organizations of aid to development.

Corruption

It is useless to pass judgment on the vulnerability of the members of a government where the so-called 10 percent (kickback) rule is in operation, when the profits from exploitation by a multinational corporation are greater than the budget of the African state in question. In some states the corruption is semi-official. In Zaire it is accepted that the more important a matter is, the higher the official to be persuaded is in the hierarchy and the more he costs; President Mobutu is said to be "beyond all price"; Nigeria has made international headlines with several famous scandals. In 1974–1975, for example, the public sector purchased some 20 million tons of cement, including 16 million for the Ministry of Defense, to be delivered only after twelve months. The resultant blockage of the ports did not end until the military government that came to power in July 1975 canceled the contracts, which enabled an enormous number of carriers to receive a high demurrage for their immobilized cargoes, much of which was only fit to be sold for scrap.[22]

Another recent scandal demonstrated the great powers of persuasion international interests exert over local authorities and their impact even on the agricultural development of the country. The explosion of a Texaco oil well off the Nigerian coast polluted the delta. In this amphibious zone, 50,000 liters of oil overran the land, swamped the stores of grain, and contaminated all the wells and canals. For more than a month (January to February 1980), several thousand isolated people were the victims of an unmitigated disaster, being deprived of food and, above all, drinkable water, but the interests involved were so powerful that Texaco was able to impose a total and enduring blackout on the local authorities. News of the catastrophe only reached the international community in the first days of March, after the well had been filled in by the help of American "air-firemen." We shall no doubt never know the price the local population had to pay for the silence, which prevented them from receiving international aid.[23]

Corruption exists virtually everywhere. One story that recently caused a stir in Senegal, a country reputed to be stable, moderate, and in certain respects democratic, is particularly revealing. In April 1980 a journalist was widely believed to have published revelations in *Le Figaro,* in an issue banned in Senegal, concerning the colossal fortunes amassed by the dignitaries of the regime. The article was in fact imaginary, but the incident shows how few illusions about the matter people have.

There is no need to refer to any particularly fraudulent activities. It is enough, in order to explain why the debts of the Senegalese peasant equal double the value of his crop, to realize the strength of the pressures exerted on rural society by the politico-religious establishment that rules the country. From these rulers, in the persons of the petty officials who hem in and in fact ransom the peasants, they are obliged to request the necessary loans to obtain seeds, manure, fungicides, and agricultural materials. In order to have prevented the 1980 peanut crop from being the poorest since the war or to have stopped the GNP from declining by an average of 3 percent a year, it would have been necessary to tackle two basic problems: that of reducing the burden laid on the country by an overgrown administration (about 70,000 officials and 35,000 semi-officials out of a population of 3.5 million inhabitants), and that of opposing the special interests of the ruling class [24] (which is to say, in the final analysis, those of world capitalism, of which the national ruling interests are merely a reflection). The authori-

ties of course favor the enterprises most promising for them, and these are
more likely to be in the industrial sphere or the sphere of prestige than in
agriculture. It is all too easy, however, to issue sweeping condemnations of
the venality or simply the interests of the people in power; the other side of
the coin is the crushing imbalance between the financial power of African
governments and that of any of the huge multinational corporations.

International Organizations

The agencies for international development increasingly show themselves
as self-devouring institutions consuming their own energy, with their activities geared to internal purposes. The running costs of these many-branched
organizations are disproportionately large, and the facilities they provide
still seem to be insufficient. For example, the budget of the World Health
Organization (WHO) for 1982–1983 was fixed at 469 million dollars, that
of the Food and Agricultural Organization (FAO) at 414 million, and that of
the United Nations at 1.25 billion. Enormous staffs, made up, to an increasing extent, of nationals of undeveloped countries for whom it often constitutes the only chance at a career, undoubtedly amass a vast collection of administrative, technical, and scientific reports in every social and economic
domain. It is not at all my intention to suggest that their role is entirely negative; contributions to knowledge have been made, along with some progress
in the struggle against world hunger and drought. But even if it were the
case—and it is not—that all the investigations met clear criteria of efficiency, they would remain fundamentally dependent on the great institutions of banking, economics, and finance (especially the World Bank and the
International Monetary Fund)—that is to say, on the sacrosanct criterion of
profitability.

The often draconian constraints imposed by the World Bank have since
1977 virtually forced the United Nations to create a financial organ for the
novel purpose, not of rendering agriculture profitable, but of "increasing
food production and raising the nutritional level of the poorest populations
in the poorest countries with a deficiency in food." This agency, the International Fund for Agricultural Development (IFAD), attempts to approach
the problem of hunger from a new standpoint, giving human factors special
attention. The stress is laid on food crops in the context of the traditional
communities and the existing social potential. Thus, in Senegal, an effort is
being made to include women in rural development by teaching them to use
mills, threshing machines, pumps, and other machinery. Moreover, those
who wish to cultivate small farms but have little capital are being given aid
(130,000 people have benefited from this in the regions of M'Bour and
Louga). Agricultural funds are redirected toward small farmers with the
loans being based on the viability of the enterprise rather than simply pos-

session of collateral. Finally, the IFAD tries to avoid creating a new international bureaucracy, by instead making maximum use of channels provided by other institutions of development (notably the FAO);[25] these efforts, unfortunately, seem to be failing.

Social-mindedness

A new spirit of social-mindedness seems to be making an appearance. It is not necessarily connected with socialism or any other particular political option, as we see from the case of the Ivory Coast. The current program, financed mainly by the World Bank and partly by the state (which diverts to it some of the revenue from taxes on the consumption of water, tobacco, and so on), beginning in 1976 but more systematically from 1979 on, has been sinking village wells, thus transforming the rural areas, and especially the lives of the women. Parallel to this program is that of the Groupements à Vocation Coopérative (GVT), which, under the control and with the financial aid of local officials of the Parti Unique, works at organizing village marketing cooperatives, with the final aim of developing production cooperatives. This second stage, it is true, seems highly problematical. Its only chance of success would be if village notables were to revive, for this purpose, forms of solidarity such as the Poro of the Senufo, or age groups.

A recent study stresses the need to cooperate with the existing structures with the hope of encouraging local initiative and to introduce appropriate techniques and projects on a village scale. In the opinion of this study, failure comes with the attempt to impose large-scale projects that have been conceived out of complex collusions of interests between financing organizations and corrupt governments. A classic case is the United Nations Development Program's reafforestation scheme in the Nigerian Sahel in 1973.[26] Since then, Niger, a vast country recently afflicted by major droughts, seems to have been the object of an intelligent effort of reafforestation, supported by a program of the United Nations Bureau for the Sudano-Sahelian Region to Combat Drought and Desertification (UNSI), which is also contributing to financing the green belt of reafforestation around Niamey and to developing the Majjia valley.

Although it is involved in large-scale programs (including the Majjia valley development scheme), the Office National d'Aménagement Hydro-Agricole (ONAHA) in Niger is primarily concerned with mid-scale rice cultivation and fish-breeding (on areas of about 500 hectares), working with the peasants to assure the necessary supply of food to the urban centers. The sources of finance are varied (the Fund for Economic Development [FED], the World Bank, the government of Belgium). Near Niamey, along the river, organized areas are farmed on a voluntary basis: the plots are distributed with the possibility (not obligatory) of using communally owned equipment at a low rental fee. Undoubtedly, the results are uneven: once the deductions have been made, the yearly profit remains small. The Zarma peasants balk at the effort of growing rice: the Chinese method of working backward in setting out plants is traditionally considered to bring bad luck. The older people regard it as "slaves' work" and for that reason reject the working methods of the Chinese, who created the plantations of Kolo at the gates of the capital. These rice plantations have therefore been given to the young people to cultivate, in an operation at once political, social, and cultural. It was launched by the regime in 1974 with the intention of "dynamizing"— that is to say, utilizing in a modern form—the traditional practice of division into age groups, in this instance rebaptized *samarya* (a word borrowed from Hausa).[27] Despite the difficulties, the results seem promising: at Lossa, Sona, Tula, Namarijungu, and the Say area the landscape presents a spectacular contrast between the often sterile plateau speckled with lateritic crust and the verdant, sparkling ricefields. The vast silos were filled to bursting point, until they were emptied in the 1986 drought. Perhaps, though, the distribution service offers the greatest hope of success for this experiment. All workers receive a monthly allowance of sacks of rice and millet at the lowest possible price. The distribution is strictly controlled, to prevent fraudulent accumulation and resale by speculators.

It would be naive to express surprise that such initiatives did not get off the ground until the 1970s. This development merely demonstrates a point that is at last becoming impossible to ignore, namely, that it is at best useless and at worst dishonest to seek to solve by strictly economic means what in reality are primarily social problems: malnutrition, hunger, unemployment, and disease in the African rural areas.

THE SOCIALIZATION OF AGRICULTURE

Faced with the problems of the rural areas, it was the socialist regimes that first and most clearly demonstrated a desire to follow a definite agrarian policy. No such policy has so far succeeded, nor even been convincing, but at least it can be said that the philosophical presuppositions underlying the socialist attempts have a more generous inspiration than those of the capitalists. The propositions are inverted: in contrast to the capitalist system, according to which an economically viable program (that is to say, a profitable one) must sooner or later have beneficial social effects, the socialists tend to believe that a socially useful program must lead to economically viable results.

The Benin Experiment

The immutability of the society and the way of thinking in the rural areas remains a problem. The peasants lack national or political consciousness;

their principal concern is survival and daily labor on the piece of soil that has been given to them. The sheer enormity and difficulty of the tasks to be undertaken, and the shortage of technicians and experts, especially at the intermediate level, too often have the effect of limiting projects to mere propaganda; much speechifying takes place, while the rural situation remains unchanged. Slogans chanted not long ago on the Guinean radio and the rudimentary Marxist speeches broadcast in Benin seem absurdly incongruous when, in the Guinea of Sekou Touré, the peasants depend on a subsistence economy and a precolonial form of barter, and the only modernization has been the industrialization of the mining sector under Western auspices. It would be wrong, however, to minimize the value of these first efforts in Benin, however uncertain they may appear to be. In any case, to some extent they preceded the revolution of 1972–1974.

Since 1961, SONADER, which has since become SOBEPALH (Société Béninoise du Palmier à Huile), has been working to improve the rural areas. On the initiative of young technicians from Dahomey who understood that past failures in cooperative organization had been due to overtight administrative control, ignorance of rural traditions and ways of thinking, and lack of peasant participation, great strides have been made in developing the oil-palm region of Mono, Ouémé, and the Gulf of Guinea. The land problems of the region were complex, ranging from the great domains inherited from the monarchies of Abomey and Porto-Novo, which were in principle undivided, to an extreme subdivision of land caused by the fragmentation of ethnic, clan, lineal, and family structures. Reallocation of lands allowed the previously scattered peasantry to regroup in development areas around schools, clinics, and sports fields. Mornings were spent in collective work on the palm plantations, and in the afternoons individuals worked on their subsistence lands. Landowners had to participate, but landless peasants could also take part. The social capital thus consisted solely of contributions in kind—soil and labor; each year, these cooperative farmers received their share of the crop, divided into "part A," the percentage of land possessed, and "part B," investment in labor provided in the first five years, a payment representing 200 days of work at about 150 francs a day. During this period of investment, the worker could take advances of up to 125 francs a day.

Mechanized techniques were used only for the oil palms. Cultivation of the half of the land devoted to food crops stressed human investment, since the lending organizations—the French Fonds d'Aide et de Coopération, the FED, and the World Bank—refused to finance this sector. The results varied. Some teams of technicians and managers proved to be remarkably effective, but conflicts often arose, with the peasants complaining that the overseers' salaries and urban way of life unduly burdened the budget of the cooperatives. The experiment, which has been taken up again by the new regime, has at least the virtue of having trained the peasants. It is enough to be present at the general assembly of the cooperative in order to be conscious of this new awareness: the peasants will no longer passively accept whatever is doled out to them.[28]

The socialist regime cannot take sole credit for the SONADER experiment, which began long before 1961. Moreover, the Benin project suffered from the drawbacks typical of a technocratic operation financed by Europeans, and it committed a number of technical and social errors. In an area of very great demographic density, at least for Africa (more than two hundred inhabitants per square kilometer), where crops had always been cultivated under the palm trees, in the first bloc they failed to allow sufficient space for food crops and they also failed to foresee that the massive clearing of thousands of hectares could cause a deterioration of the microclimate that would be injurious to the yield. Furthermore, even if the participants apparently increased their income, the forced cooperation was interpreted as expropriation of the land. Those who refused to join the cooperative were granted a yearly rent of only 600 CFA francs per hectare for their confiscated lands. The result was a drastic shrinkage of the traditional food economy of subsistence and barter, and the rigorous schedule defining hours of work and the tasks to be performed was felt to be a return to the system of forced labor. Finally, the collapse in the production of palm products (due in part, it is true, to the continued deterioration of the climate since 1972) seems to suggest that the operation could not ultimately be called a success.

In the rest of the country, the government's efforts are concerned more with rural administration than directly with production. Self-administration in the villages, it is hoped, will encourage the peasants to take the initiative in the promotion of agriculture. In the name of the three D's (deconcentration, decentralization, democratization), authority was given to local revolutionary committees, in an attempt to counteract the traditional notables and hereditary forces. Chosen by consensus in each village, each committee consists of eight young people, four men, and three women, who choose a delegate. These delegates elect the commune committees, by whom the mayor is elected, and the district and provincial committees. The committees' relative financial independence—10 percent of the direct taxes go to the village and 20 percent of the general tax revenue goes to the commune—should help in the realization of the economic aspects of the reform. The district committees have been made responsible for activities such as the policing of warehouses and the supervision of trade; and the local committees have the task of proposing schemes that, in accordance with their degree of importance, can be carried out with the means available in the villages or with the assistance of the commune, the province, or the state. At the provincial level, finally, autonomous administrative groups supervise community services such as transportation and the provision of essential products (gasoline, cement, sugar, salt).

It remains, of course, to translate these reforms into reality. Local committees and the regional or national party and planning office often do not function as they should. The financial rewards are slight, but the local labor force is expected to generate enthusiasm nonetheless. The peasants, however, appear little impressed by grouped formations or by radio broadcasts of courses of patriotic education that fail to correspond to the realities of their lives. And, contrary to the plan, a great number of former chiefs and village notables have been given responsible positions in the new hierarchy.

Since the deficiency of the program lies above all in a weak system of distribution and poor remuneration for agricultural labor, the simple but abstract plan has been suggested of "creating" a "class struggle" by increasing the wages paid to producers and salaried workers while reducing the incomes of officials and students. This measure met with violent opposition from the latter (student grants fell from 65,000 to 15,000 CFA francs) and still was unable to gather enough funds to satisfy the peasants, for world market prices were low. In 1975, the rise in the price of cotton from 40 to 45 francs per kilo and that of a worker's pay from 5,000 to 7,800 CFA francs a month seemed to be maximum,[29] and the government had to renounce its plan of lowering urban salaries.

The Tanzanian Ujamaa

The Tanzanian and Mozambican forms of socialism have at least one idea in common: that of creating autonomous and economically viable village units of production in areas where buildings are generally scattered—tiny hamlets or isolated farms—and where traditional agricultural techniques are therefore both deeply rooted and undeveloped owing to a lack of means and mutual assistance. Beyond this point, however, the plans diverge.

Ujamaa (from a Swahili word meaning family life and the kinship spirit) is associated with the "traditional models of social existence" whose particular virtues are to be made the basis of modern African society.[30] The history of the land fosters such an ideal. The German depredations, which were brutal, although comparatively short-lived, the unhappy experience of the great privileged "charter" companies, and the crushing of the last revolts—the one led by the Arabized chief Abushiri against Carl Peters's East Africa Company (1887–1890), and the violent rebellion of the Maji Maji (1905–1907), which roused the southern third of the territory against the colonialists—confirmed the peasant societies' rejection of all external influence. They had for decades been accustomed to submit to various yokes, from that of the sultanate of Zanzibar down to the slave-hunting armed bands sent out in the last third of the nineteenth century by more or less Islamized local chiefs.

The British colonizers were remarkably tolerant of the rural subsistence economy and at the same time opposed the emergence of a neo-feudalistic

type of aristocracy (contrary to what happened in northern Nigeria under
the cover of the emirates' protection). For example, in the district of Bur-
kobai, the administration split up the vast domains that migrants who had
come two or three centuries earlier from Bunyoro (Uganda) had settled in
the manner of their area of origin. The holders of these great fiefs (the
nyarabanja) had required the pseudo-serfs on their land to pay tribute in
cowries, crops, goats, and forced labor. The colonial authorities liberated
these vassals by demanding the emancipation of slaves and the registration
of lands. Like any other holders of "public lands," the possessors were
henceforth expected, in exchange for the recognition of their right of occupation, to pay yearly dues to the government.[31]

It is against this background of the maintenance and even the encouragement of small-scale peasant farming that one must understand *ujamaa,* an
idea launched in 1962 and emphasized after 1967, the year of the Declaration of Arusha, the charter of "Tanzanian socialism."[32] The principal plan
was to regroup the previously dispersed country-dwellers into rural communities whose self-sufficiency was assured by an egalitarian pooling of work
and profit-sharing. *Ujamaa* embraced three "traditional" principles: the
mutual respect of the members of the society, collective ownership of essential goods, and periodic redistribution of accumulated wealth.[33] This heritage was to be used as a dynamic instrument of rural development.

The first goal was to reestablish the balance in food production upset
since World War II by two factors: demographic acceleration; and impoverishment of the rural areas, which left peasants at the mèrcy of the droughts
that alternated with heavy rains, ruining harvests. Basic cereals—maize,
rice, wheat—had to be imported in quantities that were greatest during
1961, 1965, 1969, and especially the period of the catastrophic Sahelo-
Sudanese drought of 1973–1974, at the same time as the soaring oil prices
and increased costs of imported food products exhausted the country's foreign reserves. The movement of "villagization," which affirms the priority
given to food production, expresses a desire to "rely only on one's own
strength." It also implies a refusal to give first place to industrialization requiring costly foreign capital.

The *ujamaa* experiment was born in 1960, in the region of Ruvama in
southern Tanzania, when on a cashew plantation a group of young activists
first attempted to carry out Nyerere's instructions that "*ujamaa* villages
must be socialist organizations, created by the people and managed by those
who live and work there."[34] In 1969, this was made a standard pattern. According to the model, each dwelling was to have a plot of 2 acres of land (0.8
hectares) entirely at the disposal of the owner, who, using two-thirds for
food crops and the rest for speculative cultivation, would by 1976 have assured the self-sufficiency of his household. The rest of the land was organized into communal fields to which the peasants were expected to devote

at least half their working time. Small village industries such as brick- and tile-making and pottery were intended as a support for the agricultural activities, in conjunction with the Small Industries Development Organization (SIDO).

The organization of the work is determined by the villagers in assembly, or, if the number becomes unwieldy, by their elected representatives. The ultimate goal is to satisfy the needs of the community, with the state undertaking to provide trained staff—teachers, nurses, technicians—machinery (in 1975 it was decided that tractors and machines should be stored in each region), and heavy equipment for special projects such as digging canals.

Membership in an *ujamaa* community was voluntary, but the underbureaucracy of the party quickly assumed the dominant positions in the villages and in most cases were content to use *ujamaa* as a means to obtain grants and other payments. In 1973, the general failure of the enterprise was admitted, and the authorities consequently changed their tactics.

The economic ideal of treating the peasant as the true wealth of the country was paralleled by the political purpose of organizing the collective responsibility of the villagers in such a way that they would support the regime. Since, according to the Declaration of Arusha, socialism is "a way of life . . . in accordance with [the regime's] principles," the "excessive" privileges granted the *ujamaa* villages were criticized as inappropriate, but at the same time, "villagization" was declared compulsory.[35] This authoritarian action appears to contradict the respect professed for the traditional village autonomy, which implies both self-administration and decentralization.

The government has not been able to resolve this conflict. Certainly, great flexibility was intended: "development villages" were to be set up over three years, on a plan developed from preliminary studies of the site, soil fertility, distance from roads, availability of drinking water, and so forth. The villages became *ujamaa*, or communal, at their own pace, by gradually enlarging the collective fields at the expense of private property and by setting up production cooperatives to complement the purchasing cooperatives already established. The authoritarian approach prevailed, however: between August and November 1974, forced "villagization" became the general practice. Within a few weeks the army transported millions of rural inhabitants from lands some had already planted to distant areas of undeveloped land where they were to create fields and villages. Judging by numbers, the operation was effective, for by June 1975, nine million Tanzanians (65 percent of the rural population) had been regrouped in villages, but the total disorganization and lack of provisions caused catastrophic immediate results and deep popular discontent. Fantastic rumors began to spread about the collectivization of land, livestock, and even children.

The speed of the relocation was intended as a response to the world agricultural crisis, which was aggravated by drought in Tanzania. The operation, begun while Nyerere was traveling abroad, may, however, be seen as stemming from a clash between two outlooks: one hostile to socialism, which it wanted to discredit, and the other that of the doctrinaire Marxists who believed—in opposition to the true *ujamaa* ideology—that a radical change in outlook required a break with the traditional forms. The fact is that social opposition to the experiment was strong. Before 1973, a little over six thousand villages contained two million Tanzanians, about 15 percent of the total population, but 80 percent of these villages were situated in the poorest regions in the country. The wealthier and more populated areas, where cultivation for export had long been carried on with the assistance of well-established cooperatives, showed little enthusiasm. When the villages organized it was above all the notables who profited.

Today it is generally agreed that the program has at least partly failed. It has realized neither its economic objectives—food production remains insufficient—nor its social objectives—the reforms mainly benefited small and medium-scale agrarian capitalism—nor, finally, its political objectives— the poor, ill-used, and disappointed peasants maintain an attitude of passive skepticism, if not resistance.[36]

It is undoubtedly true that in order to increase production and improve the conditions of the rural areas, village centers must be created. The country has been given a solid agrarian structure, but the goal is far from having been achieved. In his report to the sixteenth TANU National Conference, President Nyerere strongly criticized both the peasants' inertia and the agricultural planners' incompetence. Dumont and Mottin have pointed out the basic error of making the villages too large.[37] Originally Nyerere had spoken of communities of 30 to 40 families, a reasonable number, but the optimum was soon stated to be 500 to 600 families, or 2,000 to 3,000 individuals; smaller villages were urged to group together to share tasks and equipment. Dumont and Mottin cite the case of one woman who, in order to carry home on her head the yield (1,200 kg) from her one-acre field of maize, some 8 kilometers away, had to make forty round trips: a total of 640 kilometers on foot, half loaded down, half empty-handed. In other words, with the rudimentary means village agriculture has at its disposal, a minimum unit of production that may be profitable from the point of view of mechanization and modernization makes no sense at all.

The third plan, launched in 1977, is being modified in ways that suggest that this lesson may have been learned. Agriculture is no longer the sole economic priority; industry is designated as the focus of development for the coming years. Having said this, it must be admitted that it is too early to dismiss Tanzanian agriculture as a failure. The rural program is less than ten years old, and progress, though uneven, has undoubtedly been made. Here again, Dumont and Mottin are correct in contrasting the Tanzanian atmosphere of modest goals, and the priority it gives to the rural areas, with the outrageously elitist flashiness of the Zambian urban bourgeoisie. And even if the disorganization of the state now seems to have reached a climax, it is not at all clear that the basic rural situation is worse in Tanzania than in Kenya or elsewhere. It should not be forgotten that Tanzania is faced with a tremendous challenge: it is one of the twenty-five poorest countries in the world.

The Mozambican Aldeas Comunais

Despite different presuppositions, the Mozambican experiment of the *aldeas comunais* bears many similarities to the Tanzanian *ujamaa*. It, too, stresses self-reliance, gives priority to local and regional food production, groups a scattered population into organized rural communities, and aims, finally, to turn the peasants into willing, responsible, and conscious instruments of the socialist revolution. The Mozambican model, however, includes the development of a far stronger industrial infrastructure than in Tanzania, and it is faced with the almost complete collapse of agriculture, caused by the sudden departure, since independence was declared in 1975, of a million Portuguese, and with the consequent disintegration of the interregional transport network in a country 2,600 kilometers long.

The authorities claim that it is necessary to make a *tabula rasa* of the past and expressly condemn the use of ancient "customs." "Fetishistic" manifestations and ancestral beliefs, the traditional education of girls, and the primacy of the elders are all regarded as hidebound notions that are liable to hinder construction of the new socialist society.

The peasant societies of Mozambique, even more often objects of aggression than their counterparts in Tanzania, have in the course of their history taken refuge in an increasing isolation. The process goes back several centuries, with the progressive dismemberment by the Portuguese of the empire of the Monomotapa (Zimbabwe). They began with the *prazos* (in about 1750 there were one hundred between the valleys of the Zambezi and the Tete), which were vast fiefs belonging to a few great families of settlers involved in the slave trade, who abandoned the country to the depredations of their overseers and the revolts of the slaves who had served as armed guards (the *achi-kunda*). These, transformed in the eighteenth century into bands of robbers, were finally absorbed into the political formations that came into being after 1850.[38]

The subsequent slave-owning warrior empires of the Massangano or Gorongosa to the south of the Zambezi and the Makanga or Massangire to the north were undermined by military rivalries and internal conflicts that can be traced in large part to the possession of the Western rifles distributed by the slave trade. The alien technology under inadequate control left them unable to resist the Portuguese conquest and destroyed their traditional way of life. Colonization only accentuated the disintegration by pushing the peasants out to areas of refuge, as their fertile lands were confiscated, first by concessionary companies or large-scale Portuguese settlers, then, after World War II, by the South Africans.

In the 1960s a large-scale investment in equipment for intensive cultivation of plantation crops—tea, sugar, cotton, sisal, copra—again displaced the peasants. Between 1960 and 1970, 4,600 agricultural enterprises came to own 2.5 million hectares, with a labor force that rose from 186,000 to 450,000. The rural inhabitants suffered particularly from the widespread settlement of the Portuguese soldier-farmers, the *colonatos,* whose presence was encouraged by the state as an answer both to the overpopulation of the Portuguese countryside and to the Mozambican war of liberation. In 1975, 1,315,000 hectares of the most fertile lands were taken by force from the local people and divided into small holdings of two to eight hectares each. The new settlers, supported by the state, employed paid workers and used plows and tractors.

Measures to help the local people were planned, such as improving methods of cultivation, making financing available, or creating protection against natural calamities. None of these plans was carried out. Moreover, most of the peasants worked plots of less than two hectares. At independence, 1,258,000 peasant families had to be content with 1,184,000 hectares, although only 10 percent of the cultivable land (about five million hectares) was actually being exploited. The mode of production remained particularly archaic: exclusively work with the hoe and cultivation on burnt lands, with no mechanization or even use of harnessed animals. It was an agriculture of subsistence only, less and less able to assure survival. When to the peasants' desperate situation was added the suffering caused by the war of independence itself, to rebuild rural society from the ground up became an absolute necessity.

As in Guinea-Bissau, the original idea in Mozambique was to begin with the social bases of the war, that is to say, the villages of the north where the armed struggle was organized. Waging this struggle required an efficient distribution of surpluses and an increase in productivity, both in order to supply the army, the refugees, and all those whose system of production had been disrupted by the war (with the destruction of granaries and crops through bombardments) and also to pay for the flow of arms from Tanzania. A system of production on collective blocs of land was instituted, especially around Tete. At the same time it became necessary to form cadres, to teach the peasants to read and write in order to overcome the problem of communication posed by the cohabitation of different ethnic groups (particularly in the army), and to evacuate the wounded to the liberated areas and to care for them there. Thus a certain communal existence came into being in conjunction with a state of permanent mobilization.[39]

In May 1975, a few weeks before independence, the idea was conceived of developing communal villages out of the experience in communal development gained in the war. Samora Machel, who became head of state, described them in September of that year: "The communal village is the backbone of the development of productive forces in the rural areas. . . . Through their collective life, the organized people liberate their immense creative initiative. Politically . . . it is the instrument for the materialization of the power of the workers on the level of administrative institutions, of structures of defense, of production, of trade, of education, of culture, of health—in short, of all sectors of social life. . . . We ought to know that, scattered and disorganized, we cannot exercise power."[40]

The Resolution of Communal Villages, adopted in February 1976, stressed human effort, "creativity," and use of the land. The principles evoked were self-sufficiency, to be achieved by widening the scope of food production to include orchards, kitchen gardens, and animal husbandry; investment in manpower, that is, maximum use of the local work force before calling for outside technical assistance; and conservation of the soil. Even if the ultimate goal is very different—for the intention is really to create towns in the rural areas, with all their complex and mutually complementary functions—in practice the communal villages resemble *ujamaa* in a certain number of features. For instance, production per family is limited to between half a hectare and one hectare, whether the soil is irrigated or not, and employing salaried workers is forbidden. These family plots are intended to supply the peasants with food and enable them to buy the few clothes they need. Even on this level, cooperation is encouraged within blocs of thirty to forty hectares in order to obtain the necessary funds for clearing land, hiring a tractor, or buying pesticides.

Work is also organized collectively within the framework of production cooperatives and state enterprises. Those involved cultivate food crops together and share speculative crops, the compulsory stockbreeding, and, where necessary, fish-breeding, bee-keeping, and various crafts and small processing industries such as dairies, flour mills, or canneries. These collective enterprises provide funds for repayment of credit, technical improvements, communal equipment demanded for specialized personnel such as physical training instructors or day-care superintendents, cultural and political activities, and so on.

In theory each village is organized around a cooperative and an elected assembly of the people. In practice, the village structures must adapt themselves to their varied precursors. Most of the centers grew out of the armed struggle: of the 1,500 villages that existed in 1978—of which about 500 were only in embryo, since the official number was 1,059 in 1980—with two thousand people per village and a total population of about a million inhabitants (out of six million peasants altogether), three-quarters were located in the north in the province of Capo Delgrado, where the movement seems to have won without any problem; the former combatants clearly offered a greater revolutionary potential than was to be found elsewhere.[41]

In the south, in the province of Gazu, the villages grew out of a natural disaster. The catastrophic flooding of the Limpopo caused the thousands of victims, who until then had been settled along the valley, to regroup on the slopes. The improvised and hasty manner of their settlement clearly posed enormous problems of adaptation to populations whose rhythm and mode of life had until then been very different.

Finally, the populations of certain villages present problems of integration into the plan. Those of the villages created to "retrieve" the *aldeamentos*— organized by the Portuguese colonialists for the double purpose of withdrawing support from the guerrillas and of supplying the *colonatos* with concentrations of cheap labor—are people habitually averse to any form of "collectivist" propaganda. The difficulties concerning them are far from resolved. A similar problem concerns villages made up of former migrants, both those, mainly in the north, who have returned from refugee camps where "tribalistic" antagonisms and prostitution were rampant, and the proletarianized workers in the south, especially the miners thrown out of South Africa following the economic crisis and political conflicts. These people acquired a theoretically usable professional qualification abroad (for example, driver of a tractor or ditcher), but they cannot readily be reinserted into the rural milieu.

In February 1978, the third Frelimo Congress reasserted the primary importance of the communal villages "for reconstructing the material basis for the passage to socialism." In the spring of 1980, a National Reunion of Communal Villages was held in order to make a preliminary evaluation of the experiment on the basis of information gathered over several months in villages, districts, and provinces within the three national commissions. The Reunion pointed out the relative ineffectiveness of state intervention. To be sure, the repressive character of the colonial state apparatus had virtually disappeared, but the government, they said, was incapable of persuading the population to put the official policies into practice. Moreover, they claimed, state intervention had to be cautious: more authoritarianism was regarded as undesirable, especially since representatives of the party and state too often substituted a routine-bound, supercilious, and all-invading bureaucracy for the needed materials, money, and infrastructure. Success depended both on the capacities (clearly at present insufficient) of those in charge at all levels, and, even more, on the degree of cooperation of the people themselves, which varied greatly from village to village.

The support of the peasantry can only be won by demonstrating to them the benefits of the rural policy. This means improving their conditions of life and work (in terms of such facilities as water supply, schools, and health care) and, above all, noticeably increasing their revenues so that they can satisfy needs that expand as they become integrated into the market economy.

The first of these conditions can be met fairly quickly, but the same is not true of the second: to the effects of the demands of the world market must be added the fact that a smooth-running production cooperative requires a parallel organization for distribution. In 1984 the Frelimo Congress drew attention to the central government's mistake in providing massive financing for state farms, which often gave disappointing results, while neglecting the rural communities. The difficulties in this area at the present time are tremendous, aggravated as they are both by a severe drought and by internal instability exacerbated by South African intervention.

The recent news from Mozambique is not encouraging. It suggests the reintroduction by the government of colonial practices. The revival of corporal punishment and the authoritarian rejection of village councils on the grounds that the new representatives are only the old notables in disguise do not augur well for a mutual understanding between the state and the rural areas.

Ethiopia's Agrarian Revolution

Ethiopia's case is almost unique: until the end of the empire, the peasants were subjected to a feudal domination whose politico-religious character gave them a status closer to that of the European serfs of the Middle Ages than to that of the rest of the African peasantry. The only somewhat comparable situation was that of the Hutu peasants in Rwanda, who were under the traditional domination of the Tutsi. In 1959, even before independence, a revolution stripped the Tutsi of their power. Almost immediately the pastures were converted to agricultural uses, completing the process begun under population pressure before the revolution.

In Ethiopia, traditional collective ownership existed only on a minority of arable lands; the rest were state lands which a sovereign by divine right granted as concessions to his chief vassals—the church, the army, political dignitaries. People held precarious rights over areas that could exceed several thousand hectares for a single tenant. When, after 1941, the allocation of lands as private property tended to confer private ownership on the former fiefs, there came into being a class of large-scale landed proprietors who, contrary to the expectations of the regime, did nothing to prevent its fall.[42]

The regime brought to power by the 1974 revolution did not immediately act with regard to agricultural reform, but was content to make a cadastral survey with the purpose of ultimately organizing a more rational exploitation of the soil. It was the peasants, whom this plan deprived of the slightest hope of acquiring ownership of their small plots, who one year later, on 4 March and 26 July 1975, imposed the nationalization of the land. The demand for agrarian reform, which had long been expressed in the rural areas, had become very insistent since the 1960s. The revolution gave the required impetus, and a dynamic group of Marxist intellectuals drew up the main outlines of the reform. They appropriated the lands of all the great proprietors. Although the landowners were offered the option of joining the new rural communities after a year, few did so; most lived in the city or fled abroad.

What emerged was a remarkable combination of socialist collectivization and regard for traditional African community traditions. Private property disappeared, or, rather, it was transferred, theoretically, to the nation as a whole. The only individual right that was recognized was that of use of the land within autonomous territorial associations. These correponded to the fiscal divisions (*chika*) of the former empire, because they also roughly corresponded to the ancient peasant communities.

The territorial associations had the tasks of apportioning land in accordance with the needs and capacities of the individuals or families and of organizing voluntary service cooperatives or, if the members were amenable, production cooperatives. The division of land was carried out on a remarkably egalitarian basis. Each family received the same area, which varied only according to region and availability: ten acres in the south and a little less in the north—that is to say, the average area cultivable with the means available per family production unit. For many landless peasants, this was the miracle so longed for and yet, until then, unattainable. The more well-to-do peasants who already had a horse and plow and basic equipment were constrained to lend them to the less fortunate, the former serfs. The idea was to utilize the potential of the traditional structures, in which cooperative work in the form of mutual assistance among neighbors (*debo,* a practice to which the reform made specific reference) was an ancient custom, not to be confused with collectivization of production. The Ethiopian peasant was accustomed to regard himself as master of his tools and of his work, if not of his land. Traditionally, the private appropriation of land was considered the supreme reward. Hence, in particular, a difficulty was encountered, even within the framework of the associations, of preventing the chiefs from engaging in "kulakization" of land in conformity with an old saying according to which "a man's power is to be measured by the number of hectares he possesses."

The two great principles of the Ethiopian land reform have been the egalitarian redistribution of land and, above all, decentralization, based on the peasants' self-management of modern rural units which, however, are regarded as being able to revive the traditional principles of communal labor. In order to achieve this aim, the associations have set up certain autonomous institutions. Local tribunals and militias have been given the task of executing a simple popular justice based—again, in accordance with Ethiopian rural traditions—more on publicizing the crime than on inflicting punishment. The punishments, ranging from compensation for injury to a fine or compulsory labor (for two weeks at most) or imprisonment (for no more than three months) are intended less to exclude the offender than to reestablish social harmony.

Self-administration was thus the rule from the start. The combined demands of production and politics have rendered it increasingly insecure, however, for the peasant's instinctive reaction has been to produce first and foremost for his own consumption, especially as the prices offered for foodstuffs appeared increasingly pitiful in comparison with the prohibitive prices of the manufactured goods obtained in exchange. Since 1975, a system of direct negotiation between rural communities and urban communities has been developing in order to eliminate middlemen. The government, however, has insisted on intervening directly, especially in using influence to have "politically reliable" representatives—that is, ones who support government policies—appointed in the villages. In particular, peasants who had refused to enlist in the national militia—that is to say, the troops who were to fight to safeguard national territory in Eritrea or Ogaden—were excluded from posts of responsibility.

The Ethiopian formula certainly favors the survival of rural life. It was, moreover, adopted through the direct initiative of the peasants themselves. In spite of all this, its future is not guaranteed. A military regime supported by the Soviet Union is surely developing in a centralizing and authoritarian direction less and less in conformity with its original spirit. A second agrarian reform on the Soviet model, even if minimally implemented, will cut the party off from its rural base. Yet the experiment deserves praise: although self-management may soon be a thing of the past, the fact remains that the basic social structure of the Ethiopian peasantry has been completely overturned, and that is an irrevocable achievement.

THE FUTURE OF THE RURAL AREAS

The peasants in sub-Saharan Africa must undoubtedly make changes in their way of life if they, and their countries, are to survive. The direction these changes ought to take seems relatively clear; the chances for survival, unfortunately, are more dubious.

The Transition from Past to Future

All these experiments encounter more or less the same problem, namely, how the rural areas can be modernized while retaining the best aspects of a society, several thousand years old, that is at once disoriented and passionately attached to its ancestral beliefs and practices. In short, what connections, if any, can be made between a community based on subsistence, where peasant habits of mutual aid are deeply rooted, and the dynamics of a modern production cooperative? The Tanzanian solution is ambiguous: in spite of the publicity given to developing the potential of the traditional community, the *ujamaa* villages appear to be fundamentally new structures, often artificially created and almost antithetical to the previous modes of life, even if cooperatives are being constructed with due caution. Ethiopia, though speaking less about preserving the historical heritage, seems to have more to teach on the subject.

Reformers should take care not to confuse ancient customs of communal labor with an agricultural collectivization that undermines peasant traditions. In Mozambique, for example, the government has decided that the traditional community, taken as a whole, acts as a hindrance to agrarian socialism, because it rests on fundamentally different social and ideological foundations. The traditional African rural community represents a system of production and food distribution that does indeed aim at assuring the subsistence of the group, but only within a framework of fixed social relationships and an inward-looking ideology quite unsuited to the process of modernization. Let us take the example of the ancient *foroba* system of the great Mandingo family in Mali.[43] Traditionally, the collective land tenure was in the hands of the head of the family. Each member put his labor at the disposal of the collectivity, in return for which he received his means of subsistence. The strictly regulated distribution of work and expenses took into account both agriculture and crafts, but on an inegalitarian basis of age and position in a lineage or group. The individual, who had no personal ambitions, was subject to the laws of the collectivity and the commands of its representative. The small size of the labor force ruled out any enlargement of production. The community aimed at continuity rather than improvement. Changes seemed pointless, for the collectivity owned all surplus production above what was used for subsistence and storage, for the payment of fixed obligations (taxes, etc.), and for what was in the final analysis unproductive hoarding.

The social behavior of the rural community is generally hostile to the idea of economic progress and, if necessary, resists developments resulting from outside influences. This explains the failure of the dynamic young producers who, returning from school or city, find themselves reintegrated into the traditional social relationships. Their strange zeal fades when confronted with the conscious resistance of the elders who represent traditional authority, and with the unchangeability of the inner laws of the system. As an official of UNESCO said: "For the elders, to progress was to return to the sources. The behavior of man and of society was progressing only to the degree that it was a reflection, a restitution of ancient models. . . . It is anti-progress in the modern sense of the term."[44]

A production cooperative detached from this milieu must perforce be abortive. Neither its goal, its rules, nor its leadership corresponds to that of the traditional community. Instead of introducing a modernizing or social-istic ideology into a traditional environment, it merely inspires the reutiliza-tion of traditional means to achieve conservative ends.

Experience has shown that peasants' adherence to a revolutionary party usually remains superficial in nature, especially since they enter it via the traditional representatives of the community. Thus, in Ethiopia, some lead-ers of rural associations, former chiefs of the peasant community, thought that henceforth revolutionary zeal would enable them to create a fiefdom by utilizing for their own benefit the rights over the land granted by the higher authorities—formerly the emperor, now the state, the theoretical represen-tative of the masses. In the spring of 1978, some of these people were ar-rested and their places were filled by men nominated by the government's Provisional Office for Mass Organizational Affairs (POMOA), who proba-bly proceeded to act in very much the same fashion. Similarly, in Tanzania, in areas of speculative cultivation, the more well-to-do peasants, reinforcing their present favorable position with their prestige as former traditional chiefs, turned the reforms to their own advantage by obtaining money, land, and labor from the central government and by manipulating the accounts in order to give priority to cultivation for export rather than to the food econ-omy. At best, as in the Ivory Coast, such practices favor the development of small-scale agrarian capitalism, not of a successful rural collectivism.

It therefore seems futile to seek to found a completely new political and social system on the precapitalist social relationships. As those relationships weaken, however, the process of change may be judiciously directed. For in-stance, restricted family units have increasingly gained the right of exploit-ing community land for themselves. In Mali, 13 percent of the families have gained complete autonomy from the *foroba* system and 27 percent have achieved at least partial autonomy.

The smoothest transitions take place when the traditional chiefs them-selves take the leadership in the process of innovation. A pinpoint investiga-tion between 1959 and 1967 in a large village (2,500 inhabitants) in north-ern Tanzania, not far from Arusha, is revealing in this respect. The Meru peasants there all raised coffee, and they needed to be persuaded to apply copper oxide to combat brown rot, which had been ravaging their crops for several years. All the producers belonged to the local cooperative that was to distribute the product, and although the office of head chief had been abol-ished at independence, a strong clan organization had been retained, with coordinated and hierarchical chiefs' councils. The administrative and agri-cultural experts and representatives exterior to the community made the local chiefs responsible for persuading the people to use the copper oxide. The plan succeeded insofar as the chiefs recommended use of the product, for the peasants tended to seek advice first from the traditional authorities.[45]

Here only a minor technical innovation was involved, not a revolution in the forms of production. The story suggests that innovation is a delicate matter; radical change may well prove impossible. Unless an innovation achieves almost immediate concrete results—which is rarely the case—the great majority of peasants, assailed in their most entrenched mental and ideological attitudes, are likely to put up fierce opposition.

Some Caveats

Generally speaking, a practical policy of agrarian development can only be implemented if knowledge of the rural society has been attained. The process works both ways. Just as technological action can transform a rural community, a community can absorb, reinterpret, and distort the proposed policy to such a degree as to halt the process of modernization. In other words, the tradition-modernization interaction can have infinite variations depending on the area. A traditional environment can, for instance, assimilate modern institutions such as credit unions or cooperatives simply in order to strengthen the traditional organization of labor and exchanges of goods. This thwarts achievement of the final goal, that is, an increase in agricultural production. Similarly, the techniques of acquiring land can be used by traditional chiefs as a means of reasserting their hold over their dependents: young people, women, and even, in certain cases, immigrants. Yet too great a weakening of tradition can leave the modern structures attempting to operate in a social vacuum. Thus, the Office du Niger's experiment in the Mossi colonate failed because it demanded that the migrants make a complete break with tradition, uprooting them and destroying their connection with their origins.

In short, no set formula exists for the successful transformation of traditional rural structures. No matter what ideological model is chosen, the concrete solutions must be matched to the specific social groups and forms of action under consideration.[46] I feel that a profound study of the milieu in its ecological, anthropological, and social aspects is an essential preliminary to the most important rule, that is, to act *with* the milieu and not merely *upon* it. This rule applies above all to the peasants. R. Dumont recalls the just cry of the Tanzanian minister of finance: "We are not guinea pigs, we are people!"[47] Rural development must be autocentric, that is to say, carried out with and by the peasants themselves and not simply on their behalf. The Ethiopian experiment is probably the most interesting to study just because it expressed a clearer realization of the rural situation than is to be found elsewhere. But wherever no spontaneous agrarian revolution has occurred—that is, everywhere else in Africa, except Rwanda—whatever risks may be involved in delay, the rural structures cannot be transformed otherwise than stage by stage and through a carefully chosen variety of methods. Everywhere subjected to a harsh colonial law and, before that, to the exactions of robber-chieftains and the ravages of the slave trade, the African peasants, like all the peasants of the world in precapitalist societies, learned to respond to the intrusions of the state with passivity, skepticism, and brief and violent revolts. Any authoritarian measures, however well intended, will be ill received. As everywhere else, the peasants are deeply attached to their possessions: their house, their village, their plot, their countryside. The exactions to which they are subjected and the precariousness of their existence make them cautious, distrustful, and bound more closely to their homes. They cling to their difficult lives, preferring to confine themselves to their own limits (the field, the household—in short, the primary unit of production) rather than allow themselves to be drawn into risky innovations whose failure could constitute their death warrant.

For this reason, the violent imposition of measures of modernization, whether it is merely a process of speedy mechanization—incapable of absorption in the very short run, if only because of social restrictions—or a general policy of collectivization of the means of production, can lead only to catastrophe. Flexible and varied solutions must be evolved. They must combine utilization of the peasants' considerable capacity for adaptation (vide the success of the small areas of irrigation established without disrupting the existing social structures), the introduction of well-thought-out cooperative practices in certain carefully defined sectors, and the organization of absolutely essential agroindustrial projects on condition that they primarily serve the interests of the rural sector itself. If the peasants' standard of living then improves quickly and no local aristocracy forms, success may be said to be on the way. In fact, however, this has rarely come about.

A few simple truths are in order here. The peasants are no less intelligent than anyone else and are better able than city-dwellers or employees in tertiary activities to appreciate the value of their own work. Moreover, whether consciously or not, they are today to some degree detached from traditional values, which can objectively be seen as ill adapted to the peasants' economy. They can easily recognize the significance of local achievements and are as willing to take the initiative as anyone else, as long as they see their efforts as profiting themselves rather than others. This suggests the necessity of ensuring that the agricultural economy accumulates its own surpluses. This would enable it (at least in part) to provide for its own development. Instead of this, however, plans for rural development have focused on export crops in order to subsidize the cities and industry. Indeed, except in the oil-producing countries (Nigeria, Gabon, Congo) and those producing copper or precious metals (Zambia, Zaire, Angola, and of course South Africa and Namibia), the state has looked on export crops as its main budgetary resource. This program for rural self-development may be theoretically excellent, but it is so remote from present conditions that it seems almost dishonest, or at any rate self-deceptive, to express such an idea.[48]

The Peasants' Precarious Future

The unpalatable fact is that the more than 250 million peasants in sub-Saharan Africa today are becoming ever less able to provide for their own subsistence, let alone to nourish the rest of the world. We should not delude ourselves: the criterion of capitalistic profitability and the introduction of agrobusiness are bringing to sub-Saharan Africa the Western model, based on the United States. This model is rational from the point of view of economics but is extraordinarily ill adapted to the local demographic reality. The United States is, after all, the greatest producer and exporter of food products in the world precisely because the rural society has no peasant class.

To seek, by the industrialization of agriculture, to solve the problem of the survival of African rural communities, where the peasants constitute 50 to 90 percent of the population, is thus nonsensical. No doubt, if the trend continues, the desired goal will be attained within a century, or even in a few decades, considering the present acceleration of the process. The "peasant problem" will be solved because most of them will have been eliminated by more or less violent means (famine, emigration, urbanization).

Traditional agriculture is not profitable, and the reason is as simple as it is obvious: the present "peasant crisis" in Africa is the sort that *precedes* an agricultural revolution. Contrary to the case in England in the eighteenth and nineteenth centuries, and unlike the "green revolution" that has known a certain success in contemporary India, the African migrations have not resulted from an increasing social differentiation brought about by a rise in agricultural productivity. They represent an attempt—a desperate one, considering the demographic explosion—to remedy the congestion of the overpopulated and insufficiently productive rural areas. Under these circumstances, traditional agriculture cannot compete or be brought to compete either with the mechanized agriculture of developed countries or, even less, with industry. It is economically—and thus socially—doomed.

When small-scale peasants begin to employ agricultural machinery they soon find that the resulting increase in production, subject to the crushing competition of a free market dependent on international trade, does not suffice to pay for the equipment, and they are swiftly driven to bankruptcy. Unless the government imposes tariffs to keep food prices sufficiently high (and, in our time, such protection by the customs authorities seems inconceivable), a traditional agriculture can subsist only in the most rudimentary form, that is, with minimal capital, and thus with no improvement in productivity.

By and large, no doubt, sub-Saharan Africa has reached a satisfactory level of development in such terms as gross internal product—but at what price? Many nations can buy the foodstuffs they need from other countries only by selling their own agricultural products. This frightful paradox explains why it has been these countries (Mali, Ethiopia, Somalia, Tanzania, Uganda, Mozambique) that have in the last ten years suffered most from famine.[49]

In sub-Saharan Africa the agrarian question—and first of all, the question of food production—cannot be divorced from the problem of population. It is absurd to state the problem in terms of economic rationality or profitability. It is first of all a social issue: the greatest possible number of people, with minimal means, must be able to draw subsistence from the African soil. The goal should not be to make agriculture profitable but to allow it the greatest possible autonomy and to support it with financial resources from richer sectors such as industry and oil. After all, even in the most industrialized countries the state assists modern agriculture.

The experiments in Tanzania and Mozambique inspired high hopes precisely because they tackled the problem from that angle. Optimism should not be carried too far, however, for more than one reason. The temptation of state authoritarianism seems hard to avoid in the absence of a civil society. Moreover, this socialist treatment of agriculture has every prospect of proving unprofitable as a short- or even medium-term proposition unless a still more radical change of direction succeeds in making human investment the element of primary importance. But Africa is not China: the ecological and climatic conditions, the social, historical, and cultural circumstances, and the long-standing penetration of the Western model make such a change problematical, to say the least. Guinea-Bissau provides a chilling example. Starting with a well-planned experiment in rural self-management, the country is now moving toward an agricultural giantism imported by sellers of equipment. If sub-Saharan Africa is to retain its identity, it must resist the Western reliance on economics as the universal solution. Such resistance, however, is far from guaranteed.

9

Revolt and Resistance, Collaboration and Assimilation

Peasant societies have always rejected the imposition of authority from without. In this sense the history of African peasant movements long predates colonization. Almost all studies of such movements begin with the colonial period, but it is certain that precolonial peasant revolts were frequent, although little effort has been made to trace them. We have, however, seen (Chapter 5) that Muslim intellectuals were able, as early as the seventeenth century, to manipulate peasant unrest for the benefit of the political elite. Peasants expressed resistance not only in open revolts, but also, from very early times, in their methods of adapting to circumstances. In all regions of the world and in every period, peasants showed a remarkable capacity to counter the risks that changes to their rhythms of life entailed, by means of passive techniques of either evasion or acquiescence.

Rather than speak of resistance it would be better to speak of the varied and sometimes confused expressions of peasant discontent. This was certainly a constant factor: the peasants sought desperately to resolve the internal contradictions created by rapid and radical changes in the rural economy. Even in the strongest reactions against European domination, no monolithic anti-European group ever appeared, and the agrarian movement was at the same time giving rise to conditions that favored adaptation to the modern world and thus, in the final account, began a dynamic process of assimilation. Because the period that brought it to birth was one of transition, the Mau Mau rebellion in Kenya (1950–1955) provides a good example of the interrelationship between a so-called primary movement of peasant resistance and a modern nationalist uprising.

When approaching this subject, the first problem, obviously, is to define the word *peasants*. The term tends to be used rather loosely, especially in being used to include not only sedentary farmers but also semi-nomadic herdsmen, who in some areas constituted the majority if not the totality of the rural population and whose discontent was at least as strong as that of the cultivators, for the same reasons.

At least until the First World War, almost the entire population of Africa, even the city-dwellers, engaged in cultivation and raised livestock. The towns were situated almost exclusively either in the Sahelo-Sudanese zone, with an Islamized aristocracy, or along the coasts, settled by political leaders and merchants engaged in long-distance trade across the Atlantic or the Indian Ocean. Apart from the relatively restricted areas used for government and/or commerce, these cities often resembled large villages populated by the traders' most faithful and subservient dependents and by slaves captured for purposes of war. The first compounds, mining concentrations organized from the end of the nineteenth century in the South African Rand and from the first years of the twentieth century in the Belgian Congo, exhibited a similar pattern. The rapid turnover of unskilled labor and the arrangement of the living quarters along an attempt at traditional lines made these labor concentrations into conglomerations of villagers who were still close to the soil and who intended to return to it within a few months or a few years. It seems legitimate to suppose, then, that their reactions to events may have been those of peasants rather than salaried workers.

Another problem of definition concerns the comparison inherent in the term. Are *peasants* to be understood to be "country-dwellers" who, in contrast to the "city-dwellers," derive most of their resources from the soil, often within a context of subsistence, or are they *peasants,* rather than the more general *cultivators,* only when relationships of production and class have been established between an exploited peasantry and a dominant class living partly outside the rural areas?[1]

This debate is futile. It resembles the old colonialist ethnology, which claimed that Africa had few or no workers, but only more or less pristine villagers unable to attain modernity because their cultural background neither contained the idea of progress nor the spirit of individual enterprise found in the West. If the term *peasants* means those who are exploited, it can refer only to those who live within the framework of Western societies, preferably those already of a capitalist nature. But the fact is that from the beginning of the nineteenth century, whenever speculative crops were cultivated (in West Africa above all, but also on the east coast and in Zanzibar), the African peasants, whether or not they knew it or desired it, were fully involved in the Western economic system, and self-sufficiency (in the sense of isolation), with very rare exceptions, never existed in sub-Saharan Africa. Besides, wherever agricultural production in the broad sense took place (cultivation, herding, and, among the Pygmies and San, foraging and hunting) at the same time there emerged relationships of production, usually inegalitarian, if only between the producers of complementary commodities

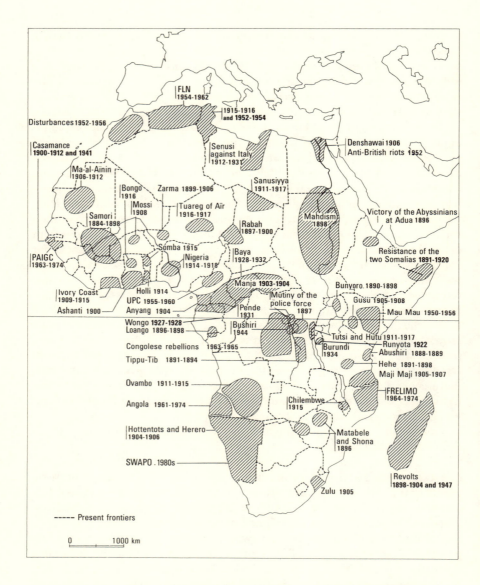

Disturbances 1952-1956

Casamance
1900-1912 and 1941

Ma-al-Ainin
1906-1912

Samori
1884-1898

PAIGC
1963-1974

Ivory Coast
1909-1915

Ashanti 1900

FLN
1954-1962

**1915-1916
and 1952-1954**

Senusi
against Italy
1912-1931

Bongo
1916   Zarma 1899-1906

Mossi
1908

Tuareg of Aïr
1916-1917

Somba 1915

Nigeria
1914-1918

Holli 1914

UPC 1955-1960

Anyang 1904

Wongo **1927-1928**
Loango 1896-1898

Congolese rebellions   1963-1965

Tippu-Tib   1891-1894

Ovambo   1911-1915

Angola 1961-1974

Hottentots and Herero
1904-1906

SWAPO . 1980s

Sanusiyya
1911-1917

Rabah
1897-1900

Baya
1928-1932

Manja **1903-1904**

Pende
1931

Bushiri
1944

Mutiny of the
police force
1897

Mahdism
1898

Denshawai 1906
Anti-British riots **1952**

Victory of the Abyssinians
at Adua 1896

Resistance of the
two Somalias **1891-1920**

Bunyoro. 1890-1898

Gusu 1905-1908

Mau Mau 1950-1956

Tutsi and Hutu 1911-1917

Burundi   Runyota **1922**
1934   Abushiri 1888-1889

Hehe 1891-1898
Maji Maji 1905-1907

FRELIMO
1964-1974

Chilembwe
1915

Matabele
and Shona
1896

Zulu 1905

Revolts
1898-1904 and 1947

----- Present frontiers

0   1000 km

Map 5. Main Twentieth-Century Centers of Revolt before Independence

or within the household itself (elders versus youngers and women). We are concerned here with this mass of people, whether wage-earning or otherwise, or whether or not they were cultivators of cash crops, whose system of life and thought and mode of production have still largely remained precolonial but who find themselves increasingly involved in the sphere of domination of Western capitalism. It is these that we are referring to as peasants.

To proceed, then: the most obvious manifestation of peasant discontent is open revolt. Rebellion itself can assume widely varying forms, however, with causes and developments that by no means always involve the peasants alone (for example, leaders may belong to the elite or the revolt be taken up by other social groups). In addition, discontent finds many other expressions: disguised revolt; passivity; individual flight or migration; social marginality and banditry; and ideologically sublimated forms of resistance that are not necessarily experienced as such by the peoples concerned, such as magical practices, revivals of sorcery, religious syncretisms, or Messianisms. In each case, it is necessary to penetrate beyond the stated aims of these movements in order to understand their significance. A combination of various factors (political systems, religious messages, social organizations, colonialist actions) will always be found to have given rise in a specified period to one particular form of resistance. Some combinations were more favorable than others to open rebellion that could both perpetuate itself and transform itself with the passage of time; it was a special set of circumstances that brought a given people the capacity to maintain a resistance that may be traced through the years from precolonial times until our own. Examining in turn the countries of animistic traditions and those of Islam, we shall attempt to determine some of these patterns.

"PRIMARY" RESISTANCE MOVEMENTS

The expression *primary* does not mean "primitive." T. O. Ranger says he used it in a purely chronological sense,[2] in reference to the resistance movements of the first years of colonialism, in contrast to the "secondary" or "modern" movements which to some degree derive from them.

Unlike the resistance movements of the precolonial state, those in the first period of colonization—roughly, from 1895 to 1915—were spontaneous uprisings of the people—in other words, peasant revolts. They were, in fact, direct responses to colonizers' concrete demands such as taxes, forced labor, or compulsory cultivation.

Contrary to the colonial myth, innumerable outbreaks of resistance took place even before World War II, and some have been prolonged until our own day. To be sure, they all failed. They seem to have resulted only in a backward-looking attitude which in its last phase produced a tidal wave of Messianic and syncretistic manifestations better suited to collaboration than

opposition. It would, moreover, be Manichaeistic to interpret the early outbreaks solely as struggles against the Whites. Some arose in societies that
had always resisted authority (this, as we shall see, was the case with the
Hollidje). Others were part of a tradition of popular resistance, principally
directed against the local chiefs, instruments of the colonialists, rather than
against colonialism per se. Thus, in the 1870s the Mbalante of Ovamboland
(southern Angola) killed their chief, abolished the chiefdom, and prevented
the Whites from entering their territory; in 1885, again, they assassinated a
particularly rapacious chief and expelled the White merchants.[3]

Other outbreaks, however, developed from spontaneous, localized movements into political movements that were more structured but also, often,
taken over by others. In this way the ground was prepared for modern resistance movements, syndicalist, political, nationalist and, later, national, including the contemporary form of national liberation struggles. The relationships between the first wave of revolts and the second thus hold great
interest for students of Africa today.

Local Peasant Uprisings

In the earliest uprisings the peasants rejected colonial laws. Everywhere
the colonizers had to come to terms with each specific group's urge to preserve its traditions. The clearest cases of peasant resistance took place in the
least centralized societies, which were the very ones that were most vulnerable and least structured to resist colonization.

Here we shall only propose a typology of these movements derived from
some typical examples. The need remains for an exhaustive study of these
uprisings, to provide us with an understanding of one of the most basic expressions of the African people's life experiences.

French Equatorial Africa offered repeated and widespread resistance to
colonization. As one observer noted in 1905, "the Congo was never conquered; vast areas of our colony have never effectively been taken over." The
situation, then, was far from one of "peaceful colonization."[4] The most unstable regions turn out to be those where the great private concessionaires or
the administration committed serious malpractices that were condemned in
1905 when the "Congo scandal," a vigorous press campaign led by the English journalist E. D. Morel and taken up by the French socialists of the
Cahiers de la Quinzaine, broke upon the international scene.

The first large-scale uprising, from 1897 to 1899, expressed the exaspera-
tion of the exhausted Loango porters on the route between Brazzaville and
the coast. In 1902, when the concessions were set up and a levy was instituted, almost everywhere serious disorders occurred, from the pillaging of
foreign trading-posts to ritualistic cannibalism as an act of vengeance, some
of the executed agents "having, sad to say, deserved death not once, but
perhaps ten times over—for each time they themselves had killed for the

pleasure of causing suffering."[5] The most violent outburst was that of the
Manja, who had been ravaged by the forced porterage in the upper Chari
(1903–1904) that linked the Congo and Chad basins. This country, normally so fragmented, put together a comprehensive movement with guerrilla
forces from every village.

Repressive operations became systematic after 1908, but "pacification"
did not fully succeed until 1913, when permanent stations were set up in the
hostile areas, and even then isolated pockets of resistance remained. For instance, the "hostile Awandjis," as they were called, revolted in eastern Gabon
as late as 1928–1929.[6] The Wongo chief had collected the levy since 1923,
but the introduction of dues and forced labor inspired rebellion throughout
the upper Ogooue: the peasants hated the militiamen, the most visible representatives of the colonial administration. The forced attendance at periodic markets for the dual purpose of supplying the administrative stations
and of levying taxes and dues catalyzed the revolt. Once again, an area
where the power of the chief rarely extended beyond the household, at most
embracing two or three families in one village, formed a cohesive and enduring resistance movement: it took two years and several campaigns to end the
harassments of the rural guerrillas in the forests. Such rebellions, sometimes
on a large scale in an area where the administration was generally few in
number, may have arisen from complex and sometimes obscure causes, but
they undoubtedly constituted responses to malpractices and reactions to colonial assaults upon traditional values.

In the Hollidje country, consisting of seventeen villages scattered in a forest ten kilometers wide to the northeast of Porto-Novo and Dahomey, with a
population of scarcely 10,000 inhabitants, we find an excellent example of
an island of insubordination characterized by a permanent rejection of any
superior authority.[7] The Hollidje were a Yoruba group who had come from
Oyo and were then driven out of Ife. As fugitives who had taken refuge in a
remote area, they had always refused to recognize the authority of the king
of Abomey. This group enjoyed a "democratic" solidarity: the representatives of the villages met in a general assembly under the authority of a
"king" who was elected from five families in rotation and whose judgement
was not always accepted. The group developed tactics suited to their natural
situation, and these enabled them, from the time of the creation of the
colony in 1894 until after independence, to refuse all contact with the government, expressed in nonpayment of taxes.

In the first years, the king simply said that his people would not obey him.
When the French made a tour of inspection, the villagers all hid in the bush.
In 1907–1908, the police made an effort to force the Hollidje to comply
with the law, but tax payment was usually demanded during the dry season,
and the Hollidje, who knew the terrain well, simply dispersed at that period.
The king sent the government a small sum and delayed sending the rest until

the rains had cut off the roads, or, that is to say, until the following year. When the administration decided to construct roads usable at all seasons, the Hollidje responded by employing guerrilla tactics against the enterprise.

The rebellion began in January 1914, when the choice between submission and revolt had become inescapable. The Hollidje undertook a campaign of harassment against the guards of the administration that continued until June. Reinforcements then arrived from Dakar, in the form of two batallions on trucks. The inhabitants were disarmed, taxes were doubled, and the chiefs were arrested. The villages were about to be disbanded when World War I was declared.

The following year a second revolt broke out after a rifleman stole a chicken belonging to the wife of a chief, and the brother of another chief was killed. The administration decided to wait for the dry season and starve the Hollidje out. By the early 1920s, open rebellion had ceased, but the population remained obstreperous. Serious troubles occurred again in 1956, and in 1963 a campaign of forced vaccination provoked yet another revolt.

The Hollidje, who traded their cotton for weapons and gunpowder, in fact could have paid their taxes, but resistance to colonization grew out of a tradition of independence. To these people, paying taxes, providing men for forced labor, and in general complying with the demands of the administration meant subservience. They refused to comply with colonization on ideological grounds, then, rather than material ones.

Examples of this type can be found with every form of colonization. The revolt led by Bambata in Zululand (Natal) in 1906 was one of many. Ending a century of stormy independence, it took as its pretext the poll tax instituted the previous year. The region flared into violence after a small force of Zulus ambushed and killed two White policemen. The uprising was ferociously suppressed: villages were burnt, crops destroyed, livestock confiscated. Bambata was killed, with as many as three thousand Africans.[8] On the other side of the continent, at about the same period (1904), war began with the massacre of 123 German merchants. The subsequent repression, which lasted until 1907, was even worse than in Zululand. Nearly all the rebel lands were confiscated as Crown lands, and the Germans drove the rebels themselves into the desert of Bechuanaland, where most of them died of thirst. In two years the population fell from more than 80,000 inhabitants to fewer than 15,000. The survivors took refuge in arid reserves, or, on the coast, became migrant workers absorbed into the colonial system. General Van Trotha had aimed at extirpating a people and a culture. Berlin finally ordered the genocide to cease, since a labor force was needed for the "valorization" of the colony. Similarly, revolts against the Portuguese penetration in Angola and Mozambique succeeded one another for over a century.[9]

Each careful case study shows that as of the beginning of the twentieth century, the colonial penetration had barely begun. Thus, in the forests of

Casamance in the extreme south of Senegal, although the colonizers decided to impose taxes in the very first years of the century, more than twenty years elapsed before they could circulate freely in relative security; every year, the levying of the poll tax gave rise to interminable arguments and often resulted in gunfire.[10] In the Belgian Congo, Maria Moï instigated the first large-scale revolt in 1915, calling for the departure of the White oppressors and a return to the days of equality among men and the laws of the ancestors (or *djamami*). The rebellions of the Bus-Blocs, the Dekesac, and the Pende followed.[11]

Similarly, and almost everywhere, the large-scale recruitment of soldiers for World War I triggered violent insurrections that expressed the peasants' discontent, which had been pent up for nearly a generation. Thus, in northern Dahomey, although recruitment was relatively light, the census of names carried out at that time for the poll tax in 1916 caused a several months' revolt in the Somba country, as well as among the neighboring Bariba; an equally violent revolt of the same kind broke out in western Volta.[12] That same year, the northeastern Gold Coast (Ghana) saw similar incidents for the same reason; forced military recruitment had been attempted there in 1915 (and was actually carried out in 1917 and 1918). The revolt in the Gold Coast reveals how great the opposition was at that time between the peasants and the rural society as arranged by the British. The movement was directed less against the British officials (whose repressions, however, did exacerbate the situation) than against the local chiefs who, recently instated in their positions in these stateless societies in accordance with the policy of indirect rule, had an unfortunate tendency to exploit for their own benefit those for whom they were responsible. They behaved more like agents of the British than like potential leaders of a stubborn resistance that had hardly ceased since 1897 and that can therefore unhesitatingly be described as popular.[13]

In the most impoverished and isolated societies, which were therefore those most slowly penetrated by the market economy, local troubles of this kind persisted until much later in the century. Although the Great Depression of the 1930s most severely affected populations already too well integrated, on the whole, into the monetary system for "primary" resistance to express itself as vigorously as formerly, certain groups such as the Pende in the Belgian Congo in 1931 and the peasants of Burundi in 1934 still resorted to this desperate means of expression.[14] A revolt of three chiefdoms of the northwest, which lasted for three months, undoubtedly sprang from the policies of financial autarchy and severity resulting from the crisis. It revitalized a local tradition of revolt bolstered by a subversive Messianism that attempted to resolve the contradictions arising out of the changes taking place in the character of "traditional" authority. As late as 1941 a violent rebellion in Casamance was caused by the combined circumstances of a difficult transitional year, the war, and the administration's requisitions of rice. This wholly peasant movement was led by a woman, the priestess Alintsinoe, who gave it a Messianic and mystical character.

In French Africa, the clearest and most frequently cited of these colonial difficulties took place in the Ivory Coast. After a brief phase described somewhat inaccurately as a "peaceful" conquest (1903–1907), characterized by progressive settlement based on negotiations and agreement, Governor Angoulvant (1908–1918) launched a campaign of conquest marked by large-scale military operations. The strategy known as *tache d'huile* enabled the French to put more than 110,000 peasant guns out of action between 1909 and 1915. The method was to move forward only after having thoroughly organized the rear around a position set up in the heart of the troubled region near a strategic crossroads that could be used as a springboard for the following stage. The idea was, as we read in a military dispatch, that "the native must see, after having clearly felt it, that the force is always there, ready to strike . . . and that there are always others further on who could come and strike at him." [15]

The Statut de l'Indigénat (Indigenous Code) of November 1904 prescribed the deportation of leaders, the imposition of collective war fines, and the peoples' surrender of all guns. The operations affected all the rebellious peoples: the Ngban of Baule, the Abbey who in 1910 had attacked the railway under construction to the north of Abidjan, and the inhabitants of the Agba country, of the bank of the Comoe River, and of the eastern province of Cavally.

In 1910 this strategy gave rise to a violent polemic in France, forcing the governor to defend himself. Referring to Gallieni, Angoulvant connected military conquest with moral conquest, and he held to the myth of "peaceful conquest." It must be understood that Angoulvant was no innovator in colonial warfare, except in his advocacy of a short war: "The most vigorous [war]," he said, "which is often the shortest, is perhaps the least harmful for the interests at stake." [16] By the eve of World War I, the colony was almost completely subjugated: with few exceptions, "primary" explosions had ceased in sub-Saharan Africa.

Most of these examples display a local character. Reflections of a fragmented social structure, they did not become expressions of a people in arms (except sometimes in tiny nations such as those of the Awandji or the Hollidje). Each of the many groups reacted sporadically to acts of political, economic, and cultural aggression, which explains both the frequency of these attempts and their inevitable failure.

Regional ‚"Political" Movements

Another sort of regional uprising developed, similar to the local peasant revolts, but connected with a ruling class that could assume the leadership of the movement or exploit it for its own benefit (which raises the question of which of these rebellions were of the people, either in origin or in character). For example, the Zarma in western Niger rebelled several times between 1899 and 1906, in reaction against requisitions and other colonialist demands.[17] The first rebellion broke out in Sargadie, a village of refuge around which the neighboring villages were clustered. Over a year, six hundred riflemen, and two cannons were needed to stifle it. A second, larger revolt began in 1905 near Sambera, led by a tall, blind marabout who won adherents throughout the area. This revolt seems to have inspired one on the Niger River, led by the chief of Karma (January 1906), then one headed by the chief of Saturu (February 1906), and, finally, a series of disturbances, around the same period, as far away as eastern Upper Volta (Fada-N'gourma) and southwestern Niger (Dendi).

Clearly, deep unrest gave rise to interconnected movements over vast areas. The immediate objective was undoubtedly to drive out the Whites, but an important, if secondary, motive lay in the overthrow of chiefs allied to the colonizers, such as the chief of Say, whose passivity amounted to collaboration, or the chief of Dosso, who participated in the repressive operations against Karma. To that degree the rebellious peasantry displayed a political and social consciousness. Since the mid-nineteenth century this area had been ravaged by wars against the Fulbe, however, leaving most actions to be ascribed to any of a mass of complex and ambiguous currents.

The new Niger warrior-aristocracy of the Wangari among the Zarma often developed an antagonistic relationship with the former authorities. Although the Zarma had always rejected the fire-lock gun, they had nevertheless elaborated an effective system of defense based on the regrouping of villages and a professional army—rather than occasional conscriptions of peasants—that increasingly came to be made up of captives of war. The Europeans of course exploited the standing conflict between the Fulbe nomads and the sedentary Zarma—the warrior-aristocracies and the traditional authorities—as a means of manipulating allegiances and dividing clans. The shock of colonialism provided the spark that set off the explosion of tensions previously held in check. To some degree, however, these movements originated with the marabouts and chiefs rather than with the masses of the people. Neither simply religious, strictly political, nor directly connected with the abolition of slavery (which took place only in December 1905), these revolts aimed at solving internal problems—differing reactions of different strata of the ruling class, conflicts of interest between captives and freemen or sedentary peoples and nomads, and so on—by providing a new focus: the rejection of the West. Since colonization had created new social cleavages as well as intensifying the old ones, however, a united front of all Africans could only be transitory, if not generally impossible.

Mass Movements

Occasionally, a united front did form, and it invariably created a massive insurrection. Large-scale peasant rebellions engulfed huge areas, expressing total rejection of an intolerable situation that overrode local ethnic and political differences. At least briefly, the peasants rallied behind political leaders, often Messianic, who expressed the fury of the rural areas and, more recently, seized the opportunity of provisionally combining the peasants' revolt with modern plans for reforming or revolutionizing the existing social structures.

We can follow the spread of these movements over the course of the twentieth century. Groups that had been distinct, scattered, and sometimes in rivalry came to join forces over a wide area in a common struggle, laying the groundwork for contemporary nationalisms. At least four major uprisings present similar characteristics, despite their separation in both time and space. These are the Maji Maji revolt in Tanganyika (1905–1907), the Kongo-Warra war in Central Africa (1927–1932), the Mau Mau uprising in Kenya (1952–1956) and the rebellions of 1964–1965 in Zaire.

The Maji Maji revolt took place in the period of consolidation of colonial power, and it represented a total rejection of forced labor in the cotton plantations and of the exactions of German mercenaries. The uprising engulfed the whole of southern Tanganyika. Tribal divisions were transcended through religious and magical practices. At a time when the traditional societies were increasingly losing their control over temporal affairs, the appearance of charismatic leaders offered the peoples a chance of reuniting with their traditions; at a time when the ancestral methods of warfare had become ineffective (as the Hehe revolt had demonstrated), Messianism appeared to endow them with new force. The Maji Maji revolt included many features of millenarianism. Kinji-kitile Ngwele claimed to have the gift of immunizing warriors with magic water (*maji*) that would also transform German bullets into water. He declared he had been sent by God to save the people from colonial oppression and that the dead ancestors would be resurrected at Ngalambe.

The uprising ended with an enormous massacre—at least 12,000 dead—that has sunk deep into the collective memory of the Tanzanian people. Its failure served as one of the earliest factors contributing to Tanzanian nationalism.[18]

The space of twenty years between the Maji Maji revolt and the Kongo-Warra war can be explained by the static condition in which the colonial administration had kept French Equatorial Africa; the expansionists themselves called it the "Cinderella of the French empire."

The Kongo-Warra insurrection began with the Baya people, who until then had lived in scattered groups. It engulfed the heart of the Federation, particularly western Ubangi-Chari but also the areas bordering on the Middle Congo and Cameroon. The country had for many years been subject to a particularly extreme degree of exploitation, mainly by the private sector in the form of vast concessionary companies, dealing in rubber and ivory, that were famous in this region for their harsh practices. André Gide, who passed through the country in 1925, gave a striking account of it in his *Voyage au Congo*. In addition to the requirements of taxation forced labor was demanded at harvest and for porterage of the rubber crop, which was almost valueless and yet exploited by the Compagnie Forestière Sangha-Oubangui (the Compagnie Pordurière, or Garbage Company, of Céline's *Voyage au bout de la nuit*), whose monopoly originally extended over seventeen million hectares (reduced to five million in 1920); furthermore, peasants were recruited to work on the Congo-Ocean railway, begun in 1921. The prophet Karnu, the "soul of the rebellion," was the catalyst, not of a spontaneous movement, but of one that came to maturity after long years of humiliation and suffering. In about 1924, Karnu began preaching an anti-European doctrine of nonviolent action whose principal points were refusal of contact with the Whites and passive resistance to colonial demands. The administration did not take note of him until 1927, when Karnu's now numerous followers, who were convinced that the *kongo-warra* (the prophet's baton of command) made them invincible, began armed revolt. More than 350,000 people joined the movement, including about 60,000 warriors. A strong sense of solidarity united villages and clans in an area hitherto known for its political fragmentation.

Karnu was killed in December 1928, but the insurrection continued to spread until 1931, when the colonizers began the last phase of the repression, a period of extreme cruelty called the War of the Caves. In 1935 the last warriors were still in hiding, refusing to leave their places of refuge for fear of reprisals.[19]

In its scale, its duration, and the number of rebels and military engagements involved, the Kongo-Warra war was the largest peasant insurrection experienced by sub-Saharan Africa between the two world wars. The administration did not deceive itself as to the implications of the war. Karnu had been working with a tribal society and therefore based his movement on traditional values, but underlying the rhetoric was a political consciousness. The refusal to collaborate with the colonizers, and especially the call for the unity of all ethnic groups, brought the rebellion to the threshold of modern times.

The harshness of the colonialist repression, however, left the country impoverished and underinhabited. The area has not yet recovered. This fact perhaps explains the apparent apathy of Central African peasants toward the tyranny of their rulers. It may also have permitted the Baya movement to be cast into obscurity both in the memories of its participants and in colonial histories, whereas the Maji Maji rebellion nourished the ideological roots of the Tanzanian resistance movement. It is true, too, that the successive regimes in Central Africa, culminating in the disastrous one of Bokassa, have hardly been of a kind to regenerate Baya nationalism.

The Mau Mau uprising in the Kikuyu country, like that of the Baya peasants, grew out of years of suffering under colonization. Despite their rapid demographic growth (the Kikuyu population doubled in less than half a century, numbering one million by 1948), their dire straits were persistently ignored by the government. Their reserves overcrowded and their lands depleted, the Kikuyu were forced to emigrate to the cities, swelling the ranks of the unemployed there. In response to this situation, the rural areas held protest marches against the agrarian policies, while urban strikes and demonstrations became widespread.

The Kenya African Union (KAU), the successor (in 1946) to the Kikuyu Central Association, proved unable to win concessions from the authorities, and in 1950 a mass uprising, the Mau Mau rebellion, broke out. It took a Messianic form, with oaths and sacrificial rites, destruction of churches, expulsion of Whites, and appropriation of lands. The first killings, of Black "collaborators," took place in 1952. The White settlers called for the extermination of the rebels, and the government responded by declaring a state of emergency, closing private schools, imposing collective punishments, and ordering that all trade unions and political organizations be disbanded. Nationalist leaders such as Jomo Kenyatta were arrested as inciting the rebellion, in spite of the fact that it had begun as a rural peasant movement. This repression only served to toughen the resistance, which was now joined by urbanized war veterans. Numbering perhaps two thousand in 1952, by 1953 twenty thousand had taken to the forests. Although a guerrilla war continued until 1960, the full-scale rebellion was crushed in 1956. By official count, eighty thousand Kikuyu were taken prisoner and ten thousand died, while fewer than one hundred Whites—soldiers and civilians—lost their lives.[20] The Mau Mau rebellion failed militarily, but it nevertheless hastened the process of decolonization.

The Mau Mau rebellion constituted a transitional movement. The Kikuyu were no longer a "precolonial" tribal group defending its traditional rights (although an ethnic bond undoubtedly did exist). Completely transformed, they had developed such extreme internal contradictions that rebellion was the only solution. The revolt must still be described as a peasant movement, however, for the dissension stemmed from conflict over land use.

The economic situation had fostered the grounds for conflict. In the Depression of the 1930s, in order to lower food prices, the state had encouraged agricultural production and had increased its control over this sector. And in the late 1940s, increased mechanization combined with the recovery of the market to reduce White dependence on Black labor and to induce

Whites to reappropriate lands that Black farmers had been working for the last two generations. Those farmers resented being transformed into agricultural laborers who had lost their rights as independent producers.

In addition to these developments in Kikuyu-White relations, intra-Kikuyu conflicts arose. Although the best land had been given to the White settlers, relatively fertile land remained in the heart of the country. The Kikuyu, who, unlike their neighbors the Masai, were traditionally sedentary, were able to profit from these areas, which were well situated—close to the road, the railway, and the expanding urban market of Nairobi with its demand for meat, vegetables, and cereals. Missionary influence in this group had created conditions suited to small-scale agrarian capitalism, and soon some Kikuyu had appropriated so much good land that others were forced either to farm for the Whites in the highlands or else to move to Nairobi, where by the early 1950s about a third of the population was Kikuyu. This social differentiation between landed and landless gave rise to a violent agrarian revolt which, although primarily a struggle between Kikuyu and Whites, included feuding among Kikuyu.[21]

The Mau Mau uprising, then, resulted from the conjunction of several sets of circumstances. First, the Kikuyu reserves became overpopulated; in consequence the soils were depleted. Second, the agricultural workers in the highlands opposed their proletarianization. And, finally, conditions in the rural areas sent many of the Kikuyu into Nairobi, where they lived as miserable squatters. Together these factors were exploited by urban leaders to fuel an agrarian and nationalist movement with rural roots, one based on a class of small-scale rural capitalists who had long been the principal dependents of the colonial state.

The Kwilu uprising in Zaire also qualifies as a primary resistance movement because of its rural origins, even though it took place under independence, long after World War II. Resistance had begun in the eastern Congo just twenty years before. A regional uprising took place in the province of Stanleyville (Kisangani). On a large scale but still "primary," it recalled the insurrection—not far distant in either time or place—of Kongo-Warra. This Stanleyville revolt was probably, despite the fact that almost nothing has been said about it for more than forty years, the most important and radical peasant revolt to have taken place in Zaire since the 1930s, if not before.[22] The insurgent regions of Masisi-Usala, Utumda, and Kisimba had always been isolated. The European presence had been confined to some prospecting for metals in the southwest of the country some ten years before the revolt, and no roads had been built. Suddenly, almost in mid-century, the peasants were faced with the full demands of the White war effort: cultivation of wild rubber (in Masisi), work in the mines for the Compagnie Nationale du Kivu (Lubutu), and a program of road construction. The response was not slow in coming. The peasants united in following the teachings of their leader, Bushiri. This man, who had worked for several years on the plantations and in the forests of the region, came forward with a Messianic message, both moral and religious, inspired by the Kitawala movement (of which we shall speak later) and calling on the elect of God for rebellion to eliminate White rule. His movement embodied the four ideas that characterize nearly all the primary insurrections: a cessation of work for the Whites; an opposition to sorcerers; an anti-White struggle; and the promise of resurrection.

The striking feature was the lightning rapidity with which the region fell in with the revolt as soon as the only European in the country—a symbol of rubber cultivation—was captured. As with the Kongo-Warra rebellion, the European authorities completely failed to notice the revolt in its early phase; in its active phase, government intervention was handicapped by delays in transmission of instructions. Military occupation of the area was ordered, but the slowness of the Belgian response, which the peasants interpreted as fear, only added to their enthusiasm.

Ultimately, however, the Belgian repression proved both effective and brutal. Several hundred rebels were arrested, and two Belgian representatives, a noncommissioned officer and an agricultural agent, were responsible for a hundred deaths by beating prisoners to extort confessions from them. Even so, four more years of military occupation were needed before submission could be considered complete.

Memories of this resistance remained in the country, and when the rural masses failed to gain freedom on independence, their reaction was commensurate with their disappointment. They had expected independence in 1960 not only to end oppression but to permit the Congolese people both the advantages of colonization and a vaguely defined return to traditional customs. The people were unwilling to accept, not an improvement, but a deterioration in their condition. The governmental corruption appalled the peasants, whose poverty was exacerbated by agricultural disasters. Faced with this dire situation, Patrice Lumumba called for a new independence that would guarantee justice and social progress for all. A rural and ethnic insurrection spread from village to village on the hope his words offered.[23]

The rebellion began among the Pende-Bambunda of Kwilu in 1962 and intensified in Kivu in the east in 1963–1964. Gizenga provided the impetus. Pierre Mulele, a native of the area and a former minister of Lumumba's, disseminated among his troops a summary of Marxist teaching that was strongly Maoist, although it revealed Mulele's Jesuit education. He decided on a strategy of all-out guerrilla war. The Conseil National de Libération (CNL), which was created in Léopoldville and met in Brazzaville in 1963, sought to coordinate the various movements of the revolt, and the leaders of the branches of the insurrection—in Kivu, in North Katanga, in Maniema, and in Kindu—proclaimed the People's Republic of the Congo.

The ideological basis of the CNL, however, was unclear. It failed to adapt socialist theory on expropriation or nationalization to the conditions of the Congo. Despite its "revolutionary and popular" aspirations, its 15 April 1964 program of "national reconciliation" amounted to little more than a standard nationalism. The constantly growing peasant rebellion filled this ideological vacuum with a strong emphasis on magical and religious phenomena. These undoubtedly served as the only remaining factors of social cohesion, for Mulele had been transformed into a legendary figure, elusive and omnipresent. The rebels of Kivu—the *simbas* (lions)—evolved into a closed order entered through initiation rites in which they received, from the witch-doctor, *dawa* (medicines) that provided immunity against enemy bullets. Terrorism became ever more violent, with waves of public executions at Stanleyville.

It is unclear to what degree the leaders were in control of the movement and how far they were driven by the forces they had unleashed. In any case, when Tshombe returned to power, his mercenaries succeeded in quelling the revolt.

This vast insurrection, with its revolutionary character (or pretensions), at least briefly combined a political movement and an authentic revolt of the peasant masses. It seemed, for a moment, to contain an immense hope and the expectation of an overthrow of the social structure, but its recourse to traditional practices to combat modern technology ended in regression, racism, and xenophobia.

PASSIVE RESISTANCE AND SOCIAL BANDITRY

The phenomenon of passive resistance in Africa has been little studied but in certain forms has, in fact, been very common and has had significant consequences. Open resistance can have somewhat ambiguous results: although the rebellious peasants become aware of their needs, the failure of the uprising hastens assimilation. Passive resistance, on the other hand, because it remains indirect, shows more lasting effects. It is also more widespread, being adopted by nearly all the rural masses. Over a long period, therefore, it acts as an extraordinarily effective barrier to outside influences.

Among the forms of passive resistance, the flight of *individuals* was a classic peasant reaction, typical of the first colonial phase. It proved the simplest way to avoid payment of taxes or being commandeered for work in porterage and was employed as long as the somewhat lax control of the colonial administration allowed it. By the time of World War I (in some of the more remote areas, somewhat later), however, individual flight gave way to *collective* migrations. From the many examples, especially in French-speaking Africa, we shall give just two. First, to avoid conscription during the massive recruitment campaigns for the European war at the end of 1915 and the end of 1917, entire villages of southern Senegal (at least 35,000 peasants) left for Portuguese Guinea and Gambia, and the peasants of Guinean Fouta Djallon went to Sierra Leone and Liberia (between 5 and 13 percent of the population). The populations of whole provinces disappeared, and others halved their numbers.[24] Second, migrations took place in response to the demand for laborers. At first most such migrations were motivated by the attempt to avoid working for others; as time went on, however, the majority were searching for a market for their labor. Thus, the Mossi laborers of Upper Volta fled from the prospect of underpaid forced labor in the Ivory Coast and went to work on the cocoa plantations of the Gold Coast. As long as the system of forced labor existed—that is, until 1946 in the French colonies and until independence in the Belgian Congo and the Portuguese territories—the villagers' desire to flee was at least as strong a motivation as the inducement of better wages in a neighboring country. Here we leave the life of the village and enter that of "modern" conditions of labor—often compulsory, but paid nevertheless. (We shall return to the subject in Chapter 10, in connection with the beginnings of the phenomenon of proletarianization.)

Like passive resistance, social banditry has until recently been neglected by historians of Africa. Precolonial African society, based on the solidarity of the group, had no place for the condemned individual. Since rights of land-use were collective, any unaffiliated person died of hunger unless he was adopted by a neighboring group as a slave. Exclusion from the community, the supreme punishment, was applied to those judged guilty of murder, debt, and other serious offenses. Seeing this, previous anthropologists have a priori eliminated the concept of marginality from the history of Africa. This amounts to a claim of uniqueness for African societies, since social banditry exists throughout the rest of the world, from Sardinia to the Ukraine, from Java to Brazil.[25]

Such a view oversimplifies the situation, especially in that phase of transition from a "traditional" rural society to a modern economy which immediately preceded the colonial takeover. The difference between the exploiters and exploited became more pronounced, even in the most fragmented societies. The standard of living of the ruling aristocracy (expressed in the construction of little "palaces," adoption of Western-style clothing, and increased consumption of liquor and champagne) rose while the masses fell deeper into poverty. To be sure, certain long-standing responses to such a situation remained valid. On the collective level, at the end of the nineteenth century extended families emigrated from Ovamboland (southern Angola) with their livestock, to settle elsewhere or to seek the protection of the White soldiers or missionaries against the *lenga* (the chief's militia). On the individual level, laborers migrated in search of employment, and especially to work in the mines of the Rand. This phenomenon was a feature of local policy: the chief's representative organized the laborers' departure and was expected to return with a substantial gift for the chief.

Certain political experiments of the period represented an attempt at conciliation: at about the time of World War I, Mandume tried to resolve the conflicts without involving the Whites, by concentrating all power in his own hands and imposing a unified system of taxation that transformed the exactions of the *lenga* into a legal code. The only result, however, was to increase discontentment in the rural areas.

At the turn of the century, peasants could still refuse to submit either to African despotism or to White domination. White soldiers and administrators were too few in number to be able to impose colonial law in the bush; for example, in 1900, after the failure of attempts at White colonization, Angola contained only some three thousand Portuguese. Southern Africa, both Portuguese (Angola and Mozambique) and British (Rhodesia), saw a great deal of banditry. There, although trade with Europe had been carried on since the sixteenth century, the Shona and Ovambo rural communities had remained in isolation until after 1870. From that time, however, the concessionary companies appropriated lands on a large scale, mines were dug in Rhodesia, and the development of cotton plantations, begun in the 1860s, became popular with White settlers. Theoretically, the government granted only vacant lands, but the itinerant and pastoral economy permitted this distinction to be made falsely.

Underlying the social banditry was an armed struggle, not just for agricultural lands, but also for pasture and, perhaps even more important, for the livestock itself, since the settlers had not succeeded in adapting imported animals. Banditry was one of the few responses the peasants could make to the introduction of capitalism. The interweaving of two contrary political and ideological systems violated revered traditional institutions, brought about political repression and economic exploitation, and left a certain number of individuals outside the new, hybrid system. These people fled to the hills and the bush. It was a mixed group. The major component, of course, was the peasants whose traditional chiefs had been arrested or replaced, depriving them of respected intercessors who could keep them in touch with their ancestors and who maintained the social order. Others were runaway slaves; a growing mass of escaped laborers who had been conscripted to work on plantations or in mines; fleeing mercenary auxiliaries (Herero and Khoi, for instance, from southwest Africa); and even soldiers who had deserted from the Portuguese army because they were badly paid, ill-fed, frequently beaten, and retained there beyond their term of service (these last provided the rebellions with a great deal of technical assistance). All these victimized, discontented, and uprooted people retained a way of life very close to that of the rural society they had left.

Little is known about these bands of rebels. They eked out a precarious survival in caves or in makeshift shelters. Constantly threatened, particularly at the end of the dry season, by a lack of food, their lives in constant danger, afraid of reprisals against their families who had remained in the village, the fugitives settled in hilly, forested, or marshy country situated, if possible, near a frontier. In Angola, the more organized groups built a series of rough fortresses (*cipaka*) on the top of rocky hills, the gaps between the hills being filled by stockades or thickets. The few women in the group— some voluntary companions, some abducted—practiced a little cultivation at the bottom of the valleys, but the chief source of subsistence was selling raided cattle to unscrupulous retailers (*funantes*), who, in exchange, provided the fugitives not only with food but with information, arms, and ammunition as well. In the 1920s, indeed, certain migrant miners in southwest Africa smuggled weapons to them.

The histories of some of these bandits can be traced. On the border between Mozambique and Zimbabwe lived a descendant of the royal family of Rovzi of Changamire. Mapondera ("he who has overcome the strongest of his enemies") had been celebrated since mid-century for putting his courage and his physical strength at the disposal of neighboring chiefs who had been unjustly attacked, or, even more romantically, for coming to the aid of the oppressed, whatever their sex or social station. Between 1894 and 1900 the European conquest turned Mapondera from a well-known guardian of the traditional order into a social bandit. His case is typical: refusing to pay the house-tax and wrongly implicated in a dispute in which a White merchant had been killed, Mapondera began a career as an outlaw, not a criminal but a victim of injustice and of White persecution. Flocking to his side came the rejects of the new society, an ever-changing and varied collection of people that rarely consisted of more than a hundred individuals. Of the thirteen of his companions finally arrested by the British, only two came from Mapondera's own village. Mapondera himself, captured but spared execution on account of his advanced age, was left to die in prison in 1903.

Mbundu, in Southern Angola, also came of noble antecedents. The nephew and heir presumptive of one of the great chiefs of the highlands, he began his struggle in 1875. Captured in 1882 and conscripted by force into the colonial army at Luanda, he deserted in 1887. As head of a somewhat loosely organized band, Mbundu became a legendary hero. When he was finally captured in a surprise attack in 1901, he was beheaded, and all the members of his *cipaka*—men, women, and children—were murdered or burnt alive.

The social bandits sought to redress injustice, but they seldom succeeded in giving expression to their potential for revolution. Although colonial accounts always represented them as frightful criminals detested by the people, in the early days the bandits were indeed largely supported by the peasants, who provided them with grains, the basis of the Shona diet; with information about the movements of patrols; and with protective "fetishes." Even so, the operations they led were seldom on a large scale: at the height of his career, Mapondera headed a band of seven hundred to one thousand men armed with European rifles, but more often they formed a little group of guerrillas ambushing soldiers and patrols, burning stores in the bush, or, at the most, attacking isolated Portuguese outposts. Perhaps the most characteristic operation was a campaign undertaken secretly at night to persuade peasants to boycott the installations of the Zambezi Company and to refuse to pay taxes to the Whites or to work for them. They could not have fomented social revolution without changing their role in the eyes of the rural societies. No longer social bandits, they would have become symbols of peasant resistance to the forces of destruction.

The bandits had more conservative aims: to defend or recreate the former order, to restore a real or imaginary lost harmony in their societies of origin. Moreover, the social bandit as robber of the rich to give to the poor was often a mythical figure, as was the bandit as avenger striking down the foes of the people, and, to an even greater extent, as the "liberator" from the colonial regime. More or less by definition, bandits operated in conquered territory, and in the final analysis it was difficult to distinguish the social bandit, in league with the peasantry against the institutions that oppressed them, from the simple brigand and outlaw pillaging all sections of society indiscriminately. The growing pressure of colonial authority made the bandits resort to increasingly rash procedures that endangered their very way of life. As a rule they may have raided neighbors who were completely unknown or hardly known at all, but a scorched-earth policy forced them to attack the people who had sheltered or protected them. In the end they even set upon the unfortunate Malawi workers on their way to the mines or the surrounding villages. In Angola by 1892, for example, Mukakapire had to abandon his *cipaka*. Condemned to a life of wandering, rejected by the chiefs of all the territories he crossed, he was shot by his own followers in 1897. Another typical story of an uneven career was that of Orloog, one of the most famous Angolan bandits, who began as a mercenary of the Portuguese as they penetrated the interior of southwest Africa and finished as a chief of the native police, receiving a regular salary. In 1908–1910 he played a role of prime importance—in the repression of banditry.

The social bandits generally had to choose between fighting or dying, though this fact is often forgotten. The popular memory tends to idealize their legendary histories. Identifying with their story, certain regions, such as the entire northeast of Zimbabwe, have turned the bandits into symbols of African resistance.

Social bandits have, then, played a role in Africa, a role the colonial sources sought to obscure. As early as the sixteenth century, social banditry appeared in the Gold Coast response to the rise of the merchant class.[26] At the beginning of the twentieth century, in Shaba (Katanga) the bandit Kasonga Niembo was supported by the Lunda peasants as a whole; and in the mountainous volcanic lands of northwestern Rwanda, bandit "head-choppers" in fact were rebels against the Tutsi aristocracy. And tactics of insubordination practiced in West Africa could fall into this same category. For instance, the insurrection of Aïr (examined below as a revolt inspired by Islam) may have been underpinned by a wave of (social?) banditry originating with nomads marginalized by the conquest of the desert and the Sahel. And the Sanusi leader Umar-al-Mukhtar in Cyrenaica, who led a large band of rebels against the Italian regime, may well merit the name of "social bandit." The recent attempt to dismiss Eric Hobsbawm's thesis as "Eurocentricity" and to argue in favor of a specifically African model of resistance does not seem to me convincing.[27] The issue of social banditry in Africa is well enough substantiated to merit further investigation.

THE USES OF THE SACRED: FROM MILLENARIANISM TO SYNCRETISM

Various forms of religion—traditional, Christian, and combinations of the two—were used in an attempt to deal with the devastations of colonization. The methods ranged widely, however, from violence to resignation.

Messianism and Millenarianism

The primary rebellions were nearly always accompanied by charismatic figures: a Messiah or prophet, claiming magical powers that would overcome European technical superiority, launched a resistance movement in the name of the divine will. This long-standing tradition expressed the inevitability of the conflict between the precolonial worldview, the social situation, and the Western economy. It was the last resort of a powerless society whose weapons had failed; hence the often suicidal quality of this type of confrontation. The first and no doubt the most dramatic instance took place in 1856–1857: the huge Xhosa uprising in South Africa. The Bantu populations of the Cape Colony, constantly pushed back by the combined expansionism of British traders and Boer farmers, desperately desired to regain their lands.[28]

The Xhosa resistance was long-drawn-out and tenacious. Between 1779 and 1881, the date of the definitive annexation, a series of wars (the Kaffir wars of colonial history) included three particularly violent rebellions that expressed the reaction of Xhosa society to its dispossession and its destruction. These rebellions were rooted in ancestral traditions. Herdsmen with a great deal of livestock, the Xhosa ritually sacrificed animals as part of a process of purification that permitted communication with ancestors. The cult of the dead, intimately linked to the whole organization of social life (marriage, birth, initiation) was presided over by the diviner—often a prophet, healer, or warrior—while the sorcerer was held responsible for all the evils that beset the group.

Without displacing these traditional beliefs, Christian influence appeared early among the Xhosa, and it took deep and permanent hold. The missionary influence was already felt at the end of the seventeenth century, and the Church Missionary Society established the first regular mission in 1816. Methodist outposts studied the local language, printed Gospels, and set up village schools. This context explains the diviners who, at the beginning of the nineteenth century, mingled elements of their ancient culture with the teachings of the Old and New Testaments. They made prophecies proclaiming a coming Golden Age: the dead, it was claimed, would form an invulnerable army of warriors who, opposing the White invasion, would restore the former territories of the Xhosa. Sometimes a prophet's influence extended far beyond the borders of his village. For instance, in 1819 Makanda declared himself brother of Jesus Christ and organized an attack upon a military outpost. Mlangeni, a great persecutor of sorcerers, began in 1847 to foretell the defeat of the Whites: their guns would be filled with water after bullocks were offered up to the ancestors.

The 1856 uprising called for a radical purification, mingling traditional practices with an apocalyptic vision derived from Christianity. Mhlakaza, its prophet, was assisted by his niece Nongquanse, who interpreted to the people the message of the ancestors. The purification entailed massacring livestock and destroying crops to such an extent that the Xhosa starved themselves. In 1857, the population dropped drastically, from as many as 100,000 to as few as 37,000 individuals. The survivors were forced to migrate to the Cape Colony in search of paid employment. By about 1870, the majority of the population already worked in mines, on work-sites, or at the ports. These profound economic and social transformations hastened the acculturation and disorganization of the Xhosa people.

This form of resistance, amounting to collective suicide, contrasts with politicomilitary reactions like that of the Chaka at about the same period. Why did one people choose the first path, and another people the second? The mental outlook, the values, and above all the history of the group concerned all played a part. Most of the primary resistance movements, even the most violent, were ambivalent, like the Temne-Mende movement in Sierra Leone in 1898 and the Zulu revolts in Natal in 1905–1906. These peasant movements were underscored by a prophetic Messianism that sacralized and popularized these reactions of desperation. Their recourse to the supernatural clearly revealed the conflict between the ideology of the rebellion and the economic and cultural realities in a rural society whose dispersive social organization countered all attempts at fundamental change.

These failures resulted in the collapse of traditional beliefs and traditional sociopolitical values, and at the same time in a recognition of the futility of resistance. The only way out was by a flight into the imaginary. This escape could take either of two forms or could combine the two. Either occult local magical practices, above all those of sorcery, were revived; or the power of the adversary was appropriated through an identification with his techniques and his religious ideology. This second approach led the Africans to convert to the new religions in great numbers. Syncretistic sects and churches flourished particularly after World War I, as the last refuge of a faltering society. The movement most strongly affected the animistic countries, which were more subject to Christian influences, but in specific forms it appeared in the Moslem world also.

Sorcery and Secret Societies

When the traditional weapons of African society proved ineffective, a typical reaction was to turn to malevolent forces, as opposed to the beneficent animistic cult and ritual represented by the medicine man. The flowering of witchcraft revealed the depth of the malaise, as we see, for instance, in the dramatic ordeals by poison (*tali*) in Casamance (southern Senegal). This practice decimated the Balant between 1909 and 1911; it began again, with renewed vigor, in the Joola country during World War I, and, again, among the Bayot in 1920, as a form of collective suicide. Similarly, almost everywhere evidence exists of the frequent practice of magical rites using water, needles, and, above all, poison.

All abominable and apparently irremediable ills were attributed to sorcerers; the cure lay in the discovery and elimination of the perpetrators. For instance, Tomo Nyirunda of Nyasaland, called Mwana Lesa, combined the supposed faculty of detecting sorcerers by means of baptism with the dissemination of the classic teachings of the Watchtower (of which we shall speak later). People who refused the test by immersion because they themselves were half-convinced of their guilt often unresistingly let themselves be drowned by their accuser. In this way Mwana Lesa was able to pride himself on having caused several hundred deaths by 1925, when he was hanged by the authorities in Northern Rhodesia (Zambia).[29]

A similar spirit showed itself in the reappearance of secret societies whose acts of violence were more or less explicitly related to witchcraft, intended as a savage revival of ancient customs. In order to gain admittance to the society of the leopard-men of Cameroon and Central Africa (Manja and Banda), the applicant had to kill a close relative (mother, son, or first wife) in preparation for a ritual festivity. The members of this society, citing the need for vengeance as their justification, abducted and murdered people who had been accused of witchcraft. For these rituals they disguised themselves as leopards, either wearing skins of that animal or tattooing their bodies with colored mixtures in imitation of leopard skins. They walked on all fours, touching the ground only with their toes, so as to make their footprints resemble the leopard's, and they voiced similar cries.[30] The same atmosphere of tension and collective terror, leading to self-destruction, prevailed in Zaire among the *amiotes* and leopard-men of the northeast, by the Ubangui River, and, in the crisis of the 1930s, in the Wamba and Bunia regions.[31]

The Syncretisms of Acceptance

The syncretistic school of thought preached an ideology of resignation that attenuated the violence of resistance. This fatalism sprang from a realization of the colonial power's invincibility, at least for the time.

Frantz Fanon has pointed out that the colonized person uses religion as a means of avoiding a true view of the colonialists and as a method of making colonization bearable.[32] Thus a political ideology develops that attempts to explain, and hence to justify or at least to render tolerable, the colonial social order. This popular vision of the colonial experience is reflected in myths of justification, which seem in most places to have appeared at the same time and in the same way.[33] These narratives were collected by administrators and missionaries when they first began to be disseminated. Stripped of trimmings concerned with the Bible, Christ, exoticism, or the benefits of colonization, the myths reveal a religious rationale. They are legends in which men and divinities intervene to justify existing power structures and authorities and to declare the finality of the established order. One recurrent theme represents the origin of the inequality of Blacks and Whites as the "test of God" or the "miraculous bath." In these legends, a first part describes either an original state of equality or else the superiority and seniority of the Blacks; in the middle part, God puts Black and White to the test—thus assigning responsibility for the present state of affairs to humanity—and the White always emerges victorious, generally through an ingenious ruse. This conclusion, while confirming the Blacks' original privileged position, explains why the Whites are rich, happy, and in a position of authority, while the Blacks are miserable, subjugated, and oppressed. The disparity, according to the legend, can be expected to be lasting, since it originates in the past and, above all, in the divine will. Blacks should accept the situation, for not only are they powerless, but rebellion would be quasi-sacrilegious. The humiliation and frustration are lessened because the submission is to God rather than to the Europeans. At most, Blacks should participate in the authority enjoyed by the Europeans by appropriating their ideals and their techniques of power—in other words, their religion.

The ideology of resignation went together with an ideology of social advancement. This belief was taught by, for example, the prophet Harris, a Liberian who from 1913 to 1915 wandered through the coastal areas of the Ivory Coast and the Gold Coast, converting the animist peoples of the area to his new religion. His message, strongly tinged with Protestantism, only concerned the Blacks, although it was not based on any form of racial opposition. According to Harris, the Whites derived their power from the Bible (in this lay his millenarianism), but after seven years of ritual practices and struggles against fetishes, the Blacks, he claimed, would reach the social and economic level of the Whites. Harrisism was entirely religious in character and never at all anticolonial. The French administration nevertheless expatriated Harris in 1915, because of the Franco-British political rivalry. Harrisism had an immediate success: whole villages converted—probably 100,000 to 150,000 people from 1918 onward—when they were visited by one of the host of lesser prophets who took the place of the master.[34]

The rise of Kimbangism in Belgian Africa was a similar phenomenon. Simon Kimbangu, of peasant origin and educated by the missionaries, became aware, in 1921, of the contradiction between the message of the Bible and the colonialist application of that message. A Messiah who said he had come to deliver the Black race, Kimbangu had two missions: the unity of the Bakongo people, and the equality of mankind. This Christian, non-syncretistic movement of promotion through religion minimized political differences, for it implied both Kongo acceptance of Western values and their desire for modernization through economic and technical progress.

To the colonial administration, however, any new ideology was ipso facto a source of subversion. That same year, they arrested Kimbangu and condemned him to death. The sentence was never carried out; instead, he was sent to Katanga, where he died twenty years later. A wave of protests followed his sentencing: altogether, from 3,000 people (according to the administration) to 150,000 (according to the Kimbangists) were deported. The effect was clearly opposite to that which was intended: the movement, thus carried far beyond the borders of the Kongo country, became interethnic and even nationwide. It never took on real political aspects, however. A revival in 1939 was tinged with xenophobia (this splinter group is today the second largest Christian denomination in Zaire), but with the coming of independence the movement evolved into a religion with no political overtones. The Kimbangist church, although it was originally an expression of "Bakongo nationalism," refused to come out in favor of the Abako, a Bakongo nationalist political movement, no doubt because it desired a religious universalism that aimed at integration into the modern world rather than at rejection of colonialism.[35]

The only sign of resistance in these movements of religious resignation was, significantly enough, an attraction for the religion not of the immediate colonizer, but of its rival European power. That is, people chose Protestant-based syncretisms (Harrisism, Kimbangism) in countries colonized by Catholics, and vice versa (as in the case of the Igbo in Nigeria, and in the Ganda country and western Tanganyika).

Religion and Resistance

In southern Africa, the spiritual refuge provided by the separated Black churches decidedly took on the character of a militant resistance. For example, the Ethiopian church, an organization in the Christian biblical tradition founded in the South African compounds in 1896, rejected all links with the West and soon became an ideological weapon against the alienation of the Blacks. Similarly, the cult of Mumbo, which appeared in Kenya in 1913, evolved into a solid anti-British opposition. Even if these movements were not basically political, they encouraged an attitude of resistance, a consciousness of oppression, and a demand for rights that transcended the diversity of languages and traditions.

The Watchtower Bible and Tract Society, or Jehovah's Witnesses, epitomizes such religious resistance movements. It originated in America but developed independently under the name of Kitawala in Northern Rhodesia and in the Congo, and as Shoonadi (Truth) or Mpakuta (The Separated) in Nyasaland during the interwar period. The expansion of the movement began at the end of 1917 with the expulsion of six members of The Watchtower from Southern Rhodesia to Northern Rhodesia. The sect's many preachers, although always hostile to the White regimes, did not advocate open sedition. Rather, they proclaimed the imminent end of the world, when "the last [the African Blacks] shall become the first": "Everything will be changed through prayer," they said; "everything will become ours, and we shall become as rich as the Whites are now." The Blacks were therefore to prepare themselves through baptism and a renunciation of polygyny, hiding in the forest and praying fervently until the Day of Judgment, the official date of which was constantly postponed. It was useless, they claimed, to till the soil or to raise livestock, especially as laborers for the Whites.

By World War I the movement had several thousand adherents and began to take action. After the German invasion, Kitawala groups in northeast Rhodesia often attacked local chiefs who collaborated with the settlers. In response, immediately after the war the colonialists declared such gatherings illegal, and they arrested 138 influential members of the movement in Northern Rhodesia. Most were imprisoned. The principal prophet in Nyasaland, Kamwana, was exiled to the Seychelles, and the Belgian Congo deported hundreds of adherents between 1932 and 1939 in order to extirpate the movement from the mines of Katanga. After the disturbances in the copper belt in 1935, in which the members of the Watchtower were supposed to have played a role, the sale of Watchtower literature was prohibited in the Congo until 1946, but the movement, offering an alternative to the harsh realities of colonialism, continued to grow.[36] As late as 1944, the Kitawala again played an undeniable role in Bushiri's vigorous movement of rebellion in the Belgian Congo.

In politically fragmented countries with scattered populations, religious opposition was the only possible unifying bond. It permitted peasants, whose social system was dispersed and whose political structures were nonexistent or destroyed, to form a body in the name of an ideology that ended a long tradition of separatism. Thus, during World War II, for the first time all the Diola of Lower Casamance united in resistance, as the priestess Alintsinoe led them in the "rice war" against the requirements of the war effort.

This religious form of resistance to oppression maintained a remarkable vitality long beyond the colonial period, giving rise to official unease. The authorities continue to watch these movements and to curb their expression to this day. Only some ten years ago, in Malawi, the Jehovah's Witnesses were mercilessly oppressed. The president for life, Hastings Kamuzu Banda, determined to eliminate adversaries who, in the 1970s, utilized a means of expressing discontent that had by then become "traditional." [37]

The Limits of Millenarianism

The millenarian temptation, through its very ambiguity, could also act as a curb to action. Deriving its strength from the rural masses' tradition of resistance, it could, in the name of respect for the past, deflect or even abort protests that held modernizing goals. Matswanism in the Congo exhibited such power.

Unlike the movements described above, Matswanism was urban and political in origin. André Matswa, a former infantryman who had fought in the Rif war, became conscious of the problems of exploitation in Africa through contact with French anticolonial circles. In 1926 he founded in Paris the Association Amicale des Originaires de l'AEF, a group for the promotion of education whose immediate program was to unify the Congolese elite. The sociocultural facade was adopted in a vain attempt to avoid confrontation with the French authorities. Matswa had addressed an open letter to President Poincaré condemning the Code de l'Indigénat, the abuses of the great trading companies, and the wretched condition of the Black population. The pretext the government used for its repression was a claim of irregularities in the collection of funds from members to finance information dissemination— seen by the colonizers as propagandizing—in French Equatorial Africa, where the group numbered about 13,000 members. Matswa was accused of embezzlement, arrested at the end of 1929, and taken to Brazzaville, where he was condemned by the local tribunal to three years in prison and ten years of banishment in Chad.[38] Despite a spontaneous general strike that paralyzed businesses and workshops and cut off the supply of goods to the city, the movement's real political force had been spent, although it did enjoy a brief period of tolerance at the time of the Popular Front (1935–1936).

Matswa himself escaped from Chad and returned to France. Wounded at the front in the early days of World War II, he was again arrested in 1940 by order of Governor-General Pierre Boisson. Tried in 1941 and condemned to forced labor for life, he died in Mayama in 1942.

At this late stage Matswa's followers took refuge in the imaginary. The ethnic group to which Matswa belonged, the Laris, refused to admit his death: since he had been buried secretly on the day of his death without a ritual ceremony, he could not, according to tradition, be recognized as having died. Two former members of his association proclaimed themselves to be the high priests of the Matswanist Church, a Messianic church whose prophet, having appeared once, was expected to come again. The focus on Matswa's reappearance changed the movement into a death cult. Its 30,000 members believed that, through a collective act of faith, contact could be maintained between the living and André Matswa. The movement achieved such a strong base that the first president of the Congo, Fulbert Youlou, indeed sought to exploit its influence politically. But although it had originally been based on a dream of Congolese nationalism, it had become only an ethnic religious sect echoing turn-of-the-century millenarianism, divested of its former dynamic political content.

THE AMBIGUOUS ROLE OF ISLAM

Islam, the dominant ideology in the Sahelo-Sudan area on the eve of colonization, proved to be, under the right circumstances, an enduring vehicle of resistance. Samori, for instance, made political use of Islam, as we have seen.

Within the colonial framework, however, Islam began to act as a means for the chief to enter into alliances with the new regime. The British administration very early sought to assure the effective collaboration of the emirates by adopting a policy of respect for their local authority and for Islamic culture in general (shown notably in the *non*-introduction of missionary schools). In northern Nigeria, Lord Lugard began in 1900 to practice his principle of indirect rule, which had first been applied in Buganda in 1890. The British followed a similar policy in the declining sultanate of Zanzibar.

The French administration took a far more ambiguous attitude. It sometimes collaborated with the local slave-trading sultans when it lacked the means for direct occupation, as in eastern Ubangi-Chari. In West Africa and in the Chad Basin, however, French imperialism overtly opposed the hegemonies of Ahmadu, Samori, and Rabah. The French saw North Africa as the paradigm: an area where Islam was an established force, to be monitored and held in check.

The colonialists credited the Moslem world with a unity of thought and strategy that it by no means possessed. Islam indeed had established a comprehensive ideological system with a hierarchy of interpreters (imams, caliphs, cadis, and so on), but it condemned the European conquest only because the Europeans were infidels. Islam offered three possible responses to the colonial challenge. The first, *hijra*, meant withdrawal to a sure place of refuge, generally in the mountains, to recoup forces in order to face the adversary. *Hijra* served as preparation for the jihad, an institutionalized war of conversion proclaimed by a Muslim sovereign. Finally, *taquiyya*, prudence, allowed persecuted sects to negotiate a status of "internal exile," an attitude soon to prevail in the colonized world as a whole.[39]

Open Rebellion: The Case of Mauritania

Hijra and *jihad* only applied clearly in the case of Mauritania, the area closest to the Maghreb. There the struggle became a national war.[40] At the turn of the century, marabouts began to give cohesion to an uprising that eventually engulfed the country as far as the Upper Niger. The initial sign of a spirit of resistance came in April 1905. The first civil commissioner, Xavier Coppolani, was murdered just after he had conquered Adrar, an act that demonstrated the refusal of the Ida or Aich to submit. These people called upon Shaykh Ma-al-Ainin, who rallied most of the Moorish tribes. Like the great Warriors of the Faith of the previous century, Ma-al-Ainin was rigorously orthodox, and he presented himself as the heir of the traditional Qadiriyya brotherhood. His conservative politics reflected his theology: far from calling for a popular uprising, he based his position on existing social values. The throne of the Sherifs, he announced, was the true Muslim caliphate. After all, the sultan of Morocco had since 1892 appointed him as his representative in the region of Villa Cisneros. Ma-al-Ainin asked the various southern chiefs to recognize the Sherifs' authority as well. What could be anachronistically called his "anti-imperialist strategy" consisted of opposing to the French an internationally recognized Islamic state—Morocco.

The ineffectiveness of the throne of the Sherifs came to appease the French, but it finally forced Ma-al-Ainin to make a truly revolutionary gesture. In 1909, he proclaimed himself sultan, at the same time declaring a jihad. By this act he made himself master of a troubled and insecure country. He fostered a new area of economic activity around the port of Tarfaya, where the restoration of old wells and the digging of new ones encouraged grazing and caravans. The region became the hub of a trans-Saharan commerce largely based on arms and slaves. Ainin did not integrate the slaves into his movement, however, as did the Sanusiyya to the east; he primarily acted as supplier to the sultan of Morocco.

The war was centered in Adrar, "a sort of isolated stone citadel in the midst of the sands."[41] Arms were supplied by German traffickers, apparently in large quantities: 40,000 cartridges were fired during the Smara column in 1913. Moroccan support—which today is used as an argument to justify Moroccan control of the western Sahara—and, above all, the Islam-encouraged growth of a sense of Mauritanian unity binding together nomadic tribes made Ainin's position almost unassailable.

By 1910 the French had decided to reverse their policy of alliance. Instead of basing it, as formerly, on the Muslim aristocracy of the great shaykhs of Trarza, who were fundamentally hostile to infidels, they henceforth entrusted the policing of the Sahara to the traditionally submissive warrior-tribes. These tribes had been won over to the French by gifts, favors, and positions of authority that inevitably corrupted traditional social values. Despite the heavy losses the Islamic guerrillas imposed on the French ("A Colonial Hell . . . Mauritania Must Be Evacuated," ran the headline of the *Petit Parisien* on 21 March 1909), the new policy proved effective. The fortress of Adar was taken, and Ma-al-Ainin's death in October 1910 decapitated the movement. The French military of Timbuktu and Mauritania joined forces in 1912 to minimize instances of social banditry, and the great drought of 1913 virtually put an end to resistance.

Mahdism: The Spirit of Resistance

The Mauritanian rebellion was exceptional not only in scale and duration, but in its leadership from above. Islam generally fomented resistance only after local leaders had been discredited in the eyes of the masses, by defeat or by their policy of collaboration. In this way the marabouts' party organized resistance in the Wolof kingdoms at the turn of the century and headed local uprisings until World War I. Such religious leaders merely guided what was in fact the Islamic version of the popular revolt. The peasants, whose beliefs were in some respects deeply rooted in the Mahdist Muslim tradition but were also not far removed from an animistic folk-culture, seized the chance of shaking off the colonial yoke.

These popular jihad movements closely resembled the rebellions prevalent at that period, and for the same reasons, throughout the whole of sub-Saharan Africa. Mahdism, which inspired various forms of popular resistance, can be equated with the recurrent Messianism of African Christian history and the millenarianism of the animistic or syncretistic movements. All these resistance movements took the form of a desperate social struggle waged partly in an imaginary sphere, in the expectation of some mighty arbiter of justice whose coming was to be announced by great disasters, the prototype of which was the European conquest. The oppressors, it was believed, would be vanquished once and for all by a purifying popular faith.

From the first days of the European conquest, Mahdism began to spread in the Nile region of the Sudan, where it fairly soon became a political movement adopted by the ruling classes. In 1881 Muhammad Aharad proclaimed himself Mahdi. He called for the restoration of the pure and just form of Islam of the days before Turkish rule, and his first victories over oppression provided a focus for discontent. The government, which became Anglo-Egyptian in 1882, was driven out, Khartoum fell in 1885, and a solidly structured new administration took over the whole country except for the ports on the Red Sea. This new regime owed its existence to a mighty reformist, mystical religious movement, but above all it embodied a Sudanese nationalism that was not suppressed until the Anglo-Egyptian conquest of 1896–1898.

Mahdism also persisted in West Africa, where it has been little studied. Scattered, fragmentary spontaneous popular movements displayed a number of specific social characteristics. They tended to assert the equality of all Muslims, to reject existing aristocracies (the foreign oppressors, of course, and sometimes also the traditional rulers), to have recourse to violence in response to popular demand, and, finally, quite often to speak for those who were displaced both from the traditional order and, to an increasing extent, from the colonial system.[42]

To give one example out of many: in the last great revolt in the Mossi country in Upper Volta in 1908, the marabout Mumani de Ramongo urged people to convert to Islam and to refuse to pay taxes. He succeeded, in the name of Islam in this remarkably hierarchical kingdom, in winning a wide variety of followers who resented the French usurpation of traditional authority.[43] Two thousand armed men advanced to within forty kilometers of Ouagadougou. Colonialist troops responded swiftly, the marabout was killed, and the allowance of the Mossi sovereign, the Mogho Naba, was reduced by one-quarter.

Islam and the French

Islamic resistance generally mingled complex religious and ethnic factors with socioeconomic and political ones. The Aïr revolt in the Niger exemplifies such a mix. Despite its relatively late date (1916–1917), it belongs to the first generation of anticolonial struggles, since the people had until then been independent. In the name of Islam, the Aïr revolt fused popular and leadership discontent. The people's unhappiness was aggravated by the coincidence of the great drought of 1913–1914 with French requisitions of millet and camels for their war effort. The appointed interpreter-intermediaries provided a focus for the hatred of the indigenous inhabitants. At the same time, although the French regarded the sultan of Agadès as submissive, he was suffering both culturally and economically. The colonial intrusion had disorganized Saharan trade and had interfered with the collection of the traditional dues that had been his main source of livelihood.

This revolt was, therefore, more than simply a religious movement, although it had a strong religious component. Kaoussan, a Targui of Damergan and a strict Senusi hostile to infidels (he had been waging a jihad in Libya since 1914) provided his military force, a little army made up of Tuareg, Toubou, and Italian and French deserters from the colonial armies. It was,

moreover, the marabouts who persuaded the tribes to revolt in 1915, even if
they did so for social and political reasons: they hoped to usurp the power
of the traditional nobility of the Imajeren.

The rebellion failed, for sedentary Black Africans who had been reduced
to servitude by the Muslim nomads joined forces with the French troops,
but it left behind a tremendous tension. At the end of 1916, the Kel Aïr
Tuareg, mostly loyal to the Qadiriyya, who had been assembled by the sultan of Agadès, and the Senusi forces of the Targui were gathered together in
the French fortress of Agadès, which was besieged for three months. The
alliance proved unstable, however, owing to the diversity of the interests involved: those of the Tuareg social system, those of the sultan—which were
not necessarily anti-French—and those of the eastward-looking Senusi religious orthodoxy. Raids and counter-raids continued unceasingly until 1931
in the northwest desert regions where the housing had been destroyed, but
the French responded promptly, beheading all the marabouts of Agadès.[44]

The beheading of the marabouts was no isolated incident. From one end
of the Sahel to the other, the French authorities in those war years displayed
an obsession with the supposed dangers of Islam. (This obsession, preserved
in documents as well as historical incidents, ultimately caused the religious
factor to be overstated in histories of the period.) In 1914, the authorities
believed they had discovered a vast Muslim anti-French plot in the Upper
Volta. It was not a new idea. In 1906 the governor had put into operation a
system for providing information about the activities of marabouts and
Koranic schools, which were subjected to considerable supervision on behalf of an anti-Islamic "policy of races" whose aim locally was to strengthen
the traditional authority of the Mogho Naba (1912).[45] Most of the accused
"leaders" of the 1914 "plot" were arrested, and heavy sentences were handed
out for "anti-French propaganda and a call for Holy War." The evidence,
however, was perceived to be inconclusive even by the French themselves,
who quickly returned to a policy of collaboration, as can be seen by the revision of the court judgments in 1916.

In Wadai, the French found the Sanusiyya yet more threatening. The
capital, Abéché, had been taken in 1909 and the evicted sultan replaced by a
French appointee. This prince, hated by his subjects, was evicted in turn in
1912. Here, as in Aïr and Upper Volta, the *ulemas* (marabouts) constituted a
nucleus of ideological resistance more or less connected with the royal family, in a situation similarly aggravated by world war and a major famine.
Following the dissemination in 1917, which was popularly known as the
Year of the Machete, of a tract in Arabic quite wrongly described as anti-
French, the authorities reacted brutally. The four marabouts principally implicated were arrested, and the militia of riflemen, let loose on the city, killed
almost the whole of the elite. The capital was emptied of its intellectuals,

and a large part of its population fled to the Sudan,[46] helping to lay the foundation for the close political and cultural ties between these two neighboring peoples.

The Rise of the Brotherhoods

By 1914 the colonialists had set up such an effective system of repression that Muslims began to be convinced that direct action would be futile. The evolution of the Islamic regions at this period paralleled that of the animist countries, with the ideological reaction becoming increasingly religious in form. Islamic areas showed themselves very resistant to the influence of Western missionaries, moving instead toward stricter Moslem practice.

This emphasis on religion did not necessarily signify opposition to the colonial regime. The common tendency toward a sublimation of the contradictions of life under colonialism found expression in Islamic regions particularly in the Taquiyya, a Muslim ideology of resignation. The major difference here was the use that the colonizers made of the movement. Contrary to the situation in the animist countries, where the administration always rejected and repressed all manifestations of African religiosity, the traditionally political nature of Islam caused it to be regarded as a complementary means of domination. Despite this fact, however, in certain cases Islam did act as an ideological resistance movement.

In the Mandingo country, the great religious leaders generally fell back on peaceful proselytism. Closely watched, they knew that their freedom depended solely on their submissiveness, which brought considerable material advantages as well. Personal rivalries, cleverly sustained by the colonial authorities, and the memory of exhausting years of vain struggle guaranteed the acceptance of a subjection that was at once a bitter trial and a source of unity. The formerly warlike marabouts showed themselves concerned henceforth with spreading their pacific influence over animist populations. The method proved to be effective: Islam made enormous progress. In Middle Casamance, for example, the Joola of the Fooni converted en masse under certain powerful marabouts, whose influence was enhanced by their foreign origin (as in the case of Shelif Yunus of Wadai). Military incidents occurred only as a result of the misplaced zeal of local officials. Thus, on the Upper River in the Fulaadu country, when in 1908 the marabout Saraxolé Suleyman Bayaga undertook to build a mosque, the administration took action. Bayaga fled to Gambia; 150 riflemen were sent after him; and he was killed. Such violence was, however, unusual.[47]

Intellectuals tended toward defensive ideological expressions of a transcendental, literary nature. Certain poems read at this period in the villages of Fouta Djallon bear witness to an Islamic culture and literature of resistance.[48] The most characteristic sign of discontent, however, was the emergence of institutions of refuge: the brotherhoods. These offered an alternative to the former chiefdoms, fostering both a sense of identity and hope for the future. The brotherhood responded to imperialism with an ambiguous counterauthority: the maraboutic leader was both a protector for his followers and an authorized representative of the colonizer. Evolution was possible in both directions: Muridism moved toward collaboration, Hamallism toward resistance.

The founder of the Murid sect, Amadu Bamba, had begun with a purely religious doctrine of Sufi inspiration, searching for salvation through inner contemplation, spiritual retreat, and maintaining a certain distance from the prevailing situation. Like most nineteenth-century leaders, Bamba was nevertheless harassed at the beginning by the French. The authorities first deported him to Gabon, then to Mauritania. In 1912 he returned to Djourbel, Senegal. At that point the administration saw his increasing popularity and finally understood that his attitude was pacific. It therefore changed its tactics and inaugurated an era of cooperation. In 1918 Bamba was awarded the Cross of the Legion of Honor (which, true to his ascetic principles, he never wore) for his success in recruiting his followers to serve in World War I.

Bamba continued to pursue meditation until his death in 1927, but his disciples seized the opportunity provided by colonial benevolence to use the labor of his nearly 100,000 adherents for their own benefit in an area suitable for the cultivation of peanuts. The Murid aristocracy set up an authoritarian, neo-feudal regime, binding the peasants to the land. The docility of the disciples gave their exploiters an economic power that made them the privileged partners of the colonial administration and, more generally, of the state. Sure of the votes of their *talibe,* the Murids exacted a high price for political support (Senegal's vote in the referendum of 1958 was called the "yea of the marabouts"). Even today, the laws and statutes of the Senegalese state are respected in the Murid area only with the consent of Shaykh Abdul Ahat M'Baké, heir of the Prophet and caliph of the Murids since 1968.[49]

This pattern was by no means unique. In the Tijaniyya brotherhood, the great traditional chiefs were similarly eager to demonstrate their adherence to the French cause. French support seemed to offer them a basis for the religious expansion that would guarantee the stability of the traditional social order. In the 1930s, the great marabout Seydu Nuru Tall, grandson of El Hajj Umar, toured French West Africa under the auspices of the colonial authorities. By escorting him and receiving him in the principal urban centers, they honored the Muslim communities, which were at once dynamic and submissive, and they supported their unifying influence. In this way they utilized the immobilizing force of an ideology that, in the name of religious obedience, demanded that its adherents display docility.[50]

Because he appeared to oppose this tendency, the colonial administration constantly harassed Hamallah. In a familiar sequence of events, his preaching was sparked by the crisis that overtook the herdsmen of Nioro du Sahel, who in about 1913 were grappling with drought and its associated food shortages and epidemics. Ignoring these disasters, the colonizers demanded that the herdsmen pay the grazing tax (*zakat*)—a Koranic institution whose collection by infidels was felt to be a sacrilege. Moreover, they controlled the wanderings of the nomads by instituting a system of passes. The marabouts interpreted this social and economic disequilibrium as a punishment from God, making fertile ground for a Mahdist movement.

Shaykh Hamallah's doctrine, originally strictly religious, was based on the Tijaniyya. He demanded a return to the original purity of religious practice, notably in the choice of formulas for the recitation of prayers (eleven rosary beads instead of twelve). Like Amadu Bamba, he was unconcerned with reevaluation of the traditional social order or opposition to colonial law. At the most, as a believer, he adopted a policy of passive resistance by means of an eloquent silence; that is to say, he tried to avoid all contact with the infidel French authorities.

The French were nevertheless worried about Hamallah's growing influence, which manifested itself on several occasions, for example, Bamako in 1917 and Nioro du Sahel in 1923. The incidents looked like doctrinal quarrels between the Tijani and the shaykh's followers. It would be absurd, however, to suppose that they were simple matters of religious interpretation. These divergences revealed, rather, Hamallah's opposition to the Umarian Tijani leaders who had collaborated with the colonial authorities. The traditional Tijani leadership, whose privileges were threatened, were the first to call for measures of repression against Hamallah and his followers. In 1925 the administration exiled Hamallah for ten years to Mauritania and then, fearing new troubles, to the Ivory Coast.

In Mauritania, in the 1930s, the movement became a form of social protest that could include the use of violence. Its leader, Yacuba Sylla, included in his preaching such egalitarian demands as the suppression of castes and the emancipation of captives (although he also called for the confinement of women), and economic requirements similar to those of the Murids. Finally deported to the Ivory Coast, he organized in the community of Gagnoa a little economic and commercial empire that still exists today.

Hamallah himself returned to Mali and in 1940 was accused of inciting violent tribal antagonisms. He was promptly deported once again, this time first to Algeria and then to France, where he died in 1943. Although no one claimed to be his spiritual successor, the movement he originated spread all over West Africa. Perhaps despite himself, precisely because he gave expression to the still confused aspirations to freedom of the populations of the Sahel he became a symbol to rally the latent forces of opposition to the colonial presence. Strictly speaking, he had no political role; no Hamallist authority tried, after the war, to recruit members for the Rassemblement Démocratique Africain, but the experience of solidarity under oppression and the personal example of Yacuba Sylla prompted many of his followers to join the nascent nationalist party.[51]

The period of the Taquiyya and the religious brotherhoods as places of refuge was coming to an end. When World War II began, Islam, from its place among the political, syndicalist, and nationalist movements then coming into being, sought to provide leadership for patterns of struggle both in the East and in the West. Once again an urban movement, the Muslim reformism in sub-Saharan Africa attached to itself a school of thought that in the Arab world went back to the nineteenth century. This original element, as yet little studied, of the liberation movements took root especially in the Mandingo areas (Mali, Guinea, Ivory Coast). It expressed in particular the desire of the Dyula bourgeoisie to create specific methods of cultural liberation, notably through the development of a competitive system of education in Arabic.

This form of Islamic resistance almost disappeared after 1950, but in the last few years it has enjoyed a vigorous revival in a somewhat different form, especially in rural areas. The Iranian religious revolution has sponsored it, in the form of the Young Murid movement, for instance, and al-Qaddafi's Libya has constructed Arab mosques and universities and has launched a lavish propaganda campaign. Here we can clearly see a development from religious dispute to contemporary political action, but in neither version were the peasants the motivating force. At most, they were an indispensable tool for urban political leaders, to whom the ever-increasing rural malaise guarantees the vast numbers of followers they crave.

CONCLUSIONS

Some generalizations can be derived from this confused, variegated picture. The local aristocracies have always sought to preserve what privileges they could, by accepting for better or worse places offered them in the new cadres and learning to manipulate them for their own benefit. The peasants in the depths of rural Africa, however, have never accepted colonization: at most, rural Africa submitted to colonization as earlier it had endured various other forms of coercion or despotism. The peasant movements, then, differed in a basic way from other forms of rebellion.

The peasant movements were ambivalent in character, being at once progressive in their demand for liberation of people and of their labor, and conservative in their archaism, which was often flavored with a millenarianism that belonged emotionally to the precapitalist world. (Such archaism, of course, commonly appears in the history of peasant uprisings in Europe and elsewhere.)[52] This peasant rejection of modernity was set against a background of hidden or open resistance. Periodically, when the situation became particularly serious massive violence broke out, motivated by an incipient nationalism that worked to unify the rural areas. In general, however, the rebellions were badly organized: even if the leader was followed enthusiastically by the masses (as in the case of a jihad), the structure of the revolt was nebulous and even its medium-range objectives were rarely defined.

A Typology of Rebellion

To make sense of the profusion of forms of rebellion, a typology is needed. To begin with, the passive forms of resistance (flight by individuals or groups, emigration, banditry) can be separated from the active forms or open revolt. The motivation also varied, including one or more of such issues as: difficulties of subsistence exacerbated by a crisis that made outside pressures on the peasantry unbearable; the struggle to retain or repossess traditional lands and to defend traditional rights; rejection of taxation; resistance to conscription; and any perceived religious persecution.

Except in Ethiopia, African peasant agitation was not generally expressed by the demand, so common elsewhere in the world, for agrarian reform. This peculiarity shows a less developed consciousness of the seizure of land, even though nowadays it happens no less in Africa than in other regions.

The forms of political organization certainly played a part. Except in those relatively exceptional cases where a "national" political structure traditionally existed, the most fragmented societies were the most ready to revolt, because it was to them that state control was most alien. These societies fostered the movements that were most popular in character, in the fullest sense of the word, bringing into play previously unrealized forces—women, and leaders who emerged from the people rather than having been chiefs or men of learning.

These most fragmented societies were less inegalitarian than the others. Their nonhierarchical social organization did not permit them to carry out the transformations that were regarded as necessary for movements of rebellion. Their traditional forms of internal regulation were incapable of handling the aggravated tensions caused by the demands of colonialism; hence they inevitably had recourse to the supernatural, to religious pressures, and to sorcery, the only paths of escape open to them.

The religion of the group also helped to determine the response to colonialism. Sometimes, though relatively rarely, the religion preached a message of social protest; sometimes, by contrast, an ideology of absolute submission to the will of God could, in the hands of a fiery interpreter, become a mighty instrument of rebellion. The level of development of a people or its degree of integration into a modern economy was also generally of significance. Either, as most frequently happened, the group in its isolation saw nothing to lose in a total rejection of the European system, or else they tried at first to profit from the system and later perceived themselves as having been the exploited ones. Finally, the process of colonization—the relative brutality, the willingness and ability of the colonizers to collaborate—affected the reaction of the peasants.

These factors explain why West Africa, which was one of the areas most affected by colonial wars of conquest, never in the twentieth century underwent large-scale peasant revolts comparable to those in Central or East Africa (such as the Kongo-Warra and Mau Mau uprisings and the rebellions in Zaire). In general, this region had been accustomed for a century or more to territorial organization more or less along state lines. Its integration into the Western economy—this was probably a crucial factor—was older and therefore more firmly rooted than elsewhere, and the style of colonization, whether French or British, was less crude; the policy did not involve legal segregation or expropriation of lands or, as a rule, abuses of forced labor.

It is, then, impossible to classify peoples according to a hypothetical "aptitude for revolt," since in the same group the factors we have listed could vary according to period and circumstances.

One feature of these peasant movements, however, has remained constant up till today. The rural community, which is bound to a tight social system by an ancient and complex network of relationships, organizes "against" something: once against the chief, then against the *commandant,* today against the bureaucrat. Whatever form the authority—that is, the state— takes, it manifests itself to the peasants through its demands and rarely or never through gifts or immediate benefits, except in the "good old days," as seen through rose-colored glasses. Neither today nor in the past has peasant resistance portended political revolution, if by that is meant the substitution of a new state—just, honest, socialist or otherwise—for an existing state that is intrinsically evil. They have been oppressed for at least a century, and probably from the beginning of their history, by the ever-increasing demands of one regime after another. Today, possibly more than in the past, African peasants, often barely surviving, aspire not to change the face of power but to reject it—which means in practice, for want of a better option, ignoring it. Herein lies the problem of peasant consciousness-raising, the difficulty of which revolutionary intellectuals so deplore. To try to change the state would merely mean to change masters—a useless proceeding. Revolutionary intellectuals brought together with rebellious peasants in African prisons have found that dialogue between the two groups can hardly be sustained, for their concepts, objectives, and modes of reasoning all differ or are even opposed.

The Three Conditions for a Peasant Revolution

The situation described above poses, in a more general way, the question of the revolutionary potential of the African peasantry—that is to say, whether it is capable of bringing about a total transformation of the existing social and economic structures. The twentieth century appears to be a time of peasant revolutions: no longer spasmodic, lawless rebellions, explosive but secondary manifestations born of frustrations like those just described, but struggles of national and social liberation aiming at changing the system of government and the distribution of authority. These are protracted struggles, involving the formation of political cadres, the training of disciplined soldiers, the creation of efficient structures of finance and provisioning, and the establishment of a broad base of resistance, both active and passive. Outside sub-Saharan Africa, a number of cases have been widely studied: China, Vietnam, Cuba, Algeria.[53] Sub-Saharan Africa offers a number of more or less localized instances of such true revolutions: in Cameroon, in Guinea-Bissau, in northern Mozambique, to some degree in Ethiopia, and, as was at one time thought, in Zaire and in Chad. The problem is to discover the circumstances in which such a development can take place and why it still happens so seldom in sub-Saharan Africa.

The first condition for revolution by a peasantry is a reasonable openness to the world economy.[54] It is claimed that the further agriculture has entered into a cycle of dependence on the international market, the greater the political consciousness of the peasants will be. Although this argument contains much truth, it is nevertheless not universally applicable, for rebellions continue to occur in areas where there is a closed system of subsistence. Such rebellions take place when peasants refuse to let the fragile equilibrium of their existence be threatened by ill-thought-out programs of development. This happened as recently as the 1950s in the northeast of Northern Rhodesia (Zambia): a peasant revolt swept over the chiefs, who had vacillated between the obligation of applying the colonial rules and the opposition from the peasants on whom they were imposed.[55]

It is nevertheless true that the more widely rural society is exposed to modernization, the more the regulation of conduct according to traditional social values diminishes, for the society progressively loses its homogeneity. The grouping according to families and lineages becomes less significant than the hierarchy separating the proletariat on the one hand (not only in the limited sense of agricultural laborers but, more generally, the exploited small peasants), and the class, in formation or already well established, of proprietor-planters or even, sometimes, entrepreneurs of industrial agriculture on the other hand. (From this can be understood the problem of the validity of the blanket term *peasant:* the concept clearly does not include all inhabitants of rural areas or all those who live off the soil.) Such villagers now live in a more complex world: the chief and notables are employed by the administration to transmit to the community elements imported from the outside. The peasants, for their part, either voluntarily or under compulsion, experience new forms of organization—for instance, cooperative farming—that depend both on new internal forms of organization of work and on external directives, subsidies, and markets.

Here is the crux of the difficulty. On the one hand, the more marked social differences are, the harder it is to achieve peasant unity, but on the other hand a relatively egalitarian framework does not necessarily ease this process. Unlike the workers in a factory, the nature of whose work promotes solidarity, the members of a rural community do not see why, in order to assure the vitality of their own unit of production, the neighboring unit should flourish like themselves. Despite some periodic collective tasks, rural life consists in essence of the individual exploitation of land.

The second condition for revolution is that it must seem to be the only possible escape from a level of exploitation that is felt to be not only intolerable but exceptional. This situation prevails when anachronistic residues of colonial rule remain (such as the Portuguese colonies in an Africa that was largely independent) or when the government is particularly inept and notoriously corrupt (as was that of the Congo in the 1960s). But conditions such as these are rare; otherwise many African rural areas would be in a state of revolution today.

In the increasingly differentiated society of sub-Saharan Africa, revolution requires a certain conjunction of revolutionary forces. This casts some doubt on the concept of a pure *peasant revolution*. The term has been said to be a misuse of language imputable both to the revolutionary leaders themselves (such as Mao, Che Guevara, Fidel Castro, or Amilcar Cabral), to the interpretations of theoreticians (Frantz Fanon, Eric Wolf), and to the mistaken idea that in the Third World there are no other significant social classes, such as workers and/or intellectuals.[56] Far from being a product of the peasantry, it is claimed, a revolution usually begins in the most advanced areas of the peripheral economy (among the proletariat of Petrograd in Russia, for instance, or in the coastal cities of China and in the capital city of Havana in Cuba). At this stage, however, the movement could still be nipped in the bud. It becomes a revolution only when the masses in the "backward" areas—that is, the rural masses—give the movement their support.

Even supposing, however, that the nucleus of the revolt was rural, the thinkers and ideologists appear to be of paramount importance. The peasants may prove able to undertake spontaneous actions that act as a call for help from the political arena in the face of a crushing exploitation, but they show little capacity for organizing the movement, precisely because the experience of the world to which they appeal can only be gained in the city and in school. Leaders of peasant revolts vanish as quickly as they appear. If the movement is not provided with a solid underlying structure, it rapidly disintegrates or turns into an unorganized insurrection. The Congolese rebellions of 1964–1965, for example, disintegrated owing to the limited political culture of Pierre Mulele and the lack of ideological clarity among the leaders.

By contrast, Cuba in the West Indies and Mozambique and Zimbabwe in

Africa experienced the type of rebellion, moderate and reformist at the start, that tended to be radicalized. Leaders such as Amilcar Cabral became increasingly convinced that unless the movement received the support of the rural majority, it would never come to anything, but it was a desperately difficult task even for these talented intellectuals, who were aware of the dynamics of rural discontent, to provide the peasants with the means to be heard.

The third condition for peasant revolutions in the strict sense, then, is an accompanying intelligentsia to organize them and to provide them with the necessary ideology. The actions, writings, and political effectiveness of the leaders of such movements often show them to be exceptional people. In Africa, we have the examples of Amilcar Cabral in Guinea, Eduardo Mondlane and, above all, Samora Machel in Mozambique and Robert Mugabe in Zimbabwe. Cabral, in particular, acted on his grasp of the need to give priority to the rural commune as a center of struggle and also of training and decision-making.[57] That was why, in its time, the populist, rural, and decentralized conception of an insurrection in Guinea-Bissau aroused so many hopes. Unfortunately, a great disparity showed itself between theory and practice. The rural community proved relatively unresponsive, because the first factor we mentioned was lacking: the rural areas of Guinea-Bissau were among those least affected by the Western economy. In contrast, the Ethiopian peasant insurrection succeeded, for a brief period at least, in its agrarian reforms, because it accomplished them by and for itself, putting aside for a while all initiatives of central power. Eventually, however, the ruling group, facing regional secessions and the demands of the military economy, relinquished the movement in favor of a system of centralization, thus halting the peasant revolution.

Wherever any one of the three factors we have described—an openness to the world economy, a situation of particular injustice and corruption, and an ideological and organizational leadership—is lacking, the peasantry must remain passive in the face of even the direst misery.

The Growth of Consciousness

The growth of peasant consciousness, as defined by their capacity to build rural institutions of reform, can be divided into three distinct stages.

The first stage, a passive one, is the state of "accommodation" dear to John Kenneth Galbraith.[58] This state does not imply submission to the exterior. On the contrary, the peasants have either proved impervious to acculturation or have been driven into a situation so wretched that they have no power to escape and cannot even rebel, beyond spasmodic and futile protests. They try as far as possible to avoid meeting the requirements of the exterior, but they believe themselves unable to influence or manipulate institutions from the inside. The notables, of course, do not fit this description, for their position as mediators predisposes them to take advantage of their situation. In sub-Saharan Africa, as in Latin America and India, for example, most of the rural areas seem to have remained more or less at this stage.

The next stage is a pragmatic one. The peasants look for individual advantages or specific social gains: an increase in the price paid for their products, an improvement in transport services, the use of tools or other equipment. Their degree of commitment to a rural organization such as a cooperative, a commune, or a trade union thus appears proportionate to the advantages they can hope to gain from it.

Passing beyond this stage depends on their capacity to conceive more elaborate demands, transcending the level of the household or the local group and bringing the community together in common action: boycotts or refusal to sell their crops to wholesalers or government organizations, or mass demonstrations for a good such as the construction or the repair of a road or a bridge. Once again, the advantages to be hoped for must appear greater than the risks involved.

To the degree that the peasants obtain satisfaction, they lose their distrust of the rural organization; more people join, and the ideological base widens. A militant role is often taken by the youngest members, who become frustrated at seeing power concentrated in the hands of the elders. They want the rapid evolution of the relations of the village with the outside world to alter the social institutions of the community. At this stage, the peasants join a movement that promises few or no immediate advantages to their group of origin, while the risk of provoking repressive governmental action increases. Now effective political leadership becomes essential. Such leaders must realize the patience and tenacity with which their aims have to be pursued; they must be determined to maintain the democratic practices that have been systematically built up from scratch; and they must be prepared to support the escalating requirements of the peasantry after the first, relatively straightforward demands (for health services and primary and general education) have been met.

Most often, the movement fails tragically before it reaches this last stage. The peasants remain at the bottom of the economic hierarchy; the new cadres appropriate for themselves the advantages that have been gained; and the chance of obtaining major collective benefits through the existing system remains slight or even diminished. The commonest reaction is a final loss of confidence in the state.

In the political and economic context, both in Africa and elsewhere, those in power, of whatever ideological orientation, generally do not believe that the development described above can be achieved. Their short-term objective is the constitution of a unitary nation-state out of many diverse linguistic and cultural forces. They wish to be able to respond to problems posed by the outside world, such as the possibility of economic dependence on major powers, or political and military threats. This is the drama of Mozambique, which along its 2,600 kilometers in length and sometimes less than 100 kilometers in breadth faces the dangers both of South Africa and of Soviet strategy in Africa. The leadership of Mozambique sees itself as constrained to impose on all its rural masses the national language of the former colonizer, the rejection of ancestral customs, and a centralized system of communal villages. Under these conditions it would be naive to believe in the rural masses' full support of the revolutionary state, except in the rare cases when they have received substantial material benefits.

Peasants are by no means the only ones in Africa to express essentially rural demands and discontents. All the primary movements (and here the term takes on not only a chronological but also a qualitative sense) used the essentially rural indigenous cultural and political background as their standard of reference in their attempts to remedy the colonial situation. The political, social, and ideological upheavals of the twentieth century brought such movements together with, and in opposition to, the "modern," post-1920 syndicalist and national movements, first by mineworkers and then in the cities. Workers and unassimilated migrants to the urban areas continued to feel themselves members of rural communities, to which they occasionally returned to engage in periodic labor.

When independence came, all these interwoven elements combined in the new political parties. Western parliamentary techniques were superimposed on a complex background in which various religious elements, millenarian and charismatic currents, and recourse to the world of the supernatural mingled chaotically with demands for immediate amelioration of the profound social and economic distress. The masses suffer from a mental and social disorientation that—even today—leads them to vote for a chief, a marabout, a prophet no less than for the ostensibly Europeanized political leader, who nevertheless makes full use of all these elements. From the time a "modern" political organization develops, no expression of discontent or rebellion is strictly speaking a peasant movement—that is to say, a movement with an exclusively rural ideology. They are all predominantly rural movements, certainly, which can still be situated mainly in the countryside, but their complex and dynamic undercurrents of, for example, urbanism, subproletarianization, or syndicalism come from the modern urban world. The result is necessarily an acceleration in changes in the way of thinking, and the final outcome can only be an overturning of traditional values.

PART IV

Labor and the City

Africa's Future

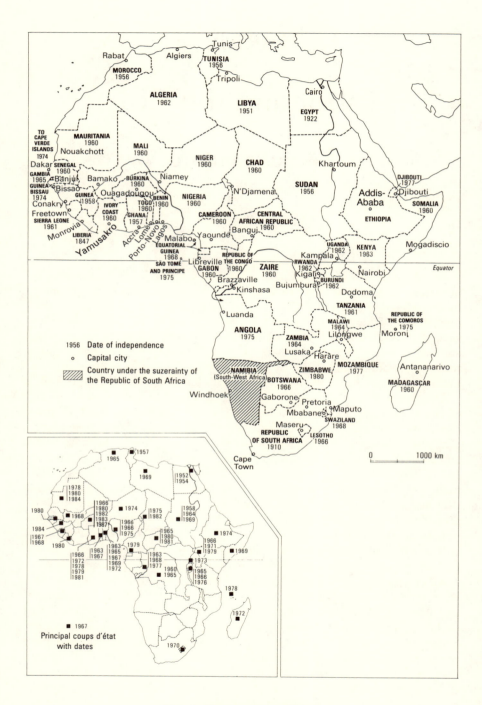

Map 6. *Contemporary Africa*

For the past half-century peasants have been abandoning the rural areas in increasing numbers. Driven out by poverty and landlessness or attracted by the mirage of a new life with regular wages, a share in the money economy, and a Western lifestyle—a radio, Western-style clothes, and activities such as football and the movies—they swarm to the cities, to the mining, administrative or industrial centers. Demographic expansion in the cities really began only in the 1930s. Since World War II in Africa, as in Asian and Latin American cities, the influx has swelled dramatically.

Until quite recently, Africa was preponderantly rural (in 1950, 85 percent of the population lived in rural areas; even in 1980, more than 70 percent were still rural). Between 1950 and 1980 the population tripled, and nearly two-thirds of this increase took place in rural areas. Between 1980 and 1990 this growth will accelerate (in the 23 years to 1960, the increase of 161 million doubled the population; between 1960 and 1980, it took 171 million to do so) and before the century comes to an end, for the first time over half will live in urban areas. Nearly two-thirds of the total growth will take place between 1990 and 2000, with a population increase of 126 million. In contrast to the rural expansion of 1950–1980, this massive increase will take place in urban areas. In other words, in the second half of the twentieth century the African urban population will have multiplied tenfold.

Of course, the trend is not distributed uniformly across the fifty-five African states. The most populated, Nigeria (around 100 million inhabitants) and Ethiopia (31 million); the largest, Zaire and the Sudan; and the least populated, Mauritania, Niger, and Gabon (which is clearly underpopulated), all face different problems. However, except for Rwanda and Burundi, two small, densely populated rural countries in the heart of Africa that are just beginning to develop their cities, and for the South African enclaves such as Lesotho and Swaziland, African states are undergoing an unprecedented wave of urbanization. The annual urban growth-rate in Kenya has almost reached 6 percent. Today this continent-wide phenomenon is matched nowhere else in the world.[1]

The African city today acts as a meeting place for social and political extremes and as a laboratory for new forms of adaptation to the "modern" world. The vague and banal expression "informal sector" does not begin to do justice to this new social reality. Sociologists have analyzed its functionings and its impediments; economists have examined its productive and obstructive mechanisms. It now remains for us to give its history. We shall proceed in four stages.

Chapter 10 examines how contemporary urbanization came into existence. Colonization brought into being a labor market. This market created and then exploited flows of migration to form a body of wage earners and an urban milieu.

Chapter 11 describes how the processes of concentration and proletarianization early gave rise to "modern" resistance movements. The Africans thus expressed their wish to regain their independence. More important, in these revolts the Africans placed themselves on the same footing and saw themselves in the same terms as the Whites. They claimed rights in a new society that they were attempting to create. Trade unionism, strikes, and protonationalism belong to this phase of development.

In Chapter 12 we see how the "modernized" literate urban elites evolved between the two world wars. These elites emerged partly from the newly Western-educated and partly from the traditional chiefdoms. They took over the role of the old elites and helped to give a political coloring to the first social protest movements. However, a huge gap remained between these elites and the largely unorganized, ill-defined, semi-proletarianized groups, who were still very close to the soil, neither truly rural nor truly urban. Soon after the end of World War II, spontaneous and transitory forms of joint action—boycotts, riots, general strikes—brought a foretaste of populism.

Chapter 13 brings all these factors together as elements in contemporary urban society. Here the "informal" or "unstructured" sector, which was formed in the course of this slow process, tends to play the dominant role. Islam, surprisingly, has little political force, except as a signal of the depth of the social crisis. It remains to be seen whether these disparate social forces can resolve the deep economic, demographic, and political problems that face Africa today.

10

Workers:
From Labor Migration to
Proletarianization

The development of a labor force began in labor migrations. Four main centers attracted such migrations: mines and their compounds; plantations; public works (road-building, ports, railways); and administration of the "colonial peace," which needed recruits to carry out its policies (e.g., soldiers, militiamen, technical personnel). These migrations acted as the sole concrete connection between two seemingly contradictory worlds, the "capitalist" and the "domestic." When the two worlds met in this way, problems inevitably arose concerning wages and living conditions, for Western capitalism spawned social and economic demands.

LABOR MIGRATIONS

The process of labor migrations, although primarily based on motivations, arose and grew from a number of factors. *Homo economicus* of course exists in Africa as elsewhere: the difference in remuneration between work in the rural areas and work in the city, between work in Africa and work in the West is clearly a factor in mobility, but it is not the only one. First, the social and historical circumstances of the original rural milieu play as large a role as does the degree of poverty. The cohesion of the group (the well-placed taking charge of the underprivileged), the system of land ownership and land distribution, and the accepted values can act, to an equal degree, as an incitement or as an impediment to migration. Above all, the migrant flow was always socially differentiated. Not only the poorest workers—illiterate peasants driven by demographic pressure from the areas most neglected by capitalist development—emigrated. The children of notables—administrative chiefs or small-scale planters—also left, in search of a skill or a profession corresponding to their aspirations. People hoped that the city would provide them not only with a means of subsistence but with a different quality of life, the guarantee of individual independence and of a certain social prestige connected with "modernity."

As of the early 1920s, this attitude was taken by the very small minority of aides to the colonial administration (clerks, interpreters, and so on), who were mainly based in economically weak colonies such as Dahomey and in small colonial urban centers, rather than in the areas of concentration of the labor force (compounds, ports, railway stations). Changing conditions, both in the place of origin (such as kulakization of the rural areas) and in the place of immigration (for example, the development of urban strata), contributed to the appeal of migration. After World War II, the intensity and the diversity of migrancy increased as the city offered more social and cultural opportunities to the migrants (see Chapter 13).

Seasonal Migrations

Even before the colonial period, seasonal agriculture necessitated labor migrations. In the indigenous rural economy, by the middle of the nineteenth century *navetanes* supplied labor for peanut cultivation for export. In 1930 about 30,000 of these workers from Upper Volta and Guinea were working in Senegambia. Similarly, the Ghanaian cocoa plantations at the turn of the twentieth century practiced the *abusan* system, using immigrant sharecroppers, and the same system became widespread a generation later on the Ivory Coast.

The seasonal ebb and flow of agricultural workers preserved their rural identification. The urban workers, too, remained close to the soil, because they had no specific new locus. They went wherever work was to be found: in the rainy season, to the fields; in the dry season, to the cities. They had not as yet learned to differentiate clearly between the life of the town and that of the country.

A qualitative analysis of rural and urban hourly wages in Senegal in the 1920s shows that rural wages for peanut production exceeded urban wages. The low and unchanging level of urban wages made such work attractive only when there was a crisis of subsistence (as in 1921 in Senegal). At other times the rural areas provided not only their own subsistence but that of their migrants. The city served as a center of consumption rather than of production. It won a labor force only by simultaneously controlling labor supply and demand and regulating its flow, although without assuring either its maintenance or its reproduction.

This urban migration remained temporary and seasonal, as is shown by an analysis of the passenger-load on the Dakar–Saint Louis railway, which passed through the great peanut-producing area of Cayor. In 1922, the total passenger-load was equal to an impressive 43 percent of the population of the colony (which of course is not to say that the number of *individuals* using the railway was that high). The numbers fluctuated seasonally: in the rainy season (June to October) most of the country-dwellers engaged in cultivation in their own fields. Movement started again during the peanut sea-

TABLE 4.   Hourly Payment of Workers in Senegal
(100 = wages of an urban worker, 1919)

	City (worker in Dakar)	Rural areas (peanut cultivator)
1919	100	270
1920	107	126
1921	152	119
1922	115	207
1923	122	300
1924	137	455
Average	122	283

SOURCES: M. Lakroum, *Le Travail inégal: Paysans et salariés sénégalais face à la crise des années 30* (Paris, 1983); André Vanhaeverbeke, *Rémunération du travail et commerce extérieur: Essor d'une économie paysanne exportatrice et termes de l'échange des producteurs d'arachides au Sénégal* (Louvain, 1970).

NOTE: Urban wages are defined as the minimum hourly sum paid by the colonial administration; rural wages are calculated according to the amount of annual work necessary for raising peanuts, estimated at the time as roughly 480 hours of labor per ton.

son and increased throughout the dry period. The Africans did not drain continuously and irreversibly into the cities; rather, the city seasonally turned into a sort of population storehouse. Moreover, cities did not grow linearly: a trade crisis, an epidemic, or a war like that of 1914–1918 could put a halt to expansion.

Dakar was quite typical, and Kano, Nigeria, one of the large towns of the interior, was equally representative, although the timing of growth differed there. In Kano, rapid growth of the peanut trade caused a fairly fast process of urbanization in the 1920s (the average annual rate of increase equaled 1.4 percent between 1911 and 1921, 6.1 percent between 1921 and 1931). Then the Depression years of 1931–1935 saw a definite decline (−3.6 percent). The Kano-Nguru railway (inaugurated in 1930) extended to new peanut-producing areas, and a succession of rainy years enabled a still unsettled population to respond to the economic crisis by returning to the bush under relatively favorable conditions.[1]

The "Push-Pull" Movement

This migration between the cities and the rural areas was implicitly preserved by the colonial powers and by traditional rural constraints. The "push-pull" movement has been described by British and American economists and anthropologists: economic factors had a centrifugal effect, while the social system had a centripetal one. The interplay of these opposing forces resulted in a continual oscillation between the agricultural community and the external economy.

Economic pressures in the rural areas forced people to the cities to earn money for feeding and supporting the family, paying taxes, and meeting such social requirements as proving worth or demonstrating virility. In Namibia, for example, miners with families usually remain in the compounds twice as long as bachelors.[2]

At the same time, the necessity of maintaining agricultural production, land rights, and family connections and the desire to live in familiar surroundings encourage the migrant worker to return to the village. The workers find it unpleasant to be separated from their families, even if social, cultural, and economic factors make such a separation desirable. For example, the wives must remain to tend the land and livestock, on which the family's survival depends; city education is perceived as "corrupting" the children; and the migrants do not wish their families to share the workers' humiliations. The emphasis given to magical practices and the frequency of dispatches of "medicinal" herbs that guarantee a wife's fidelity testify to workers' homesickness.[3] Yet, the role of social pressure ought not to be exaggerated. To some extent it is put forward simply as the best excuse to give to the Whites. It would be dangerous to say that the workers were leaving because they had earned sufficient money (that might cause their employer to reduce their wages) or because they found the attitude of the White supervisors unbearable. These reasons, although unpresentable, doubtless generally prove paramount in the workers' decision to return home.

In areas of concentrated population, water pollution and poor sanitation rendered survival uncertain until these problems were tackled in the 1920s. Before World War I, epidemics of typhoid, influenza, and pneumonia killed about 25 percent of the urbanized Congolese of Elisabethville (Lubumbashi). It was hardly surprising, therefore, that when an epidemic of influenza broke out in 1913, half the workers left the city. The Mossi migrants of the Upper Volta had a proverb illustrating the terrible dangers they had to face: "The White man's work eats people up." In short, for many years, urban-dwellers faced higher deathrates than did the peasants who had remained in their traditional surroundings. Fatigue, sickness, and accidents convinced workers to return home. In the gold mines of Southern Rhodesia, out of a total of more than 17,000 workers in 1906 that rose to 36,000 in 1920, 2,000 died of accidents within the first twenty years of the century, and more than 18,000 died in the compounds of disease (7 percent of them during the Spanish influenza epidemic of 1918).[4] Such statistics, to be sure, no longer hold, but the myth of the devouring city survives.

The urban center nevertheless attracts, because of its real or imagined opportunities for work. Employers draw their employees from the rural areas in order to keep salaries low and to avoid having to provide for the needs of families. Legal restrictions have enabled the system to be preserved. In the colonial period, limitations on the length of contracts guaranteed a rapid turnover. Today, states such as South Africa and Namibia prohibit families from settling in areas of production.

The Urban Labor Market

The impoverishment of the rural areas generated the conditions for the overgrowth of cities characteristic of the Third World today. The expansion of the coastal cities, at least, can be traced directly to the Depression of the 1930s. Such cities can be regarded as "overgrown" only when the inflow of migration takes place without a corresponding increase in opportunities for work (in the West, unlike the Third World, the growth of cities in the nineteenth century was also spectacular, but opportunity paralleled population growth). When work became scarce in the early 1930s, poor peasants began to form the basis of an urban subproletariat. In the Maghreb the first *bidonvilles* (shantytowns) began to appear;[5] in French West Africa, the cities began to inflate as the global rhythm of demographic growth plunged from an increase of one million between 1926 and 1931, to an increase of only 200,000 between 1931 and 1936, out of a total of 19.6 million in 1936. In sharp contrast, the population of the three principal ports swelled. Dakar doubled and Abidjan sextupled its rate of increase, and even Conakry, reversing its previous tendency (a decrease of 7.5 percent between 1926 and 1931), doubled its rate of increase from 1931 to 1936.

In Africa, population mobility and shifting job opportunities are by no means new. Long-term migrations, however, appear to be a purely contemporary consequence of the very unequal development of adjoining areas. In West Africa (apart from Nigeria), probably 5 million inhabitants moved from the north to the south between 1920 and 1970, accentuating the contrast between the relatively barren Sahel and the "useful" coastal areas. In the same period, the overall population nearly tripled, from 15.2 to almost 40 million. The population of the interior only doubled, while that of the coastal regions nearly quadrupled (from 5.1 to 18.7 million). Much of the relatively slow rate of growth of the inland areas can be attributed to the flow of emigration. The rhythm of urban growth accelerated. In Nigeria, a country that had long been remarkably urbanized, in the decade 1950–1960 the rate jumped from the 2.1 percent of 1920 (hardly more than the general rate of demographic growth in the country at that time) to 5.5 percent. In the twenty years from 1950 to 1970, then, the Nigerian towns, which had previously been sustained by their own demography, absorbing few immigrants, took in more than two million.[6] Rhodesia underwent a similar large-scale absorption of reserves of cheap labor.[7]

Coercion and forced labor have long ceased to act as precipitating factors in labor migration. From World War II on, the problem, on the contrary, has been to control the inflow of Africans who voluntarily came to look for work in the cities. The economic factor plays a large part. The comparative cost of the act of migration itself has decreased considerably in the last half-century. In addition, the temporal and cultural distance between the rural areas and the cities has lessened. In 1930, an immigrant from the northern Gold Coast needed two or three weeks to reach Kumasi. Today, by truck, it takes only one day to go as far as Accra. Finally, health measures and mass inoculations have improved the rate of survival in the cities, and the death-rate has become lower there than in the bush.

Migration has a "snowball" effect: one migrant attracts another, and each subsequent one receives a great deal of assistance from members of his family or social group who are already established in the city. Above all, after the young people—those who are most productive, most open to inno-vation—leave a particular area on account of its poverty, stagnation sets in, further impoverishing the area. Moreover, as in southern Nigeria, the ex-penses of education for migrants to the cities plus the assistance they receive, both in money and in kind, from their families in the rural areas may exceed the sums the city-dwellers sent back to the country: the richer area receives a net transfer of capital.[8]

Finally, a land shortage developed. Since the 1960s, probably half the continent and at least half of its population have felt the effects of demo-graphic pressure. Today, forty-eight of the fifty-two African nations suffer in differing degrees from a lack of land, and for twenty-three of them it has become a national problem.[9] The cities contain a stratum of unfortunate, landless young men from rural areas who, if they find nothing in the city, have nothing to lose there either. Migrants who have long been settled in the city, they are desperate, little educated, and forced into the most marginal activities. Even in countries, such as Tanzania and Kenya, that are not con-sidered overpopulated, the problem exists. In Tanzania, a 1971 study of 5,000 people in seven large towns showed that one-quarter of the male in-habitants possessed no land,[10] and a 1976 study of more than 3,000 heads of families in a dozen urban shantytowns in Kenya revealed that about half of them had less than one hectare apiece. Many possessed less than 0.1 hec-tares, while from 6 to 20 percent had no land at all.[11] In all, at least two-thirds of the squatters of Nairobi and Mombasa are landless and earn their living in the "informal" (noncapitalist) sector.

Namibia, an Extreme Case

We now come to the most contemporary and the best example of the in-exorable process of labor migration.[12] Namibia has enormous mineral re-sources, which have been mined since World War II. Diamonds have been discovered, particularly in the south, as well as lead, zinc, copper, and, recently, uranium in the central region around the capital, Windhoek, the only sizable city. In 1946, mining products accounted for 13 percent of the gross national product; the figure rose to 40 percent in 1960 and 60 percent in 1973. The mining industries of this underpopulated country employ only migrant workers from the overpopulated "homelands" of the north, a practice that has been systematized since the 1960s. Migrant Ovambo constitute about half of the total population (46.5 percent). The system of working under contract has nearly quadrupled the number of Ovambo in Namibia, from 91,000 in 1921 to 342,000 in 1970. The homeland has 367 people to the square kilometer. Permanent migration is prohibited but, under international pressure, South Africa has made considerable investments in the reserve over the past fifteen years. These improvements have caused the number of Ovambo migrant workers to decline slightly. Nonetheless, at least a third, if not half, of the active population today do not return to the territory (compared to 4 percent before World War II and 10 percent in 1955).

The size of the Namibian labor force has gradually increased, from 47,000 individuals in 1938, just over 50,000 in 1971, to nearly 70,000 today—about 10 percent of the total population. During the same period, the proportion of work under contract doubled, rising from 42 percent to 83 percent. In other words, Namibia depends on migrant labor if it is to mine its resources. The rural areas pay very little for this labor. The lowest wages in South Africa in the 1970s were paid to the miners (hence a crisis occurred in mine employment); the Namibia miners, despite a considerably higher cost of living, received even lower wages, due to Namibia's lack of a minimum-wage law.

At least for the lower-grade workers, return to their "homeland" in the rainy season (January–February), the time of agricultural labor, remains a necessity. The workers therefore prefer the six-month contract, the shortest form, and nearly half of them leave the compound after less than three months. Although the workers detest migrant labor, they regard it as inescapable. Virtually every man from the north has been involved in it at one time or another. To avoid it altogether, enough money must be accumulated to start a small business or to buy the truck that will enable its owner to enter the monetary economy immediately. Such an opportunity, however, rarely occurs. The common fate is that of the migrant worker trapped in a vicious cycle, with each new contract meaning an absence slightly longer than the one before.

This spiral continues indefinitely. The shortage of manpower (resulting from the rapid turnover and the employers' methods of organization) causes a systematic redeployment of recruited workers, which in turn inspires a policy of low pay and long hours. Unskilled and oppressed, the workers are frustrated by the poor wages, the irregular bonuses, the extra hours, and the

early end to their careers. Moreover, the Whites' control is all the more in-
trusive in that the manpower is unqualified, inexperienced, and insufficient
in number. To these disadvantages of the work itself can be added the attraction their original rural milieu holds for the workers, who must leave their
families there. Everything, then, encourages workers to return home in desperation as soon as possible, especially as the rapid turnover of manpower
and legal prohibitions make it almost impossible to establish protective
trade unions.

At the end of 1971, this intolerable situation brought the workers under
contract to engage in a general strike. It lasted two months and, for the first
time, brought out of their international obscurity the 13,000 to 20,000 migrants involved. (Namibian workers had struck at least eighty times since
South Africa took control in 1915; over seventy strikes took place after
1940, and twenty managed to attract the attention of the authorities.) The
1971 strike—apart from an immediate savage repression by order of the
state—only resulted in placing the responsibility for making contracts (formerly the task of the National Labour Office) on the traditional authorities
of the Bantustans. Supposedly, the workers can thus negotiate the conditions
of their employment on a more personal basis. In fact, however, the South
African government has been clever enough to saddle the native authorities
with a highly unpopular task. As of today, the basic system of migrant labor
has not been affected.

International Migrations

African migrant industrial labor does not confine itself to White southern
Africa. Particularly in West Africa, it is today predominantly—and increasingly, despite the parallel rise in unemployment—an international migration. If we take into account clandestine employment, perhaps a quarter of
the workers—and, in some sectors, as many as half of the unskilled or semi-
skilled workers—in France, Switzerland, Germany, and Belgium migrated
from Africa. They come to the centers of industrial capitalism, where they
earn far higher wages than they do at home, because they can no longer survive in the lands of their birth. This "reserve army" of workers guarantees
the elasticity of the capitalist system: replacements are cheap, they can
readily be exploited, and they are dismissed first in a time of crisis.

Authoritarian measures similar to the "colour bar" (British immigration
quotas, Swiss racial referendums, the attempts of Giscard d'Estaing's government to keep families apart) are, if not always applied, at least continually reintroduced. The local working class tends to approve such measures; its classic defensive posture of xenophobia and racism is, after all, not
very different from that of the "poor Whites" in South Africa. The migrants'
inferiority, highlighted by their assignment to jobs disdained by the local

population, their substandard living conditions, and their lack of political rights, contributes to a rapid turnover that results in incapacity to assert social claims and a great vulnerability to repression.[13]

ORIGINS OF THE PROLETARIAT

Unskilled Workers

Clerks and unskilled workers, few in number though they were, were the earliest wage earners of the colonial regime. Outside the mining areas, the carpenters, masons, porters, and diggers were, at least until the 1930s, the principal laborers for the colonizers. In French West Africa at the outbreak of World War II, these wage earners constituted little more than 1 percent of the population (167,000 workers), nearly all employed in places of administration—that is, the urban centers. The ambiguity of the situation can be seen in the following question: can this mass of low-wage earners justifiably be called "proletarians" or a "working class" in the making? On the one hand, these assistants to the colonizers were by no means the most impoverished members of the community. On the other, unskilled workers tended to be recruited from among the disadvantaged of the traditional milieu. When a construction project was planned, the administration notified the chiefs, who collected the slaves, the rebels, people of low standing, and handicapped people of all kinds. When these people had been exploited as laborers and had been separated from their rural origins for several years, they could be said to be ipso facto members of the proletariat, that is, those who have no means of surviving except by their physical strength.

Many of these early "collaborators" reaped the maximum material and social profit from their position at the intersection of two systems. Although they were very lowly wage-earners in European terms, in the eyes of his kinsmen and his village every petty clerk of the administration was invested with a scrap of the White man's authority. Remaining close to his original milieu, which continued to satisfy basic needs, he was able to play a double game. Hamadou Hampaté Ba tells a historical story of the irrepressible rise and misadventures of the interpreter Wangrin. Thanks to his position, he accumulated bribes and livestock, only to lose everything in an unequal procedural struggle against the Whites. In these origins lies the ambiguity of the role played by these "white-collar men" throughout African social history up to our own day, when trade unions operate on behalf of officials rather than workers.

Unskilled workers connected with the cities can clearly be treated as a proletarian group. Considering the sometimes extreme underemployment, they do appear to be relatively privileged. The debatable concept of a *labor aristocracy* seems inapplicable, however, for the wages of a single person must support a whole extended family. Evidence for these workers as a proletariat can be found. For example, one of the first recorded professional organizations was formed by the carpenters of the city of Saint-Louis, Senegal. The carpenters grouped themselves around their most senior and respected member, the master carpenter Thioblet Ndiaye, who was unhappy at the state of subservience in which, despite his relatively important position, the European master carpenters kept him. In 1885, 114 workers drew up a petition requiring any carpenter who wanted to recruit a worker for the Upper River to obtain Ndiaye's authorization. Despite the guild-like character of this petition ("companions" gathering around the "master" of their craft), the initiative expressed a collective professional demand—a sign that this socioprofessional group was becoming conscious of its rights.[14]

Shortly thereafter, the unskilled workers of Lagos also demonstrated solidarity, in one of the earliest strikes yet studied.[15] In 1897 they ceased work in protest against two decisions by a new Governor: to lower their wages and to change their working hours.[16] The scarcity of manpower forced the administration to capitulate after only three days of demonstrations. The municipality of the large port of Lagos, with its nearly 3,000 craftspeople and unskilled laborers, was at that time by far the largest employer in the region. The workers, however, had only recently become city-dwellers. Most were survivors from the slave trade, which had been suppressed in the Lagos area by the annexation of 1961, and many of these people had been employed as servants in African households. The British expansion in the hinterland aided the emancipation of this precolonial labor force. Many managed to set themselves up as small independent planters, while an as yet limited number were drawn to the city by the prospect of a small cash salary. The government employees formed a single independent group, but because they were paid by the day or worked under short-term contracts, most of them remained temporary migrant workers midway between the rural areas and the city, and their organization never passed beyond the rudimentary stage. Although a few professional associations have been recorded in Lagos at that period, their brief unity did not evolve into trade unionism. It did, however, reveal the aspirations of an embryonic proletariat.

The African bourgeoisie of entrepreneurs and traders failed to share the workers' aspirations. On the contrary, they supported the colonial administration through the local press. These careful and prudent prenationalists restricted themselves, in fact, to asking for constitutional reforms favorable to the elite that they represented.

Agricultural Workers

Agricultural workers had existed in Africa for many years. Their status was somewhat ambiguous, however, since the absence or underdevelopment of a monetary economy encouraged practices closer to sharecropping than to a wage system in the strict sense. The *navetanes* of Senegambia have already been discussed. The properous slave-trading economy drew migrant labor to Buganda from the more populated French-speaking areas (the Belgian Congo, particularly the territory of Ruanda-Urundi) and English-speaking ones (Tanganyika, Sudan). These migrations have been recorded from at least the beginning of the colonial period.[17] Since the colonizers generally employed these people as porters, that name came to be applied to them whether their function was agricultural or urban, domestic or commercial.

As late as the 1950s, three-quarters of the several hundred thousand annual immigrants still worked on cotton and coffee plantations, half of them for the Bugandans. This percentage, unusual for Africa, resulted from the Colonial Agreement of 1900, which transformed the provincial chiefs into great landowners. Three different forms of contract were in use (the present tense cannot safely be used for this recently battered country). The commonest form was by the job. The oldest form, mentioned by nineteenth-century travelers, was an agreement to work on a given piece of land in exchange for an allocation of two or three days' worth of food. Most recently a trend appeared toward a regular system of work by the month. Workers' dwellings were provided near the main house. Each worker owed three or four hours of work a day and the fulfillment of a few domestic tasks such as provision of wood and water or babysitting.

Only a few wealthy planters could provide stable employment in this form. At all periods and throughout the area, most laborers were transients. In 1938, out of 86,000 migrants, only a fifth had been there for more than two years, although 18 percent of those interviewed had lived there uninterruptedly for more than ten years. Most, however, returned home every year or two. Moving from place to place, they were essentially temporary workers, unlikely to foster an active movement of social or economic protest.

In a country such as Kenya, colonized by Whites, agricultural work did become the most common form of labor. Even in the Highlands, where Africans were permitted only as employees of the Whites, sharecroppers and wage-earning agricultural workers could not always be regarded as belonging to the proletariat. Since it was traditionally considered a humiliation for a peasant to have to work for someone else, the workers saw their condition as a transitory one. They became agricultural workers only under duress and they quit as soon as possible (when, for example, enough money had been earned to discharge a debt or to pay a dowry). Moreover, as colonization developed, agricultural laborers joined the little local bourgeoisie of planters and traders or migrated to the cities, rather than uniting into a proletariat.[18]

Miners

A true proletariat first formed in the mines. Mining had played a part early in colonial history. Diamonds were discovered in South Africa in 1867, and gold in the Rand in 1886; in Rhodesia, gold had been mined since 1893. The first mines in Namibia (southwest Africa) date from the same period. In the Belgian Congo, mining of copper at Shaba (Katanga) and of diamonds at Kasai began in the first decade of the twentieth century. In Northern Rhodesia (Zambia), the Copperbelt started production in the 1920s, and diamonds were discovered in Angola in 1912 and in Sierra Leone in the early 1930s. The mines, although great consumers of manpower, were often situated in underpopulated areas. The chronic shortage of labor led to a systematic organization of migrations, and compounds were established that housed large concentrations of workers. In Southern Africa, first Indians were brought to work on the sugarcane plantations of Natal. Next, Chinese were recruited. By 1905, 27 percent of the workers in the gold mines were Orientals. This proved to aggravate the racial problem, however, and soon the mines ceased to employ Chinese.

Thus, in the interior of the continent there arose the scourge of recruiters, who at an early stage organized the first great labor migrations. South Africa obtained workers chiefly from Nyasaland (Malawi) and Mozambique; in 1929–1930, 10 to 12 percent of the budget of Mozambique derived from the 50,000 emigration permits officially negotiated with the Transvaal via the Witwatersrand Native Labour Association (WNLA), created by the Chamber of Mines. These 250 recruiters had the right to engage up to 80,000 Mozambicans a year. Between 1913 and 1930, 900,000 workers left for the mines, and of these a third returned with injuries. By the 1930s the WNLA had exhausted the local supply of manpower and was forced to broaden the scope of its recruitment. Of 31,000 miners recruited abroad in 1952, nearly half came from the Portuguese territories, compared to 23 percent from Malawi, 16 percent from Tanzania, 10 percent from Namibia, and 6 percent from Zambia. Of 371,000 miners in 1969, foreigners constituted 68 percent, of whom 27 percent were from Mozambique and 18 percent from Lesotho. The South African miners were also migrants: up to 24 percent came from the Cape Province.[19] Most of these were worker-peasants who had come to obtain a little ready money to supplement subsistence agriculture; the employers found that by diversifying their reserves of these part-time workers, they could maintain salaries at the lowest possible level.

The Union Minière du Haut Katanga held an official monopoly on recruitment in the eastern province (Maniema) and in the Belgian-mandated territories of Rwanda and Burundi, where in 1936 the population density was 68 per square kilometer (compared to 4.1 in the Congo). In 1930, out of a total of 350,000 Hommes Adultes Valides (ablebodied adult males) in Rwanda-Burundi, 7,000 resided in the Congo, of whom more than 4,000 worked at Katanga. The usually rapid turnover was slowed somewhat by the relatively attractive terms of the contract: 3,400 Belgian francs for three years' work, with an advance for the payment of dowries and—a new clause—an offer of immediate reengagement.[20] (This policy of recruitment, with its assignments to precise geographical locations and its tendency toward stabilization of manpower, early differed from that of the Rand.)

Nevertheless, the generally unstable employment in the mining industry hindered the emergence of a class consciousness that could give rise to effective syndical and political action. Because the category of salaried worker was as easy to leave as to enter, the migrants did not develop a sense of identity as workers.

Dockers and Railwaymen

It was not in the mines, but on the docks and, above all, on the railways that African workers became class conscious. The emergence of such a consciousness required a permanent proletariat with a limited but relatively organized, or organizable, group whose function at the heart of the communications system made them both especially aware of their economic importance—hence of their power—and able quickly to disseminate information and instructions.

After World War I, the French-speaking areas showed the influence of those who had become acculturated through wartime mobilization. The actions of certain of the 160,000 war veterans were decisive, owing to their openness to new ideas, their Westernized outlook, and their privileges. Exemption from the Code de l'Indigénat and, for some, the acquisition of French nationality enabled them to express their ideas in the press—in 1920 Dorothée Lima founded the first newspaper in Dahomey—to make the first demonstrations—in 1916 in Conakry Abdoulaye Mara launched the SCOA dockworkers' strike—and to found the first militant organizations—in 1925 in Paris, André Matswa, veteran of the Rif war, founded the Amicale des Originaires de l'AEF, and around the same time, in France Lamine Senghor, also a former worker, laid the groundwork for African communism. Their roles were at least as important as those of the mere 25,000 South African Blacks who fought with the British in the war and were undoubtedly influential in bringing about the great Black strike of the Rand in 1920.

THE AWAKENING OF CONSCIOUSNESS

Unlike the situation in liberal and industrial England and France, in Africa movements of social protest grew up within a coercive system that forbade the workers to express their grievances directly until a late stage. Consequently, secret, inarticulate, and ill-organized forms of resistance such

as desertion or underproductivity have a special importance in the development of the African workers' consciousness.[21] Historians must therefore be-
ware of the ethnocentric temptation to reduce African social movements to
syndicalism and to reduce labor action to strikes. Undoubtedly, the number,
frequency, scale, and length of strikes, the number of workdays lost, the
rhythms of turnover, the rates of trade union membership, the size of street
demonstrations, and the adoption of radical positions are indications of social unrest, but to limit the picture to these active forms of labor militantism
imposes on the African proletariat the model of European social history as it
has developed since the middle of the nineteenth century, just when new
schools of thought among Western historians are insisting, on the contrary,
on the necessity of drawing attention to phenomena that indicate the emergence of a general popular culture.[22]

The chronological evolution of social movements in Africa does not con-
form to any single pattern, but varies according to the locality, the colonial
context, the centers of activity, the cultural heritage, and the motives of the
social groups concerned. We can nevertheless propose a typology, each
phase of which represents a stage in the integration of the worker into the
system that employs and controls him.

Rejection of Compulsory Labor

The first stage of the integration of the worker into the system was a negative one. Faced with sudden colonial demands and receiving a miserable
compensation for their work (virtually nonexistent wages, corporal punishment, and so forth), the Africans at first refused to allow themselves to be
incorporated into a form of employment in which they could find neither
purpose nor interest. Compulsory labor forced them to abandon their own
forms of subsistence and sources of revenue (agricultural subsistence, ped-
dling, crafts); it opposed their lifestyle and way of thinking, their customs of
kinship, their religious traditions, and their attitude toward time and work.
The colonial authorities responded with brutality to the Africans' rejection
of such labor. At this stage, African resistance was hardly distinguishable
from peasant revolts. How could workers respond, except by rejection, to
the recommendations of the Labor Code of the Portuguese colonies (1914),
according to which the state should "have no scruples about obliging and,
if necessary, forcing the savage Negroes of Africa to work—or, in other
words, to improve their situation through work so as to gain the best means
of existence in order to civilize themselves"?[23]

The colonial administrations made a number of attempts to regulate labor recruitment. Portuguese legislation made a subtle distinction between
"correctional labor" (for convicts) and the "moral and social obligation" of
at least six months' labor a year for men between 14 and 60.[24] The Belgian
Congo officially fixed the rate at 25 percent of the ablebodied adult men and

lowered it to 10 percent in the mid-1920s because of the shortage of man-power. French Equatorial Africa limited recruitment by the administration itself to "a third of the ablebodied male population that had reached adult age" and by 1926 warned the new exploiters of the forest areas that they were setting up their work sites "at their own risk and peril and in the knowledge that they were in danger of not finding the necessary manpower on the spot." [25] The official rates of recruitment were generally exceeded, however, by a variety of methods. The concept of the ablebodied male, for example, could be interpreted loosely, as it merely referred to "individuals who had reached an adult's normal [?] development." [26]

Especially in central and southern Africa, where the confrontation with capitalism was more recent and more brutal than elsewhere, the first colonial phase belongs to "proto" African social history. That does not mean that the African workers were not acutely aware of being exploited, but they did not yet articulate this awareness in the Western manner. Two reactions were dominant: flight and passivity, of which the first was most common as long as the traditional world was able to offer refuge.

Primary resistance was characterized by collective rejection. Whether this expressed itself as a "tribal" war, a religious movement, or a general boycott, it was primarily a struggle connected with work: refusal to allow the traditional lands to be expropriated, refusal of obligatory cultivation, refusal to work at porterage, refusal to leave for the mines or for work on the railways or in the forests. Especially at the beginning, this refusal took the straightforward form of flight aimed at cutting off contact, a ploy that worked best when an ethnic group spanned a frontier. Between 1895 and 1907, more than 50,000 Shona and Chewa of the valley of the Zambezi fled to Rhodesia and Nyasaland (Malawi), while the Ovambo and Bakongo fled from Angola in order to escape Portuguese domination. Sometimes "escapee populations" created autonomous enclaves like the West Indies maroon communities of runaway slaves. An example was the *mitanda* (or Bushmen) of Northern Rhodesia (Zambia), who jealously guarded their independence. We have also seen that in the gold mines of Southern Rhodesia, whose exploitation began in 1893, the miners' discontent was closely linked to the revolt of the Shona in 1896–1897, which halted industrial development. The episode was repeated. In one of the first mines to resume its activities, at the end of 1898, when twenty-one workers died of pneumonia almost simultaneously, the belief spread rapidly that the place was cursed. No miner went near the mine for two months, and it was forced to close. Again in 1901, a boycott followed a serious accident and closed the mine for most of the year. At the beginning of this century, conditions in the mines were so deplorable that it was almost impossible to attract Shona workers from the surrounding areas despite the crisis of subsistence caused by several years of drought. [27] In southern Africa as a whole, the employers' constant complaint about the shortage of labor undoubtedly reflected the local demographic situation, but it also obviously indicated a form of collective resistance that encouraged the creation of the system of long-distance labor migrations.

The second form of rejection of forced labor involved desertion or individual flight, and this, too, was the subject of constant complaints by the first employers. In a world over which the worker had no control and in which he was excluded from all responsibility, desertion was one of the few positive actions he could take. The percentages of desertion, then, in all kinds of labor were very high—from 20 to 40 percent. In 1909, the Portuguese officials were able to find only 300 of the 5,000 porters commandeered by the governor of Tete, and even those all fled before reaching their destination.[28] Kikuyu on the colonial farms of the Highlands of Kenya, workers on the railways in Nigeria or on the Congo-Atlantic railway, and miners in the Rand and the Copperbelt all escaped. For instance, more than 25 percent of the 8,400 workers engaged by the Rhodesian Labour Office in 1900–1901 deserted. Even the army saw its share of this form of rejection, as in the desertion or self-mutilation of the conscripts for labor on public works in French West Africa from the 1920s onward.[29]

Desertion was not merely refusal to work, as the Europeans so conveniently interpreted it. A direct correlation existed between rates of desertion and wages: in Rhodesia, many more desertions occurred in the Shona country than in the Ndebele country, where wages were higher, and many workers braved the dangers of a journey of several hundred kilometers to the mines of the Rand, where working conditions were much less terrible.[30]

Even today, the majority of Namibian miners leave their jobs before the end of their contract. Among the mining teams, moreover, those that have the harshest supervisors tend to have the highest worker turnover rate. Their mode of departure is also suggestive of their attitude. To receive a gratuity on departure and the testimonial necessary for their reengagement, the miners must give 24 hours' notice. They prefer to undergo these losses by leaving without notice, however, in order to cause the employers as much inconvenience as possible.[31]

The reaction of passivity was expressed primarily in the workers' extremely low productivity. Contrary to the beliefs of the colonizers of the period, the truth was not that the Africans had to be underpaid because they were "congenitally lazy" or unable to comprehend "the benefits of work," but that they worked badly because they knew they were being exploited. The idea that increases in wages would accelerate the turnover rate (because the migrants would want to return to their land as soon as they had attained the minimum sufficient for their needs) showed an unawareness of the adaptability of the labor force. African wage earners were no more indifferent to money than any others, but the wages they could earn were too low to provide any incentive to labor. Examples therefore abound of slothfulness and neglectfulness at work, for example, in connection with agricultural workers of the Company of Mozambique and of the Zambezi and with employees of the South African railways. Desertion was succeeded by absenteeism. The inspectors of the colonies recognized, however, that every time a less miserable wage was offered, the workers' productivity improved. Similarly, today, the Consolidated Diamond Mines in Namibia, which offer the best pay, are the only ones where all the workers are reengaged and the only one that can boast, despite difficult conditions of work in inhospitable natural surroundings, of an ever-growing waiting list of candidates for migrant labor.[32]

Semi-proletarian Resistance

The second stage of the integration of the worker—the most common in the interwar period—was one that was semi-rural, semi-proletarian. Ill adapted both to their employment and to life in the cities, these workers formed an integral part of the system. They continued, individually or collectively, to protest, in new ways but within a still largely traditional framework. The workers of La Forminière in the Belgian Congo, for instance, very early understood the social and financial advantages that the company offered them in comparison with life in the rural areas under a colonial administration. While they now accepted the concept of wage labor, however, the workers continued to object to their working conditions. They rejected the spirit of competition, as expressed in production quotas (Namibian miners formed a brotherhood to oppose such quotas). Workers demanded time enough to do their work properly, that is to say, they set a pace closer to agricultural or craft practices than to those of industrial production. If the employers balked, the workers resorted to sabotage—a brutal method of retaliation—or to theft.

Theft, which has been extremely common, represented an attempt to correct exploitation by supplementing wages with anything useful and movable that could be taken from the job site, such as candles or explosives (to be used in fishing). In the diamond mines of South Africa and Namibia, advanced techniques of detection have been installed, and in the mines of Rhodesia it has been observed that the value of the gold smuggled varies inversely with wages.[33] The motivation is not necessarily purely economic: a successful theft proves the worker's ability to mislead the Whites. Being able to deceive the master bolsters self-esteem.

A number of phenomena that have as yet received little attention reveal the workers' difficulties in material and moral adaptation. The undue frequency of accidents—twice as high for Blacks as for Whites in the gold mines of the Rand—and of illness can be ascribed to objective causes such as malnutrition and inadequate inspection procedures, but can they not also be seen as signs of psychological resistance, of workers unconsciously trying

to deprive the employer of their labor? When the situation becomes desperate enough, oblivion through alcohol, drugs, or suicide enables workers to
escape an unbearable situation.

Theft, alcoholism, suicide, and magical and religious practices are clearly
symptoms of a profound malaise, of maladjustment, of psychological resistance. They are not, however, necessarily objective manifestations of *social*
resistance showing the emergence of a proletarian consciousness; they are
just as much means of accommodation to the system. Moreover, each of
these practices carries within it the power of self-destruction. Because in a
coercive framework these indirect forms of resistance cannot express still
vague grievances, they remain equivocal and can easily be manipulated or
neutralized by the authorities.

We have already seen, when speaking of the peasants, the ambivalence of
the religious factor. The separated Black churches preach an ideology of resignation, but by their very separateness they generate consciousness of an
alternative to absolute submission to the colonizer. Thus we see Ethio-
pianism and the Watchtower spread from the mining concentrations of
southern Africa, and the independent churches being forbidden in the Rhodesian compounds.

The workers' emotional displacement leads them to invest their new
wages in modern versions of traditional magic. The Namibian miners offer a
striking example. Unable to resolve the contradictions with which they are
confronted, they spend a large part of their income on "medicines" (or fetishes) sold by specialized (not always African) firms in South Africa. These
"medicines" address their particular fears and wishes: getting good jobs,
avoiding debt, gaining protection from sorcery, succeeding with women. A
third of the packages received on the compounds contain such "medicines,"
although the smallest costs a fifth of an unskilled worker's monthly wage.[34]

Drinking together is a ritual that confirms the workers' solidarity. They
see such gatherings as a confraternity in which the members exchange
friendship, for enemies do not drink together. They also drink for other reasons, however—first of all, because there is very little else to do. In the eve-
nings or on weekends, they meet in the "hotels" of the compound, which are
traditionally surrounded by open spaces so that they cannot be taken by surprise by the Whites. These spaces provide somewhere to retire to if the meeting degenerates. Any happening—a departure, for instance—is seen as sufficient reason to get together for a drink. Drinking together is also an effective
means of resolving conflicts: tensions are dissolved in an exchange of insults
under the influence of drink. What the Whites like to describe as a "tribal
war" is, on the contrary, the occasion for a collective regeneration of a confraternity that was momentarily strained. But these drinking bouts have
their darker side. The bored migrants drink in order to forget, and the traditional beer only increases their depression. Meetings generally end with

often terrifying stories from home in which fears about the fidelity of the workers' wives and the consequences of their absence can be detected.

Coming together to drink or to dance, with its contribution to friendship and solidarity, is one aspect of a working-class culture that reveals the emergence of a social consciousness. The creation of a system of mutual comprehension helps the workers to endure their wretched fate and at the same time to work out a common strategy of resistance. This counterculture is subtle and difficult to grasp. It is made up of in-jokes and a unifying code language. For instance, the miners of Namibia, to the confusion of their employers, each use four or five names: their childhood name, a nickname, a name used at work, and one used when dealing with the boss.[35] The ostensible reason is to provide a Christian name for the Whites' use, but this custom is related to a traditional practice for deceiving the enemy. For much the same reason, the workers on the East African Railway, of very varied origin, all spoke Swahili in front of the British.[36]

The work songs that break the monotony, the drinking sessions, and the dancing associations have provided opportunities for the workers to be alone together, away from the world of the Whites. Thus, the Beni dance societies that existed throughout East and Southern Africa created a living art-form out of African words and music and symbols taken from the White apparatus of authority (march rhythms, honorific hierarchies, discipline, uniforms).

For nearly a century the Ngoma dance has reflected the great social changes brought about by colonialism: the devastations of World War I, the misery of the Great Depression, the first strike, the beginnings of political struggle. Beginning in Tanganyika under the Germans, the dance, accompanied by songs in Swahili—the principal common language—first spread in rural areas under the influence of soldiers demobilized from World War I. Migrant workers, especially in the 1930s and later, brought it to the Mombasa and Lamu, stressing its carnival aspect. At this point, a social rupture developed, widened by the warnings of the British authorities: the white collar urban petite bourgeoisie preferred to belong to Anglo-Saxon–style civil service associations, while the dances formed the migrant workers into a cohesive group. In 1918–1920, Nyasa miners from Malawi introduced the Beni into the compounds of Southern Rhodesia and Katanga. There the dance associations assumed important social functions, serving as a mutual aid fund for the exchange of gifts, food, and clothing. The Beni also gave rise to imitators: in the Copperbelt in about 1940, the Bemba of the north danced the Beni, the Bisa danced the Kalela, and the Nyasa danced the Nganda.[37]

The dance societies left the participants in a "tribalistic" isolation, but at the same time they generated a certain social dynamism that provided activists with a rallying point. The first mutual aid societies in the Rhodesian compounds derived from the Beni dance societies.[38] The mining companies, like the administration, worried about the "subversive" role played by these societies. In 1934, public dances were forbidden in Elisabethville; in Southern Rhodesia, the Chamber of Mines stressed the societies' role in fomenting social protest among labor. In at least one case, their participation was clear—in the disturbances in the Copperbelt in 1935. The activists did not, of course, go on strike because they were members of the Beni, nor did they belong to the Beni because they were activists, but they did become leaders precisely because they held positions of responsibility in the dance associations. The Beni served as a center for the formation of political activists until independence, when syndical and political organs became institutionalized.

Protest within the System

When the most proletarianized and urbanized workers—those most thoroughly assimilated into the capitalist system—ended by accepting its legal and political structures, they formulated their demands within the framework which had been imposed on them. From that time on trade unions and syndicates, the open forms of labor action, prevailed. The symbols of protest were the strike, the agricultural boycott, and the urban riot with a political connotation. This was not a new phenomenon: the first strikes had taken place at the very beginning of the twentieth century.

It was, paradoxically, in West Africa, by far the least industrialized part of the continent, that trade union action evolved most continuously and, perhaps, most effectively. This was due at least in part to the relative freedom from coercion enjoyed in that area. It is a remarkable fact that in 1947–1948 Senegal had a strike lasting five months, the longest in the history of African trade unionism. In South Africa, on the other hand, where labor action by the miners began early, the harshness of the repression caused these manifestations, though violent, to be sporadic and inconsequential. The trade union movement saw some success in South Africa at the beginning of the 1920s, but it was broken by savage legislation based on apartheid that virtually stamped out all active forms of labor resistance. And in Central Africa, the movements of social protest were thwarted by regimes (in Southern Rhodesia and Namibia) that were perhaps even worse than that of the Rand, or by the preservation at a late date of traditional structures (in the Copperbelt), or by the efficiency of Belgian paternalism. For these reasons secret resistance long prevailed, for in these areas, which were far less urbanized than South Africa, only that form could be utilized.

Finally, in sub-Saharan Africa as a whole, it was not until after World War II that one critical factor emerged. Two phenomena, which up to that point had developed rather independently, fused. Social action—spontaneous or organized, indirect or syndical—merged with political action, the foundation of the nationalist parties and the national liberation struggles.

Because the social bases of these two forms of action differed vastly, however, they developed in contrasting and in some cases even antagonistic fashion. The nationalists, who had emerged from a more or less assimilated petite bourgeoisie of officials and planters, demanded participation in the colonial government. They found it difficult and go on finding it difficult to identify with a popular base, still closely connected to the soil, whose demands differ from their own. All these elements, then, weave together in complex and fascinating ways in the origins and development of the African social movements.

11

Labor Action: Social Protest to the End of World War II

THE MINERS

The mines were the earliest concentrations of labor in sub-Saharan Africa—first in South Africa, and then in the Belgian Congo and Northern Rhodesia (Zambia). The size of the compounds in South Africa from an early date and the specific character of apartheid make that country's struggles particularly dramatic. Even today, the connection in South Africa between social protest and the forces of national liberation remains uncertain. South Africa provides a classic example of urbanization and proletarianization and of the now universal rise to social and political importance of the "informal" sector.

The Struggle in South Africa

South Africa toward the end of the nineteenth century was a colony with a relatively large White population: nearly one million Whites and the same number of "colored people"—Indians, mulattoes, and others—and only four million Blacks. The heart of the South African industrial economy was, and still is, the Rand, whose gold mines played a central role in the rise of South African capitalism. The evolution of the Rand reflects that of the country as a whole. The system of coercive labor based on the color bar (transformed in 1949 into the political model of apartheid) and the overlapping of class and race relationships make it the prototype of the formation of classes in southern Africa in the urban setting of White cities and Black townships.

The Western Origins of White Trade Unionism.   Working-class people of European origin earliest and most strongly manifested a tradition of social struggle. Anglo-Saxon workers were inspired by the example of the British trade unions; a little later, immigrants and refugees from Eastern Europe expressed a European radicalism influenced by the ideas of Marx, the anarchists, and the social democrats. The problems of the Blacks were overlooked by both these groups, since they were preoccupied with the fundamental contradiction between capital and labor, in which the semi-rural Bantus were not yet involved. The White miners, relatively few in number, were confronted, like their Black counterparts, with an efficient apparatus of coercion and repression. For their strikes to succeed, they had to present a homogeneous front, and thus they were absolutely opposed to the practice of employing African "blacklegs" (strikebreakers). In the gold mines, the White miners struck to protect themselves from competition from the Blacks, who were lower-paid and easier to manipulate. In 1893, the first color bar was created, on the insistence of the White workers; in 1897, a wave of discontent followed reductions in salaries; and in 1907 the White laborers called a strike against the employment of Blacks for skilled labor. Again in 1913 and in 1914 large-scale strikes were held by White workers. Each time, workers and management clashed violently, and shots were fired, but the White miners finally succeeded in having their unions recognized. This helped to validate the color bar. Most important, the Mines and Works Act of 1911 gave only Whites the right to perform skilled labor and made striking a crime for Black workers under contract (including piece-workers and day laborers). This law henceforth dominated the social history of South Africa. Meanwhile, the influx of African immigrant labor from nearby territories reduced the cost of replacing "native" workers from one-half to one-sixth of that of proletarianized Whites and encouraged employers simply to dismiss disobedient workers.

In 1913, following the success of the Whites, the Blacks defied the law and went out on strike.[1] This action was the first sign of the awakening of a Black workers' consciousness; hitherto, with few exceptions, the Black miners had expressed their discontent in presyndical forms, most frequently by desertion.[2] In 1913, however, some 9,000 miners stopped work for three days. The strike was rapidly put down by the authorities, but it made a strong impression on both the Black workers and the administration. A Commission of Enquiry was immediately set up, and this first strike succeeded in obtaining from the government what ten years of previous efforts on the part of officials and entrepreneurs had failed to achieve: increased rations, better working conditions, medical assistance, and better housing. The major problem of the Black miners, however—their subordinate position—remained unaffected. Their situation worsened with the collapse of agricultural productivity in the reserves and with the runaway inflation of the war and postwar period.

Sporadic localized strikes continued in 1915 and 1916. In the eastern Rand in 1917, the workers organized a boycott of the compound stores, which, taking advantage of their virtual monopoly, were raising prices even faster than the overall rate of inflation. Not only did wages not keep pace with prices but, in the rural areas, the rapid penetration of capitalism completed the disorganization of an agricultural economy that had become incapable of adapting.[3] An outbreak of plague among the cattle on the coast in 1912 had already caused the migration to the Rand of some 60,000 wretched peasants. Southern Mozambique, a great supplier of labor, suffered, like the rest of the continent, from two successive years of severe drought in 1912 and 1913, followed in 1915 and again in 1917 by some of the most disastrous floods of the first half of the century. The epidemic of Spanish influenza wreaked havoc in 1918: of the 158,000 Black workers on the Rand, a third were hospitalized and nearly 2,000 died. The culminating disaster, in the years 1919–1920, was an unprecedented drought. The miners, migrant workers who until then had been more or less rural people, had henceforth to depend on their wages alone to support their families. They were transformed into a class of quasi-permanent, urbanized workers. Some of these lent a willing ear to the teachings of the Socialist International League, which was winning converts among the new Black petite bourgeoisie. The influence of the League on the miners began to appear in 1917 after a series of courses the League gave to Black workers in Johannesburg. The courses led to the formation of the Industrial Workers of Africa (IWA), the first major Black trade union, which immediately became involved in the wave of protests at the end of the war.[4]

Black and White Strikes, 1920–1922.   A long period of malaise and resistance came to a head in the strike of 1920. In Johannesburg, the unrest reached a peak in 1919, when the White municipal employees succeeded in obtaining a 25 percent increase in wages and the Black roadsweepers were sent to jail for asking for sixpence a day more. The Transvaal Native Congress (a local branch of the ANC, which had been founded in 1912), the IWA, and the Industrial and Commercial Union (ICU, an organization of Black workers created in January 1919, which was to replace the IWA), all sprang into action. On the first of July, a strike by 15,000 workers employed in three mines was broken up by mounted police. In the following months the government appealed to the African chiefs and notables to restore calm, for the unrest in the cities was being carried to the compounds by the foremen, who lived outside the compounds. In an attempt to head off disaster, the government granted the mining companies permission to increase Black wages slightly.

It was too late. The Black miners' strike began on 16 February 1920 and continued, with ups and downs, until the twenty-eighth. The peak day was 23 February, when 37,000 absences were registered. Altogether, 71,000 miners took part in the strike, of whom 30,000 participated for six days and 25,000 for at least a week. Mobilization was essentially but not exclusively along ethnic and regional lines. The necessity of living together on the compound could intensify rivalries between regional groups, but at the same time it encouraged an interweaving of relationships and interests. From a very early stage, the miners were also aware of internal social differences: however unskilled the work, a hierarchy existed, ranging from the simple worker to the foreman. (Similarly, in the mines of Rhodesia, the workers recruited under contract by the Labour Office, who were too poor or lived too far away to pay for their journey themselves, constituted a lower order within the proletariat, as was shown by their generic nickname *shibaro* or "slave," which had become synonymous with "forced labor." This attitude of contempt was fostered by the employers as an outlet for aggression.)[5] In 1920, the most militant among the miners came from East Africa; they were also the largest group (80,000 out of a total of 206,000) and the most stable (three-quarters of them had come there for the second time and remained for an average of nineteen months). The Sotho of the Transvaal, who had been particularly severely hit by the agricultural crisis and had been working longest in the Rand, were also among the most active. All this bears out the interconnection between urbanization and workers' consciousness.

The Black miners were no match for their opponents, especially since the White miners sided with the government. An effective repression left three dead and fifty wounded. This time the Blacks won no concessions. On the contrary, in 1921 the purchasing power of the Blacks' wages was 13 percent lower than in 1916.

The anti-Black attitude of the White workers did not earn them a privileged position. The higher wages of White workers made their situation precarious: the ratio of Blacks to Whites in the mines of the Rand had risen, between 1910 and 1922, from 7:7 to 11:7. The South African Communist Party, which was almost exclusively White, was established in 1921 and immediately asked to be affiliated with the Communist International. It took the lead in advancing social claims but continued to uphold White privilege. The crisis of the early 1920s, when the price of gold collapsed from 130 shillings an ounce in 1919 to 95 in 1922, brought this conflict into the open.

The major capitalists of the mining industry—as opposed to the agriculturally oriented, protectionist nationalists—advocated solving the economic crisis through a policy of free trade, with lowest cost as the determining factor. White miners' wages were slashed by between 25 and 50 percent, their paid free days were eliminated, and the work was covertly redistributed so that Blacks performed some semi-skilled jobs, in violation of the agreement concluded between the Chamber of Mines and the unions in 1917.

White miners began a strike in January 1922. A current slogan revealed the ambiguity of the situation: "Workers of the world, unite for a White South Africa!" The enemy was identified as a contradictory mixture of elements that included the magnates of the Chamber of Mines and the Black hordes. "The Black workers," the Communist party had to explain, "are not your enemies but potential allies against the capitalist class."[6] The extraordinary violence of the conflict bordered on civil war. The government prevailed only in mid-March, after four days of armed struggle in which 25,000 White miners were confronted with 7,000 troops accompanied by bombardiers. There were 153 fatalities, more than 500 wounded, and 5,000 arrests.

Although it was broken by force, the strike was a political success for the Whites. It marked a turning point in South African history, from colonial imperialism to national capitalism. The first phase was dominated by the mining capitalists, while in the second the nationalist bourgeoisie was able to assert its power.

Proletarianization and Politics in the Interwar Period.   The strikes, especially those of the Whites, had considerable long-term effects on the color bar. It led to the Industrial Conciliation Act of 1924, which reaffirmed White trade unionism as a movement specifically excluding the Blacks, and to the Color Bar Act of 1926. The strikes also contributed to the defeat of the mining party in the elections of 1924, bringing to power a labor/nationalist union government that transformed the state into the instrument of the "White nation."[7] This confrontation between mining corporations and nationalists was one of the permanent features of South African politics. The requirements of rationality and economic viability in international trade had taught the capitalists of the mining industry (represented by the Chamber of Mines, which grouped together the varied companies in the tradition of chambers of commerce) the advantage of utilizing Black labor and thus of encouraging progressive training of Blacks and a flexible interpretation of the color bar. The nationalists, however, insisted on a hierarchical, racial division of labor.

The nationalist government of the late 1920s tightened the segregation laws. This paralyzed official Black trade unionism. The labor movement had no means of action except through collaboration with the anticolonial political struggle waged by some nationalist leaders from other social classes.

No more Black strikes on any scale took place in the Rand until a quarter of a century later, in 1946. The Whites began at this time to radicalize their labor policy. Because the Communist party sought a united front of workers beyond differences of color, it addressed itself to the Black workers of the ICU and the Black nationalists of the ANC. Militants joined forces interracially. For instance, the little Federation of Non-European Trade Unions organized the first major mixed-race strike, that of the textile workers of Germiston. The evolution was undoubtedly slow. The Communist International, under the influence of White South African activists, at first hung back. In its 1927 debate on "the revolutionary movement in the colonies" (an echo of Lenin's "National Question" of 1920), the South African delegation, invited to compare the "proletariat" of the capitalist countries with the "masses" of the colonies, claimed that there was little difference between them, but the following year they had to accept the party's decision that it would work in a determined and consistent fashion for the creation of an independent *native* (Black) South African Republic.

The Profintern, the trade union section of the Comintern, which was created in the Soviet Union in 1921 to encourage proletarian trade unions in the colonized countries, in 1926 established a subsection, the International Committee of Negro Workers. In its fourth congress, in Moscow in 1928, it debated the national problem and especially the "Negro question." A new wave of young South African activists—for the first time including Whites born in South Africa and Black communists from the Young Communist League—participated in these debates. Among these early activists were Albert Nzula, who in 1929 became the first Black secretary-general of the South African Communist party, J. B. Marks, and Moses Kotane. These people assumed the leadership of the party.

The Great Depression exacerbated internal conflicts between South African reformist nationalists and the evolving Soviet Communist party. In 1930 the African National Congress broke with its radical wing. The moderates took control of the congress, which they ran until the 1960s. The Soviet Union meanwhile ordered the dissolution of the League of African Rights, which Nzula founded in 1929 to promote the popular struggle against the passes, travel permits required of Black workers. This move proved disastrous, for the league was the only effective link between the Communist party, the ICU, and the ANC.[8]

Despite all these setbacks, some large-scale activity did take place. A huge meeting followed by a large demonstration was organized in Johannesburg at the end of 1929, in protest against a violent tax-collecting operation in the African townships of Durban supported by 700 policemen armed with cannons and tear gas. In 1930, the anti-pass campaign occasioned vigorous meetings; some 3,000 workers, of whom a third were White, gathered on 1 May of that year.

The relative quiescence of the following years, due in part to the Depression, was also caused by a certain inability to link political combat with social struggle. The urban bourgeoisie of petty shopkeepers and government employees (who still constituted less than 1 percent of the Black population) fell back upon a patient and moderate "constitutional" opposition.

In these difficult years, interracial political radicalism was quite unable to reflect workers' claims on a popular level, and the ICU, which was constantly persecuted by the government, finally collapsed. The last strike it organized, that of the East London railway workers and dockworkers in 1930, lacked political and financial support and was a complete fiasco. As political perspectives narrowed, the Communist party, too, lost strength. In 1931 it "purged" its membership. Henceforth, it saw itself as an integral part of the movement of national liberation. In 1938, it transferred party headquarters from Johannesburg to the Cape, and Blacks, Indians, and Coloureds came to play major roles within the party while White trade unionists—the only ones recognized by the state—fell away.

This is not to say that Black labor agitation disappeared, but in the years 1930–1945 it was affected by a profound transformation in South Africa. The boom in gold, which began in 1933 with the abandonment of the gold standard, and the wartime economy not only mitigated the effects of the world economic crisis but encouraged the growth of the industrial sector, which from 1943 on became more important than the mining sector. Between 1933 and 1946 the number of industries rose from 6,500 to 10,000. The equipment industries expanded at the expense of the food industries and others, and industrial production rose by 140 percent on two occasions: between 1933 and 1939, and again during the war, while the gross national product tripled.

This period saw the creation of an urbanized proletariat. The number of Black urban employees rose from 400,000 in 1933 to 800,000 in 1939, and from 1921 to 1946 the Black urban population tripled. By 1946, one Black out of four was a city-dweller, and Blacks outnumbered Whites in the cities. Urban "control" thus became an urgent matter for the government.

The great syndical coalition that had grown out of the ICU collapsed, and, especially in the Cape and in Natal, parallel White syndicates took the Black trade unions under their wing. Governmental nonrecognition of Black unions left them open to all kinds of interference, yet labor activities nevertheless developed on a local scale within each industrial enterprise; in 1945 the Federation of Non-European Trade Unions boasted the affiliation of 119 trade unions comprising some 158,000 members, or more than 40 percent of the 390,000 Blacks employed in trade and industry.

An activism developed that was limited to raising wages and improving working conditions. This form of protest increased twofold during the war. From 1930–1939 to 1940–1945, the number of non-White strikers increased from 26,000 to 52,000, the number of days of absence per striker increased from 2.7 to 4.2, and the total number of days of absence rose from 71,000 to 220,000. Between 1942 and 1944, when martial law, facilitated by the war, made Black strikes not only illegal but liable to heavy punishment, about sixty took place. Since unskilled labor was easy to replace and the Black trade unions had no resources, these strikes were difficult to sustain: Black strikes were more numerous than white ones, but their duration was shorter.[9]

The Black Strike of 1946.   The growth of the industrial sector in the 1940s provided employment for the 100,000 poor Whites, and the earnings of Black workers in the private sector, which had increased only by 10 percent between 1930 and 1940, jumped by 52 percent between 1939 and 1946. Owing to the temporary shortage of skilled labor during the war, for the first time the salary differential between the two races shrank.

The eruption of demands for higher wages in 1946 did not take place within this new urbanized labor-force but among the miners of the Rand. These workers were supposed to have remained rural migrants: their contracts specified that they were to return to their reserves after fourteen months (now lowered to twelve). From the time of the Land Act of 1913, which restricted the area of the Black reserves to 13 percent of the land in South Africa, rural productivity had collapsed under the stress of overpopulation: 2,400,000 Blacks were classed as "peasants" in 1936. This number fell to 830,000 in 1946 and to 447,000 in 1951. (The decline from 1936 to 1946 is exaggerated by the fact that women, regarded as "dependents," were not counted during that period.) In other words, the miners had little choice: they returned less often to their reserves, and the labor rotation imposed because of social conservatism simply turned them into badly paid and wretched proletarians. In 1943, out of 300,000 miners, three-quarters received less than the maximum wage; increases in pay depended on the overseer's goodwill; and no social benefits were provided—neither sick leave, nor severance pay, nor overtime, nor compensation for injuries.

On the initiative of Communist activists, during the war a syndicate was created among this still largely unorganized mass: the African Mineworkers' Union, which in 1944 counted 25,000 members. As a result of the pressures it exerted, in 1943 a government-nominated Commission of Enquiry was set up. The commission, while supporting the system of migrant labor since it was regarded as particularly profitable, recommended raising the wages of the lowest-paid miners to at least subsistence level. Seven hundred trade-union representatives examined the commission's conclusions in 1944. They criticized its shortcomings but demanded immediate implementation of the measures recommended. The following year, a mass conference repeated the demand. The catastrophic agricultural situation hastened an explosion, and in 1946 2,000 delegates presented new wage demands, including one for two weeks of paid vacation. The Chamber of Mines failed to respond, and a strike broke out on 12 August 1946.

The crisis of 1946, like that of 1922, was a turning point in the social struggle, but this time it was the Whites who would not budge. They appeared to stand in a very advantageous position: between 1911 and 1969 their purchasing power had increased by 70 percent, while the Blacks' had diminished by 25 percent. More than 60,000—perhaps as many as 72,000—workers went on strike, and the Federation of Non-European Trade Unions of the Transvaal called for a general strike. The government, led, as in 1922, by General Smuts, flatly rejected the recommendations of its own Commission of Enquiry. This time, the White miners were the strikebreakers. Smuts, adapting the tactics he had used a quarter of a century before, treated the strike as a revolt, proclaimed martial law, and, taking violent repressive action, crushed all resistance within six days. By official count, 12 people died and more than 1,000 were wounded.

The strike was a failure; no increase was made in wages until 1949. The state and the entrepreneurs joined to keep labor costs low—with the exception, already, of Harry F. Oppenheimer, president of the Anglo-American Mining Company, whose more modern structure profited from a relative stabilization of manpower. The sole positive outcome of these events was to encourage the industrial sector to try to stabilize employment in the industrial sector as a means of increasing the availability of skilled labor and heightening productivity. The return to industry after the war of 45,000 Whites and 7,000 Coloureds, however, slowed even this progress.

This episode drew the Whites' attention to the social dangers of the rapid growth of the South African economy, and it encouraged a violent reaction in the form of the victory, at the end of 1948, of the Afrikaner Nationalist party over the United party of General Smuts. For the first time, the Afrikaners monopolized power. They now planned a systematic dismantling of Black opposition, beginning with the African Mineworkers' Union.

Despite its failure to achieve its immediate goals, the strike of 1946 nevertheless marked a turning point in the social and political history of South Africa. The most important strike in the history of the country, at least in size, it showed the degree to which the mass of migrant workers had become proletarianized. By bringing growing contradictions out into the open, it forced the Black resistance to reconsider its strategy, and the political evasiveness of the legalistic elite gave way to mass action and passive resistance. The first sign of this new attitude was the refusal of even the Native Representative Council of chiefs and notables to assemble.

Apartheid and Terrorism. The Action Program launched in 1949 by the ANC advocated mass action in the form of strikes, boycotts, and manifestations of defiance based on Ghandian nonviolence. In 1950 in the Rand the first political general strike occurred. In 1959, a radical, nationalist, pan-African wing broke away from the ANC. The Pan-Africanist Congress (PAC) practiced a more aggressive policy toward the government and organized another campaign against the pass laws. In 1960 the government responded to this campaign by a violent repression in the townships of Sharpeville and Langa that resulted in sixty-nine deaths and several hundred injuries.

After this action, nonviolent resistance gave way to armed struggle. The labor struggle in the strict sense was collapsing: by the end of the 1950s there

were fewer than 60,000 Black trade union members.[10] The only possible solution appeared to be political—a struggle for national liberation—but in
the following decade the workers as a whole seemed too disorganized, or
too disheartened, to act as its spearhead. Beginning in 1961, it was the radical nationalist wing, grouping the radicals of the ANC, the Communist
party (SACP), and other similar bodies, who went on the offensive. They
instigated a campaign combining sabotage of government installations with
guerrilla tactics in the rural areas. This agitation only increased the electoral
strength of the nationalists, giving them a free hand to complete the destruction of the Black opposition with a series of legal measures prohibiting all
meetings and manifestations, suppressing communism; and driving the
ANC underground through the Unlawful Organisation Act of 1960. The
radical resistance movement thus failed because the governmental repression
discouraged the masses from following the handful of heroic revolutionaries.

Yet, the great mining concerns did attempt to address this new wave of
labor unrest by trying to improve Black workers' skills and wages. Once
again, it was the issue of productivity that spurred them to action. The dis-
proportion between the wages of Blacks and Whites had risen sharply. In
1922 the ratio was 1 to 11.2; in 1946, 1 to 12.7; in 1956, 1 to 14.7; and by
1969 it had become 1 to 20. The lack of training for Blacks meant that their
skill levels failed to keep pace with the modernization of the equipment. The
overwhelming majority of workers (67 percent) were unskilled; 20 percent
were semi-specialized; and only 11 percent were overseers.

Most observers at the time believed that the great business concerns, led
by liberal multimillionaire Oppenheimer, would oblige the nationalists to
improve the terms of employment and the wages of the Blacks.[11] However, a
first attempt to raise Blacks' wages (in the hope of increasing their output)
again caused the Whites to go on strike. From 1966, the White trade unions
successfully fought to retain their excessive privileges; the unassailable legal
basis of their position enabled them to win all their cases in court.

The nationalist government believed that the interests of private capital
were identical with the general interest: not only capitalism in general but
the specific forms it assumed in South Africa were regarded as an integral
part of public order. In the national interest, a correlation between economic
and political measures, between capitalism and apartheid, not only was considered necessary but was embodied in law. Any modification of a worker's
status—residential, professional, or relating to wages—thus became primarily a legal matter. The system was given definitive form by the Bantu
Urban Areas Consolidation Act, which placed the distribution of the labor
force under state control. In addition, the Bantu Act of 1952, which transformed the traditional pass into a "reference book," drastically limited the
workers' mobility, resulting in more than 600,000 prosecutions and 30,000
expulsions annually.

From the beginning of the 1960s, this system was reinforced by a series of laws permitting unprecedentedly repressive police action. These laws included the Emergency Act (1960), which allowed anyone to be arrested in the interests of order and public security; the Terrorism Act; and the Internal Security Act of 1976, a new version of the Suppression of Communism Act. This effective apparatus of repression built upon the "Hostility Clause," dating from 1929, by which any actions or even words liable to provoke a feeling of hostility between natives and Europeans are punishable with a year's imprisonment and/or £100 fine. Black workers were thus effectively silenced: the least important trade-union leaflet would almost inevitably have been repressed, and any identifiable leaders risked "relegation," a discretionary governmental measure that specifically forbids them to participate in any political or public activity.

The Strikes of the 1970s.   In the 1970s, Black labor unrest, aggravated by an intensification of apartheid and by the world crisis, has found formidable expression, despite the laws, in strikes and violent disturbances.[12] Developments in the international arena—the independence gained in the 1960s by the ex-protectorates of Bechuanaland, Basutoland, and Swaziland, the wars of national liberation in Angola and Mozambique, and the military escalation in Vietnam—revived hope among Black workers. Above all, after years of continuous growth since the end of the war, the world crisis of the 1970s came as a crushing blow to the South African working class. The runaway inflation that had begun in 1964 had brought great hardships to the most underprivileged workers; the recession now made their situation intolerable. South African economic policy was faced with an alternative: either to curb inflation, thus eliminating many jobs and lowering wages, or—the solution adopted at the beginning of the decade—to increase inflation, which would elevate the cost of living. A survey of 1971–1972 revealed that 79 percent of the Black workers lived below the "poverty datum line," that is to say, earning less than the absolute minimum necessary for an average family, and 92 percent fell below the "minimum effective level," that is, they earned just enough to provide for a few needs such as schools and health services.

The history of the South African labor movement is divorced from the usual model of class struggle of the Western proletariat of the nineteenth and twentieth centuries (that is, a first phase of increasing demands and successful strikes, in an era of economic growth; and a lessening of activism in the subsequent recession). The reason is probably that the material and moral wretchedness of an undeveloped milieu has little in common with the troubles of the workers in a Western economy, however harsh the conditions of the emerging proletariat at the time of the industrial revolution may have been. At the beginning of the 1970 recession, the South African workers saw their families in danger of dying of hunger in a land where others were wealthy; no alternatives were left to them except death or revolution. Thus a wave of Black strikes mounted—the first for half a century—this time in the industries that had developed since the 1930s, as well as in the mines. The movement started in 1972 among the dockworkers of Durban and the Cape. It culminated in the strikes in Durban in 1973: the 160 strikes involved more than 60,000 workers in all sectors of industry. The key role fell to the Coronation brick and tile factory, where the movement began on 9 January: a series of strikes succeeded one another for three months, some of them lasting for at least a week, despite their illegality. Despite a multitude of intimidatory measures by the authorities, who condemned this action by "a handful of antigovernment agitators," in three-quarters of the strikes the strikers won an increase in wages. Only in seven strikes did they lose their employment.[13]

Not only did other workers strike—the transport workers of Dundee, textile workers in East London, and bus drivers in Johannesburg—but many employers decided to take the initiative and adjusted wages, thus sometimes succeeding in averting trouble. Moreover, miners' wages quadrupled between 1972 and 1975, although this was chiefly in order to make them competitive with urban industrial wages, so as to remedy the increasing scarcity of migrant labor. In other words, if labor action began and remained in Durban, it was because, thanks to the events in Durban, other areas had less about which to complain.

The only real political gain was in the failure of the police to take effective on-the-spot repressive action. Orders had clearly been given to hold back, an unusual situation for South Africa. Concessions were minimal: inflation rapidly eroded the value of the agreed-upon raises, and the Trade Union Law of 1973 once again prohibited, except in very specific cases, strikes by Black workers. The Black trade unions, although no longer illegal, were still not recognized by the Ministry of Labour and thus were not empowered to put forward the economic demands of their members. At the most, provision was made for an indirect and stratified representation of Blacks through strictly controlled "liaison committees." The employers had difficulty in coming to terms with a factor that is inherent in the ever-increasing participation of the workers in the capitalist system—namely, that winning a few concessions could only urge the workers to further demands. Certainly, in the following years, the worsening recession and the increasing unemployment (the numbers rose from one to two million Blacks between 1970 and 1976 and increased the turnover of migrant workers) by no means favored the propagation of strikes. Yet they continued, although never on the scale of those in Durban. More than 1,000 strikes were called between 1973 and 1976, involving, it is true, a smaller number of workers (98,000 in 1973 and 23,000 in 1975) and increasingly short interruptions of work (the number of days lost fell from 229,000 to 18,000 in the same period).[14] The sporadic and isolated character of these strikes increased the strikers' vulnerability. In this war of attrition the capitalists, made wary by the decline in profits and backed by the government, were little inclined to give way and least of all to recognize Black trade unions as valid partners in dialogue. The confrontations were generally violent: nearly all of the at least twenty-three strikes in the mines between September 1973 and March 1975 involved deaths.[15] A general sense of desperation led to large-scale disturbances that culminated in the Soweto riots of June to September 1976.

Ghettoes and Disturbances.   After this impressive period of revival, Black protest in South Africa seems to have passed from labor militancy to the expression of a desperation which was certainly violent but was ideologically and practically unstructured—in short, from class struggle to racial disturbances. It remains to be explained why Black resistance in the 1960s took the form of strikes in Natal but of tumultuous riots in the Rand and waves of urban squatters in the Cape (just as it had in Johannesburg after World War II).[16] Could the differences in form result from variations in regional economic development?

It would be wrongly simplistic to imagine the Rand as consisting solely of mines, Black proletarians, stores, and compounds. From the genesis of the labor force, urban migration and the policy of geographical segregation made the Black townships the center of South African Black social history. The townships continue on the level of day-to-day living, culture, and ideology the system that the color bar imposed on places of work. The inhabitants living there side by side range from a petite bourgeoisie of traders, teachers, officials, and so forth to the mass of squatters, subproletarians, and fringe elements—a complex and various Lumpenproletariat. In the townships the concept of class oppression tended to be replaced by that of national and racial oppression, for not only were the classes juxtaposed, they were bound together by their common experience, resulting from their separation from the Whites and embracing all areas of life—social and economic, and also cultural, political, and ideological.

Within and in relation to the townships, a "ghetto" culture has developed (it is specifically claimed as such by movements such as Black Consciousness). The internal tensions and contradictions between the various groups, the White liberal current that has brought elements to such popular forms of culture as football, music, and dancing, the influence of an important subproletariat on daily life (in such forms as alcoholism, prostitution, insecurity, and marginality), and the ascendancy of the local petite bourgeoisie, which advocates education as the only means of social advancement, are all factors helping to explain the relatively late appearance of a "workers' consciousness."

The township is an effective form of social control, for the ghetto forms a self-enclosed mental universe. It is doubtful whether the movements of protest that take place within it, such as that of the squatters, could transcend their limited economic objectives. A sign of ghettoization was the outcome of the Black Consciousness movement, whose desire to unite the Blacks, as an oppressed people, against White racism was expressed in social and political objectives.[17] The range of social strata in the movement prevented it from forming any program of precise demands. It therefore based its action on sheer militancy. Its passionate appeals to the masses could not suffice, however, to transcend the limits of the intellectual petite bourgeoisie among which the movement had originated. Its Black Allied Workers' Union recruited only a few hundred members.[18]

To be sure, the black ghettoes are also capable of extraordinarily violent revolts, as was demonstrated by the events in Soweto in 1976. In this vast black township of Johannesburg with its well over 500,000 inhabitants, the discontent began with the young people. This was not surprising. At least since 1968, when Black students broke from the National Union of South African Students to form the Black Consciousness movement, political militancy had won over the youth. Most of these radicals were the children of workers, rebelling against being deprived of their elementary rights as citizens. The start of the action was a campaign waged for several weeks against the compulsory teaching of Afrikaans (the language of the Boer colonizers) in the schools. A mass meeting on 16 June in the great stadium of Soweto was attended by at least 15,000 young people. A policeman fired, killing a thirteen-year-old boy. Havoc ensued: the young people, armed with stones, attacked the police station, public buildings, and those associated with the White establishment—liquor shops, churches, stores—shouting: "No more alcohol! Better schools!" The police fired upon the crowd, whose fury rendered them indifferent to the danger. The workers—men and women— who returned to their township at night found it in a state of riot that lasted three days. More than 100 died; more than 1,000 were wounded, and another 1,000 were arrested. The police repression of the following months took what was probably a similar toll. Similar disturbances nonetheless took place in most of the townships of the Rand and even of the Cape.

The new and significant factor in this case was the budding alliance between college students, high school pupils, and workers. The problem was complex: the Black population is made up of an overwhelming majority of urban workers, a scattered, declining rural population, and a tiny middle class. Owing to education and social position, the intelligentsia can undoubtedly exercise a political influence incommensurate with their numbers. But to do so they must arrange some form of liaison with the masses of the people.

In the summer of 1976 the young people and the young intellectuals first violently expressed the dissatisfaction of the Blacks as a whole. They set up the Representative Council of Students in Soweto, and this group gave the movement its cohesion and its force. The problem was to discover how the liaison with the workers could be effected and whether the students would be able to grasp that the only way they could give concrete expression to their anger was by co-opting the working masses, who alone were in a position seriously to threaten the country's economy. As long as the struggle was limited to high school students, it could be repressed without much difficulty; the state had only to isolate them from the adults and discredit them in the eyes of the rest of the Black population.

The young people had close links to the workers. For the most part, they were the children of workers, and they could expect to become low-paid laborers themselves. The workers saw their children being killed, their town beleaguered by the police, their dignity flouted. Nevertheless, at the beginning of August they refused to go out on strike when the young people called on them to do so. They had good reason: the young people's actions in pulling up tram-lines and damaging pick-up trucks hardly served to convince the workers of the necessity for a strike. Especially in view of the spontaneity required for a Black strike in South Africa, a body of workers had to be prepared to stop work simultaneously, despite all obstacles. Previously they had done so only when they had specific demands, and the situation had been less complex; their aim had been to obtain from an employer—a definite second party—within a particular enterprise, concessions that had been set out by their trade union.

None of this applied in Soweto. There the students wanted a general political strike. When they realized their problem, they put out a comprehensive and specific program asking for the liberation of prisoners and freedom of education as well as the elimination of the color bar and of passes. This time, the joint action culminated in the massive strike of 23–25 August. The rate of absenteeism in Johannesburg was about 80 percent. Despite some police provocation aimed at stirring up tribal quarrels within Soweto, a second general strike, even more fully observed than the first, took place from 13 to 15 September. This strike, recognized by employers and the government as a mass demonstration, brought together more than half a million workers. A sister strike that took place at the Cape was the prime example in South African history of a joint protest by Blacks and Coloureds. But this was also the last demonstration of any size: unarmed students could not defy the police and the army indefinitely. They had achieved a fusion with the workers at one moment and on one occasion. In order to have made any further progress, an organized working class would have had to propose a joint program to the Council of Students. At no time, however, did the trade unions intervene as they had done during the great strikes of the preceding years. The manifestations of August and September 1976, due as much to the spontaneous indignation of the workers as to the militancy of the students, had no sequel, for they lacked a solid substructure. The firm cohesion of the state and the capitalist enterprises overpowered the protesters.

The problem remained, then, the absence of any large-scale labor organization that could coordinate a coherent program and strategy. The repressive laws make the formation of such a vast association inconceivable, and thus the struggle is liable to be limited for some time to mere discontent and disturbances.

The Future of the Labor Movement.   The labor movement, despite the inequality of the forces involved, has in the last ten years or so developed a strategy adapted to the difficult circumstances under which it is forced to function. The Durban strikes were decisive. In view of their defiance both of the government and of their employers, the workers, seeking as far as possible to avoid retaliatory measures, were unwilling publicly to nominate representatives or to give prior notice of their action. They held impromptu meetings and transformed the strikes into mass demonstrations that assembled the workers at their workplaces, rather than persuading them to stay at home. Such techniques of spontaneous action were practiced and popularized, giving the trade union movement a new, totally democratic character. Nothing seemed to suggest that the movement received its instructions from an organized center, and yet it is obvious that when the strike pickets resorted to violence they were expressing the feelings of an overwhelming majority toward a few recalcitrant members.

Since then, "spontaneous" strikes have become the rule, especially in the Rand, where despite an increasingly systematic repressive apparatus there has recently been a resurgence of militancy. After a first strike in May 1982 that affected 1,600 workers, in July a massive protest in eight mines in the Johannesburg region involved some 30,000 strikers driven to desperation. For the first time in the ten or so years that the companies had been attempting to narrow the gap between the wages of Black and White workers (today the average monthly wage for Blacks is 216 dollars; for Whites, 1,060!), the percentage of increase of the wages of the Blacks was lower than that of previous years. Moreover, whereas all Whites and the Blacks who worked underground received a 12 percent increase, Black workers aboveground received only an 11 percent raise.[19] Strikes sometimes continued for more than a week at a time, despite at least ten deaths, hundreds of arrests, and the massive deportation of miners, who were replaced without difficulty with the thousands of unemployed festering in the Bantustans or pouring in from the neighboring states of Swaziland and Lesotho (in the same way, in 1980 the South Africans had responded to the strike of the municipal workers of Johannesburg by deporting more than 10,000 of them). The 15,000 workers in the automobile industry in Port Elizabeth also struck, paralyzing the assembly plants of Ford, General Motors, and Volkswagen. In other words, despite the gravity of the recession, which weakened, if not the fighting spirit of the workers, then at least their capacity to counterbalance the increasing numbers of the strike-breaking unemployed, the trade union movement seemed once again to have gained momentum.

The events of Soweto illustrated the fact that the alliance of the national movement with the labor movement has become a necessity. Among the Black population, the working class is by far the most important, both because of its numbers and because of its political impact. Even though the political distribution of the Black population in 1970 was officially 8,200,000 in the "White" areas, compared to 7,100,000 in the reserves (including 4,000,000 women), the economic policy of the apartheid system is to allow only the "economically active" population to settle in the vicinity of cities. In 1970, of 5,000,000 Black workers, probably hardly more than 1,700,000 worked in agriculture and only 800,000 lived in the reserves. The number of urbanized migrants is probably underestimated by 20 percent, due to concealed employment.[20] They constitute at least two-thirds of the workers compared to only 5 percent of "employers" (there are hardly more than 20,000 Black tradesmen) and only 4 percent of petty officials and members of the liberal professions.

In South Africa, the proletariat has no need to ally itself with the peasantry and the oppressed middle class. The working class is today a vast majority, and a peasant revolt in the reserves would have no chance of success. The whole oppressive South African apparatus is organized to isolate those areas, which would be as easy to subjugate militarily as they are negligible economically. The peasantry and the middle class of South Africa now depend on the working class, not the other way around. Hence the importance of an alliance that makes every Black resistance movement first of all a workers' movement, supported both by the radical elite and by the poor peasants of the reserves. Obvious in the case of the Blacks, this is also true, though to a lesser degree, of the Coloureds and Indians (in 1970 the Coloureds comprised 13,500 employers and nearly 700,000 workers, and the Indians 17,000 employers and 160,000 workers).

This principle has now been understood by the political parties. The "Freedom Charter" of the African National Congress drew some conclusions from it, adding to such democratic requirements as universal suffrage and educational and professional liberty such basic workers' demands as the right to organize trade unions, a minimum national wage, a forty-eight-hour week, and an annual vacation. Even though the African National Congress claims to represent Africans as a whole and not only the working class (for which it is reproached by the South African Communist Party), its program suggests an immediate revolution of social structures, as is emphasized by the inclusion of a few socialist reforms such as nationalization of the mines and changes in agrarian policy.

Since the 1950s, however, the policy of apartheid in the strict sense of the word has triumphed, a triumph that has culminated today in the creation of Black states (ex-Bantustans). This process, which began in 1976 with the independence of Transkei, was destined in the long run to turn the approximately 18,000,000 Blacks into foreigners in their own country, to be described at best as migrant workers in the "White" areas. The struggle for national liberation is thus an urgent one. An organization must be developed that can find expression on the political level, and yet today the Communist party, the ANC, and the SACP are outlawed. The fight nevertheless continues. It is carried on—not without painful ruptures—by clandestine organizations or ones based, of necessity, beyond the frontiers of South Africa. This, as we know, by no means puts them out of the range of White vindictiveness. Nevertheless, inside South Africa itself, the recent gathering of nearly all the Black trade unions into a single federation bodes well for their future.

The Rand miners' strikes of 8–30 August 1987 bring to mind the struggles of 1920 and 1946. Although the figures repeat those of the earlier outcomes—10 dead, 350 wounded, about 40,000 fired—these strikes were the longest, largest, and had the most repercussions of any ever staged in the Rand. The National Union of Mineworkers (NUM) succeeded for nearly three weeks (seventeen days) in maintaining a united front of about 340,000 strikers in fifty-six gold and coal mines, out of the ninety-nine under the jurisdiction of the Chamber of Mines. It is true that the settlement terms fell below even those that had earlier been emphatically rejected by the strikers. The principal issue, that of wages, was not addressed; the miners received only accidental-death benefits and an increase in paid vacation. Nonetheless, the NUM proved itself to be the first union capable of holding its own against the Rand mining industry. The officials of the Anglo-American Mines refrained from the usual talk of "victory." Most of the discharged miners were rehired. And, significantly, just when the strike began, Parliament revoked the statute that banned non-Whites from thirteen jobs in the mines. The Rand mines will no doubt be long in banishing all evidence of apartheid, but the achievements of the strikes of August 1987 must not be undervalued.[21]

Belgian Paternalism

The Belgian Congo practiced a policy that, although seemingly very different from that of South Africa, was no less effective: colonial "paternalism," admired by Western economists up to the very eve of independence. This method can best be seen in the workings of the great copper-mining Union Minière du Haut-Katanga.[22] The Union Minière and its financial backers, the Société Générale de Belgique, contributed lavishly to the budget of the colonial administration (10 percent in 1924, 25 percent in 1930, 28 percent in 1938). In the 1920s the Union Minière developed an understanding both with the administration and with the Benedictine mission that left it free to exercise absolute control over all its personnel, both European and African.

The first White workers came from South Africa. They were quick to advance demands; in 1919 and 1920, their strikes for higher wages paralyzed production. The policy of the company was to give preference to Belgians, who accepted lower wages and were more reliable politically (in 1920, 44 percent of the employees were Belgians; by 1930 the figure had risen to 97 percent). A colonial decree denied the right of association to all workers except administrative employees. This excluded White miners and railway workers—as well, of course, as Blacks—from trade union activity. The company held its personnel through its health and welfare programs; it maintained a strict social hierarchy, from the upper echelons to the technicians; and it even sponsored workers' leisure activities, such as clubs and football teams.

The company's control over its African employees took longer to organize but resulted in an even more complete subjection of the workers. The main problem was the shortage of labor. The company at first adopted a method similar to that used in the South African mines or in railway construction projects that took a high toll in human lives: unskilled workers were recruited on contracts of only six to nine months, to be replaced by new recruits when their strength had been exhausted. Between 1922 and 1924, however, production rose from 43,000 to 86,000 tons of copper. To maintain production levels, the company needed to double its manpower, from 7,000 to 14,000 miners. The task was made difficult by the very low demographic density of the region, the shortcomings of the recruitment network, and the competition of other firms. The severe shortage of labor was exacerbated by administrative measures that protected natives by denying assistance to recruiters and prospectors in the less inhabited areas. At the end of 1925, restrictions on emigration to the Congo introduced by Northern Rhodesia in order to keep its workers in the Copperbelt sparked a radical change of social policy. Henceforth the company attempted to offer attractive terms, in order to maintain a stable workforce recruited from a relatively restricted area.

The first task was the reorganization of the camps. Within three years, two-thirds of the staff and agents dealing with native recruitment had been replaced by others less wedded to coercive methods. Wages were increased and the camps were put under the joint control of a production manager, a physician, and an organizer of leisure activities. Their guiding principle was to increase production through cooperation with the personnel; as a result, between 1926 and 1927 the cost to the company of each worker jumped by 40 percent (but wages accounted for only one-fifth of the increase).

The next step was to create stable families. In some cases, the recruiters even refused to renew the three-year contracts of bachelors. This policy bore fruit by 1930 when, for the first time, there were more births than deaths in the camps. Each family lived in a little brick house and was provided with health services. In 1925 the Benedictine missionaries took on the direction of the boys' schools in Elisabethville, and the following year, in return for a monopoly on evangelization in the camps, they signed a contract giving them the task of teaching "Christianity, loyalty, and obedience, as well as reading, writing, and arithmetic"[23] in the entire network of Union Minière primary schools. The company paid mothers a monthly allowance on condition that they took proper care of their children and sent them to school.

Events during the Great Depression enable us to appreciate the company's hold over its employees. Between 1931 and 1932, the company, by agreement with the international cartel, reduced its production by half, from 120,000 to 54,000 tons. Over 11,000 Black personnel were laid off. The Union Minière first got rid of the employees who were the least dependable workers and the least reliable politically—those whose housing lay outside the camps, and foreigners (Zambians and workers from Rwanda-Burundi). In 1931 the Blacks, in an unprecedented rebellion against these dismissals, staged three uprisings. That of the underground mine of Prince Leopold, the most modern mine and the one whose workers were most highly paid, brought 1,500 workers from Kasai into conflict with 1,000 workers from Rwanda. These revolts demonstrated the success of the company's social policies.

The ethnic character of the disturbances caused the management to favor interethnicity over the previous policy of housing workers by region of origin. People from any given area were systematically divided among the camps; the only membership recognized was that of the "Union Minière tribe." Finally, the companies instituted "marriage assistance," in which the head of the camp undertook to conduct negotiations for the fiancé's family. Under this program, 133 marriages were concluded in 1935, and as many as 243 in 1938. The employer's domination over the workers' lives extended as competition over the size of dowries arose between urban workers and rural workers and between miners and the agricultural workers of the wealthiest cotton plantations. Thus, the company ended by playing "both the role of chief, of father and of maternal uncle. One could have money, new clothes and a brick house—all this in return for absolute submission."[24]

The system worked: in 1940, nearly 80 percent of the employees of the camp of Lubumbashi had been there for more than three years, and more than a third had worked at least ten years for the company. The death rate fell from 20 percent in 1928 to less than 2 percent in 1939. The schools, however, aimed solely at producing "good" workers; tests in 1940 disclosed that the children could barely read, write, or speak French. The system thus created survived, more or less intact, until the beginning of independence.

The Zambian Copperbelt:
Conservative Neo-traditionalism

In Zambia (Northern Rhodesia) copper mining began in 1912, but it became firmly established only after 1924, when the British government took over the territory of the British South Africa Company. Eight principal mines were worked by a number of companies, of which the most important was the Anglo-American Company.[25]

The economic crisis of 1929 swelled the ranks of migrant workers. Between 1927 and 1930 the attraction of higher wages raised the number of miners from 8,500 to nearly 30,000. The White miners, still the more numerous, sought in the cities a more comfortable place to live and readily available welfare services, while the Blacks, who lived in overcrowded huts thatched with straw, were chiefly drawn by the mirage of a comfortable life in the city. They had also been affected by the collapse of cash crops: prices had fallen dramatically, while taxes had been maintained at the same level or even increased; land had come to be in short supply; and the agricultural market had shrunk (between 1934 and 1936 the frontier of Katanga had been closed owing to epidemics, thus cutting agricultural produce off from its traditional outlets). All this drove unskilled workers toward the compounds; in 1937, the mine of Roan Antelope turned away two-thirds of the applicants.

Most of the workers earned enough money only for an individual without a family. Very low at the beginning, wages rose fairly rapidly but soon reached an inadequate ceiling. The low wages, combined with the employers' policy of rapid turnover, forced the workers to adopt a strategy of survival that involved continuous movement between the cities and the rural areas. Thus the Africans took maximum advantage of both modes of production, the rural "traditional" model and the "modern" urban one. A tendency to desertion, the workers' usual response to a coercive system of wage-earning, contributed to the cross-migration. In the 1930s, its rhythm was accelerated by an extension of underground mining, the dangers of which (silicosis, accidents, harsh penalties) provided an added incentive to leave. Apart from skilled workers, only 10 percent of the miners stayed for more than three years. Unskilled workers were the rule, for what little training was offered had to be acquired on the job.

Only Chilean copper was cheaper than Zambian. In order to maintain this low price, the companies employed as many Blacks as possible, even in skilled jobs. Competition between Black and White miners intensified. The Whites, who were associated with the South African White labor organizations and adopted their slogans, in 1936 finally established an offshoot of the Mining Union of the Rand. The Rhodesian Mine Workers Union (NRMU) rapidly transformed itself into a national trade union and sought to impose the rule of the "closed shop" or color bar.

The success of the Whites in turn pushed the Blacks to strike. The imme-

diate causes of the strike were layoffs due to the Depression, and a discrimi-
natory tax aimed at reducing urban overpopulation. The rate of taxation
was increased by 50 percent in urban areas and lowered by 25 percent in
rural areas. Under these new economic hardships mobility no longer compensated for the deterioration in working conditions, and opportunities in
the informal sector became increasingly curtailed.

In 1935, three strikes were declared. At Roan Antelope, the most modern
mine (the turnover was half as rapid as in the other mines, while the average
wage was half again as high), a drastic policy of layoffs (elsewhere they had
been content to stop recruitment) gave the movement a particularly desperate character. The Bemba, an ethnic group from the northeast, where agriculture was devastated by the closing of its frontiers, were represented in
large numbers. The authorities condemned the Bemba dance association,
the Mbeni, as the principal organ of transmission of news and ideas, along
with the Watchtower, another focus of strike organization.

The strike expressed the accumulated resentment of the workers. It
brought together in a violent protest the unemployed and the marginal elements as well as the miners themselves, although it did not yet express a
clear consciousness of relations of production. The Commission of Enquiry
nominated by the government sensed this and seized the occasion to an-
nounce that to form a Black trade union would be premature at that time.
The commission proposed at the most the nomination of "tribal representatives" who would transmit to the management the grievances of the African workers. This plan cleverly utilized traditional institutions for dialogue, but in a "tribal" framework that would guarantee a conservative
form of society. British paternalism aimed more at controlling the African
miners than at assuring their well-being as the Belgians did.

A new stage was reached in 1943, with the creation of "Boss Boys' Committees," liaison committees between African workers and European cadres.
They survived only until 1947, when the British government dispatched an
official instructed to assist the development of the African trade-union
movement. That same year, four Black trade unions came into being. Their
White counterparts tried to restrict the operation of the Black unions and
then to neutralize them by proposing to federate them with the White
NRMU. In 1949, all African miners were represented by the North Rhodesian African Mine Workers Trade Unions, which were recognized the following year by the mining companies. This marked a very important stage
in Zambian trade unionism, but the movement remained focused on local
working conditions. Political factors came into play only later.

Diamond Mine Strikes in Sierra Leone, 1938–1939

West Africa saw comparatively little mining until a late stage. It was only
in Sierra Leone that the discovery of gold and, especially, diamonds in the

1930s led to an exploitation comparable to that of Southern Africa.[26] The Sierra Leone Development Company (DELCO) engaged 4,000 workers and the Diamond Exploitation Company employed 2,000. Altogether, including those employed in the smaller mines, 13,500 Africans were involved in mining, and 6,000 of these were employed as miners, out of a total population of fewer than 3,000,000.

As elsewhere, the difference in wages between the White skilled workers and the unskilled Blacks was enormous, but here nothing more than a wage/skill differential was involved, for the color bar had no legal existence in West Africa. Hence, in the early stages trade union activity was often intense. In 1938 the workers of Pepel DELCO went on strike for a fortnight for higher wages, and those of Maranya did the same, putting forward their demands in a six-point document. The colonial administration failed to act on its promises but, as we shall see below, the strikers were able to benefit from the experiences of the railway workers, whose continuous struggle since the beginning of the century had just then resulted in the establishment of the Sierra Leone Youth League. The league at this precise time was able to provide an effective framework for making political and social demands. Under the leadership of Wallace Johnson, at the outset of World War II the league gave the signal for a mass movement that affected all sectors.

THE RAILWAYMEN

West Africa and its railwaymen were among the pioneers of African trade unionism. Two main factors help account for their role. The first was the absence in West Africa of any segregationist legislation. One possible reason for this was the extensive French presence in this area: they, like most of the Latin countries, officially disavowed this type of racism. The Code de l'Indigénat was of course aimed specifically at the natives, but their ostracism was less a matter of color than of culture. Assimilation was ostensibly the goal, both under the French administration and under the Portuguese, whose form of colonialism was nonetheless among the harshest. The absence of any policy of colonial settlement also prevented excessive competition for land or employment as in South Africa or Kenya. The absence of segregation cannot be accepted as a complete explanation, however, for the case of Algeria embodies all the abuses of colonization with the sole exception of legal racial ostracism. The absence of racial legislation that would codify the inferiority of the Blacks did, however, leave them free to make demands like those of the Whites, that is, to attempt an assimilation which, if it was not achievable, was at any rate conceivable.

The second factor, also specific to West Africa, was the antiquity of relations—originally commercial—with the West. From the earliest days of the slave trade, interactions were based on an—admittedly illusory—equality of one power with another. In the nineteenth century this developed into the more complex form of a trading economy in agricultural products. Africans retained the monopoly of an agricultural export economy (which began earlier here than elsewhere) and were thus protected from any outside acquisition of their land. The policy of the large European concessions of French Equatorial Africa failed in French West Africa, and the British administration explicitly forbade such activity in Nigeria and Ghana, so as not to disorganize the economy. A close analysis shows that in French West Africa the granting of small concessions (less than 100 hectares) benefited the Africans at least as much as the Europeans, who enjoyed no legal superiority.[27] A "creole" culture thus grew in the West African coastal centers, similar to that which had existed in Mozambique under the Portuguese as *prazos* or Crown states. These had originally been given to Portuguese settlers or overlords (the *prazeros*) but by the middle of the eighteenth century had changed their racial and cultural identity. Increasingly involved in the slave trade, those areas were controlled by half-castes whose chief preoccupation was to carve out for themselves more or less autonomous principalities.[28] Similar experiments in acculturation might have succeeded everywhere, but, for historical, cultural, and ecological reasons, they were not encouraged elsewhere by the British.

Hence, an elite, or at least a middle class, emerged earlier in West Africa than in the rest of the continent, especially in those British areas with the best systems of education in Africa. This educated elite hastened the growth of "consciousness," so that it had become impossible to suppress it between the two world wars, as was done in Eastern and Southern Africa, by the coercive apparatus of "multi-racialism."

The absence of a color bar permitted the professional associations, first established by the Europeans, to admit Africans. The Africans took advantage of this opportunity, particularly in the postal service, the teaching profession, and the railways. This pre–trade unionism began as, and remained, a professional syndicalism of officials of the colonial administration. On all levels, the positions of responsibility in the syndicates were held by people who accepted colonization as a system to be improved rather than opposed. This characteristic later shaped the political role of trade unionism.

These facts explain why, for better or worse, the labor movement in West Africa—the least industrialized part of the continent, where mining was almost nonexistent and even the railway system was less developed than elsewhere—was, if not the most dynamic, at least the best entrenched and thus best prepared to play a political role at the beginning of World War II.

Nigerian Trade Unionism

The situation in Nigeria, whose center of trade union development was the great port of Lagos, demonstrates the solidity of the labor movement in West Africa.[29] Toward the end of the nineteenth century, the workers were either government employees (this group, consisting mainly of creoles from Sierra Leone, was the best off) or artisans and unskilled laborers working in the public sector: Kru dockers from Liberia and, to an increasing extent, migrants from the Yoruba and Ibo countries (in 1930, these migrants made up the second largest group in the city). The only common denominators of this varied collection of people were that they were badly paid and under-privileged in comparison with the White workers.

These wage earners remained closely attached to their land and their family group. They often returned to their villages, and they utilized family connections heavily in their search for employment. Some professions were the monopoly of an ethnic group; up to 1933, for instance, all firemen were Kru. A broad social hierarchy ran from unskilled day-laborers and clerks paid by the month to graded professionals such as railwaymen, mechanics, and sailors.

Labor activity began early. A mechanics' mutual aid association came into being in 1893, and a branch of the National African Sailors' and Firemen's Union was founded in the early 1920s. One of the most active organizations was the Nigerian Civil Service Union, an association of various groups which in 1946 became a trade union in the strict sense.

By World War II, about twenty-five major work-stoppages had taken place: twelve in Lagos, six in the east of the country, four in the west, and three on a nationwide scale. We have mentioned the strike of the unskilled workers in Lagos in 1897. One of the most characteristic was the strike of 1904, begun by railway officials in protest against a new contract that eliminated sick pay. One official alerted his colleagues by railway telegraph; by the time the return message arrived, a supporting group had been formed. Even if the general strike was broken by blacklegs, it gained much publicity, thanks to the *Lagos Weekly Record,* which was edited by the father of one of the leaders. In short, the workers on a number of occasions proved their capacity to defend their interests and organize resistance.

In the period between the two world wars, the Communist International exerted a limited but real radical influence. In 1928, with the effective support of the Profintern, the influence of the International Committee of Negro Workers began to spread in South Africa, reaching West Africa as well. The impetus came from George Padmore, a Marxist from Trinidad who established the Negro Workers' Bureau in Hamburg to recruit Black cadres and disseminate Marxist literature in the colonized world. He probably contacted the workers of Lagos through the Seamen and Harbour Workers' International and the British section of the Anti-Imperialist League. In 1930 he traveled incognito along the western coast to recruit delegates to the first International Negro Workers' Conference, held that year in Hamburg. When workers in Lagos were found to possess copies of the organization's journal, *The Negro Worker,* the Nigerian government accused the journal of having contributed to the disturbances in Aba. One of Padmore's traveling companions was the son of the Nigerian Herbert Macaulay, of whom we will see more. A nationalist from the beginning, he attended the Fifth Congress of the Profintern in Moscow with three other Africans. His successor in 1931 was Wallace Johnson from Sierra Leone who, the following year, also traveled to Europe and visited Moscow.

The limited impact of the pre–trade union organizations caused certain activists to look for a local political answer to their demands. The creation in 1922 of the Nigerian Labour Corporation, which published a bulletin to "defend the cause of labour," can be seen as a first draft for a labor party. Wage earners, however, constituted less than 4 percent of the population of Nigeria. The corporation was subject to the persecution of the employers and the incomprehension of its members, who wanted to use it as an employment agency or a source of financial assistance rather than as an instrument of militant action. Another attempt was made by Wallace Johnson, editor of the *Nigerian Daily Telegraph,* in 1930, but his appeal for radical economic solidarity in an African Workers Union to put an end to foreign exploitation only recruited 200 members. Police repression then forced him to leave the country.

Communist influence was much less in evidence than a search for an alliance with the emerging local middle class, the only one whose delegates to the colonial government could claim to be chosen in a representative manner. Undoubtedly class antagonism did exist; for example, several wealthy Lagos entrepreneurs exploited cheap Black labor on their cocoa and kola plantations. Yet, the Blacks were conscious of their overall position of subordination, and the bourgeois leaders put forward their claims on behalf of everyone. Thus, Herbert Macaulay founded the Nigerian National Democratic Party (NNDP) and placed his intellectual talents at the service of wage earners both in his *Lagos Daily News* and on the Legislative Council. In 1935, the NNDP succeeded in pressing for the creation of a Commission of Enquiry on Underemployment. The commission discovered that only half of the 4,000 workers questioned had been born in Lagos and that nearly 4 percent of the active population was unemployed, while 50,000 unskilled workers were employed in the public sector and 3,000 clerks in commerce.

The NNDP accomplished very little for the workers during the Great Depression, for it was opposed to direct action and thus to strikes. Distrustful of the masses, it advocated representative constitutional action through legal participation of the urban elite in the colonial government. After 1934 it was overshadowed by the more active Lagos Youth Movement, which set up a Labour Bureau and demanded not only political reforms but economic ones. These, it is true, were chiefly concerned with defending African businessmen against the Europeans and with protecting the peasants (through the creation of cooperatives and the organization of credit and support for

the planters and transporters of cocoa), but the movement did establish connections with one of the best-organized trade unions of the 1930s, the Railway Workers' Union. The votes of the wage earners put members of the
movement in the majority among the Africans on the Legislative Council
in 1938.

The Lagos Youth Movement eventually fell victim to internal strife, but
by 1938 the prenationalist political parties had understood the need of an
alliance with the trade unions. This strategy brought success to a new party,
Azikiwe's National Council of Nigeria and the Cameroons (NCNC) just
after the war. In Nigeria as elsewhere in Africa, henceforth trade unionism
entered the political forum.

The Turning Point: World War I

Virtually everywhere in West Africa, the beginnings of urban and proto-
industrial action and wage demands date to the last years of World War I or,
more clearly, to the interwar period. This must be understood in relation to
the economic unrest of the time. Unprecedented unemployment was aggravated—especially in French West Africa—by the return of the servicemen
and rates of inflation averaging 300 percent, while the wretchedly low wages
remained almost unchanged. On the Dakar-Niger railway, for instance, the
wage index for unskilled labor, fixed at 110 from 1914 to 1916, rose to 228
in 1920, while the price index for imported basic consumer-goods such as
cloth, drinks, tea, and rice rose to 1,222. The cumulative effects of runaway
inflation, of the wage freezes, and of many other forms of deprivation during
the war gave rise to the first disturbances. In Dakar the workers of the Senegal Company struck in December 1917; at about the same period, a strike in
a depot lasted two days, followed by an attempted general strike on January
in the following year and a bricklayer's strike in Rufisque in February.[30] Unrest showed most strongly among the war veterans, the most acculturated
workers. To be sure, their action was ambiguous because of their consciousness of being privileged, with prior rights to employment, but generally
speaking they played a dynamic role in social agitation. Their first activity
took place in the repatriation camps, where demobilization still dragged on
in 1919. Delays in payment of wages, combined with a resentment of unkept
promises, led them to revolt.

Most of West Africa, including British West Africa, was affected by the
same malaise. Two waves of unrest spread throughout the area. The first
began at the end of the war as a result of inflation (hence the often mixed
character of these manifestations in which Europeans and Africans found
themselves side by side): the dockers' strike in Conakry in 1918; the strike
by the Nigerian Mechanics' Union in 1919, which was renewed the following year throughout the railway system in Senegal; in Gambia from 1921 on;
and in 1923 in Porto-Novo. The second wave took place in 1925–1926, the
years of the "great strikes," as they are called. At that period, the contrast

had grown intolerable between the Africans' poverty and the colonizers' obvious prosperity in those last years before the Great Depression. The unrest began to be accompanied by anticolonialist political demands, for the workers' discontent found an echo in the incipient claims of the relatively well-established middle class of the creoles of Sierra Leone and the *Originaires* of Senegal.

Development and Repression in Sierra Leone

The labor movement in Sierra Leone began in 1919 and was at first confined to the wage demands of a very specific professional group, the day-laborers on the railways.[31] The war bonus the administration granted at the termination of hostilities to all socioprofessional groups except this one in any case proved inadequate to offset the economic crisis. The price of rice had risen by 400 percent: one measure cost a full day's pay. The day-laborers petitioned for an increase in wages; when it was refused, they called a general strike on 17 July 1919. After only two days, the administration agreed to a substantial increase, but the gesture came too late. Discontent turned to riots directed against the Syrian-Lebanese merchants who had been settling in the country over the previous twenty years and who were accused of profiteering in the crisis. In most of the urban centers, looting of their stores continued through the end of the month.

The complete success of this action, marked by an increase in wages and no sanctions, led to the founding of the Railway Workers' Union, which declared a second strike the following year. This time the forces of repression won: the army and police intervened and sixteen leaders of the movement were fired.

The strike of 1926 had much more the character of a social movement with political undertones. It too was organized by the Railway Workers' Union, and it took place within the framework of colonial legality. In 1925, Blacks and creoles had been given the right to occupy positions of responsibility previously reserved for Europeans alone. The effect of this was to make them aware of the fact that they received lower pay for identical work. The subsequent general strike included day-laborers and permanent employees, engine drivers and train crews, station officials and administrative staff, and nearly all the telegraph office employees.

What was new here was the support of the creole intelligentsia of Freetown, who were sympathetic to the grievances of the masses. A Committee of Support was set up and the local press devoted extensive space to letters from readers. The opinion a "returned exile," formerly a businessman in Accra, expressed in the *Weekly News* was revealing. He affirmed his attachment to law and order but opposed the government's demand for absolute submission, which, he said, was starving the workers. He had therefore supported the strike financially.

The strike was on a large scale. It lasted six weeks and, in the course of time, acquired a political dimension, expressing the accumulated resentment of the creole elite and their capacity to recognize the workers as potential allies against colonial oppression. The administration understood this and responded with political sanctions. Since 1895, the creoles of Freetown had enjoyed considerable communal liberties, electing a City Council directed by a mayor and aldermen. This council was a cradle for the political ambitions of the rising class, especially as, since 1924, a limited number of Black members had been admitted to the Legislative Council. Now the constitution of 1924 was suspended; the City Council was dissolved and was replaced by a council entirely appointed by the government—an arrangement that lasted for twenty-two years, until 1948. The Blacks were censured and debarred from recruitment to public office and from promotion.

The setback of 1926 for many years ended trade union activity, which was now regarded by the authorities as a springboard for political agitation. When, a little later, Wallace Johnson tried to use the disturbed situation during the Great Depression to instigate a strike, the repression was rapid and violent. The major African party, the Congress Movement, was prevented from utilizing its popular basis to act as a mass party.

Trade Unions in French West Africa

During World War I, French West Africa provided more than 160,000 recruits for the army, as well as economic assistance in the form of requisitions to be sent to France (although they were often abandoned on the docks) that made considerable inroads into the local production.[32] Although they were not yet numerous, the wage earners, because they were most fully integrated into the monetary economy, were most aware of the decline in their standard of living. The dramatic inflation of the franc caused a rapid deterioration in purchasing power. The price of imported rice from Indochina, which had become the basic food in the cities, had soared, while local wages and incomes had remained stationary.

Senegal, unlike the rest of sub-Saharan Africa, had a unified European/African trade union. No doubt this was because in Senegal alone the French colonizers had adopted a policy of assimilation, whose most remarkable and singular expression is associated with the four "free towns" or "communes": all "natives" (originaires) of the towns of Saint-Louis, Rufisque, Gorée, and Dakar were granted French citizenship in 1916.

Senegal at that time was the most industrialized French colony in Africa, but it was undeveloped compared to South Africa and Zambia. Nonetheless, the railwaymen of Senegal took a leading role in the fight for equality. In regard to Black workers—originaires and others—the official idea of assimilation implicitly affirmed, or at least allowed workers to lay claim to, the same civic, intellectual, and therefore political identity as that enjoyed by Whites. After World War II, the French administration proclaimed a second policy, that of centralization, which reinforced the Black workers' claim. By unifying the French West African railways into a single system, the RAN (also called the Régie des Chemins de Fer de l'AOF), the colonizers themselves moved the issue of equality beyond the borders of Senegal.

Two separate associations, one European and one indigenous, originally existed. The first received official recognition in 1918, and the second—limited to the Dakar–Saint-Louis railway line—only in 1927. Their professed objectives were professional: to protect the workers' wages and to negotiate with management. But the indigenous association soon demonstrated its political sympathies by joining the Ligue de Défense de la Race Nègre, created in Paris in 1927 by the Senegalese communist activist Lamine Senghor out of the year-old Comité de Défense de la Race Nègre.

The absence of a color bar favored the emergence of the trade union spirit. Where wages were concerned, it was not the color of workers' skins that counted, but their country of origin. A French Black from Senegal could not obtain a *prime coloniale* (colonial pay differential), but a French Black from the West Indies had just as much right to it as a French White from the mother country. Moreover, wages were more or less equal for equal work; it was the system of bonuses that doubled or more than doubled salaries, and it was differences of rank—from the unskilled African worker to the French managerial staff—that stretched the scale of remuneration.

Professional Agitation in the 1920s

The first joint action in Senegal took place in April 1919. It was led by the French, who demanded the inclusion of the bonuses in the salaries and asked for the creation of a retirement and contingency fund; the Africans would have been content with a raise of 0.50 francs a day and a cost-of-living allowance. The strike had lasted only three days when the administration at least partly satisfied the demands. With mounting inflation, various forms of agitation began again some months later among the African railwaymen. Once again, 80 percent of their demands were met. The Europeans renewed the issue of an eight-hour workday, which had rarely been practiced since, as a conciliatory measure, it had been decreed in 1919.

As in Sierra Leone, numerous relatively major strikes were held between 1919 and 1924, and in the period 1924–1926 they became political in nature. The demonstrations following the revolt of the Bambara workers on the Thiès-Niger line in 1925, for example, subsided only when the ringleaders were released. The campaign launched by the Communist party against the Rif war in Paris and the preparation of elections in Senegal in 1925 for the Colonial Council and for the municipality of Saint-Louis brought on a wave of anticolonial activity. Labor unrest affected all groups: day-laborers; temporary workers; railwaymen; postal employees, who went on strike in 1919 and again in 1925; and sailors, who distinguished themselves by a seventeen-day strike in 1928. Increasing economic malaise, however (the prices of speculative crops began to drop in the second half of the decade), prevented the success of these activities and heralded a period of retreat that lasted through the Great Depression and on to the era of the Popular Front. Trade union activities, after all, prosper best when profits are rising; when jobs are scarce and profits shrink, employers are reluctant to show generosity.

The Popular Front.   The greatest impetus to trade unionism was given by the government of the Popular Front when in 1936 it legalized the application in French West Africa—at least for "Europeans and the assimilated"[33]—of the laws of 1884 and 1904 that established syndicalism in France. The approach diametrically opposed that applied in Indochina. There an earlier awakening of Communist militancy, more threatening for the authorities, caused the socialist government prudently to delay the measure. The innovation in Senegal resulted in the immediate appearance of numerous trade unions. In order to join, the Africans theoretically had to prove that they knew how to read and write, but the terms of eligibility were liberal, although the differences between Africans and Europeans in employment, wages, and trade union training and experience made day-to-day functioning sometimes difficult. Paradoxically, this upsurge of trade unionism led in 1937 to a split into European and African railway trade unions; periodic attempts at renewed fusion proved futile.

A successful strike would often result in the creation of a new trade union. Altogether, by the end of 1937, nearly 8,000 trade union members (that is to say, 10 to 13 percent of the wage earners, a considerable percentage for the period) belonged to forty-two unions and sixteen professional associations. The devaluation of the franc, which caused prices to rise considerably, accelerated the movement. The struggle also represented a form of opposition to the colonial administration, even though the trade union leaders tended to avoid embarrassing the left-wing government.

The dockworkers of the port of Dakar and subsequently of Rufisque, Saint-Louis, and Kaolack, the bakers, and the oil and soap manufacturers of West Africa each in succession brought some 1,500 to 2,000 people out on strike. They won assorted social reforms, including an eight-hour workday (it was nine hours in the rest of West Africa), workmen's compensation, legislation regulating the employment of women and children, and the organization of an efficient staff to monitor the application of labor laws. Employers, trade unions, and the government, in coordination with the chambers of commerce, began extensive negotiations that covered such basic issues as wages, the application of the eight-hour workday, and job discrimination. Most of these negotiations were peaceful. The harshest demonstrations took place among the most underprivileged groups, and the only real violence came in the January 1937 strike by the truckdrivers of Kaolack, a great harbor in the Sine-Salum peanut area. Despite their excellent organization, with pickets and road blocks, the administration succeeded when it confronted them with their traditional rivals, the camel drivers and ass drivers.

In 1938, after the Popular Front collapsed, a bloody confrontation in Thiès brought an end to this brief period of social euphoria and toughening of Black demands.[34] Until the Thiès strike, the trade unions had only a small active membership, but in this strike the day-laborers, whose condition was the worst of all the railway workers, came to the fore. The strikers of Thiès belonged to the "indigenous" trade union of the Dakar-Niger railway, a huge enterprise employing some 7,000 to 8,000 workers, 2,000 of whom lived at the main station of Thiès. Day-laborers and auxiliaries, illiterates and temporary workers were excluded from employment security and collective wage agreements. They worked nine hours a day under deplorable conditions.

They had made a prior attempt in 1936, and when they reactivated their movement two years later, the political situation proved unfavorable. It was the time of the Munich Conference and war seemed imminent. The administration therefore refused to tolerate a strike that could prevent transport of conscripts. A confrontation left 6 dead and 119 wounded, including 49 policemen. The strike announced the emergence of a trade unionism no longer French but supported by the most wretched African groups. This new body of activists could, particularly in the English-speaking countries, be drawn into the anticolonialist struggle.

Post–World War II Assimilationism. Curiously, the labor movement subsequently became politicized less rapidly in Senegal than elsewhere, despite an enormous strike by the workers of the RAN, the greatest colonial enterprise of the period, with 20,000 wage earners (a tenth of the salaried population of French West Africa). The strikers included workers on the Dakar-Niger railway and those from the Ivory Coast, Dahomey, and Guinea, as well as workers and unskilled laborers from the docks.[35]

The strike was most widespread in Senegal, and it lasted there for an unprecedented five months, from 10 October 1947 to 19 March 1948. The reasons for the strike were clear. The standard of living had fallen abysmally; to the salary freeze during the war was added the staggering rise in prices following reestablishment of contact with Europe. The creation of the colonial franc with a local value twice that of the French franc did not compensate for the high price of imported consumer goods.[36] The essential motivation of the strike could have led it toward a political outcome: the Africans sought to obtain identical treatment to the Europeans—a right that had been officially recognized six months earlier. This vast movement to reject racial discrimination was, moreover, supported by the population as a whole, who

contributed to a solidarity fund that allowed the railwaymen an income
equivalent to their salary throughout the duration of the strike.[37] In spite of
the favorable conditions and the impetus provided by the defeat of Nazism,
however, the strike never passed beyond its institutional framework to become a larger political movement.

The tenacity of the Senegalese was not shown on the Ivory Coast. The
planters protested against the commercial paralysis resulting from this
strike, which occurred just as the coffee-trading season began. Local politicians and colonial administrators joined forces to curb the strike there,
where it affected far fewer workers (about 500 railwaymen and 1,700 dockworkers). Work was resumed in the Ivory Coast at the beginning of January.

Why was there no specific juncture between social and political aspirations, which at that point were nationalist? Partly because the assimilationist
myth still held sway in Senegal both among the politicians and among the
workers who formed part of the monetary economy. To seek equal treatment meant asking to be accorded the rights of a French citizen rather than
opposing French rule. Moreover, the time was not ripe for a fusion between
trade unionism and nationalist politics. The Communist International, true
to the line it had adopted since the beginning of the 1930s when European
fascism was coming to power, avoided setting itself openly against the colonial powers and did not wish to operate a nationalist movement from behind the scenes. No doubt the wholehearted support of the CGT (Confédération Générale du Travail) for unaffiliated trade unions was effective,
but the French Communist party preferred to limit its struggle to social and
economic matters in the tradition of colonial trade unionism. After all,
the persistent factor in the labor history of the Senegalese railwaymen since
the turn of the century had been the fight against unequal wages. Even if the
strikes were in fact aimed against colonial exploitation and even if they implied a national struggle, social and political forces had not yet merged.

12

Trade Unionism and Nationalism: The Slow Growth of Sociopolitical Movements

The long-standing divergence between the political activists and the popular movements can readily be explained by their differences in origin, culture, determination, and objectives.

THE ELITES

Some elite groups were reformers, others were radicals. All, however, belonged to the educated class. They had attended French-run schools, and they acted as cultural mediators between the African natives and the Europeans.

A Reformist Bourgeoisie

The elites had long been urban and acculturated. They represented two concepts that were both contradictory and complementary: resistance and collaboration. The term *elite*—which draws attention to Western cultural influence—is somewhat unsatisfactory. These people undoubtedly constituted a middle class of diverse origins that aspired to the rights and status of a European-style bourgeoisie. The colonial system had, however, largely denied them both economic and political equality. Until World War II, this group nonetheless aimed, not to reject the Whites, but to assimilate their knowledge, to be accepted as their equals, and to participate in the exercise of a power divested of its "abuses" and opened to African representatives.

To see the prewar elites as a "nationalist" resistance is anachronistic in the same way as attributing an anticolonialist ideology to the Popular Front would be. The concept of nationalism came into being only when activists openly revolted against the colonial regime in the hope of becoming the legal masters of their national destiny. Before World War II, at the most a struggle took place to modify certain unbearable features of an accepted system. The elites did not recognize themselves as "natives" any more than the colonial officers did, but they asserted that they had emerged from the natives and consequently should represent them—and dominate them. In short, the overwhelming majority of the prewar elites held to the reformist school of thought.

The example of Dahomey (Benin) admirably illustrates both their aspirations and their limitations. Although it has been studied a great deal, this case was in no way exceptional. Throughout Africa, small or medium-sized cash-crop plantations and colonialism brought into being similar elites (for example, the creoles of West Africa, the agrarian petite bourgeoisie of Kenya, the merchant entrepreneurs of the ports and caravan routes, the petty officials of colonization). Their political ambitions grew in proportion to their social and economic importance. It was these new notables, in fact, who nurtured and finally harvested the fruits of decolonization.

By the 1920s, the Dahomean bourgeoisie gropingly sought new forms of expression. One sign of this search was the demonstrations in Porto-Novo in response to the crisis of 1921–1922, aggravated by the will of the administration to balance the commercial deficit through a poll tax, sale of marketing licenses, and a tax on the European-style residences of the notables. After World War I, the first generation of graduates of the schools of Dakar (Louis Hunkanrin was one) began to denounce colonial abuses, first on wall posters, then in petitions of agrarian protest against the omnipotent administration, and finally, in 1917, by creating the first Dahomean newspaper, *Le Récadère de Béhanzin*. In February 1923, these Jeunes Evolués succeeded in rousing the people to action. The Franco-Muslim Committee was supported by princes who were political adversaries of King Toffa (who had died in 1908) and of his descendants, especially Sonigbe, who claimed to be his legitimate heir. This group, with the local section of the Ligue des Droits de l'Homme, led the population to refuse to pay the increases, to demonstrate in the streets, and to boo a delegation of cantonal chiefs. The employees in the private sector and the dockworkers at Cotonou went on strike. There was a brutal reaction: a state of siege was declared, the ringleaders were banished, and the heavy collective fine of 360,000 francs was imposed. The movement was quashed for several years.[1]

The new social class made up of graduates of schools was not restricted to the petty bureaucracy. In lower Dahomey, known at that period as the Latin Quarter of French Africa, the elite, as elsewhere, was mixed. It began with Afro-Brazilians, former slave-traders who had turned to the oil trade and, as merchants or interpreters, acted as ideal intermediaries for the colonizers. The loss of their former source of economic power had made them eager to adopt the culture of the new rulers. Living in the European manner and sending their children to the Catholic school, they formed the basis of a little bourgeoisie of literates. "For us Blacks," they wrote, "education is a matter of life and death."[2]

The bureaucratic stratum was made up of the personnel of the local administration and commercial firms (secretaries, interpreters, instructors, nurses, postal employees, managers, cashiers). Dahomey contained 299 of these officials in 1914, 433 in 1924, 603 in 1929, and 776 in 1936, which then constituted nearly half of the *évolués,* who were ready to claim advancement in the social scale.

Side by side with these appeared a new type of small tradesman, retailer, or rural broker. The colonizers' concern to limit the possible competition of African trade to the expatriated firms fostered the consciousness of this group, which financed the local press and contributed to it. Finally, planters, descendants of the great Brazilian and royal farmers and administrative chiefs enriched by the conquest, sometimes were truly wealthy. Maximilien Quenum, for example, sent two of his sons to study in France while the third subsidized *La Voix du Dahomey;* Simon Akinde used his paternal fortune to publish Allada's *L'Echo des Cercles.*

Distinguished by their literacy, social status, and way of life, the *évolués* (*akowe*) expected to influence the evolution of the community, either through assimilation into the colonial bourgeoisie or, less commonly at that period, through an alliance with the incipient urban proletariat via trade union action. Their preferred mode of expression was the press.

The first Dahomean newspaper, *Le Guide du Dahomey,* which appeared in 1920, was a short-lived vehicle for the views of a naturalized ex-infantryman, Dorothée Lima, whose slogan was "Dahomey for the Dahomeans." The failure of the labor demonstration of 1923 then curbed the tendency to radicalism for several years. Not until the Great Depression did the malaise of the elite express itself in a proliferation of newspapers (fourteen!). The chief of these was *La Voix du Dahomey,* which had been founded in 1927. In 1933, its steering committee comprised seven commercial employees, thirteen businessmen and tradesmen, four farmers, one artisan, and only one official. Its first critical article dealt with the tax on the turnover of trade. A self-appointed "organ of defense of the general interests of the country," not by "revolution" but by "evolution," the newspaper, beneath its careful self-censorship, covered all the fundamental questions. It discussed the function of the elite (35.5 percent of the articles), and, as a secondary consideration, educational policy (6.8 percent); the defense of the masses, ill-treatment of the natives, denials of justice, and so forth (46.2 percent); and, finally, fiscal and economic questions (11.5 percent). A novel feature was the establishment of local committees scattered throughout the country to garner material support for the journal.[3]

Although the newspaper had only about 2,000 readers, or 2 percent of the population, the administration waged a struggle against this weapon for the arousal of consciousness on the part of the colonized. Governor de Coppet, who was otherwise known for his pro-Black and socialistic policies, noted in a memorandum in 1933, "[The newspapers] show sympathy for certain extreme forms of Communism. . . . Their influence is detestable. I have decided to fight them."[4]

The journal defended itself against this charge. "We are neither rebels, nor revolutionaries, nor Communists, but servants of France." The government nonetheless held the newspapers responsible for the passive resistance to taxation, which was really due to the peasants' destitution. The administration staged a surprise search of the newspaper premises, arrested the directors, and initiated long-drawn-out legal proceedings based on the accusation that the paper had a "pernicious effect on the indigenous masses." The affair roused strong feelings. Some members of the opposition, such as Louis Hunkanrin, vigorously supported the newspaper. The verdict, handed down in the far more liberal political atmosphere of the Popular Front (June 1936) at the end of a court case that was followed with passionate interest, finally granted the victory to the elite.

The lack of fighting spirit shown by this Dahomean elite after its victory contrasts surprisingly with its former vitality. Perhaps because of the war, during which the Vichy regime suppressed any signs of resistance and reduced nationalism to an unimpeachable loyalty toward the French "mother country," the Dahomean reform movement seemed to have reached the limits of its development. The politicized elite, imbued with French culture, accepted the colonial ideal of the French socialists and sought only a collaboration with the colonizer that would guarantee them administrative autonomy. In Senegal, the presence of Black French citizens from the four "communes" made the imitation of the French model even more obvious. After the social stimulation of the Popular Front, the railwaymen's strike in Thiès in 1938 and its violent consequences revealed the deepening rift between the middle classes, who had been won over to the government's labor policy, and the popular activists, who gave rise briefly to the fear that through the blood that had been shed they might succeed in fundamentally challenging the colonial system.

The Birth of Radicalism

Until the war, anticolonial African radicalism remained very much a minority movement. Continent-wide censorship almost completely blocked the infiltration of "pernicious" Western ideas of liberty and independence, and a repressive apparatus rendered political expression virtually impossible except in the four "communes." The Belgian Congo still remembers how Patrice Lumumba found in the French Middle Congo in the 1940s (which was hardly a paragon of open democracy at that period) a freedom that he had not known existed.[5]

We have mentioned the difficulties encountered in English-speaking West Africa by a few clandestine internationalists such as George Padmore and Wallace Johnson. Even in the Gold Coast, where proto-nationalists had been speaking out, in attempts to gain autonomy, since the end of the nine-teenth century, fighters for independence were still, in 1940, very few. The most remarkable among them was Dr. Joseph Kwamé Danquah, who had earned a doctorate. He organized the Gold Coast Youth Conference, whose political aim was to seek recognition as a dominion. His program, which was moderate, included a democratization of the Legislative Council, whose twenty-nine members included only nine Africans (six elected by the chiefs and three landowners, one from each of the three coastal towns); he pro-posed two chambers, one elected and the other composed of chiefs who pos-sessed the power of veto. He also demanded that Africans be recruited into the civil service.

When a few English-speaking graduates left Africa, they encountered the Afro-American concept of pan-Africanism. Kwame Nkrumah, son of a blacksmith in the southwest, in 1935 left his job as a schoolmaster in Achi-mota to make the "great leap" to the United States. He spent ten years in American universities, then studied for two years in England. During his exile from Africa he was searching, as he put it, for "a formula by which the whole colonial question and the problem of imperialism could be solved." He devoured the writings of Marx, Lenin, Mazzini, and especially Marcus Garvey and worked extensively as an activist in the African diaspora. As president of the African Students' Organization of the United States and Canada, he played a leading role in the Pan-African Congress in Manchester in 1945. He began political activity in his own country only in 1947.

French-speaking activists found their forum in the Communist party or the International in France. A Dahomean, Kodjo Houenou, the brother of one of the supporters of *La Voix du Dahomey,* founded in France the Ligue Universelle de Défense de la Race Noire (the Universal League for the De-fense of the Black Race). Their journal, *Continents,* was brought to trial by Senegalese Deputy Blaise Diagne. Since the 1930s the Communist party had been trying to reach the Black African workers and war veterans in France through the Union Inter-coloniale. When he went to France in 1922, Lamine Senghor (not related to the ex-president), a former infantryman who had been gassed in World War I, became active in the group. He participated in the first manifestations of the intercolonial antimilitarism, apropos of the Ruhr and the Rif campaigns. In the Workers' and Peasants' Congress of the Paris Region, Senghor's rousing speech and the embrace he shared with Hadj Ali implied the rejection of a fratricidal war between pariah peoples. In 1925, the Communist party ran Senghor, then one of the few Black leaders of ability in the Colonial Commission, as a "colonial candidate" for the thir-teenth *arrondissement* in Paris. He appeared in a leading role in the Brussels Congress, and he was elected to the board of the Anti-Imperialist League.[6] In 1926, he gathered a nucleus of Young African Communist students, among the best from the William Ponty School of Teachers, who had been sent to study in Aix-en-Provence. They established, along the lines of Indo-Chinese and North African organizations, what was to be named the Ligue contre L'Oppression Coloniale et Impérialisme and its newspaper, *La Voix des Nègres*. In France, however, the group did not succeed in converting either the intellectuals or the workers in the party. Senghor's intense effort to propagandize among the Black seamen of Marseilles, Le Havre, and Bordeaux came up against clientism and was aborted by the police, aided by informers who hunted out even the mildest anticolonial organizations. In 1927, the moderates, with police help, ousted Senghor (who was arrested in that year), along with his few revolutionary companions.

The movement had little more effect in Senegal, although the socialist Lamine Gueye related the difficulties of these students in the journal *L'A.O.F.*, but it touched most of the African activists who passed through Paris. In 1919 a branch of the Ligue was founded in Cameroon by a somewhat questionable activist of Guianan origin, Victor Ganty, who had first tried to found a spiritualist "church," the Science Chrétienne Réunie du Cameroun. At one point he earned the distinction of uniting the hostility of the modernist school of thought with the traditional opposition of the Duala notables, when he succeeded Richard Manga Bell as the leader of the Association France-Cameroun. In 1931 he addressed a petition to the League of Nations entitled "Defense of Black Cameroon Citizens."[7]

André Matswa, an infantryman in the colonial war in the Rif in 1925, may well have been moved by the same influence when he founded the Amicale des Originaires de l'A.E.F., although the moderation of his demands, like those of the Senegalese, reflected the mirage of (equal) citizenship. Matswa had outstanding success among the Bakongo in Brazzaville and afterward in Libreville and Bangui, where the Amicale counted 13,000 members in 1929. The numbers of demonstrators on the worksites brought about a repression, and in 1930 Matswa was condemned to prison and deportation.

In France, Tiemoko Garan Kouyate succeeded Lamine Senghor as the leader of the Young African Communists in 1927. He refused, for the sake of African unity and independence, to "enter the [colonial] system." He worked in the Confédération Générale du Travail for the creation of autonomous Black trade unions; put forward the idea of an Institut Nègre in Paris; organized an Exposition Anti-coloniale, in response to the Exposition Coloniale Internationale of 1931 sponsored by Blaise Diagne and the Colonial Ministry; founded a school of Marxist studies in Marseilles; and participated in the Congress of the Third International. Most important, in 1931 he began to publish *Le Cri des Nègres,* and the following year, in the midst of the Great Depression, he established the Union des Travailleurs Nègres. This marked the start of a period of revolutionary propaganda in Africa in which newspapers and tracts smuggled from Europe exercised an influence in the cities. The appeal known as *L'Histoire d'un merle blanc* ("The Story of a White Crow") from the name of the booklet whose cover was used to conceal it, served as the program of the Ligue de Lutte pour la Liberté des Peuples du Sénégal et du Soudan. The Ligue was founded by Kouyate in Dakar in 1933 on the instigation of the colonial section of the French Communist party. Its *Merle blanc* appeal appears to have been the first call for national independence. "We are fighting for the right of the peoples of Senegal to self-determination," it proclaimed, "by forming an independent national state. . . . The groups of the Ligue are preparing the workers and the peasants for the great decisive battles of the Senegalese peoples."[8]

At the end of 1933 Kouyate was expelled from the Communist party for refusing to adhere to the party line, but he continued to work for the emancipation of the African continent. He collaborated with George Padmore in planning the Congrès Mondial Nègre (which was postponed until after the war). At the end of 1935 he founded the journal *Africa,* and he took advantage of the Popular Front to establish the Fédération Française des Jeunesses d'Afrique Noire and to address a "Plan for Decolonization" to the governor-general in 1937. Just before the war, he founded the first Association des Etudiants de l'Ouest Africain. He was deported, and he died in 1942.

After 1936, the local and international situation no longer favored political expressions of anticolonialism. The young Black intellectuals in Paris usually reacted against acculturation by asserting their African identity. The French assimilationist policy made Africans' integration dependent on their rejection of traditional values; they were recognized as citizens only on condition that they Westernized their outlook. Since they had no political outlet, these Black intellectuals adopted a literary form, publishing the review *L'Etudiant Noir* in 1934. In 1939 this journal launched the idea of *négritude,* invented by the West Indian poet Aimé Césaire and the Senegalese Léopold Sedar Senghor. From that time until independence, this movement was to play a considerable role as a weapon of struggle in French Africa.

The Communist Study Groups

World War II had a crucial effect on African "consciousness." The number of those conscripted was much smaller than in World War I, but the Africans sent abroad, especially to the Japanese front, learned from contact with new peoples and ideas. Part of the native African elite was quick to apply Soviet and American anticolonialist propaganda to their own situation. The Atlantic Charter signed in 1941 by Churchill and Roosevelt, on the latter's insistence, proclaimed the right of all peoples to self-determination in the name of democracy and freedom, and this principle was reiterated in the United Nations Charter in 1945. The message was adopted and elaborated by a new generation of nationalist militants.

The Groupes d'Etudes Communistes were organized in the capitals of French Africa from 1943 on in support of the Free French government. They were especially active just after the war, when the few French Communists stationed in the Empire wished to continue their militant activism after leaving the Resistance. The composition of these groups was as diverse as their origins, and some members subsequently adapted themselves to the colonial system. Many of the study groups evolved from those set up by Communist activists to consider the role of the Communist Delegation to Algiers in 1943–1944. Africans, of course, were included in these activities, and after the expulsion of the French Communists between 1947 and 1950, the groups became entirely African.

A small nucleus of French workers from Toulon and Ferryville lived in Dakar. Involved in their private activities and belonging to the Dakar dockworkers' union, reestablished in 1943, they had little contact with the Africans. Railway workers, teachers (including Camille Souyris, later deputy director of education in French West Africa), a few officers, and a professor from the School of Medicine also formed study groups. These groups had contacts with certain African organizations: in the Ivory Coast, with Félix Houphouët-Boigny's syndicate of African planters, and in Dakar, Thiès, Bobo-Dioulasso with the Comité d'Etudes Franco-Africaines. This all-African organization, whose motto was "Africa Mater," consisted entirely of members of the elite. It covered its activities by adopting a conformist name and pursuing cultural objectives (the study of African languages), but in fact its intentions were anticolonial. In October 1946, after the constitutive Congress at Bamako, it was succeeded by the Rassemblement Démocratique Africain (RDA).

In Abidjan, the Groupe d'Etudes Communistes originally brought together people opposed to the planters and suspicious of Houphouët-Boigny. Here Jean Lambert, an administrator connected with Governor André Latrille, for some years formed a link between the agricultural syndicate and the Groupe d'Etudes Communistes. In Dakar, the Groupe d'Etudes played a more limited role than it did in the Ivory Coast. It was confronted with a political movement inherited from the four "communes" and the federation of the Section Française de l'Internationale Ouvrière (SFIO) in Senegal. The Senegalese, who had been ruled by the French since the seventeenth century, had no wish to take orders from the Ivory Coast. They saw the RDA as "anti-Senegalese." Communist political activity was thus limited to a small and marginal party, the Union Démocratique Sénégalaise (the Senegalese section of the RDA), founded in 1948. This group attempted combined action with Léopold Senghor's party, the Bloc Démocratique Sénégalais, with which it fused in 1946, at the time of the Loi Defferre. They separated again in 1958, at the time of the vote on the constitution. The Union Démocratique Sénégalaise, no longer affiliated with the RDA, then gave birth to the

Parti du Regroupement Africain du Sénégal, which no longer exists. All the parties outside the RDA constituted the PRA (Parti du Regroupement Africain). Another party professing Marxism, the Parti Africain de l'Indépendance (PAI), was founded in 1957 by students returning from France. These were more dogmatic than the Marxists of 1947–1948 from the William Ponty School, and most were exiled in the 1960s. The founder of the party, Mahjemout Diop, whose Marxism, learned in Rumania, was ill adapted to Africa, took refuge in Mali. The party had to change its name to the Parti de l'Indépendance et du Travail (PIT) when its initials were usurped by a little group, trained by a former secretary-general, which was banished, and then recalled by Senghor in order to serve as a controlled legal opposition. The Groupe d'Etudes Communistes still existed as late as 1950, Ousmane Ba having succeeded Jean Suret-Canale as its director.[9]

In Senegal, Communist activity was limited by its lack of influence on the trade unions as institutions, but in Cameroon trade unionism took on a political character exceptionally early. Colonial oppression was harsh. Even after the war, political activity remained impossible. Unlike in Senegal, in Cameroon meetings were forbidden, and censorship and informing were commonplace. The first activists, some twenty people from Cameroon and a few Europeans led by Gaston Donnat, a Communist teacher of Algerian "pied noir" origin, began to meet clandestinely in Yaoundé in 1944. This little circle came out into the open in 1945, when it gave birth to the officially recognized Groupes d'Etudes Communistes. Its activists, who included the future revolutionary leader Ruben Um Nyobe, had already planned the structures of trade unions to be established as soon as official permission was granted.

The war also developed the labor force. In view of the vital strategic role of Africa and the difficulty of obtaining supplies, the Allies had to intensify local exploitation of strategic products (the iron of Sierra Leone, the tin of Nigeria) and, above all, to develop processing industries. The foreign trade of British West Africa thus doubled between 1938 and 1946. Moreover, pending the return of French West Africa to the Free French, the Vichy government wished to annex the activities that in France had fallen into the hands of the Germans. Its desire to industrialize manifested itself in industries aimed at producing economical products, at recycling, and at substituting local manufacture for imports.[10]

Thus in French Africa trade unions began to be affiliated with radical political parties such as the RDA, an exceptional interparty and interterritorial common front whose members were associated with the Communist groups in the French Parliament in the period 1946–1960. The Union des Populations Camerounaises (UPC, affiliated with the RDA) owed its effectiveness as a catalyst of national sentiment to the enthusiasm and organizational abilities of its leader, Ruben Um Nyobe, a former trade unionist of the Confédération Générale du Travail, but the movement was primarily a peasant rebellion. Similarly, it was only the support of the impoverished owners of small cocoa plantations that assured Nkrumah the victory of the Convention People's Party in 1951.

At the same time, the growing masses of the subproletariat in the cities, revealing their discontent in a series of disturbances, continued to arouse in the elite a distrust tinged with disdain but not devoid of apprehension.

URBAN CONFRONTATIONS

Urban confrontations were no new phenomenon in Africa. The most remarkable before the war were those in West Africa instigated by women. This was by no means an accident. Women traditionally played a distinct and important role in the regional economy, running the trade in food and fabrics, the articles of commerce whose trade was both the oldest and conducted on the largest scale.

The "Women's Wars" or "Aba Riots," Nigeria

The "women's wars" or "Aba riots" revealed in a fascinating manner a deep social malaise, in a transitional period midway between the precolonial Igbo society and the emerging Nigerian society. The women felt their role to be seriously threatened, first within the traditional system (in 1925), but also by colonial economic policies (in 1929).

The women's associations, within the traditional patrilineal context, upheld the order of life in the villages they entered by marriage. They also enabled the women to protect their own interests. It was through these associations, for instance, that Igbo women on the coast of Benin were able to keep their profits. The women cultivated taro, the basis of the local diet, and while the men gathered the palm nuts, the women extracted the oil and sold it. Moreover, the village market was controlled by the women: they did the selling, fixed the prices, and traveled great distances to trade their goods.

Thanks to the parallel decision-making apparatus, a woman could win a case against a man: one who regularly beat his wife, for instance, or who allowed his animals to graze in his wife's field. Finally, by maintaining links with the association of married women of their villages of origin, women benefited from an information network that went far beyond the boundaries of the village.[11]

Colonization threatened this well-organized system on three fronts. First, through the missionaries, the Europeans spread the ideal of a Victorian subjection of the woman to her home. Second, the oil presses of the British merchants robbed the women of their chief source of income. The third and principal destabilizing element was the introduction of currency, which devalued the cowrie shells traditionally used as a medium of exchange. When the British tried to introduce marketing licenses at Calabar in 1925, the women attacked Europeans and foreign Africans and, when the market was shut down, decided not to sell to Europeans.

It was not until 1927 and 1928 that taxation was introduced in the last five southern provinces. What particularly incensed the women was the appointment of warrant chiefs answerable to native councils, each presided over by a British officer. These councils were supposed to dispense a pseudo-native justice, impose fines, and convey the orders of the colonial administration—but without any reference to the traditions concerning women. The women thus found themselves dispossessed of their political and economic roles.

The rebellion of 1925 was still a movement of a primary sort, with a religious connotation. The women besieged the Native Courts and went to the homes of the warrant chiefs, singing and dancing and bringing them the message of their supreme spirit, Chineke. They sought a return to a pre-colonial way of life with the old religion revived and Christians excluded. They also demanded the reactivation of the traditional trade routes, the restoration of cowrie shells as the medium of exchange, and a reduction in bride-price—which the introduction of European currency had rendered prohibitive—and its payment in the traditional form. Finally, they wanted their right to fix the prices in the markets to be recognized.

The revolts of 1929, in contrast, whose immediate cause was the women's fear that they too might have to pay taxes, had an explicitly economic objective. The women, reacting to a sudden fall in the price of oil, demanded an end to the monopoly by European firms and the abolition of marketing licenses. The speed with which the news of the rebellion spread throughout the country from October on bore witness to the effectiveness of their information network. In December, more than 10,000 women from distant villages converged on Aba, and 6,000 on Owerrinta. The main object of their attack in town was always the Native Court, but they also assaulted other symbols of colonial rule—banks, post offices, warehouses. It was clear that the movement was by no means spontaneous, for the spokeswomen of the village organizations were the chief negotiators during the demonstrations. Sometimes a few concessions were granted, such as an agreement not to tax women or to require licenses, but a vigorous and effective repression followed: some sixty women were killed, twenty-nine of them at Opobo, on 16 December.

The British sought to explain these demonstrations as having been provoked by a secret organization of the Igbo men, who had sent their women as proxies out of a conviction that no repression would be aimed at women. An inquiry in 1930, however, proved that the rebellion was entirely the work of the women. The action was set firmly in the tradition of the village protests in which, if the women were displeased with a male member of the community, all the women together would mock him.

The protest action began with the women because, involved as they always had been in the trade of the region, they were more directly subjected to the vexations of colonial rule and more sensitive to falling prices than the men were. The men could profit from monetarization, because they participated in the wage-earning system and were engaged in more speculative cultivation. Finally, colonization offered those men who were able to read and write an opportunity for social and professional advancement that was denied to the women. The women, then, were conscious of being the chief victims of the new system.

There were other similar episodes that are less well known, such as the role of the women in the anti-pass campaign in South Africa in the years 1913–1918. The women's riots in Lomé (Togo) in 1933 were in the same category. We know the importance of women as traders in wholesale clothes; they are nicknamed "Nana-Benz" because of their ostentation, represented in our day by the possession of a Mercedes-Benz.[12] Heirs to a long tradition, they are businesswomen who amass fat bank accounts through a trade that has remained largely informal. In the 1930s, when the economic crisis hit tradespeople with full force, the women once again were the first to go into the streets to demonstrate their fury at the blind coercion and impossible financial demands of the colonial government. Yet other examples are the movement of the women of Saint-Louis who, under Soukeyna Konare, a cousin of Lamine Gueye's, on 4 May 1930 led a demonstration that, despite attempts at intimidation, allowed the elections for the Colonial Council to take place, or that of the women of Abidjan who, under the leaders of the women's committees of the Parti Démocratique de la Côte d'Ivoire, on 24 December 1949, after months of disturbances, undertook a long march to the prison of Grand-Bassam to demand the liberation of prisoners. In the same tradition, the "evicted" women of South Africa today confront armed police with their bare hands.[13]

Boycotts in Ghana and Uganda

The boycott was used as an intermediate form of protest, linking the rural areas and the city, the riot and the strike. The first boycotts were held in the rural areas or among the rural people in the cities. One of the earliest recorded boycotts took place from 21 to 25 May 1914. The Lebou truck-gardeners, fishmongers, and traders refused to supply the Dakar market, in reaction against the threat to their lands posed by the Council of Hygiene's drastic measures to combat the plague. They ended the boycott only when they received a promise of "a type of cheap and healthful housing that would be suitable for the Blacks."[14]

The boycott was used most often in the two countries with the strongest trading economies: Ghana (then the Gold Coast) and Uganda. There, more than elsewhere, the only direct contact of the peasants with the colonial world was through commerce. In the first major boycotts, which showed undeniable planning, the Ghanaian cocoa producers reacted to a collapse in prices by refusing to sell their product. In 1930–1931, again in 1934, and particularly in the years of recovery, 1937–1938, when the planters became aware both of being exploited and of their own economic force, they kept a freeze on exports for several months. Ultimately, the British authorities had to intercede between the producers and the expatriate firms. The necessity for price controls began to be felt, and during the war the idea of a stabilization fund took hold. Such a fund at last came into being in the 1950s, in the form of the marketing boards.[15]

After the war, political unrest was incited by the middle class of Ghanaian entrepreneurs and was increased by the persistent shortages. The boycott proved a powerful weapon against expatriate importers: in January and February 1948 it forced the Accra Chamber of Commerce to agree to a compromise. The notables, however, were overwhelmed by the populace: demobilized soldiers, the unemployed, and subproletarians responded to police repression by looting British and Syrian firms. The rioting and arson destroyed nearly all the goods accumulated during the war (but most of these had already gone bad). Fifteen people died and another 115 were wounded in similar disturbances in Kumasi. Kwame Nkrumah seized this opportunity to launch the "national reconciliation" of the Convention People's Party.

In the cities, trade—semi-wholesale and, above all, retail—was run by foreign minorities: Lebanese and Syrians in West Africa, Greeks in Equatorial Africa, and Indians in East Africa. In times of crisis, when the price of food was high and purchasing power low, popular anger directed itself against these scapegoats, just as it had in Freetown in Sierra Leone in 1919 against the postwar profiteers. This element can be found in nearly all the urban riots.

Trade boycotts and the looting that followed often triggered further protest action. In the absence of established political or trade union organizations (which often were prohibited by law), the boycott served to unite a heterogeneous population of administrative employees and those in the private sector, wage earners and unemployed, subproletarian migrant peasants who often believed their recent urbanization to be merely temporary, and—most important—women, burdened with anxiety about how to feed their families. Xenophobia, combined with economic resentments, guaranteed the success of the boycott as a method.

Buganda presents a vivid example of the boycott used methodically. There, as in the Gold Coast, an agricultural trading economy dominated.

Based, in this case, on cotton and coffee, it was maintained by small plantations created by the British laws of 1900 and 1927 that encouraged the division of lands. The native planters had always resented the foreigners who
collected and marketed their produce. When they arrived in the cities and
found these foreigners monopolizing the retail trade, the planters revolted.
They rioted in 1945 and again in 1949, under the joint leadership of the
bataka and the African Farmers' Union (AFU). Instructions were given to
boycott the European and Indian merchants, who—especially the latter, the
most visible intermediaries between the cultivators and the wholesalers—
were accused of exploiting the local people.[16] We find in this case a curious
intermingling of political and economic demands: they asked that more authority be granted to the Lukiiko (the traditional council of the Ganda king)
and at the same time that the marketing of agricultural produce be placed in
the hands of the Africans themselves. The action from the start took an urban form. During the riots, the police had to intervene to save the *kabaka*'s
palace.

These tactics were revived ten years later, this time for openly political
ends, by the Ugandan National Movement. The dual aim was to unify the
country and to win its independence. The political elites agreed on a general
boycott of non-African shops and the masses followed suit. The movement
spread rapidly to other spheres such as transportation and beverage sales.
The protesters performed many acts of intimidation; for example, they
burned down a Catholic school that disregarded orders when making pur-
chases. It was suggested that Indian trading activities be taken over by thirty
Ugandan wholesalers. Calm was restored when the Bugandan monarchy
gave its support to the repressive British policies, but for nearly a year—
from March 1959 to February 1960—the movement had succeeded in
fusing all the political stances of the country into a single unified force.

Finally, Idi Amin Dada expelled the Indian and other minorities from
Buganda. It was not an impulsive act but was rooted in Bugandan colonial
history. The opposition to the colonialists or neo-colonialists gained widespread support both from exploited proletarians and from the middle class,
whose political ambitions had been thwarted. The Nigerian government's
dramatic expulsion of nearly a million small-scale Ghanaian traders followed the same pattern.

The Douala Riots of 1945

The Douala riots were not the only ones of their kind to take place after
World War II. In Kankan in Guinea, for example, at the end of 1947, a populist agitator, Lamine Kaba, controlled the town for two days: and in Thiaroye
in December 1944, a basically similar uprising occurred.[17] What the events
in Douala brought out particularly clearly, however, was the role of the city
as the place of social confrontation par excellence.[18] At least three groups

were involved in the Douala unrest: the trade unions and the local pre-nationalists, mainly Duala who had lived in Douala for years; the unorganized and not well-established new immigrants, "de-tribalized city-dwellers" in the informal sector; and the as yet secure but increasingly threatened group of colonists, who sparked the affair.

The town had grown more rapidly during World War II than in the whole of the preceding quarter-century. The African population rose from 25,000 to 40,000 between 1914 and 1939, and by 1945 had reached 60,000. However, whereas the original Duala population had remained remarkably stable (2,000 in 1914, 2,300 in 1943), the immigrants, who equaled them in number on the eve of the war, rapidly became a majority that had tripled by 1956. Europeans were encouraged by the Fonds d'Investissement pour le Développement Economique et Social (FIDES) to immigrate: at the end of the war Douala had 3,300 European inhabitants (constituting half the Whites in the country); in 1948 there were 5,800; and by 1956 their numbers had grown to 17,000.

Each of the groups—natives, immigrants, and Europeans—held a separate socioeconomic position, as can be seen from their geographical distribution in the town. In 1911, the Germans expelled the leading Duala-Bell clan from the well-situated Bali and Joss plateaus in order to set up European quarters near the port. The French returned the Bali plateau to the Duala, who then made a profit by renting their land. A middle class of Duala landed proprietors became integrated into the colonial system as administrative clerks, small-scale entrepreneurs, or employees in the private sector. They constituted an elite that collaborated with the colonial administration.

At the beginning of the war, in response to the German threat, the colonial authorities created a movement of support among the Duala, the Jeunesse Camerounaise Française (Jeucafra), under the leadership of an employee of the public works department, Paul Soppo Priso. The main impetus was given by the Free French government, which granted the French colonies as a whole the freedom to form trade unions; previously, only French West Africa had been permitted to unionize. Trade unions flourished: postal employees, customs officials, medical service staff, railway workers, and teachers, led by a small nucleus of activists of the CGT and the French Communist party, in 1945 united in the Union des Syndicats Confédérés du Cameroun. At the same time, the Jeucafra, which supported assimilation to French culture and the French political system, nevertheless acted as an agent of Cameroon national consciousness: the middle class of Duala elite became aware of its growing power.

The recent immigrants were people from the inland regions who were despised by the Duala, whom they disliked equally. They took advantage of the ambiguous legal status of the Bell plateaus to cluster further west in the area behind the port, which became known as the New Bell. The immigrants were an unstable population who suffered from a lack of regular employment and, after the war, a shortage of essential foodstuffs (rice and fish) and a rapid increase in prices that halved purchasing power. Their poverty and general sense of deprivation easily fostered social unrest.

The protest movement began with this subproletariat. The day-laborers on the railways launched a wildcat strike. It was supported by the wretched inhabitants of the poorest and most remote quarter, the Bonaberi, who had been cut off from the rest of the town by the collapse of a bridge and thus lost their marginal activities of marketing bananas and manioc. Rumors and unrest built up throughout the weekend, despite the trade unionists' attempts to negotiate. On Monday, 24 September, a crowd surged out of New Bell, armed with sticks, ready to loot any symbol of property-owning. The crowd found itself faced by an organized band of 200 Whites (was this deliberate provocation?) who were panicked by the growing threat to their privileges. In response to the Conference of Brazzaville, they had just organized an interterritorial conference in their town, called the States-General of Colonization. At this conference they rejected the recent Code du Travail Outre-Mer, condemned the cooperative spirit of the mutual aid societies, and deplored the emergence of a Black proletariat. Having seized a hundred rifles at the police station, they engaged in a massacre: sixty to eighty people were killed. When the Whites learned that the Union des Syndicats was negotiating with the governor, they invaded the house of a French leader of the CGT, and in the shoot-out that followed the secretary-general of the Chamber of Commerce was killed.

The riots were quickly suppressed. The trade union leaders were arrested but protected from the wrath of the European settlers, and a collective fine was imposed on the African population. This episode had briefly united the people of Cameroon: trade union leaders and the rebellious masses. The subsequent expulsion of French Communists enabled the nationalists to take over. Ten years later, in May 1955, Ruben Um Nyobe's Union des Populations Camerounaises first played a part in new disturbances, more violent and on a larger scale, that marked the beginning of the struggle for nationhood.

Urban Disturbances in Zaire

It was also at the beginning of World War II that the center of social discontent in Zaire shifted from the rural areas to the towns. During the Great Depression, the spectacular fall in agricultural prices—about 80 percent—and the increase in taxes had caused such explosions of violence among the peasants as the Pende and Dekesse-Kote rebellions in 1931 and the Mboon-Ding rebellion in 1933–1934.[19] At the same time, an urban subproletariat of dismissed workers, uprooted persons of various origins, and the unemployed was forming: in three years, 15,000 had flocked to the cities. The administration was concerned. "The Blacks must be made to work hard," they decided. "Held in check both by the administration and by the agricultural agents of the companies, they will no longer be able to foment revolts." [20]

In 1941, in spite of the stability of the labor force, strikes erupted in the compounds of Katanga. Despite their violent suppression, they achieved noteworthy results (wages increased 26 to 50 percent for the lowest-paid workers). At the end of the war, the number of incidents rose: strikes in Léopoldville (Kinshasa); the *complot des clercs* ("clerks' plot"), as it was called, in Elisabethville (today Lubumbashi in Shaba) in January and February 1944; mutinies in the police camps in Luluabourg, Kanima, and Katanga; and various disturbances in the principal centers of the Lower Congo, from Léopoldville to Matadi in November 1945, which spread along the railway of the Great Lakes to Kindu from December 1945 to January 1946. The authorities reasoned that these occurrences were unorganized and xenophobic, and "no element enables one to discern the existence of discontent." "On 26 November," they reported, "a strike that broke out at Matadi immediately degenerated into a disturbance, for the Blacks do not know how to strike and for them it means waging war on the Whites." [21] The administration blamed the influence of religious sects—Kimbangism, Kitawalism, Kalingism—and ascribed the subversion to "foreign elements."

In fact, these events signified the emergence of a proletariat. The only areas affected were the economic centers, which were also the oldest urban concentrations: the complex of the Union Minière, the railway stations, the Kilomoto gold mines, the capital city, and the port. The end of the war brought economic and social distress. The influx of former soldiers who now had no jobs was augmented by those who had been involved in the "war effort" in the rural areas (forced labor, compulsory cultivation, heavy taxation). Urban living conditions consequently worsened: flimsy shelters became permanent homes, and no garbage disposal, public utilities, or sanitation was provided. In 1947, a Belgian senatorial commission described the "atrocious misery" in Léopoldville (which at that time had a population of 100,000, a number that had quadrupled by 1960). Until then, the colonial authorities, who aimed above all at a "society without conflict," had been careful to abort any attempt to create a working class, whether Black or White. The war breached this "empire of silence," but, owing to the strictness of administrative control, the new force was able to express itself only in spontaneous, uncontrolled fits and starts.

GENERAL STRIKES

The boycott and the riot can bring together social forces with disparate tendencies, but they are spontaneous, short-lived occurrences that may alarm but seldom have lasting consequences. General strikes, however, mass manifestations supported by established professional or syndical organizations, are able to direct the expression of discontent. They occurred frequently in the postwar period, the predecolonization period, and finally at the beginning of the first independent regimes. These strikes were able to unify the whole country on a specific issue and at a given moment of its history, but no lasting collaboration between wage earners and political leaders was achieved. In the cities, the general strike was a spectacular phenomenon, but it generally lacked consequences, as was seen in Zanzibar in 1948, in Ghana in 1950, 1951, and 1971, in the Ivory Coast in 1948 and 1959, in Nigeria in 1945 and 1964, in Kenya in 1950, and in Senegal in 1952, 1953, and 1969. In certain cases, it did hasten the process of decolonization or play an immediate role in the fall of a political regime, as in Sudan in 1958, in Brazzaville in 1963, in Upper Volta in 1968, in Madagascar in 1972, and in Ethiopia in 1974. In most cases, however, the government passed rapidly into the hands of the army. If we except Ethiopia, it can be said that only the "Trois Glorieuses" ("three glorious days") in Brazzaville in 1963 had, strictly speaking, a revolutionary impact.

Reformism in the Ivory Coast

The events in the Ivory Coast demonstrated the differences rather than the points of convergence of various social groups.[22] The point of departure was the strike of 1947. Social protest movements, by worrying the leaders of the rising bourgeoisie, accelerated a change of policy of the Parti Démocratique de la Côte d'Ivoire–Rassemblement Démocratique Africain. The huge Rassemblement had originally (in 1946) aimed to coordinate all the political groups in French-speaking Africa in their anticolonialist struggle, which was supported by the French Communist party. Despite the abolition of forced labor—confirmed by the second Constituent Assembly (May 1946)—and the granting of the status of "imperial citizens" to all French subjects, the gap between the workers and the middle class dominated by the planters had widened. Houphouët-Boigny, president of the Planters' Syndicate and leader of the PDCI–RDA, having undergone harassment by the authorities, decided that it was safer to pursue a policy of class collaboration. In 1947, he unsuccessfully proposed a rapprochement to the governor, and in 1948 he suggested to the parliamentarians of the RDA that they should split from the Communists. For a time he was placed in the minority. The left wing of the party reaffirmed in its second congress, in 1949, the alliance with the French Communist party and the French working class, but that policy changed with the popular urban unrest in 1949 and 1950, centered in Treichville, Bouaflé, Seguela, and Dimbokio.

The first incidents were violent brawls during a political meeting held under the auspices of pro-French sympathizers on 6 February 1949 in Treichville, a Black area of Abidjan that was undoubtedly controlled by the RDA.

The colonial authorities took this incident as a pretext for arresting the entire steering committee of the PDCI–RDA and organizing the repression of the party nationwide. A series of strikes and demonstrations took place, and overall several hundred people died, in shootings, arrests, and by sentence following the large trials in 1950. This social disturbance also had a political objective. The more active agitators wished to pressure the leaders into radicalizing the party. Because of the anti-Communism of the colonial administration (which forbade any public action by the RDA), the result was just the opposite. In contradiction to the "Marxist revolutionary policy" advocated by Gabriel d'Arboussier, and following negotiations in Paris between Houphouët-Boigny, spokesman of the agrarian bourgeoisie, and François Mitterrand, minister for overseas territories, the PDCI–RDA signed a "colonial peace," accepting the Union Française and a break with the French Communist party to the benefit of the Union Démocratique et Socialiste de la Résistance (UDSR). This was a rapprochement with people of the Socialist party who had come from the Gaullist Mouvements Unis de Résistance and had rejected the fusion of the two attempted in 1944–1945 within the Mouvement Unifié de la Résistance Française. This represented acquiescence to the colonial policies of the Fourth Republic. The support of the party was obtained for the Loi Defferre of 1956 and the referendum of 1958 founding the Communauté Franco-Africain.

Then the general strike of 1959 erupted. The Ivory Coast had 310,000 wage earners, of whom an impressive 60 percent belonged to trade unions. The immediate cause of the strike was the arrest of one leader of the local branch of the Union Générale des Travailleurs de l'Afrique Noire (UGTAN), a trade union close to Guinean positions and opposed to the reformism of the Ivory Coast. When the interunion organization of the public services began a seventy-two-hour protest strike, the authorities declared the strike illegal and ordered the police to disperse the participants. The strike ended with one person dead and 23 wounded, 213 officials dismissed and 319 suspended. The government, supported by the PDCI–RDA, made many arrests. This episode marked the definitive rupture between the reformist bourgeoisie and popular demands.

Trade Unionism and
Tribalist Regionalism in Nigeria

Because of its major urban centers and a long-standing urban tradition, Nigeria had a particularly large number of wage earners, and trade unionism began there earlier than elsewhere in Africa. The largest single employer was the great port of Lagos. The western areas, the site of the ancient Yoruba kingdoms and the foundation of the agrarian capitalism of the country (since they supplied 90 percent of the cocoa), had long also had an urban civilization. In 1952, 47 percent of the population of those regions lived in urbanized village centers containing more than 5,000 inhabitants. Anglican Christianity was the dominant religion, and a large number of small groups were engaged in trade, administration, or the liberal professions. Southeast Ibo—a Catholic area with a decentralized administration, scattered dwellings, and poor soil, where the schools were the only route to social promotion—produced a steady stream of petty officials eager to absorb Western techniques and ideas.

Nationwide, the public services were by far the largest employer, but only 6.4 percent of the employees belonged to a trade union. The wage earners, who might have amounted to a considerable political force, were not grouped together in a single association; each enterprise, each group, each area had its own union. The ideological diversity of the leaders was accentuated by very strong regional peculiarities. Petty local quarrels, division of interests over local, personal, and ethnic factors, and general underemployment led the workers to place more confidence in their "tribal" allegiances than in "modern" organizations. The political parties, too, failed to recognize the political potential of the trade unions, which engaged in frequent but sporadic violence. Negotiations between the unions and the management over professional claims, in the British trade-unionist tradition, were seldom politicized.

In Nigeria, as in the rest of the continent, the war and the postwar period marked the beginning of serious disturbances.[23] In 1939 the colonial administration authorized the formation of organizations for the defense of the rights of wage earners; by 1941, forty-one trade unions had already been founded. In 1942, after the workers of Lagos went on strike, Michael Imodu, radical leader of the railway union, was imprisoned and then was banished for having continued agitation in prison. From 1943 to 1948, the various trade unions were amalgamated into the Trade Union Congress of Nigeria (TUC).

In 1945, employees of the public sector in Lagos held a two-day general strike. They demanded, in addition to a 50 percent cost-of-living increment, a substantial increase in base wages. The TUC, however, was unable to keep control: the masses responded to the administration's threats by acts of violence such as derailing trains. The government finally yielded and created a commission of enquiry.

The following decade saw a succession of strikes (which were sometimes bloody in their consequences, as in the miners' strike of 1949). The pattern was always the same. After demands from a trade union, the government created a commission of enquiry, and at the same time trade union action increased in order to put pressure on the authorities. Thus 1945, 1955–1956, 1960–1961, 1964, and 1967 were peak years in numbers of strikes and strikers recorded. Between 1945 and 1970, wages were raised four times.

Trade unionism and politics came together in these struggles for higher wages, whose outcome was of electoral significance. After independence, trade unionism, which demonstrated the power of the workers, had a genuine political impact. This was shown by the general strike of 1964.[24] Allowing for altered circumstances, the situation in 1964 was similar to that in 1945: increases in wages had not met the trade unionists' hopes. Since independence, the political leaders—who ran the country for their own benefit, with a great deal of corruption—had shown a notable indifference to social problems. At the end of 1963, the Joint Action Committee (JAC) was created. It again demanded a commission of enquiry on wages (including those in the private sector) and threatened the federal government with a strike. The government, underestimating the degree of discontent, proclaimed a state of emergency following an outbreak of popular demonstrations. A general strike was begun two days later. It lasted for two weeks and ended with the victory of the strikers.

The strike coincided with a period of intense political unrest. The federal system created at independence had accentuated regional differences: since the most populated areas were best represented, rigged elections became the rule (sometimes involving as many as 10,000,000 votes). This practice gained special notoriety in the elections of 1962–1963. By then there were fewer trade unions and only three dominant political parties, none of which was able to gain a clear electoral majority. The National Convention of Nigerian Citizens (NCNC), formed in 1944 by uniting about 100 tribal and syndical organizations, represented a pragmatic form of socialism that had taken deep root in Lagos and among the Ibo immigrants in the north. The Action Group had broken away in 1950 on the initiative of Obafemi Awolowo, who was frustrated at being kept out of office. It called for a "democratic socialism," gathered together the ethnic and syndical malcontents, and became very dominant in the west. Finally, the Northern People's Congress (NPC) had since 1949 been the party of the northern Hausa and Fulbe Moslems, who were conservative and regionalistic. The NPC could gain a majority if it won the support of a southern party, and since the elections of 1959, its coalition with the NCNC connected it with the politically active world of the docks.

There was a serious economic crisis in the west, where the Action Group was out of office. The resultant social disturbances of May and June 1964 contributed greatly to a switch of alliances in the elections: the NCNC was reconciled with the Action Group, and the NPC, breaking the somewhat unnatural alliance with the NCNC it had formed in 1959, united with Akimbela's party, the Nigerian Democratic Party, to form the Nigerian National Alliance (NNA). This multiplication of little parties was symptomatic of the general malaise.

The growing popular opposition made a boycott of the elections a success: at the end of 1964, out of 20,000,000 electors, only 4,000,000 voted.

President Azikiwe refused to choose his premier from the winning opposition coalition, the NNA. The last act of this political farce came when the NNDP rigged the votes outrageously and then declared itself victorious in the elections. Thus, General Ironsi's "coup" of January 1966, officially carried out in order to end the repression, was welcomed by the workers. His "populism," favored by the workers, came to a sudden end six months later, however, when he was assassinated.

Underemployment, always chronic, was becoming epidemic. The number of wage earners had tripled in twelve years, but the number entering the workforce also mounted; in 1963, 44 percent of the population was under fifteen years old. The country was badly run, the administration corrupt, the resources inefficiently exploited, and the wealth unevenly distributed. Nigeria was a rich country inhabited by poor people. Much resentment had accumulated against the middle class of politicians who as yet were scarcely involved in the economic process and whose rival groups systematically resorted to clientelism and corruption.

Despite the oil boom, the total Africanization of the public sector, and the appearance of young Nigerians in positions of responsibility in large companies with foreign capital, the situation did not improve. In 1970, after the civil war, a wave of demands for social justice swamped the administration: 600 unions and associations submitted their grievances. Mounting inflation once again led to the appointment of a commission of enquiry, which proposed that a cost-of-living increment of 30 percent should be paid in two installments to the public employees and recommended that the private sector do the same. The great European companies arguing that "wage adjustments" had been made in the previous years, at first refused to comply, but after a number of major strikes had been called, the military government forced them to adopt the policy.

Why, despite the relative success of these popular movements, did a "revolutionary" political syndicalism never come into being? The first reason was the absence of unity (the TUC had come to an end by 1951, and the All-Nigerian Trade Union Federation, created in 1953, was no more successful). Above all, the trade union reformist tradition preferred wage negotiations to violent action, which was resorted to only out of desperation. There has been talk of a "labor aristocracy," but the Nigerian industrial worker is incontestably a proletarian. In the industrial area of Ikeja, not far from Lagos, 20,000 workers, mainly Yoruba, were concentrated around some fifty factories (such as that of the United African Company) with advanced equipment and high productivity. These factories represent various sectors: construction, textiles, paint manufacture, beer manufacture, pharmaceutical industries.[25] The workers, attracted by the relatively high wages, often come from the railways or public works. They are experienced and organized, and the young workers have completed at least a limited primary education. There is almost no professional mobility. Workers soon reach their limit of advancement, and the only way for an individual to earn higher wages is by recourse to the trade union. The workers are capable of taking action (as in 1970) over some specific local issue. In their speeches and declarations they often refer to imperialist exploitation and the glaring inequalities of Nigerian society, but for the moment they do not consider overturning the system. Their almost unanimously expressed desire is to quit the factory, but this stems from a petit-bourgeois ambition of becoming independent entrepreneurs. It is a strategy of adaptation within the existing system.

Political Syndicalism to Reformist
Trade Unionism in Kenya

As in South Africa, social policies in Kenya until the 1930s were entirely repressive, but the International Convention of Labour of 1930, which condemned forced labor, was ratified by Great Britain the following year. Urban troubles had already begun: the first African general strike—a one-day but impressive event—occurred in Nairobi as early as March 1922.[26] Under pressure from the Indian workers—especially the Sikh railway workers—the British government (at about the same time as the French government in West Africa) legalized trade unions, although they were still very tightly controlled (the registration procedure allowed for the possibility of future exclusion from the union). This period of crisis was one of increasing urbanization. The population of Nairobi rose from 25,000 inhabitants in 1930 to 40,000 in 1938. Three-quarters of the population were unemployed, and the first strikes of Asiatic workers were in protest against the poor living conditions (there was neither a water supply nor, of course, electricity, and worst of all was the problem of municipal latrines). The first union, which was founded in 1934, was the Indian Trade Union; the following year it became the Labour Trade Union of Kenya. The union, led by the Indian Marxist Mikhan Singh, held a series of strikes. One two-months-long strike succeeded in obtaining from the authorities an increase in wages for building and transport workers. Seeing this success, African workers began to develop interest in the unions.

The port of Mombasa, above all, took over the movement. Labor unrest came from three main groups of workers: the dockworkers, the railway workers, and those employed by the public utilities. The working conditions and sanitation were worse there than anywhere else. In 1937, there were serious disturbances; these came to a head in 1939, when strikes spread from one port to another (to Dar-es-Salaam, Mombasa, and Tanga). For the first time, Africans—mainly Kikuyu—took an active part in the demonstrations, and a social solidarity came into being that transcended racial divergences.

The number of African trade unions increased during the war in those professions where a comparison was possible. These sectors—transport, taxis, and building construction, and among tailors, hairdressers, and domestic servants—displayed obvious disparities between similar social groups of different color. In 1947, as in the Copperbelt, an official of the Ministry of Labour was given the task of organizing "responsible" trade unions, that is, ones whose aims were not political. Priority was given to work committees and staff associations.

Kenya in this period was the country where Black trade unionism was most politicized. The Africans became increasingly aware of the racial barriers to their economic progress, and they began to feel that their situation would not improve under the existing colonial regime. The unrest culminated in Mombasa. In January 1947, a general strike there lasted for eleven days. Beginning with the dockworkers and railway workers, it rapidly took in virtually the whole of the African labor force, including the domestic servants. This strike by 15,000 people paralyzed the city. The movement spread by word of mouth, for no well-structured organization existed, but it gave birth to the African Workers' Federation, which in turn supported the nationalist aims of Jomo Kenyatta's Kenya African Union. In this way, African trade unionism passed from interracial class-consciousness to nationalist rebellion.

This change did not take place without incident. Repression threw the movement off balance. Watched by the authorities, the African unions sought the support of the powerful Asiatic federation, the Labour Trade Union of East Africa, in which the leading role was played by the printers' and press unions and whose leader was still Mikhan Singh, who was influenced by South African Communist trade unionism. He had sought for years to organize the Kenyans on interracial lines and in accordance with their work: his slogan was "equal pay for equal work," with a minimum wage for Africans equal to that of everyone else, an eight-hour workday, and a forty-five-hour week.

Interracial trade unionism had a momentary success in May 1949, when the East African Trade Union Congress was founded with the support of Jomo Kenyatta's party. Singh was made its secretary-general, and Fred Kubai became its president. The congress functioned well in those cases where the Indians were badly paid and the Africans were few in number, but it had little success when racial competition was great or when there were many qualified Asiatics (as on the railways or in the administration).

The climax came in 1950. In May of that year, the congress launched a week of mass boycott, calling for immediate independence for a democratic Kenya. The arrest of the two principal leaders brought on a general strike involving 6,000 workers that lasted for nine days in Nairobi. This was a political strike, although wage claims were included.

The strike was declared illegal. The repressive policies of the government weakened the congress, but they also gave new life to Black political consciousness. In contrast to the Indians, who were divided between employers and wage earners, the Blacks' class allegiance was obliterated by racial allegiance. The Black trade unions, in collaboration with the Black petite bourgeoisie, moved clandestinely toward participation in the nationalist political struggle that underlay the Mau Mau rebellion.

This rebellion was far from purely a peasant affair, even if nine-tenths of the Kenyan population were still rural-dwellers,[27] for the city-dwellers and the rural people were closely linked. In Nairobi in 1953, only 11 percent of the wage earners had held their jobs for more than five years, and the overpopulated reserves constantly renewed the supply of semi-proletarianized workers. At least 10 percent of the Nairobi labor force was unemployed. The rapidity of the cross-migration between wage-earning jobs in the city and work in the rural areas was beginning to decrease considerably, because the growing difficulty of getting onto the land left no alternative to the insecurity of employment in the city. The city-dwellers were always hoping to return to the rural areas, however, because most of them were unskilled workers close to the minimum subsistence level (50 percent of those in the private sector and 30 percent of those in public employment) who spent at least three-quarters of their wages on food.

Urban social unrest thus played its part in the popular uprising, but after independence the Kenyan working class, in a pattern that has become typical in sub-Saharan Africa, was neutralized by the ruling class. The rulers imposed a one-party system and compulsory membership in the national trade union. Thus, the state was the direct heir to the colonial tradition: after the rebellion was crushed, between 1952 and 1963 only the federal syndical body, the Kenya Federation of Labour (KFL) was permitted to express political demands, and that was only because its leader, Tom Mboya, enjoyed the approval of British liberals. Any signs of unrest or political agitation were severely repressed from the start.

In the same tradition, Kenyatta's Kenya African National Union (KANU) government was supported by most of the leaders of the KFL to the disadvantage of the Kenya African Democratic Union (KADU). After 1963, however, the government relegated the KFL to the role of responsible economic partner. This was the first task of Tom Mboya, who was both president of the KFL and minister of labour under the new regime. In 1966, under government auspices a new labor confederation, the Central Organisation of Trade Unions (COTU), was set up. It ended the split, reflecting the political differences of their leaders, between the two branches of the KFL. Henceforth, the workers were controlled by their trade union. Labor unrest did not disappear, but the union leaders, now engaged in subtle machinations as they balanced their political ambitions, based on clientism, with the necessity of responding periodically to the wage claims of workers taunted by the conspicuous consumption of the ruling class. The leaders thus maintained a fragile equilibrium between the popular base and the government.

"Trois Glorieuses" of Brazzaville

This equilibrium was shattered in Congo-Brazzaville in 1963. The typically neo-colonial regime of Fulbert Youlou was particularly corrupt and unresponsive to the workers' grievances. The city-dwellers at that period constituted 40 percent of the population, a remarkable proportion for sub-Saharan Africa, and their number was rapidly growing, having doubled in less than five years. The population of Pointe-Noire had risen from 20,000 inhabitants in 1949 to 80,000 in 1963, and Brazzaville had seen the greatest influx, its population rising by a third between 1959 and 1963, when it counted 150,000 inhabitants.

The number of jobs failed to keep pace with this rise in population. The city harbored a multitude of unemployed: those who had lost their jobs or who had not found one, in addition to the young people who had just reached working age, constituted the majority of ablebodied men in the capital (nearly 20,000 out of 36,700). This high unemployment rate was more or less repeated in the other cities: of Pointe-Noire's 80,000 inhabitants in 1963, 33,000 were unemployed; and the figures for Dolisie and other cities are similar.[28]

These unemployed people could be enlisted in any kind of urban demonstrations and could be manipulated by politicians. In recent months, political discontent had increased. Fulbert Youlou's party, the Union Démocratique de Défense des Intérêts Africains (UDDIA), brought together the petite bourgeoisie of the center and south. At first the UDDIA based itself on the Lari-Bakongo ethnic regionalism of the followers of Matswa. In 1957 it superseded Tchicaya's Parti Progressiste Congolais, which, as the local section of the RDA, had affinities with the SFIO. In the late 1950s, however, Fulbert Youlou used the negative attitude of the Matswanist extremists, who were opposed to any collaboration with France, as a pretext to rid himself of his opponents by arresting them and deporting them to the north of the country. In 1962 he again tried to impose the Parti Unique, a single-party system. From then on, all political expression was stifled. The trade unions alone retained the ability to pressure the government, for although the urban labor force was in the minority (16 percent of the population were wage earners and 4.5 percent artisans and small tradesmen, compared to 68 percent peasants), wage-earning had a relatively long-established position in the Congo.

As late as 1940, the Congo had neither a bourgeoisie nor a working class. Petty administrative employees, soldiers, and workers in the depots constituted at the most a potential proletariat. When a proletariat did come into being, it was in an urban and politicized form. Unlike developments at the same period in the Belgian Congo around Simon Kimbangu, André Matswa's Amicale was first political, with wage claims and demands of a modern nationalist type, and not a Messianic religious movement (it was to assume this character only after 1940, when political action had failed). This very early politicization of the proletariat occurred partly because the wage earners, a group that developed quickly, were also very vulnerable. There were two main groups of wage earners: minor municipal officials in Brazzaville, who were at that period the only literate personnel in the Federation (in 1938, scarcely 10,000 attended school out of a population of some 5,000,000— that is, only 0.2 percent); and construction workers on the Congo-Ocean railway, a body of workers of very varied origins in the heart of the Middle Congo. In the 1930s working conditions in Brazzaville improved. Like Dakar in French West Africa, it was the administrative capital, and it was a center for the tertiary industries throughout French Equatorial Africa, as it remained until independence.

The country, then, was urbanized, with a relatively large wage-earning population, but at the same time particularly impoverished, or at least ineffectively exploited and barely subsisting from a feeble trading economy. The situation was opposed to that of the neighboring territory of Gabon. Gabon possessed a labor force of limited size which easily found employment, and wages there, wretched though they may have been, were undoubtedly higher than in the Congo, whose larger labor force felt its more threatened position. These factors promoted a growth of consciousness in the Congo.

The Great Depression resulted in a general revision of colonial policies, and after 1946, the French government's economy of plunder gave way to an emphasis on large-scale investments in the industrial sector. A particular effort was made in the Congo, where the Brazzaville Conference was held: it was the center of the Federation; moreover, its government administrators very early joined the Free French, forcing Gabon to follow suit. Rewarding the colony meant granting special advantages to the settlers. The Fonds d'Investissement pour le Développement Economique et Social became active, especially in the processing industries (food, assembly, and so forth). This encouraged rapid social change, accelerated the growth of the urban labor sector, and resulted in its relative combativeness.

At the same time, in the federal capital the tertiary sector of service jobs expanded and a small local administrative and commercial petite bourgeoisie emerged that was heavily dependent on the rapidly growing French economy. This bourgeoisie was to abandon itself wholeheartedly to collaboration with the West. The principal result of the excesses of the Youlou regime, then, was an early class struggle that gave rise to bitter social antagonisms. In the "trois glorieuses" of 1963, it was—exceptionally for sub-

Saharan Africa—the unions that went into the streets and brought about a political revolution.

In the early 1950s the Congolese unions affiliated with the three French groups of unions: the FO, the CFTC (which had thirty-one affiliated unions in 1958), and the CGT (which had twenty-three affiliated unions). The unions belonging to the CGT were centered on the Congo-Ocean railway, the ports, and the municipal services; they were nationalized in 1957 as the Confédération Générale des Travailleurs Africains (CGTA). Only about 10 percent of the Congolese labor force belonged to unions, but the unions were solidly supported by youth associations that were founded as Christian groups but had recently been radicalized and secularized. Most important of these was the Association Scolaire du Congo (ASCO), created in 1959, made up of high school pupils whose "moral and material" interests ASCO claimed to defend in the manner of a trade union. This combined structure disseminated a certain consciousness of the situation in the country and assisted the rapid propagation of the uprising of August 1963.

Socially and economically, the country had reached an impasse. The Youlou government's main answer to increasing unemployment was the Kouilou dam project, the preparatory work for which was carried out in 1961 and between 1958 and 1962 attracted 25,000 people to Pointe-Noire in search of employment.[29] Owing to lack of funds, however, the project came to a halt. Faced with rising discontent (the urban riots of 1959 pitting Laris against Mboshis), Youlou banned the CGTA, which had Communist sympathies and was accused of endangering state security, and sought in June 1959 to promote the Parti Unique. The CGTA responded by creating a "revolutionary political party." The activists of the party, seeing the impotence of the existing regime, succeeded in transcending the trade union framework and in momentarily uniting the union with high school pupils, the unemployed, and nonunion workers. In 1961, this Syndicat Professionel des Agents des Services Publics began to threaten a general strike.

The event that sparked the strike was the visit of President Sékou Touré, who in June 1963 at Brazzaville City Hall made a speech strongly condemning the "reactionary" policies and extravagance of the Congolese leaders. He was acclaimed with cries of "Long live the President of Africa!" The following month, the Comité National de Fusion Syndicale of the labor organizations in a meeting at the Labor Exchange issued a manifesto proclaiming its determination to play a "dominant and active" role in the fight against "all colonial or procolonial regimes and on behalf of social advancement and the consolidation of the independence that has been gained." Forced to recognize the Comité de Fusion, Youlou tried to stifle the political demands of a provisional government (following the dissolution of Parliament) by the creation of a new Parti Unique that would absorb both the groups of syndicates and the youth associations. Seeing his failure, he publicly condemned any political role for the trade unions. An ordinance forbade all political gatherings until the Parti Unique was established.

The trade unions responded by ordering a general strike. Arrest of the union leaders caused the explosion. On the morning of 13 August, despite police cordons that prevented the strikers from reaching their meeting place, a crowd began to surge in from Bacongo and Poto-Poto. Policemen and soldiers, refusing to obey orders to repress the action, joined the demonstrators. The crowds swarming towards the presidential palace gave the trade union leaders the main role in negotiations; popular pressure forced the president to resign. The union leaders, who had not expected such an outcome, were neither organized nor self-confident enough immediately to assume the responsibilities of government. Instead, a provisional government of "technocrats" was formed, setting up a mechanism for a future revolutionary process.[30]

This decisive political role of the unions has remained the exception in Africa. Today, the working class in general hardly seems to be a political force. In the interaction of the social forces that confront one another in the cities, the workers appear to be no more than one group among many. The classic picture of opposition between the bourgeoisie and the proletariat in capitalist countries has become most inadequate to cover the complexity of the fabric of urban society in the Third World, as elsewhere.

13

Cities, Social Classes, and the Informal Sector: The Future of Poverty

The African city is a place of recent emigration, going back one or two generations at the most. Between 1950 and 1975, the population of Kinshasa, for example, rose from 200,000 to more than 2,000,000 inhabitants. In analyzing the various elements among the urban masses, then, primary importance must be given to the relationship between migration and identification with the city. This criterion enables us to distinguish three main levels of integration into urban life.

First, the city-dwellers proper, the most fully integrated inhabitants, are born in the city in a mixed society. The smallest group, they constitute an embryonic middle class, for they earn enough to support four or five people. These inhabitants willingly disregard ethnic relationships in favor of intercultural voluntary associations such as sports clubs and trade unions. They feel little obligation toward their kinsmen in the village and detach themselves from them.

Second, new city-dwellers maintain a dual allegiance, to the village and to the city. They belong both to associations based on traditional allegiances and to urban organizations. With mid-range or low salaries, they assume a heavy burden of family assistance and struggle to resolve the conflict arising out of their dual attachment.

Third, the proletarianized rural migrants—most of whom are foreigners—generally live below the poverty line, and they are as yet very little integrated into city life. Cut off from their village, they stay in their own quarter, where they attempt to replicate their ethnic and religious environment. Most survive by dealings in the informal sector.[1]

This division may be valid, but it has the disadvantage of neglecting social analysis in favor of a quasi-mechanical chronology. The social fabric is both more dynamic and more complex than this grouping suggests. A large body of other criteria, such as the extreme variety in origin of the migrants, the various movements that develop among them, and their social and professional status, must be taken into account.

THE INFORMAL SECTOR

The vague term *informal sector* is used to designate a social grouping that is in reality complex, hierarchical, and disparate. We will attempt here to sort out the various strands of this sector, which deserves a more accurate term— perhaps *extralegal* or *marginal noncapitalist*—than the imprecise catchall *informal*.

Social Ambivalence

We cannot limit our analysis of the situation to the contrast between the "modern" and the "informal" sectors. This dualism existed from the first days of colonization, and the recent rural migrants to the cities, who were merging into a proletariat, did not themselves see these as contradictory lifestyles.[2] On the contrary, the sectors embodied the ambivalence of the migrants' condition: they were dependent both on the peasant system that maintained their families and supplied part of their subsistence and on the Western capitalist system that provided them only with a "supplementary" income (calculated, until very recently, without considering the expenses of supporting a family). In Kenya, it was only in about 1954 or 1955 that the colonial government began to pay African workers—and, even then, only those who had reached a certain age—enough to support a small family in the city; hitherto they had been paid as though they were bachelors living alone.[3]

Even when city-dwellers of long standing have clearly become proletarians (as is the case for industrial workers), a great ambiguity remains. The worker becomes at the same time an integral part of "modern" capitalist society, of the rural world, and of the urban "informal" sector. To be sure, since the 1950s the annual rate of turnover has greatly diminished in the large firms and the public services (from 15 to 5 percent). Even workers more permanently based in the city become only partially proletarianized, however, both because workers retain rights to their land and because they maintain family ties. The connection with the land always persists: the more thoroughly workers become integrated into the capitalist system, the more tenaciously they preserve their rural ties. In East Africa in the late 1960s, three-quarters of the workers owned land. In Tanzania, a recent survey revealed that only 18 percent of the workers in the modern sector had no land of their own, compared to 39 percent in the informal sector.[4] The city-dwellers return to the village to visit their relatives and to bring them gifts and money, to find wives, and to build houses. They continue to offer their country relatives hospitality and to give them 10 to 20 percent of their own income. If they are well enough paid, they bear the costs of improvements in the village infrastructure or the ethnic association in the city.

The modern/informal symbiosis is experienced every day in every house-hold, by every couple and every individual. Even today the modern sector does not provide enough for the family's needs. It is not unusual—in Kin-shasa, Lomé, and elsewhere—for an official's wife to supplement her hus-band's income by practicing the most informal petty trades (selling cooked food such as fritters or bananas) or for a salaried worker to offer marginal repair services in his spare time.

The maintenance of ties to rural life and a preference for the informal sector are not expressions of a timid conservatism but, on the contrary, a rational response to the insecurity of the urban sector—a kind of insurance of the right of reentry into the traditional economy.

Traditional Solidarity and Class Identity

The emergence of a class identity requires an awareness of common eco-nomic interests opposed to those of at least one other class, so that specific collective actions are taken to defend those threatened interests. Close con-tact with the rural areas, the feeling—even after a long period of resi-dence—that life in the city is only a temporary measure, and the persistence and even the reinforcement of the ties of kinship all hinder the emergence of such a class-consciousness. And yet, class-consciousness does show certain signs of development, such as a vocabulary of class relations in languages where this terminology did not previously exist. Thus, in Nairobi they dis-tinguish in Swahili between the group of people (*wananchi*) composed of poor folk (*wakini*) and that of the rich or *wazungu* (Whites). The middle class is called *makarani* ("clerks," the educated). Even in a miserable suburb such as Pumwani, they distinguish between the petite bourgeoisie of land-lords and small tradesmen (*matajari,* the rich, or *mananojiwega,* those who have possessions) and those who possess nothing (*makarani,* mini-tenants). In Tanzanian cities the vocabulary is even more explicit, for TANU propa-ganda uses pejorative terms for the well-to-do. Some form of this phenome-non is to be found in nearly all the major African cities.[5] Other signs of an emerging class-consciousness are the various institutions set up by diverse elements of the urban population to defend particular interests: not only trade unions, but societies and associations of friends, of apprentices, of small shopkeepers, and even of subproletarians such as beggars and prosti-tutes. Finally, class conflict becomes obvious in cases of industrial action such as organized strikes, while wildcat strikes, demonstrations, and riots are also forms of social confrontation.

It no longer suffices to oppose the "bourgeoisie" to the "proletariat," to place the "intelligentsia" in a separate category, and to give the "subprole-tariat" a dangerously ambiguous status, outside the society but manipu-lable by the authorities. As this "marginal" group, described by terms as various as they are vague ("floating proletariat," "Lumpenproletariat," "in-formal sector," "unstructured," "uncontrolled") becomes almost the major-ity, it fundamentally influences the society, both by its role in relations of production and by its social aspirations.

Criteria of the Informal Sector

In a number of Latin American cities, the majority of the population works in the informal labor force (nearly 70 percent). Although that level has not yet been reached in Africa, at least one-third of the active population is unemployed or survives through "marginal occupations." In most cities, the percentage is nearly half: it was 31 percent in Abidjan by 1970, more than 50 percent in Lagos and 50 percent in urban Senegal in 1976, 37 per-cent in greater Dakar in 1975, 38 percent in Lusaka in 1974, 44 percent in Nairobi in 1972, and more than 60 percent in Kumasi, Ghana, in 1974.[6] Considering the slow rate of increase of employment, these figures can only grow.

Apart from defining the informal sector negatively, as engaging in sup-posedly noncapitalistic activities, it is difficult to establish criteria. The in-formal sector operates a market of commodities and services providing an irregular and unverifiable income, in which the dividing line between the licit and the illicit is often difficult to discern (for example, cases of traffick-ing, receiving stolen goods, moneylending, smuggling, and so forth are com-mon). Their activities are generally small-scale, usually run by a family or a single individual, rarely employing more than ten people, and drawing on local, not external, resources. They make up for lack of capital and tech-nological equipment by a relatively abundant informal labor force that is recruited for work by the day or by the job. This labor market is irregular and terribly vulnerable, for it has no formal protection and it is highly com-petitive, but it is infinitely easier to enter than the capitalist sector. The skills needed are generally rudimentary and can be acquired outside the official educational and professional system. Little analyzable data is available, since these informal establishments normally elude current criteria of statis-tical investigation such as a fixed location, a license, payment of taxes, and eligibility for state assistance.

Informal enterprises undergo a number of hardships that result from this extralegal status. They cannot obtain loans from banks, so they are forced to pay moneylenders' usurious interest rates. Unlike modern firms, they re-ceive no assistance with infrastructure (water supply, electricity, railway freightage). On the contrary, troublesome regulations (health laws, taxes on revenues, licenses for street vendors) make them liable to penalties such as arrests, fines, and eviction. The extreme competition gives them only minimal margins of profit, and they cannot afford any insurance or social benefits.

The Informal Social Scale

The informal sector contains several distinct strata. At the top are the small capitalist entrepreneurs, that is, those who own their means of production, although the equipment is generally old, rudimentary, and patched up.[7] The labor is usually provided by family members who are paid little or nothing, and they are active in two fields: production (small manufacturers and artisans) and distribution (small shopkeepers and carriers). They thus operate in a very limited area left relatively open by "peripheral capitalism," which controls both input—raw material, loans—and output—the manufacture of industrial commodities using "modern" techniques of commercialization. At the bottom of the scale are the workers—family helpers, apprentices, casual employees engaged for the day or by the job. These constitute the actual or potential labor force (potential in the case of adolescents, delinquents, and so on).

Manufacturers sometimes head enterprises, but more commonly they are artisans who pay others by teaching them their craft. The artisan, who has a direct relationship with a particular clientele, enters the market only to buy his raw materials and to purchase a means of production (a sewing machine, a gem cutter) or to find a location for it. This contact becomes almost nonexistent when the artisan repairs or maintains some common article. Such an operation requires virtually no capital, either fluid or fixed, for if some spare part needs replacement, the client is generally expected to pay in advance. Small manufacturers such as furniture makers work more directly for the market, but the work is always organized in a paternalistic manner through relationships of kinship and dependency.

It is only when a little capital has been accumulated that the stage of petty capitalist production, aimed exclusively at the market, is reached. Three paths are then open to new entrepreneurs. They can return to the land, to which they are closely allied, and where their land rights may allow them to embark on speculative agriculture (plantations, agroindustry). They can invest in property in the city like those who first run a "maquis" (as a cheap restaurant is called in Abidjan), then furnished lodgings or a hotel involved in prostitution, and finally—if luck or intelligence leads the entrepreneurs to combine economic activities with the cultivation of influential political friends looking for a straw-man—buy a luxurious motel complete with villas or rented apartments. Finally, they can try to enter the industrial sphere. Since techniques there are advanced and competition is stiff, this is generally done through subcontracting. The firms in the modern sector profit from utilizing the services of these enterprises, which can cheaply answer a diversified micro-demand (for example, as motor mechanics, builders, or small-scale textile manufacturers) because they hold down production costs by evading labor laws and paying minimal wages.

The proletariat of the informal sector is generally paid, if at all, by the day or by the job. The most regular workers are the apprentices; they are generally young migrants from the rural areas or primary school dropouts who belong to the boss's family or social group. They are paid little or nothing, but work in order to learn a skill.

Similar strata can be identified among those who work in distribution: petty traders and small-scale transportation enterprises are frequently employed by the large firms. These distributors formerly linked the rural producers and the import-export trade. Today, however, with the creation of marketing boards to handle agricultural products for export, most goods go direct from the international market to the small consumer. Among the poorer distributors there are many gradations, from the delivery person with a decrepit van, ox-drawn cart, or taxi, down to the wandering stall-keeper or "table-man" carrying pack or stall from place to place or the illicit street-vendor selling colas or packets of cigarettes. The goods sold by these vendors are generally supplied by a wholesaler whose own sources are shrouded in secrecy, whether the goods are smuggled or imported from every part of the world. Senegalese peddlers of supposedly "exotic" craftwork (formerly Italian, but now increasingly from Eastern Asia) are firmly controlled by a few entrepreneurs, often Murids.[8] (Such pieces are found all over France and now even in New York.) Each peddler offers a limited selection of products acquired that day from a wholesaler who himself belongs to the informal sector. The mass of petty traders are the main element of the "floating" workforce, for those who have been unable to find any other source of support can always resort to this no-capital form of trading. In Ghana one-eighth of the labor force is entirely or partly involved in trade; in the Adjame quarter of Abidjan, as much as one-third of the active population engages in trade.

In addition to unemployed young men, women are increasingly entering this sector. Trading run by women is a well-established tradition in West Africa; moreover, the women's lack of formal education and the men's domination of more profitable "modern" activities encourage women to make petty trading their special preserve in the labor scene of the city.

This group is particularly resistant to any attempt at organization, because its first concern is individual survival. The case of Nairobi, where several associations of peddlers and traveling salesmen have come into being, appears to be exceptional in this respect.[9]

The labor force in the informal sector is fluid and to a great extent occasional. Most members oscillate between intermittent employment, exercise

of individual ingenuity, and unemployment. In Accra, only 15 percent of the
people working in enterprises with fewer than ten employees are wage earners, and a study of the unemployed youth of Lagos found that, in 1970, more
than one-third had practiced some petty trade in the preceding month.[10] Urban underemployment or unemployment shows a clear connection with
poverty and delinquency. In Kenya, for instance, although 90 percent of the
population was still rural in 1970, almost half the crimes (43 percent) were
committed in cities. In the city of Kampala, Uganda, of the 6,000 people
arrested in 1968, about half were unemployed men; only one-quarter of
them were engaged in unskilled labor; and 60 percent of the offenses against
property were committed by the unemployed.[11] Certainly, unemployment is
not the only reason for delinquency. As is true worldwide, the disruption of
the family, exacerbated by divorce, alcoholism, and other such manifestations of urban tension, contributes its share. In Africa, as in the most industrialized nations, a sense of urban insecurity tends to turn wealthy residential
areas into fortresses surrounded with high walls reinforced with fragments of
broken bottle or barbed wire and protected by iron bars, watchdogs, and
guards. We cannot, however, interpret the delinquency—particularly juve-
nile—of the poor in the cities as a more or less conscious but awkward expression of class aspirations. The sense of insecurity exists just as strongly in
the most poverty-stricken areas, where an atmosphere of mutual suspi-
cion prevails that is particularly unpropitious for the emergence of class-
consciousness. Similarly, in the great American cities, the "gangs" seldom
come out of the ghetto.

The Dependence of the Informal Sector

Does this complex and varied mass of people harbor any combination of
factors that would favor the emergence of class-consciousness? The over-
arching characteristic is dependence on the Western world. Almost all the
small manufacturers derive their equipment or their raw material from the
West, whether it is imported or salvaged (cooking-pot makers' scrap iron or
shoemakers' plastic). Moreover, most of them learned their trades in the
modern sector; in Dakar, for example, this is true of 70 percent of the furniture makers and 55 percent of the mechanics. Finally, some, such as tailors
and dyers, supply their products—nearly always consumer goods—to the
supermarkets.

This relationship between the informal and the modern sector works to
the advantage of the dominant mode of production, primarily because
small-scale local concerns offer commodities and services inexpensively,
organizing a form of distribution that adapts to the demands and daily purchasing requirements of the small retail trade and adds to its choices.[12] To
the extent that the informal sector offers cheap food and other subsistence
commodities to urban workers, it lowers the labor cost in the large enter-

prises. Has the question ever been asked, for instance, why so few of the public or private firms have cafeterias, and why the workers—who buy their meals from sidewalk vendors—have never asked for them? The informal sector, which is expected to supply much of the market of commodities, offers the employees of the modern sector themselves the opportunity to save some money while making their informal activities possible by the tightness of their budgets. The reserve of floating labor held in the informal sectors assures a supply of labor for periods of expansion without raising wages. Finally, subcontracting—even if it is still far less common in sub-Saharan Africa than in Southeast Asia—reduces costs of both production and distribution by employing women, children, and jobless youths. The consequent chain of exploitation works very much to the advantage of Western capitalism. One example of this phenomenon is the foreign building enterprise that, having obtained a contract to construct a number of buildings in Dakar, merely provided the site and overall supervision. The actual building was subcontracted to Senegalese entrepreneurs, who in turn gave part of it to micro-entrepreneurs. The chain of subcontracting became a chain of exploitation, with wages dropping at each stage: the masons earned very little, and the apprentices nothing whatsoever. The profits went to the original contractor, who neither paid the officially determined salaries nor provided benefits.[13]

To be sure, examples can readily be found of intermediate artisanal activities becoming mechanized, absorbed by the capitalist sector but assured of profitability (as in the case of the shoemakers). And, in contrast, many industrial units have failed or owe their survival only to state assistance (for example, manufacturers of ready-made clothes) or have had to abandon production of certain "low-level" goods. Thus, in Abidjan the Bata leather sandals were progressively eliminated by the cheaper, imported "Ho-Chi-Minh" plastic tongues; the traditional craftsmen could only survive, as at Lomé, by making "Dunlop" sandals out of old tires.[14] In such cases, subcontracting is not marginal but is undeniably linked to the modern sector, even if adaptability to the African market influences it more than does its doubtful profitability.[15]

The importance of the informal sector should not be exaggerated, however. It is grafted onto the capitalist economy, certainly, but its elimination would probably not be a fatal blow to the capitalist mode of production; its primary aim is the survival of its own membership.

The "Involutional" Prospect

The small manufacturers of the informal sector show great inventiveness and an extraordinary capacity for adaptation. Far from being stagnant or unproductive, this sector has changed the structure of society by giving employment to the urban and rural masses. The sector's long-term prospects, however, look far less hopeful. All indicators point to the likelihood of an ever-increasing influx of unemployed to the city, where they will have to resort to increasingly shaky subterfuges in a labor market that is developing at a much slower pace. Statistics show that the modern sector will not be able to develop quickly enough to absorb workers if the nationwide rate of population growth exceeds 2.5 percent a year. If new arrivals on the labor market are to be incorporated into the industrial society, half the active population have to be regular wage earners; in most African cities, the number is only 10 to 20 percent.[16] Therefore many economists speak not of *evolution* but of the opposite, negative process of *involution,* in which a growing population shares a relatively fixed pool of jobs and goods.

This, precisely, is what makes the evolution of the cities of the Third World so different from that of European industrial centers in the nineteenth century. It is less instructive, in fact, to point out the analogies between the two than their fundamental dissimilarities.[17] In sub-Saharan Africa, urban and industrial development has been neither preceded nor accompanied by a rapid and sustained parallel development of rural productivity: the "agricultural revolution" has not yet occurred. The exodus from the rural areas owes little to an accentuation of social differences resulting from an increase in agricultural profitability. On the contrary, the world prices of agricultural products for export fail to keep pace with those of industrial goods (the opposite relationship to that in Western Europe throughout the nineteenth century). This results in an "unequal exchange" between the rural areas and the city, as the rural areas not only fail to feed the cities but themselves grow dependent on urban commodities and on imported foodstuffs. Finally, contrary to the situation in nineteenth-century Europe, the African urban migrations do not represent a "thinning" of the rural demographic surplus. Even if the rural population growth does not equal the influx into the cities, the rural areas are in a state of crisis and consequently feel increased demographic pressure. From now until the end of the century, migration will increase, in accordance with the rule of the annual 2−4−8 (2 percent total increase of population, 4 percent increase in the cities, 8 percent increase in the squatter areas). The world has never before been faced with so great a challenge in such a short period of time.[18]

The second difference between Africa and the West is a direct result of the first. The disparity in the cities between the demand for jobs and the supply, and thus between the forces of production and the internal consumers' market, is growing. The technology of the nineteenth century was a great consumer of labor: the influx of migrant workers driven by the impoverishment of the rural areas was gradually absorbed into the emerging industries (although there was undoubtedly a certain lapse of time that led, for at least one or two generations, to intense urban poverty). Moroever, the high deathrate in the cities—which continued to increase in London throughout the eighteenth century [19]—counterbalanced a rural population growth that was, generally speaking, moderate compared to the formidable rates today in the Third World (where the deathrate in the cities is, on the contrary, lower than that in the rural areas). Not only does this "natural demographic control" no longer exist, but other means of controlling employment also no longer exist. In the eighteenth and nineteenth centuries, the surplus man-power created by the demographic upsurge and the agricultural revolution had the additional major outlet of the New World. From Ireland and Scotland first of all, and then from the rest of continental, central, and southern Europe, millions emigrated to America, proportionally far more than the number of migrants from the Third World who are today absorbed by the industrialized Western countries.

The operations now carried out in the Third World by the multinational companies, even if they continue to take advantage of the low cost of a super-abundant labor force, provide many fewer jobs than formerly. The complex of factors results in an extroverted economy, that is to say, one that is primarily oriented toward export, exacerbating the process of unequal exchange.

This brings us to the third major difference. In the nineteenth century, the Western countries created strong systems of government with the aim of protecting and consolidating local industry and encouraging its expansion into foreign markets. By contrast, the African colonial governments deliberately restrained industrial development. Today, despite occasional attempts to promote a protected national industry, the usual course is to continue the policies of the colonial era. When industrialization does take place in Africa—and it is not yet the general rule—it does not fundamentally alter the system of dependence.

Increasingly futureless jobs—and hence resources and markets—are divided among increasingly impoverished masses. Certainly, capitalist accumulation provides an opportunity for a few individuals to make fortunes; the biographies of a few African multimillionaires recall the American self-made men of the end of the last century. Nevertheless, even the most active of the small entrepreneurs have great difficulty in accumulating sufficient capital to enter the modern sector. Competition and underemployment and, thus, instability of employment are on the rise; as real per-capita income falls, the chances of escaping the vicious circle of poverty—namely, low productivity, assuring a miserable income, which reduces productivity further—diminishes. Hence the precariousness of the position of the small employer or self-employed worker: Western competition constantly threatens them with redundancy, underqualification, and, consequently, subproletarianization. Thus, in Lomé, the competition of Bata forced the leatherworkers to abandon their traditional craft and put together "Dunlop sandals." [20] Similarly, in

Dakar, the small-scale manufacturers of Medina footwear found themselves reduced to piecework, depending on Bata for their supply of leather and on Lebanese wholesalers for plastics.[21]

At best, the result could be a radical transformation of social and economic structures that transcend centralism and the pressures of international capitalism. Is that where we are heading?

THE PRICE OF CLASS-CONSCIOUSNESS

The Obstacles: Individualism and Accommodation

Even today, class-consciousness has only reached an embryonic stage among this complex and varied mass of people. This is due to two related factors: an individualistic survival structure aiming, at best, at social success on the petit-bourgeois model, and the influence of various forms of social and cultural conservatism.

The informal sector feels no impetus to conceive the future in any other way than in the image of the surrounding society. The only ambition is to succeed in terms of the existing system and then to reproduce it. This results in a "present-centered" attitude;[22] the passivity of the informal sector has even earned it the description "black hole." In short, the area and the period lack hope; the situation is one of historical sterility. The result is a process of accommodation rather than revolution. We can only ask how long and to what degree this pattern of behavior can contain the contradictions of an increasingly inegalitarian society. Will it last long enough to see the beginnings of a lessening of demographic pressure?

The position of the small entrepreneurs is essentially ambiguous. On the one hand, their success, such as it is, depends on shameless exploitation of the poorest among them; and, on the other hand, the meddlesome control of their activities by the public authorities causes them to resent the ruling classes. Within the confines of the informal sector, their often very similar social origins, their close family ties, and their residential proximity to the urban and lumpen proletariat give the entrepreneurs a feeling of solidarity with them, but their immediate interests are served by the maintenance and even the reinforcement of the current mode of exploitation.

As for the mass of workers, the state of intense competition the labor market forces on them hardly encourages them to unite. Their ambition is to reach the level of the "little boss." The unemployed lack solidarity, for looking for work is a notably individualistic activity that makes all others into rivals. As long as those looking for work are convinced that they have a chance to succeed, they are unlikely to present a major political threat based on a reasoned ideological and political radicalism. Thus the only chance of revolution remains a general populist uprising.

Because they lack any clear aims, the people have the tendency to take

refuge in a familiar system of values. The city-dwellers turn to the traditional beliefs to find the explanation and the reassurance they need to cope
with the insecurity of employment and the day-to-day difficulties of life in a
foreign world. If they have found employment in the modern sector they
must live in this alien world from the moment they leave their households
and (more or less ethnic) quarter in the morning and enter the "world of the
Whites" (in both literal and metaphorical senses). The proliferation of medicine men, soothsayers, marabouts, and other traditional practitioners reveals the importance assigned to precolonial beliefs. Their clientele, moreover, is by no means restricted to the underprivileged inhabitants of the
suburbs, but comes from all social strata. Members of the elite avail themselves of the services of both modern medicine and traditional healers (like
the director of a clinic in Gabon, who consults the medicine man before
taking an airplane).

Above all, the last few years have seen a new wave of conversions to more
or less syncretistic religions. Thus, in the outlying areas of Abidjan can be
found Celestial Christianity and the New Church, along with a multitude of
sects and "prophets" with smaller followings. This phenomenon, among a
wretched mass of people whose original culture no longer fits the society in
which they have to survive, is more than a simple ethnological curiosity. It is
the means of reducing or of channeling in an apolitical direction the tensions
created by a very inegalitarian society. The existing social order is in practice
strengthened by these faiths, for their dominant feature in this prescientific
conception of the world is personification of the source of pain. That is to
say, a given injustice is deemed to have been perpetrated by a guilty individual. This person can be identified and punished through some religious or
magical process. The method for dealing with social ills, then, would not be
a program of collective political action but the repetitive execution of appropriate religious techniques. Religion, to be sure, is not necessarily the "opiate
of the people," but the millenarist version rarely leads to revolution.

The traditional social practices tend to emphasize cross-allegiances. Each
person is encompassed by ties that provide him with a certain security: his
allegiance to his village, to his family, his religion, his language, and his
place of residence—in short, to his group of origin. Certain elements such as
the ethnic group or the religion can exercise a decisive influence, especially if
the latter binds together the members of a foreign minority as Islam does in
Abidjan.

Allegiance to a religious or ethnic group does not necessarily contradict
class allegiance. It is neither unusual nor necessarily uncomfortable to belong at once to a professional trade union (these are nearly always multiethnic), to a regionalist association based on the ethnic group, and to a religious community. In such a case, however, political activity is dissociated
from the trade union, which is restricted to purely professional matters. A

good example of this phenomenon is found in Nigeria where, despite the general strike of June 1962—an impressive demonstration, at the time, of interethnic solidarity—the workers all voted in the general election of December of that year according to their regional identity.[23]

The political exploitation of ethnicity is expressed in clientism, which binds the client closely to his patron and prevents him in the name of tribalism from recognizing himself as a member of a class. It is a phenomenon of conservative origin. The ruling classes exert their authority over the masses by reference to the cultural heritage of a solidly structured society with a strongly hierarchical tradition.[24]

Clientism is often exploited by strong totalitarian governments that promote nationalist concepts such as a classless society or order or national unity. The absolute power of the state is justified by archaic tradition. It directly controls the various communities by incorporating into the state apparatus the popular organizations that developed in the course of colonial and postcolonial struggles—first of all, of course, the trade unions.

Attractive though the idea may be, under these circumstances it is hard to believe that the informal sector will catalyze future social upheavals. Although it is impossible to predict the future with certainty, this argument seems more like a declaration of faith than a statement of reality.[25]

Populism and Revolution

The arousal of class-consciousness seems to be connected, in Africa as elsewhere, with a combination of the aspirations of the underprivileged masses and an organized political leadership. The same rule applies to urban societies as to the twentieth-century "peasant revolutions": what is needed is a political leadership that can express popular demands in ideological terms while remaining closely connected with its base; the latter makes the difference between populism and revolution. Two unequally matched forces, the intelligentsia and the working class proper, take part in this process.

The intelligentsia, at least in its origins, differs from the mass of "preproletarians" of the informal sector. African intellectuals of the new generation also have little in common with their middle-class predecessors of the colonial era, who desired to reform the existing system. Most present-day intellectuals, like their fellows the world over, still remain eager to adapt to a society that gives them material advantages and social prestige. A change, however—also worldwide—is taking place that is likely to alter the situation radically: young graduates are finding it harder to get jobs and many are thus condemned to marginalization. For university graduates, the process began in the early 1970s (in Dakar it is known as the *maîtrisards'* problem)[26] and it is affecting a growing number of high school pupils, for whom matriculation formerly guaranteed a job in the administration, that panacea of underdeveloped countries with a paucity of industrial employment. The number of graduates who are forced into the informal sector is hard to determine, but it is by no means negligible.

The city appeals to a wide social spectrum. A definite connection can be made between level of income, level of education, and migration: the more affluent rural families are, the more lands planters have, the more likely they are to send their children to school in the city. The classic model is undoubtedly that of a poor family in which the parents deny themselves essentials in order to invest in the education of the oldest son in the hope that his future position will somehow ensure the survival of the rural family group. Thus, in the relatively densely populated area of eastern Kenya, "semi-urban" villages have proliferated that, although a few hundred kilometers from the capital, depend on the graduates of the family, who provide financial aid for the rural families and pay educational and other expenses for the less fortunate or less talented members who have remained on the land.[27]

This pattern is even more marked among the families of notables, whose sons and, increasingly, daughters—eager for a new type and quality of life— go to the city to obtain their secondary and higher education and the diploma that until recently guaranteed them their social, financial, and thus political prestige. It could be said that the more highly educated peasants are, the more likely they are to leave for the city. In Tanzania, 60 percent of the adults are literate, but the literacy level reaches nearly 90 percent among recent urban immigrants, two-thirds of whom spent at least five years at school.[28]

The phenomenon of overqualification exists today on a scale large enough to produce a strong sense of personal frustration among these young people looking for a job. Most of them see themselves as belonging to a misunderstood elite. Ideologically they are closer to the petit-bourgeois, white-collar workers with whom they dream of identifying themselves than to the miserable mass to which they in fact belong. And yet, almost everywhere in recent decades, high school students have played a crucial role in civic disturbances—in South Africa, in Brazzaville, in Dakar. Could not some of these students, fired with an ideology of revolt against the state apparatus and the oligarchy in power, transcend their individual grievances and create a collective movement full of revolutionary potential? Something of the kind seemed to happen during the riots in Soweto.

These "displaced intellectuals," however, can do nothing on their own. The example of Soweto demonstrates the importance of an integrated industrial proletariat. It is true that everywhere except in South Africa, this latter group is gaining strength less rapidly than the urban informal sector, but large-scale industrial concentrations have formed around certain economic centers such as Lagos, Abidjan, Mombasa, and Nairobi. The size of the industrial proletariat varies enormously according to the degree to which the economy of a country is developed. Industrial workers constitute nearly a third of the active population in Zambia, but only 5 percent in Mali and little more than that in Niger (although there the uranium mines definitely increase the numbers). On an average, the workers in the modern sector still make up less than half of the urban labor force, but proletarianization of these newly urban peasants has increased rapidly in these last ten years. Moreover, these people cling to the dream of individual enterprise. Everyone wants to "set up on his own"; as a result, a great deal of interplay takes place between the modern and the informal sector.

The industrial workers cannot be subsumed under the vague term, used in a confused way in Africa, of *labor aristocracy,* for that would preclude these people "privileged" with regular wages from being regarded as proletarians. The differential between the wages of unskilled workers or peasants and those of skilled workers at the top of the wage scale remains extremely small.[29] The workers, who seldom give up the rights to their land, support a disproportionate number of the impoverished in the rural areas and the cities (at least 20 percent of their income to others). In addition, the advantages they enjoy in relation to the peasants are dwindling, especially with the high cost of subsistence in the city (charcoal for cooking, food, rent), which is generally greatly underestimated.[30] Finally, the purchasing power of urban wages continually falls: in Ghana—an extreme case, but Zaire is even worse—it has dropped by 45 percent since the 1960s. In the Ivory Coast, a study of 1,000 workers in the food industry has demonstrated that a very low standard of living leads to absenteeism and reduced productivity.[31] Many workers are able to survive only by complementing their wages through direct or indirect (via their wives and/or children) recourse to the informal sector.

It is true that some workers in industry receive relatively high wages; the miners in Zambia used to enjoy an income double that offered in other sectors of industry, although industrial wages as a whole have increased twice as fast as those in the rural areas. Their political role, however, is, if anything, more active than that of more poorly paid workers. Often skilled workers, who are the best organized, are the foremost in making demands (as in Kenya and Ghana).[32] We have indeed come far from the Marxist models of the beginning of the century. It is clear that in present-day Africa, class-consciousness, if not nonexistent, is at any rate sluggish and confused. In at least one case, that of South Africa, we can be sure that in the future the labor movement, which already has numerical superiority, will play a crucial role, but no one can predict whether it will take a radical or a reformist direction. Until now, White repression has prevented any follow-up to labor demonstrations.

Elsewhere, politicization is still in its infancy. The trade unions on the one hand accept the rules of capitalism and thus help to integrate the proletariat into the existing system, and on the other hand impose class identity on a national scale.[33] The efforts of the state, as in colonial times, to emasculate the trade unions constitutes a proof by inference of their potential for resistance. (See Chapter 12.)

African workers do not become proletarian, in the Western and Marxist sense, simply because they earn wages in a city. Rather, the more city-dwellers are integrated into the capitalist sector (as the salaried workers are), the more they turn to elements connected with their original societies. More than others, they maintain their rights to their land; they participate in rural life as much as or more than the others of the informal sector, either personally or through relatives; they maintain membership in ethnic associations as well as in trade unions (even if only 5 percent of them are activists). Beyond an appearance of modernity manifested in property, salary, and lifestyle, the most integrated city-dwellers are giving rise to original (African?) syncretic urban practices that can no longer be associated simply either with residual rural customs or a Westernization of manners.[34]

Because the workers are denied formal outlets for grievances, they are forced to express themselves through wildcat strikes and urban riots, which are undoubtedly interconnected. The riot, which is sporadic and localized, transitory and quickly dealt with, in most cases, by the military authorities, demonstrates the impasse populism has reached today;[35] but it also offers a means of allying the workers with the impoverished, the representatives of the modern sector with the fringe elements of the informal sector—whose interests are far more closely connected than may at first appear. After all, the places of residence, means of subsistence, ways of life, and, finally, the aspirations of the two have much in common. Apart from the miners and railwayworkers, they all live together in the same cramped, unhealthy quarters, belong to the same family networks and professional associations, are involved in similar activities and petty trades, and face the same problem—the impossibility of acquiring capital. Thus the entire milieu could give rise to new forces and forms of protest, if at the same time there arose a coherent political consciousness, properly organized and directed. Needless to say, this is still far from being the case.

Nevertheless, from now on the turbulence of uncontrolled or little-controlled urban growth is destined, in sub-Saharan Africa as elsewhere, to become the principal generator of upheavals. Whether we like it or not, it is in the cities that people, work, and systems of organization are now concentrated, that economic and cultural institutions develop, and that political power is established. It is there that the decisive social dynamics of the future will come into play.[36]

Conclusion

From this huge yet incomplete inventory, this at present somewhat disappointing balance sheet, this unfinished and unfulfilled evolution, what conclusions should be drawn?

These societies are in the throes of metamorphosis. On the one hand, the historical roots of underdevelopment go back to the first days of a system of international mercantilism that has always drawn most of the surplus outside the country. This system extends from medieval Islam to contemporary Western capitalism and includes Portuguese, Indians, Greeks, Lebanese, and Syrians. On the other hand, the African societies have not yet adjusted to the swift and traumatic changes to which they have been subjected in the period from colonization to independence. For some African nations, the entire process has taken less than a century. Their adjustment to these trying changes was actively thwarted by the totalitarian colonial regimes, which immobilized both the economy, by imposing quotas determined in Europe, and the culture, by emphasizing "tribal" differences. Whether from an economic, social, political, or ideological viewpoint, the systems and outlooks that govern the operation of the African states seem contradictory, for elements inherited from the sometimes distant past coexist and interact. Some of these factors are no longer workable, and others belong to a future more desired than expected. The difficulties of the present confuse the picture further. All that can be said for certain is that the changes now taking place have every likelihood of proceeding at an accelerated pace for another generation, if not longer.

Does that mean that the African societies are headed toward economic and cultural absorption by the capitalist "monster," and the final outcome will be a uniform "suburbanization" of the world? That is undoubtedly a risk. It would not be the first time a dominant civilization absorbed the outlying regions it controlled, even if the hope exists of a later counter-movement that in turn will foster a new and greater flowering of culture. Did not Rome finally fall to the barbarians, giving birth to the Western world of the present day?

The worldwide scale of the phenomenon is unprecedented, however. Africa shares her dilemma with developing nations around the globe. The pattern is familiar: a nation-state, an industrialized economy, a productive agriculture without peasants, a consumer society, and the triumph of urbanization—and their corollaries, the decline of oral tradition, the "folklorization" of the regional past, denatured survivals of older social and economic structures, and the blossoming of cults symptomatic of the prevailing malaise.

To the burning question asked by so many historians, so many students, so many African intellectuals—"What is to be done?"—is there really no answer, except to let history take its course? Because Africa is economically and politically so fragile, that would mean, to put it crudely, that what is to be expected is increasing exploitation of resources near a few fantastically overpopulated cities, while the rest of the continent degenerates into "tribal reserves" wracked by malnutrition and disease.

If the mechanisms that have been set in motion are allowed to continue to operate, it is indeed difficult to see any other future. The process can only be stopped by deliberate action. And, historically, is that not how all great social changes have occurred? England became the first industrial nation in part because a century earlier its brief political revolution had liberated the necessary social forces. France's bourgeois revolution of 1789 freed it from the restraints inherited from feudal times. The Soviet economic burgeoning surely owed much to the revolution of 1917. Finally, China, too, used violence to change the course of its history.

It is probable that sub-Saharan Africa will be unable to halt the progress of underdevelopment without a radical revolution, first of its social, then its political, structures. The issue is extremely complex, however, first of all because Africa does not exist as an entity except in a purely geographical sense. The Organization of African Unity, to be sure, must not be discounted. It has proved its effectiveness in national liberation struggles, but its internal and external divisions today prevent it—this is the least we can say—from generating radical change. The jealous, competitive nationalism of unequally matched countries that are sometimes excessively restricted or underpopulated makes success for pan-Africanism appear unlikely in the near future.

The great powers' strategies of undermining African attempts at forging independence and of competition work to perpetuate the weakness and divisiveness that make the African continent the most vulnerable area of international rivalry. It is obvious that as long as the Horn of Africa and Chad are considered sites for strategic confrontation by the Soviet Union, Europe, the United States, and China, as long as Nigeria and Zaire are treated as objects of economic wagers, and as long as Zambia, situated at the heart of the continent, bordering so many actually or potentially socialist countries (Tanzania, Mozambique, Angola, Zimbabwe, Namibia), and neighboring Zaire are regarded as important pieces on the Western chessboard, the internal political life of these countries is bound to be weakened and distorted.

Any collective solution must involve a fundamental revision of concepts that today are taken for granted but in fact only apply to the Western capitalist system. The Western model of consumption has to a great degree been assimilated, but is the division of labor as it is today internationally defined the only one possible? Must the cities and the rural areas continue to be regarded as two separate entities connected by relations of hierarchy and dependency (the city fed by the rural areas, the rural areas supported by the city)? Can they not instead be perceived as an indissociable complex that binds together a mass of interdependent currents and networks that assure both the equilibrium and the survival of the whole? Finally, is the nation-state the only political model possible? On the contrary, the central authority, the administration, in other words, the officially recognized state is daily losing not only its effectiveness but its credibility. A growing section of the African masses is now turning to other forms of power management, to small-scale society and economics based on neighborliness and proximity. The formidable growth of the so-called informal sector with its parallel institutions, innumerable sects, and so forth displays this tendency clearly.

These progressive changes, indistinct as yet, although sometimes taking place in sudden spurts, might ultimately prevail, supporting new political concepts. Some leading country—Nigeria, for instance—through its economic, demographic, and hence strategic importance might conceivably exert a decisive influence, drawing the others after it. Or some violent cataclysm might take place that would radically alter African geopolitics. Such an outcome could only be produced by the South African "volcano." Despite the violence of the underlying conflicts, however, it is no doubt equally possible to suppose that the present unstable situation, held in check by the White army and police, may continue to exist for some time.

There remains one at least relatively unknown quantity that may be destined to play a crucial role in the evolution of the future map of Africa: the demographic factor. Will the Black demographic explosion continue long enough to submerge the White regime in South Africa? Will it be sufficiently long-lasting and on a sufficient scale to force the miserable urban masses radically to alter their way of life and their manner of surviving? Or may not a controllable population growth, reabsorbed over a long period, create more favorable conditions for development? It is still too early to say. At the present time, we can only make short-term forecasts about Africa, and the short run, we must admit, gives little ground for encouragement.

The road to be traveled is long, and the liabilities are heavy. Any number of accusations can be leveled at Africans. They display neither a European sense of initiative, nor an Asian willingness to work, nor the modern state's concept of the public good. All these attributes, however, and many others as well, can be acquired.

The fact is that societies, groups, or classes in Africa are today in the making. The immediate situation looks bleak. The standard of living is likely to continue to fall until 2005 or 2020; the few reserves of money and goods are fast disappearing; infant mortality is rising—and that is not even to mention the modern black plague, AIDS. But major changes are under-way, beginning with the demographic factors just mentioned. Faint signs of an agricultural revolution can also be detected. The diverse cultures are meld-ing. Finally, Black Africa is becoming transformed in the urban melting-pot, far more rapidly than, for example, China has been. In twenty years every aspect that defines Africa today will have undergone an alteration that can-not be foretold by our present means of analysis. The pessimism undeniably called for in the short term, then, cannot validly be extended to the longer term.

To bear out such optimism, of course, Africans must succeed in taking control of their own destiny. They must overcome a variety of obstacles as they face, and to a large extent oppose, the "developed" world. And here South Africans may lead the way.

Appendix:
The Sources of African
Demographic History

The only indisputable fact about demographic history is that the question is extraordinarily difficult.[1] The sources are by no means nonexistent, but they are scattered, disconnected, and unreliable. Annual data are available at least beginning in the 1920s and sometimes from the beginning of the colonial era (particularly in English-speaking Africa), but they are unreliable, as those in all underdeveloped countries today still are, due to the difficulty of making a scientific census in the Western manner. All too often, the colonial administrators proceeded by guesswork or automatically added some increment to the figure for the preceding year, arrived at heaven knows how. Not only were the technical means lacking for making an accurate countrywide assessment, but the "natives" tried by every possible means to avoid being counted, since a demographic census was associated with the collection of the poll tax, which was levied per capita. Parish registers, some of which are old, obviously dealt with only a part of the population. Even the more recent official registers cannot be relied on, for registration is by no means a universal practice. Some societies (notably those that have been Islamized) have a strong tendency to "forget" the females or are traditionally disinclined to divulge stillbirths.

When we are dealing with the twentieth century and sometimes with the nineteenth, it does become possible to argue from figures. In Luanda, for instance, the Portuguese systematically collected meteorological data beginning in 1857, and we have a complete account of the annual rainfall from 1878.[2] Censuses, even if questionable, at least exist in this period, in addition to such official documents as tax registers and conscription lists. Earlier than that, nothing of the kind exists. In certain localities, we find some very early data. There are ancient chronicles recording the great events which marked the history of the region, among which great demographic calamities (famines, epidemics, invasions of locusts) have an important place. Typical examples are the chronicles written by the *ulemas* (Muslim scholars) of

Timbuktu, particularly the *Tarikh es-Sudan* and the *Tedskiret en-Nisian,* which date from the period from the end of the sixteenth century to the middle of the eighteenth century,[3] and the *Chronicles of Walata* or *Tichit,*[4] which concern the southern edge of the Sahara in the nineteenth century. Similarly, in Angola, seventeenth-century missionary sources quite regularly noted droughts, epidemics, and rises in population in the kingdom of Kongo (but how dependable are they?), and for the great slave center of Luanda we possess an almost complete account of divergences from normal rates of rainfall and sickness in the seventeenth century.[5]

The problem is not solved. If we possess a relatively continuous set of statistics for an early period, we must evaluate its significance. Thus, we find that in Walata and Tichit in the nineteenth century, twenty-two years were marked by calamities, including fifteen years of epidemics, four of famine, and one of sharp price increases. In the first twenty years of the century there were only two calamities, and between 1834 and 1854 all was calm. The most difficult periods were the 1820s—early 1830s, and the second half of the 1800s. The general picture of vulnerability that emerges from the chronicles results from both the large number of calamitous years and the excessive shortness of the periods of recovery, but it must be asked whether these observations of two localities about 350 kilometers apart can be projected onto the whole region and, if so, to what degree.

This is still a relatively reasonable example. But, for the precolonial centuries, the typical source is the Arab or European "traveler's tale," which is usually as vague as it is colorful. We are told of a "populated countryside," but we are not given the demographic density. And the most famous observers exaggerated wildly; Stanley, for example, claimed that there were some 40,000,000 inhabitants in the Congo Basin.

Oral sources are sometimes the most important, but they are always incomplete. The collective memory recalls major events such as severe epidemics or long droughts that may have caused major structural changes, but incidents seen as normal are not transmitted to future generations. Nothing is said about recurrent food shortages that give rise to malnutrition and sporadic illnesses. Finally, memories do not go back beyond the seventeenth century, and even that is very rare. For earlier periods, the sources at the most enable us to perceive the main lines of development and to make working hypotheses.[6]

Archaeological sources provide important local information concerning sites of settlement, their expansion or contraction, and their material culture. Many more excavations are needed, however, and dating remains uncertain. Moreover, it is difficult to tell whether a discovery represents an original settlement or a resettlement (for instance, the eleventh-century cultivated areas in the bend of the Niger recently discovered by an American team).[7] Better use could also be made of historical and demographic analysis of ancient maps and especially of aerial coverage by the Land Satellite System. Although they are generally used for military purposes, these photos can reveal the ancient division of land into portions and the ancient tracks; in short, they bear witness to the history of land use. Much could be learned, with a sufficient investment.

Linguistic study of vocabulary and the history of borrowings can suggest the centuries-old or even millennial development of contacts and exchanges. The spread of the language generally, though not always, corresponds to a population expansion. Reconstitution of a "proto-vocabulary" provides a means of estimating, through a glottal chronology, the character of linguistic and demographic dispersion, as we see in some celebrated studies of proto-Bantu and of the populations speaking these languages from about the first millennium B.C.[8]

A study of the history of cultivated plants and agricultural technology, if it is related to the evolution of the soil and climate, can give us some idea of the periods when an agricultural revolution—which may suggest a change in climatic or political conditions—affected the production of food crops, which could then feed more—or fewer—people.

The history of climate provides grounds for speculation. Certain climatologists today suggest that the repeated droughts from 1972 onward may mark a definite turning point. In reply, the historian can only point to similar long periods of repeated drought as early as the end of the sixteenth century and again in the last decade of the nineteenth century and at the beginning of the twentieth century.

Notes

Introduction

1. Pat McGowan and Thomas H. Johnson, "African Military Coups d'Etat and Underdevelopment: A Quantitative Historical Analysis," *Journal of Modern African Studies* 22, no. 4 (1984): 633–56, and "Sixty Coups in Thirty Years: Further Evidence regarding African Military Coups d'Etat," *Journal of Modern African Studies* 24, no. 3 (1986): 539–46.

2. Bill Warren, *Imperialism, Pioneer of Capitalism* (London, 1980).

3. Some persuasive examples are Tibor Mende, *From Aid to Recolonization: Lessons of a Failure* (New York, 1973); Jean Ziégler, *Main basse sur l'Afrique noire* (Paris, 1978); Gérard Chaliand, *Struggle for Africa: Conflict of the Great Powers* (London, 1982); and René Dumont and Marie-France Mottin, *Stranglehold on Africa* (London, 1983).

PART 1

Chapter 1

1. Cf. R. F. Stevenson, *Population and Political Systems in Tropical Africa* (New York, 1968). Our present knowledge in this area was summarized in two symposia at the University of Edinburgh that resulted in the publication of *African Historical Demography*, 2 vols. (Edinburgh, 1977, 1981). Cf. R. J. Rathbone and R. P. Moss, eds., *The Population Factor in African Studies* (London, 1975); G. W. Hartwig and K. D. Patterson, eds., *Disease in African History: An Introductory Survey and Case Studies* (Durham, N.C., 1978); and K. O. Zachariah and J. S. Conde, *Migration in West Africa: The Demographic Aspects* (Oxford, 1982). See also the work of the round-table conference Sécheresse Africaine: Climat et Société, Paris, Ecole des Hautes Etudes en Sciences Sociales, December 1982.

2. J. C. Miller, "The Significance of Drought, Disease, and Famine in the Agriculturally Marginal Zones of West-Central Africa," *Journal of African History* 23, no. 1 (1982): 17–61. See also Philip Curtin, "Nutrition in African History," in Robert I. Rotberg and Theodore K. Rabb, eds., *Hunger and History: The Impact of Changing Food Production and Consumption Patterns of Society* (Cambridge, England, 1985).

3. J. B. Webster, ed., *Chronology, Migration and Drought in Interlacustrine Africa* (London, 1979).

4. D. C. Ohadike, "The Influenza Pandemic of 1918–19 and the Spread of Cassava Cultivation on the Lower Niger: A Study in Historical Linkages," *Journal of African History* 22, no. 3 (1981): 379–91.

5. Cf. J. C. Caldwell, "Major Questions in African Demographic History," in *African Historical Demography*, vol. 1, pp. 7–22.

6. C. Wrigley, "Population and History," in *African Historical Demography*, vol. 2, pp. 17–32.

7. This section should be reevaluated in the light of the new data and hypotheses offered in an excellent work edited by D. D. Cordell and J. W. Gregory, *African Population and Capitalism* (Boulder, Colo., 1987).

8. Wrigley, "Population and History."

9. Esther Boserup, *The Conditions of Agricultural Growth* (London, 1965); Esther Boserup, *Population and Technological Change: A Study of Long-Term Trends* (Chicago, 1981); and Esther Boserup, "Economic and Demographic Interrelationship in Subsaharan Africa," *Population and Development Review* 11, no. 3 (1985).

10. Monique Chastanet, "Les Crises de subsistance dans les villages Soninke du cercle de Bakel, 1858–1945," *Cahiers d'Etudes Africaines* 23, no. 1–2 (1983): 5–36.

11. Cf. C.-H. Perrot, "Traditions orales et démographie historique: A propos de la population du Ndenye aux XVIIIe et XIXe siècles," in *African Historical Demography*, vol. 2, pp. 433–56.

12. B. Riccioli, *Geographiae et hydrographiae reformatae* (Bologna, 1661; Venice, 1672), appendix "De verisimili hominum numero," pp. 630–34. Cf. E. Ducreux, "Les Premiers Essais d'évaluation de la population du monde et l'idée de dépopulation au XVIIe siècle," *Annales de Démographie Historique* (1977): 421–38; Jean-Noël Biraben, "Essai sur l'évolution du nombre des hommes," *Population* 34, no. 1 (1979): 13–24, reprinted in Hervé le Bras, ed., *Population* (Paris, 1985), pp. 56–68. See United Nations, *Demographic Yearbooks*.

13. Cf. P. Curtin, *The Atlantic Slave Trade: A Census* (Madison, Wisc., 1969).

14. W. F. Willcox, ed., "Increase in the Population of the Earth and of the Continents since 1650," *International Migrations*. Vol. 2: *Interpretations* (New York, 1931), pp. 33–82; A. M. Saunders, *World Population: Past Growth and Present Trends* (London, 1936); and cf. F. Lorimer, W. Brass, and E. Van de Walle, "Demography," in A. Lystad, ed., *The African World, a Survey of Social Research* (New York, 1965), pp. 271–303; J. D. Durand, "World Population Estimates, 1750–2000," *Proceedings of the World Population Conference, Belgrade, 1965*, vol. 2 (New York, 1967); J. D. Durand, "The Modern Expansion of World Population," *Population Problems: Proceedings of the American Philosophical Society* 3, no. 3 (1967): 137, 152–53.

15. W. A. Hance, *Population, Migration and Urbanization in Africa* (New York, 1970), pp. 16, 35. The more recent evaluations give a total of 680 million inhabitants toward the end of the seventeenth century (Biraben, "Essai sur l'évolution," p. 16).

16. Greighton Gabel, "Demographic Perspectives on the African Pleistocene," *African Historical Demography*, vol. 1, pp. 71–104.

17. Thurston Shaw, "Questions in the Holocene Demography of West Africa," *African Historical Demography,* vol. 1, pp. 105–21.

18. M. Malowist, "The Social and Economic Stability of the Western Sudan in the Middle Ages," *Past and Present,* no. 33 (1966): 3–15; A. G. Hopkins, "The Western Sudan in the Middle Ages: Underdevelopment in the Empires of the Western Sudan," *Past and Present,* no. 37 (1967): 149–56, and Malowist's rejoinder, pp. 157–62. Cf. the further treatment of this idea in C. Coquery-Vidrovitch and H. Moniot, *L'Afrique noire de 1800 à nos jours,* 2d ed. (Paris, 1984), p. 285.

19. Hance, *Population.* Cf. P. Chaunu, *La Civilisation de l'Europe classique* (Paris, 1966), and J. Dupâquier and M. Dupâquier, *Histoire de la Démographie* (Paris, 1985), pp. 109, 149.

Chapter 2

1. P. Curtin, *The Atlantic Slave Trade: A Census* (Madison, 1969).

2. See in particular J. E. Inikori, "Measuring the Atlantic Slave Trade," *Journal of African History* 17, no. 2 (1976): 595–627.

3. The figures are no longer based on the number of slaves that arrived at their port of destination, but on the number carried by the various transporters (British, French, Spanish, Portuguese, Danish) from Africa. This method of computation has been made possible by new archives at our disposal. In the eighteenth century, 6.1 million slaves were transported, with the British carrying 41 percent, the Portuguese 29 percent, the French 19 percent, the Germans 6 percent, and the Danish 1 percent. P. E. Lovejoy, "The Volume of the Atlantic Slave Trade: A Synthesis," *Journal of African History* 23, no. 4 (1982): 473–501.

4. See R. P. Dieudonné Rinchon, *La Traite de l'esclavage des Congolais par les Européens: Histoire de la déportation de 13,250,000 Noirs en Amérique* (Paris, 1929).

5. The American cotton industry, also founded on slave labor, developed in the nineteenth century, that is, after the prohibition of the slave trade (1807–1815). To an increasing degree, the supply of slaves came from their reproduction in the Southern states rather than from Africa.

6. Cf. P. Manning, "The Enslavement of Africans: A Demographic Model," *Canadian Journal of African Studies* 15, no. 3 (1981): 499–526; P. Manning, *Slavery, Colonialism and Economic Growth in Dahomey, 1640–1960* (Cambridge, England, 1982).

7. According to J. D. Fage, "The Effect of the Export Slave Trade on African Populations," in R. P. Moss and R. J. A. Rathbone, eds., *The Population Factor in African Studies* (London, 1975), pp. 15–23; but a little less, according to Caldwell, "Major Questions."

8. Demographic estimate of P. K. Mitchell and P. Curtin discussed by J. D. Fage, "Slavery and the Slave Trade in the Context of West African History," *Journal of African History* 10, no. 3 (1969): 399–400. It is difficult to understand how this last writer, dealing with these same figures, can claim that the drain in population was about equal to its natural rate of growth, unless he is assuming that the rate of growth was exceedingly low or nonexistent (about 0.1 percent)—that is to say, itself adversely affected by the slave trade.

9. Cf. J. E. Inikori, Introduction to J. E. Inikori, ed., *Forced Migrations: The Impact of the Export Slave Trade on African Societies* (London, 1982), pp. 13–60. By 1500, the Saharan traders had already taken more than four million slaves.

10. L. M. Diop, "Le Sous-peuplement de l'Afrique Noire," *Bulletin de l'IFAN* 40B, no. 4 (1978; appeared in 1980): 718–862, and "Méthode et calculs approximatifs pour la constitution d'une courbe représentative de l'évolution de la population de l'Afrique noire," in *African Historical Demography*, vol. 2, pp. 139–52. Concerning the relative prosperity (and hence density of population) of the rural areas before the sixteenth century, cf. M. Tymowski, "Les Domaines des princes du Sonrhaï (Soudan occidental): Comparaison avec la grande propriété foncière en Europe au début de l'ère coloniale," *Annales ESC 25*, no. 6 (1970): 1637–58.

11. J. E. Inikori, "Underpopulation in Nineteenth-Century West Africa: The Role of the Export Slave Trade," in *African Historical Demography*, vol. 2, pp. 283–314. It is only fair to stress that Inikori does not base his assertion of a general demographic decline on the effects of the slave trade alone but on the combination of these with natural calamities.

12. Figures from R. Austen, "The Transaharan Slave Trade: A Tentative Census," in H. A. Gemery and S. J. Hogendorn, eds., *The Uncommon Market: Essays in the Economic History of the Atlantic Slave Trade* (New York, 1979), pp. 23–76.

13. J. Thornton, "The Demographic Effect of the Slave Trade on Western Africa, 1500–1850," in *African Historical Demography*, vol. 2, pp. 690–720.

14. Compare the figures with the general analysis of H. S. Klein, who has traced in their entirety the figures for the annual export of slaves from the ports of Luanda and Benguela in the eighteenth century ("The Portuguese Slave-Trade from Angola in the 18th Century," *Journal of Economic History* 32, no. 4 (1972): 894–918, republished in Inikori, ed., *Forced Migrations*, pp. 221–41). Cf. J. Thornton, "The Slave Trade in XVIIIth Century Angola: Effects on Demographic Structure," *Canadian Journal of African Studies* 14, no. 3 (1980): 417–27.

15. Jill Dias, "Famine and Disease in the History of Angola, c. 1830–1930," *Journal of African History* 21, no. 3 (1981): 349–78.

16. M. Mason, "Population Density and Slave-Raiding: The Case of the Middle Belt of Nigeria," *Journal of African History* 10, no. 4 (1969): 551–64.

17. P. Manning, "A Demographic Model of African Slavery," in *African Historical Demography*, vol. 2, pp. 371–84.

18. The earlier pottery culture (or Earthworks ware) is characterized by two levels of large earth constructions situated on hilltop sites (in contrast to the later tradition of the Ashanti, who regarded high areas as subject to evil influences). This belongs to the transition between the Later Neolithic Age and the Iron Age. The later culture (Atwea ware) is directly related to the present-day pottery of the people who speak Twi and also (especially since the end of the nineteenth century) to that of the neighboring Denkyira, Asini, and Ashanti: D. Kiyaga Mulindwa, "Social and Demographic Changes in the Birim Valley, Southern Ghana, c. 1450 to c. 1800," *Journal of African History* 23, no. 1 (1982): 63–82.

19. See J. D. Fage, *A History of Africa* (London, 1978), pp. 244–88. Gemery and Hogendorn's assessment of the enormous cost of the slave trade in West Africa in the nineteenth century (*Uncommon Market*, pp. 145–62) confirms this pessimistic analysis.

20. The slaves were emancipated in 1836 in the British possessions, in 1848 in the French colonies, in 1863 in the United States, and in 1888 in Brazil.

21. This estimate, arrived at by synthesizing various colonial surveys, should be treated with caution, but it nevertheless serves as an indicator: A. G. B. Fisher and H. J. Fisher, *Slavery and Muslim Society in Africa* (London, 1970), p. 13.

22. Cf. C. Meillassoux, "Le Commerce précolonial et le développement de l'esclavage à Gumbu du Sahel (Mali)," in Meillassoux, ed., *The Development of Indigenous Trade and Markets in West Africa* (Oxford, 1971), pp. 182–98.

23. E. A. Alpers, "Futa Benaader: Continuity and Change in the Traditional Cotton Textile Industry of Southern Somalia, c. 1840–1980," in Catherine Coquery-Vidrovitch, ed., *Entreprises et entrepreneurs en Afrique, XIXe et XXe siècles,* vol. 1 (Paris, 1983), pp. 77–98.

24. Cf., in this connection, among other sources, F. Cooper, "The Problem of Slavery in African Studies," *Journal of African History* 2, no. 1 (1979): 103–25; S. Miers and I. Kopytoff, *Slavery in Africa: Historical and Anthropological Perspectives* (Madison, 1977), discussed by M. Klein and P. Lovejoy in "Slavery in West Africa," in Gemery and Hogendorn, eds., *Uncommon Market,* pp. 181–207; and C. Meillassoux, ed., *L'Esclavage en Afrique précoloniale* (Paris, 1975).

25. C. Coquery-Vidrovitch and P. Lovejoy, *Workers of Precolonial Long-Distance Trade* (Beverly Hills, 1985).

26. Cf. G. Mcsheffrey, "Slavery, Indentured Servitude, Legitimate Trade and the Impact of Abolition in the Gold Coast, 1874–1901: A Reappraisal," *Journal of African History* 24, no. 3 (1983): 349–68; and D. Bouche, *Les "Villages de liberté" en Afrique Noire française (1887–1910)* (The Hague, 1968).

27. For more information on this multifaceted issue see, e.g., C. Coquery-Vidrovitch, "La Mise en dépendance de l'Afrique noire, 1800–1960," *Cahiers d'Etudes Africaines,* nos. 61–62 (1976): 7–58; and C. Coquery-Vidrovitch, Introduction to *Entreprises et Entrepreneurs,* vol. 1.

Chapter 3

1. Helge Kjekshus, "The Population Trends of East African History: A Critical Review," in *African Historical Demography,* vol. 1, pp. 352–64, and especially Helge Kjekshus, *Ecology Control and Economic Development in East Africa: The Case of Tanganyika, 1850–1950* (London, 1977). Cf. R. Van Zwanenberg and Anne King, *An Economic History of Kenya and Uganda, 1800–1970* (London, 1975).

2. Cf. R. W. Beachey, "Some Observations on the Volume of the Slave Trade in Eastern Africa in the 19th Century," in *African Historical Demography,* vol. 1, pp. 365–72.

3. C. Thibon, "Démographie historique," in J. P. Chrétien, ed., *Histoire rurale de l'Afrique des Grands Lacs* (Paris, 1983), p. 255.

4. R. W. Beachey, "Observations." Cf. Edward Alpers, "The Impact of the Slave Trade on East Central Africa in the XIXth Century," in Inikori, ed., *Forced Migrations,* pp. 242–73.

5. Abdul Sheriff, *Slaves, Spices, and Ivory in Zanzibar: Integration of an East African Commercial Empire into the World Economy, 1770–1783.* Athens, 1987.

6. G. W. Hartwig, "Demographic Considerations in East Africa during the 19th

Century," *International Journal of African Historical Studies* 12, no. 4 (1979): 653–72.

7. Ibid.

8. Cf. J. Christie, *Cholera Epidemics in East Africa* (London, 1876).

9. R. F. Burton, *Zanzibar, City, Island and Coast,* 2 vols. (New York, 1967; orig. pub. 1872), vol. 2, p. 345.

10. R. Pankhurst, "The History and Traditional Treatment of Smallpox in Ethiopia," *Medical History* 9 (1965): 344–45.

11. See J. Ford, *The Role of Trypanosomiasis in African Ecology* (Oxford, 1971).

12. L. White, "A Chronological Symptomology of Venereal Diseases in Panwani, Nairobi, 1914–1950," in *African Historical Demography,* vol. 1, pp. 429–36.

13. Jill R. Dias, "Famine and Disease in the History of Angola, c. 1830–1930," *Journal of African History* 21, no. 3 (1981): 349–78.

14. Cf. R. Pélissier, *La Colonie du Minotaure (1845–1961),* vol. 1 (Orgeval, France, 1976 [published by the author]), pp. 678–716.

15. C. Coquery-Vidrovitch, "Population et démographie en A.E.F. dans le premier tiers du XXᵉ siècle," in *African Historical Demography,* vol. 1, pp. 331–51. For a more general picture, see Catherine Coquery-Vidrovitch, *Le Congo [A.E.F.] au temps des grandes compagnies concessionnaires, 1898–1930* (The Hague, 1972).

16. Anne Retel-Laurentin, *Un Pays à la dérive: Une Société en régression démographique—les Nzakara de l'Est Centrafricain* (Paris, 1979).

17. G. Sautter, *De l'Atlantique au fleuve Congo: Une Géographie du sous-peuplement* (Paris, 1966), p. 624. Cf. Martin, Leboeuf, and Rambaud, *Rapport de la mission d'études de la maladie du sommeil au Congo français, 1906–1908* (Paris, 1909).

18. Moyen-Congo, *Rapport annuel* for 1911 and 1913, in Coquery-Vidrovitch, "Population et démographie," p. 335.

19. Huot, Marzin, Ricau, Grosfillez, David, "L'Epidémie d'influenza de 1918–1919 dans les colonies françaises (suite). 2. Groupe de l'A.E.F.," *Annales de Médecine et de Pharmacie Coloniales* 19 (1921): 443–78.

20. Sautter, *De l'Atlantique,* p. 968.

21. The recent research of Steven Feierman, kindly described by the author, deals with this subject.

22. The annual rate of increase was 1.5 percent in 1926–1958 and 3 percent in the decade 1948–1958. Cf. D. Domergue, "La Côte d'Ivoire: Essai de démographie historique, 1905–1945," in *African Historical Demography,* vol. 1, pp. 295–330.

23. The case of Senegal, for which there are abundant and longterm sources, owing to an exceptionally early colonization (the French were established in Saint-Louis from the middle of the seventeenth century), deserves to be studied in depth. More will be known with the completion of the thesis of Elikia M'Bokolo on epidemics, famines and ecology in French West Africa. Cf. J. C. Miller, "The Significance of Drought, Disease and Famine in the Agriculturally Marginal Zones of West-Central Africa," *Journal of African History* 23 (1982): 17–61.

24. K. D. Patterson, *Health in Colonial Ghana: Disease, Medicine and Economic Change, 1900–1955* (Waltham, Mass., 1981).

25. R. Headrick, "French Health Service and African Health in French Equa-

torial Africa," 1977 (mimeo.); and D. Domergue, "Les 20 Premières Années de l'action sanitaire en Côte d'Ivoire," *Revue Française d'Histoire d'Outre-Mer* 65, no. 238 (1978): 40–63.

26. United Nations, *Demographic Yearbooks*. The estimates vary in the various editions (1954, 1964, 1974). I have used conservative figures.

27. K. D. Patterson, "The Democratic Impact of the 1918–1919 Influenza Pandemic in Sub-Saharan Africa: A Preliminary Assessment," in *African Historical Demography*, vol. 2, pp. 401–32.

28. Cf. L. J. Bruce-Chwatt and J. de Zulueta, *The Rise and Fall of Malaria in Europe* (Oxford, 1980). Until recently, the literature on malaria in Africa has been scanty: R. M. Prothero, "Population Movements and Problems of Malaria Eradication in Africa," *Bulletin of the World Health Organization* 24 (1961): 399–403; S. Feierman, "Struggles for Control: The Social Roots of Health and Healing in Modern Africa," *African Studies Review* 28, no. 2–3 (1985): 73–148; P. Curtin, "Medical Knowledge and Urban Planning in Tropical Africa," *American Historical Review* 90, no. 3 (1985): 594–613; and John W. Call, "Anglo-Indian Medical Theory and the Origins of Segregation in West Africa," *American Historical Review* 91, no. 2 (1986): 307–35 (based chiefly on a study of Europeans' fear of malaria). See also W. Cohen, "Malaria and French Imperialism," *Journal of African History* 24, no. 1 (1983): 23–36; and Dennis G. Carlson, *African Fever: A Study of British Science, Technology, and Politics in West Africa, 1787–1864* (Canton, Mass., 1984).

29. Idrissa Kimba, "Histoire de la colonisation au Niger, 1898–1920," Thèse d'état, Université Paris VII, 1988; Gado Boureima, "Crises alimentaires et stratégies de subsistance en Afrique sahélienne (Burkina-Faso, Mali, Niger)," Thèse, Université Paris VII, 1988.

30. A. Sarraut, *La Mise en valeur des colonies françaises* (Paris, 1923).

31. M. Sellier, "Notes sur le peuplement et l'histoire du cercle de Niamey," ms., 1951, p. 84, quoted in F. Fuglestad, "La Grande Famine de 1931," *Revue Française d'Histoire d'Outre-Mer* 61, no. 222 (1974): 25.

32. J. C. Caldwell, "The Sahelian Drought and Its Demographic Implications," American Council of Education, Overseas Liaison Committee Paper no. 8 (Washington, D.C., 1975).

33. Quoted by Fernand Braudel, *L'Identité de la France: Les Hommes et les choses* (Paris, 1986), vol. 1, p. 153.

34. The Food and Agriculture Organization lists thirty-two countries: Angola, Benin, Botswana, Burkina-Faso (former Upper Volta), Burundi, the Central African Republic, Chad, the Comoro Islands, Ethiopia, Gambia, Ghana, Guinea, Guinea-Bissau, Kenya, Lesotho, Malawi, Mali, Mauritania, Mozambique, Niger, Nigeria, Rwanda, São-Tomé, Senegal, Sierra Leone, Somalia, Sudan, Swaziland, Tanzania, Togo, Uganda, and Zambia. To this list should certainly be added Djibouti and the Bantustans.

PART 2

Chapter 4

1. An approach to this question was attempted in the symposium Pouvoir et Etat en Afrique Noire: Catherine Coquery-Vidrovitch, "Les Structures du pouvoir et la

communauté rurale précoloniale," *Revue Française d'Histoire d'Outre-Mer* 68, nos. 250–53, (1981): 54–70. See also Eric R. Wolf, "Modes of Production," in his *Europe and the People without History* (Berkeley and Los Angeles, 1982), pp. 73–100.

2. Cf. J. Pouchepadass, "Le Village et l'État en Inde," in C. Coquery-Vidrovitch, ed., *Sociétés paysannes du Tiers-Monde* (Lille, 1981), pp. 91–110.

3. P.-P. Rey, "Bapuni et Bakugni: Articulation des modes de dépendance et des modes de reproduction dans deux sociétés lignagères," Colloque sur les Relations de Clientèle et de Dépendance Personnelle, Ecole Pratique des Hautes Etudes, 1968 (mimeo.).

4. The latest theory, however, (P. Garlake, *Life at Great Zimbabwe* [Harare, 1982]) sees these societies as much less centralized than was common some years ago.

5. E. Terray, *L'Organisation sociale des Dida de Côte-d'Ivoire* (Abidjan: Annales de l'Université d'Abidjan, series F, vol. 1, no. 2, 1969); cf. M. Augé, "Statut, pouvoir, et richesse . . . dans la société alladian," *Cahiers d'Etudes Africaines* 9, no. 35 (1969): 461–81.

6. J. F. Bayart, "Les Sociétés africaines face à l'Etat," *Pouvoirs* (special issue entitled *Les Pouvoirs Africains*), no. 25 (1983): 23.

7. C. Meillassoux, "Essai d'interprétation du phénomène économique dans les sociétés traditionnelles d'auto-subsistance," *Cahiers d'Etudes Africaines* 1, no. 4 (1960): 38–67; republished in his *Terrains et Théories* (Maspero, 1978), pp. 21–64.

8. J. Cabot, "Développement et espace vécu: Le Tchad," *Sociétés paysannes du Tiers-Monde,* pp. 381–88.

9. See the analysis in vol. 4 of the oral traditions or *Histoire des Rois* in F. Raison-Jourde, *Les Souverains de Madagascar* (Paris, 1983), Introduction.

10. M. Rosenberger, lecture in the seminar Connaissance du Tiers-Monde, Université Paris VII, 1979.

11. E. Mworoha, *Peuples et rois de l'Afrique des lacs* (Paris, 1977), pp. 132–41.

12. Dan Sperber, "Les Paysans Clients du Buganda," Colloque sur les Relations de Clientèle et de Dépendance Personnelles, Ecole Pratique des Hautes Etudes, 1968 (mimeo.); and M. Le Pape, "Le Buganda," *Cahiers d'Etudes Africaines* 9, no. 35 (1969): 356–63.

13. C. Oliver, "Le Kabaka Mutesa, dernier souverain absolu du Buganda," in C. A. Julien et al., *Les Africains,* 12 vols. (Paris, 1977–1978), vol. 1, pp. 261–92.

14. M. J. Herskovitz, *Dahomey, an Ancient West African Kingdom,* 2 vols. (New York, 1938); cf. K. Polanyi, *Dahomey and the Slave Trade: An Analysis of an Archaic Economy* (Seattle, 1966).

15. C.-H. Perrot, "Hommes libres et captifs dans le royaume Agni de l'Indénié," Colloque sur les Relations de Clientèle et de Dépendance Personnelle.

16. Mworaha, *Peuples et rois de l'Afrique des lacs,* pp. 183–210; J. P. Chrétien, "Echanges dans l'Est africain," *Annales ESC,* 29, no. 6 (1974): 1327–37.

17. Augé, "Statut, pouvoir, et richesse," and Meillassoux, "Essai d'interprétation."

18. Cf. Rey, "Bapuni et Bakungi."

19. A. Adler, "Essai sur la signification des relations de dépendance personnelle dans l'ancien système politique des Mundang du Tchad," *Cahiers d'Etudes Africaines* 35 (1969): 441–60; and his *La Mort est le masque du roi* (Paris, 1982).

20. H. d'Almeida-Topor, *Les Amazones: Une Armée de femmes dans l'Afrique précoloniale* (Paris, 1981).

21. F. Pouillon, "L'Ankole," Colloque sur les Relations de Clientèle et de Dépendance Personnelle.

22. Mworoha, *Peuples et rois,* pp. 141–42; and Adler, "Essai sur la signification."

23. Marc Abeles, "In Search of the Monarch—Introduction of the State among the Gamo of Ethiopia," in D. Crummey and C. C. Stewart, eds., *Modes of Production in Africa: The Precolonial Era* (Beverly Hills, 1981), pp. 35–68.

24. C. Vidal, "Le Rwanda des anthropologues ou le fétichisme de la vache," *Cahiers d'Etudes Africaines* 9, no. 35 (1969): 384–401.

25. Sperber, "Les Paysans Clients," and Le Pape, "Le Buganda."

26. C. Tardits, *Le Royaume Bamoum* (Paris, 1980).

Chapter 5

1. See the collection of biographies edited by C. A. Julien et al., *Les Africains,* 12 vols. (Paris, 1977–1978), and the series of mini-biographies edited by Ibrahima Baba Kaké, published in Paris in the early 1980s.

2. Cf. Yves Person, *Samori—une révolution Dyula* (Dakar, 1968).

3. T. O. Ranger, "Connections between 'Primary Resistance' Movements and Modern Mass Nationalism in East and Central Africa," *Journal of African History* 9, no. 3 (1968): 437–54. Cf. Chapter 9, below.

4. Cf. H. Moniot, "Rabih," *Les Africains,* vol. 4, pp. 285–309.

5. J. P. Chrétien, "Mirambo," *Les Africains,* vol. 6, pp. 129–57. Cf. A. D. Roberts, "The Sub-Imperialism of Buganda," *Journal of African History* 3, no. 3 (1962): 435–50.

6. See W. G. L. Randles, seminar, Université Paris VII, 1977. Cf. S. Marks, "Shaka Zulu," *Les Africains,* vol. 2, pp. 279–309.

7. Cf. I. Wilks, *Asante in the Nineteenth Century* (Cambridge, England, 1975).

8. J. K. Fynn, "Ghana-Ashanti," in M. Crowder, ed., *West African Resistance,* (London, 1971), pp. 19–52.

9. J. M'Leod, *A Voyage to Africa* (London, 1820), corroborated by R. F. Burton, *A Mission to Gelele, King of Dahome,* 2 vols. (London, 1864), and J. A. Sketchly, *Dahomey As It Is* (London, 1874).

10. A. R. Dunbar, "Kabareja aux prises avec Soudanais, Bugandais . . . et Britanniques," *Les Africains,* vol. 4, pp. 193–226.

11. R. Pélissier, "Mandume et la résistance Ovambo au colonialisme portugais," *Les Africains,* vol. 7, pp. 205–36. Cf. G. Clarence-Smith, *Slaves, Peasants and Capitalism in Southern Angola, 1840–1926* (Cambridge, England, 1979), pp. 80–81.

12. Neither medieval Mali nor, even less, medieval Ghana corresponded geographically to the present-day states of those names.

13. This section of the book owes a great deal to J. L. Triaud, "L'Islam en Afrique de l'Ouest," Colloque de l'Association pour l'Avancement des Etudes Islamiques, Paris, 27–28 March 1981. Cf. also C. Meillassoux, "Le Rôle de l'esclavage dans l'histoire de l'Afrique occidentale," *Anthropologie et Société* (Quebec) 2, no. 1 (1978): 117–48.

14. Meillassoux, "Le Rôle de l'esclavage."

15. C. Meillassoux, ed., *L'Esclavage en Afrique pré-coloniale* (Paris, 1975). Cf. Chapter 2.

16. A. G. Hopkins, "Economic Imperialism in West Africa: Lagos 1880–1892," *Economic History Review* 21, no. 3 (1972): 419–41.

17. M. A. Klein, "Social and Economic Factors in the Muslim Revolution in Senegambia," *Journal of African History* 12, no. 3 (1972): 419–41.

18. On El Hajj Umar, see S. M. Cissoko, "El Hadj Omar Tall et le mouvement du jihad dans le Soudan occidental," *Revue Sénégalaise d'Histoire* (Dakar) 1, no. 1 (1980): 39–69, and B. Barry, "Le Mouvement omarien et le renouveau de l'Islam militant," ibid., pp. 70–81.

19. M. J. Tubiana et al., *Abd-el-Karim, Propagateur de l'Islam et fondateur du royaume du Ouaddaï* (Paris, 1978).

20. J. L. Triaud, "Les Résistances contre l'Occident," Cahier Afrique Noire, no. 2, Laboratoire Connaissance du Tiers Monde, Université Paris VII, 1979, pp. 53–54 (mimeo.).

21. See his biography, "Mohamed Abdul Hassan," by N. Lecuyer-Samantar, in the series edited by Kaké (Paris, 1980). Cf. P. Decraene, "Afrique: Guerriers, rebelles et conquérants," *Le Monde Dimanche,* 1 February 1981.

Chapter 6

1. See Catherine Coquery-Vidrovitch and Alain Forest, eds., *Décolonisation et nouvelles dépendances: Modèles et contre-modèles idéologiques et culturels* (Lille, 1986), and in particular the contributions of M. Chemillier-Gendreau ("Le Modèle et la représentation de l'Etat," pp. 65–80) and E. Le Roy ("Le Modèle européen de l'Etat en Afrique francophone," pp. 81–110), on which the opinions expressed here are largely based.

2. This remarkably accurate and significant expression is taken from Le Roy, "Le Modèle," p. 96.

3. Chemillier-Gendreau, "Le Modèle," p. 70.

4. G. Clarence-Smith, *Slaves, Peasants and Capitalists in Southern Angola, 1840–1926* (Cambridge, England, 1979), pp. 76–82.

5. E. de Dampierre, *Un Royaume Bandia du Haut-Oubangui* (Paris, 1967).

6. J. Suret-Canale, "La Fin de la chefferie en Guinée," *Journal of African History* 7, no. 3 (1966): 459–94.

7. A. Duperray, *Les Gourounsi de Haute-Volta* (Stuttgart, 1984).

8. Memorandum concerning the occupation of the colony, Journal Officiel de l'AEF, August 1909.

9. J. Guyer, "The Food Economy and French Colonial Rule in Central Cameroun," *Journal of African History* 19, no. 4 (1978): 577–98.

10. Memorandum of 15 August 1917, *Bulletin du Comité de l'Afrique Française,* nos. 1–2 (December 1917): 20.

11. A. Summers and R. W. Johnson, "World War I Conscription and Social Change in Guinea," *Journal of African History* 19, no. 1 (1978): 25–38.

12. See the memorandum from the vice governor-general in connection with the political and administrative role of the native chiefs, in "État indépendant du Congo, gouvernement local," *Recueil Mensuel* (1904): 75–77; the memorandum, dated 18 August 1906, clarifying the administrative decree of 3 June: *Bulletin Officiel* (1906): 395–99; and, above all, the memorandum concerning the correct policy to

follow toward native chiefs and subchiefs, in *Recueil Mensuel* (1915): 95. See Abemba Bulaimu, "Le Mode de production lignager face à la traite arabe et à la colonisation: Le Cas des collectivités locales au Maniema," *Cahiers du CEDAF* (Brussels), nos. 6–7 (1979): 32–38.

13. F. Zuccarelli, "De la chefferie traditionnelle au canton: Evolution du canton colonial au Sénégal, 1855–1960," *Cahiers d'Etudes Africaines* 13, no. 50 (1973): 213–38.

14. R. Delavignette, *Les Vrais Chefs de l'Empire* (Paris, 1939), p. 35.

15. J. F. Bayart, *L'Etat au Cameroun* (Paris, 1979). On the history of Duala nationalism, see E. Ghomsi, "Résistance africaine à l'impérialisme européen: Le Cas des Douala du Cameroun," *Afrika Zamani*, no. 4 (1975): 156–202; and, on the ambiguity of the phenomenon, R. A. Austen, "The Metamorphoses of Middlemen: The Duala, Europeans, and the Cameroon Hinterland, ca. 1800–ca. 1960," *International Journal of African Historical Studies* 16, no. 1 (1983): 1–24. Cf. F. Quinn, "Charles Atangana of Yaoundé," *Journal of African History* 21, no. 4 (1980): 485–95.

16. Cf. F. Verdeaux, "L'Aïzi pluriel: Chronique d'une ethnie lagunaire de Côte d'Ivoire," Thèse de 3ᵉ cycle, ORSTOM-EHESS, 1981.

17. J. P. Dozon, "Les Leçons de l'histoire ou l'ethnologie dans tous ses états," ORSTOM-Abidjan, 1977 (mimeo.).

18. Verdeaux, "L'Aïzi pluriel," pp. 80–86.

19. Cf. E. Mbokolo, *Le Continent Convoîté* (Paris, 1980), p. 118.

20. P. Biarnes, *L'Afrique aux Africains* (Paris, 1980), p. 441; cf. R. Lemarchand, *Rwanda and Burundi* (New York, 1970).

21. R. Lemarchand, "Myth and Realities of the Zairian Crisis," paper submitted to Howard University, Washington, 1984. Cf. Fred Warren Riggs, *Administration in Developing Societies: The Theory of Prismatic Society* (Boston, 1964), and his *Prismatic Society Revisited* (New York, 1971). Note that C. Van Onselen, approaching the subject from a different angle, had already advanced the idea of an "urban faction": see his "The Political Economy of Tribal Animosity: A Case Study of the 1929 Bulawayo Location," *Journal of Southern African Studies* 6, no. 1 (1979): 1–43, on factional strife and urban conflicts in the ghettos of South Africa.

22. B. Verhaegen, "Impérialisme technologique et bourgeoisie nationale au Zaire," *Connaissance du Tiers-Monde* 10, no. 18 (1978): 347–80.

23. My knowledge of Islam owes much to J. L. Triaud. Cf. also J. Coulon, *Les Musulmans et le pouvoir en Afrique noire* (Paris, 1983).

24. See Barbara J. Callaway, *Muslim Hausa Women in Nigeria: Tradition and Change* (Syracuse, N.Y., 1987).

25. Cf. Roger Chemain and Arlette Chemain-Degrange, *Panorama critique de la littérature congolaise contemporaine* (Paris, 1979).

26. E.g., Sony Labou Tansi, *La Vie et demie* (Paris, 1979).

27. Henry Lopes, *Le Pleurer-rire* (Paris, 1982).

28. Ibrahima Ly, *Toiles d'araignées* (Paris, 1982).

29. In this connection, cf. P. Bruckner, *The Tears of the White Man: Compassion as Contempt* (New York, 1986).

30. Despite the proven effectiveness of elementary teaching in the mother tongue, with gradual acquisition of the official Western language as a foreign tongue, this practice is nonexistent elsewhere. Today Zaire is thinking of reintroducing the sys-

tem, using four selected languages (this experiment was considered several years ago but was halted owing to the intervention of then French president Giscard d'Estaing).

PART 3

Chapter 7

1. A complementary outline of the ideas expressed here can be found in C. Coquery-Vidrovitch, "Les Paysans africains: Permanences et mutations," in C. Coquery-Vidrovitch, ed., *Sociétés paysannes du Tiers-Monde* (Lille, 1981), pp. 25–40.

2. Cf. A. Emmanuel, *L'Echange inégal* (Paris, 1969); C. Meillassoux, "Modalités historiques de l'exploitation et de la surexploitation du travail," *Connaissance du Tiers Monde* (Paris, 1974), pp. 136–60; S. Amin, *L'Accumulation à l'échelle mondiale* (Paris, 1970); and B. Jewsiewicki, ed., "Mode of Production: The Challenge of Africa," *Canadian Journal of African Studies,* special issue, 19, no. 1 (1985).

3. G. Hyden, *Beyond Ujaama in Tanzania: An Uncaptured Peasantry* (Berkeley and Los Angeles, 1980).

4. See the excellent case studies in S. Amin et al., *L'Agriculture africaine et le capitalisme* (Paris, 1975), in particular the contributions of J. Weber ("La Région cacaoyère du Centre-Sud Cameroun"), J. Boesen ("Les Paysans et l'exportation du café," on Tanzania), M.-L. Mazoyer ("Développement de la production agricole marchande," on the Ivory Coast), M. Keita ("Interventions en milieu rural," on Niger), and P.-P. Rey ("Les Formes de la décomposition des sociétés précapitalistes du Nord Togo").

5. C. Raynaut, "Le Cas de la région de Maradi (Niger)," *Sécheresses et famines du sahel,* vol. 2 (Paris, 1975), p. 27.

6. D. J. Morgan, *The Origin of British Aid Policy* (London, 1980), vols. 4 and 5.

7. Cf. Chapter 8.

8. M. Tymowski, "Les domaines des princes de Sonrhaï (Soudan Occidental): Comparaison avec la grande propriété foncière en Europe au début de l'ère féodale," *Annales ESC 25,* no. 6 (1970): 1637–58. On slavery, cf. Chapter 2. Studies that have recently brought the subject back under consideration include Meillassoux, "Modalités historiques," and P. Lovejoy, *Transformations in Slavery: The History of Slavery in Africa* (Cambridge, England, 1983).

9. Cf. J. Vansina, "Towards a History of Lost Corners in the World," *Economic History Review 35,* no. 2 (1982): 165–78; Marcia Wright, "Technology, Marriage and Women's Work in the History of Maize-Growers in Mazabuka, Zambia: A Reconnaissance," *Journal of South African Studies 10,* no. 1 (1983): 55–69, and her "Bwanika: Consciousness and Protest among Slave Women in Central Africa, 1886–1911," in C. Robertson and M. Klein, eds., *Women and Slavery* (Madison, Wisc., 1983).

10. For details of pledge transactions and the changes brought about by British and French land legislation, cf. C. Coquery-Vidrovitch, "Le Régime foncier rural en Afrique noire," in E. Le Bris, F. Leindorfer, and E. Le Roy, eds., *Enjeux fonciers en Afrique noire* (Paris, 1983), pp. 65–84; and F. G. Snyder, "Land, Law and Economic Change in Rural Senegal: Diola Pledge Transactions and Disputes," in I. Hamnett, ed., *Social Anthropology and Law* (New York, 1977), pp. 114–57.

11. On the case of the Baule, see Mazoyer, "Développement," pp. 143–66.

12. A. Zajackowski, "La Famille, le lignage et la communauté villageoise chez les Ashanti de la période de transition," *Cahiers d'Etudes Africaines* 3, no. 12 (1973): 458–73.

13. Cf. S. Amin, *Le Développement du capitalisme en Côte d'Ivoire* (Paris, 1967), pp. 94–95.

14. M. MBodj, "Un Exemple d'économie coloniale: Le Sine Saloum (Sénégal) de 1887 à 1940. Cultures arachidières et mutations sociales," Thèse de 3ᵉ cycle, Université Paris VII, 1978.

15. J. I. Guyer, "The Food Economy and French Colonial Rule," *Journal of African History* 19, no. 4 (1978): 577–98.

16. A. Schwartz, "Grands Projets de développement et pratique foncière en Côte d'Ivoire: L'Exemple de l'opération San Pedro," in Le Bris et al., eds., *Enjeux fonciers en Afrique noire*, pp. 293–300.

17. E. Le Bris, "Surpression démographique et évolution foncière: Le Cas du sud-est du Togo," *African Perspectives* (Leiden) 1 (1979): 107–26.

18. H. Derrienic, *Famines et dominations en Afrique noire: Paysans-éleveurs du Sahel sous le joug* (Paris, 1977), p. 142, discussed by G. Belloncle, "Quel avenir pour le Sahel?" *Esprit* n.s. 2, no. 26 (1979): 51–57. Cf. Raynaut, "Le Cas de la région de Maradi," pp. 5–43.

19. J. Pouchepadass, "L'Economie paysanne et le marché dans l'Inde moderne," in Coquery-Vidrovitch, ed., *Sociétés paysannes du Tiers Monde*, pp. 91–100.

20. J. Cardoso, *Finances et crédit de la colonie de Mozambique* (Lourenço-Marques, 1931), p. 29.

21. R. First, *Black Gold: The Mozambican Miner, Proletarian and Peasant* (New York, 1983), pp. 28–34.

22. R. Pourtier, "Le Gabon: Développement et organisation de l'espace," in the Symposium on Equatorial Africa, S.O.A.S., University of London, May 1979. See also his thesis on Gabon, University of Paris I, 1986. More or less comparable examples of the decay of the rural areas are given in R. Palmer and N. Parsons, ed., *The Roots of Rural Poverty in Central and Southern Africa* (London, 1977).

23. H. Deriennic, *Famines et dominations*.

24. See G. Kitching's fascinating study, *Class and Economic Change in Kenya: The Making of an African Petite Bourgeoisie, 1905–1970* (New Haven, 1980).

25. Boesen, "Les Paysans," pp. 138–39.

Chapter 8

1. See P. Hill, *Studies in Rural Capitalism in West Africa* (Cambridge, England, 1970).

2. Cf. C. Coquery-Vidrovitch, "De la traite des esclaves à l'exportation de l'huile de palme au Dahomey," in C. Meillassoux, ed., *L'Evolution du commerce en Afrique de l'Ouest* (Oxford, 1971), pp. 107–23.

3. S. Amin, *Le Développement du capitalisme en Côte d'Ivoire* (Paris, 1967), pp. 73–111. Although these figures are debatable and at best only approximate, considering the unreliable nature of statistics on Africa, they do give a sense of relative scale.

4. Schwartz, "Grands Projets de développement en Côte d'Ivoire."

5. Quoted by P. Biarnes in *L'Afrique aux Africains* (Paris, 1983), pp. 190–91.

6. See ibid., pp. 183–205.

7. R. Dumont and M. F. Mottin, *Stranglehold on Africa* (London, 1983), pp. 205–8.

8. See J. Copans, *Qui se nourrit de la famine en Afrique? Le Dossier politique de la faim au Sahel* (Paris, 1974); J. Copans, ed., *Sécheresses et famines au Sahel*, 2 vols. (Paris, 1975); Guy Maton, "La Politique des grands barrages hydro-agricoles," *Actuel-Développement,* no. 3 (1974): 32–37; and D. Daley and R. J. Harrison Church, eds., *Drought in Africa* (London, 1974).

9. R. Francke and B. Chasin, *Seeds of Famine: Ecological Destruction and the Development Dilemma in the West African Sahel* (Montclair, N.J., 1980).

10. Véronique Lassailly, *Espace utile et transfert de population en amont du barrage de Kossou (Côte d'Ivoire)* (Paris, 1980). Cf. S. Soulama, "Socio-économie d'une expérience de développement rural en Haute-Volta: Aménagements et mise en valeur des Vallées des Volta (A.V.V.)," Thèse de 3ᵉ cycle, Université de Lille, 1982.

11. In fact, the financial backers, before releasing the funds, waited until the cost of all the operations needed to operate the dams had been calculated. Cf. a recent account in Guy Belloncle, *Participation paysanne et aménagements hydro-agricoles* (Paris, 1985), pp. 57–105.

12. P. Gourou, "Une Expérience d'agriculture mécanisée en Afrique orientale: Le Plan des arachides," *Cahiers d'Outre-Mer* (1955): 105–18; J. S. Hogendorn and K. M. Scott, "The East African Groundnut Scheme: Lessons of a Large-Scale Agricultural Failure," *African Economic History,* no. 10 (1981): 81–115.

13. C. Aubertin, "Note on the Sugar-Producing Areas in the North of the Ivory Coast," ORSTOM interdisciplinary seminar, Paris, December 1980.

14. Dumont and Mottin, *Stranglehold on Africa,* p. 224.

15. FAO conference in Harare, July 1984.

16. C. Meillassoux, "700,000 Paysans de la Vallée du Sénégal," *Le Monde Diplomatique,* no. 314 (May 1980): J. L. Boutillier, "L'Aménagement du fleuve Sénégal et ses implications foncières," in Le Bris et al., eds., *Enjeux fonciers en Afrique noire,* pp. 301–7.

17. F. Kiamenga, "Etude des transformations agricoles récentes d'un village Zaïrois," Thèse du 3ᵉ cycle, Université Paris VII, 1978.

18. Report of Edmond Giscard d'Estaing on his mission in West Africa, 1931–1932, Archives Nationales, Section Outre-Mer, Affaires Politiques, 539.

19. Memorandum by Marius Moutet, August 1936, and Rapport sur le fonds d'équipement colonial de la Conférence des Gouverneurs Généraux, Archives Nationales, Section Outre-Mer, Affaires Politiques, 2529.

20. Works of the Subcommission on Production of the Economic Organization Commission, Brazzaville Conference, Archives Nationales, Section Outre-Mer, Affaires Economiques, 101.

21. P. Biarnes, in *Le Monde,* 16 April 1980.

22. Announcement of the Federal High Commissioner of Nigeria, *Le Monde,* 6–7–8 December 1975.

23. Cf. *Daily Times* (Nigeria), 3 March 1980.

24. Cf. P. Biarnes, in *Le Monde,* 16 April 1980.

25. E. Sauvignon, "Le FIDA," *Annuaire français de Droit International* (Paris, 1978), and "Aider les pays les plus pauvres," *Le Monde Diplomatique* (May 1980).

26. H. Raulin and E. Raynaud, *L'Aide au sous-développement* (Paris, 1980), pp. 232–40.

27. Diouldé Laya, "Impact de la tradition sur le développement de l'Afrique," Centre d'Etudes Linguistique et Historique par Tradition Orale, Niamey, undated note. See also G. Frélastre, "Une Etape importante dans le développement rural africain: Le Séminaire de Zinder (nov. 1982), et nouvelle stratégie de la République du Niger," *Le Mois en Afrique* 18, no. 211–12 (1983): 69–106.

28. See A. Mondjannagni, *Campagnes et villes au sud de la République Populaire de Bénin* (Paris, 1977).

29. IDEP seminar, Cotonou, October 1975, on the problems of socialist planning, held at the request of the government of Benin.

30. J. K. Nyerere, *Freedom and Socialism* (Oxford, 1973).

31. C. K. Meek, *Land Law and Custom in the Colonies* (Oxford, 1949; republished London, 1968).

32. Text in J. K. Nyerere, *Ujamaa* (Oxford, 1968), pp. 13–37.

33. J. K. Nyerere, *Ujamaa Vijinini* (Socialism in the Villages) (Dar es Salaam, 1967).

34. See Dumont and Mottin, *Stranglehold on Africa,* pp. 101–41; C. Allen, "Tanzanie, les illusions du socialisme," *Esprit* n.s. 2, no. 26 (1979): 37–50.

35. "Living in villages is now an order. . . . It is a decision of TANU": *Daily News,* 7 November 1973.

36. G. Hyden, *Beyond Ujamaa in Tanzania: Underdevelopment and an Uncaptured Peasantry* (Berkeley and Los Angeles, 1982).

37. Dumont and Mottin, *Stranglehold on Africa,* p. 132 n. 37.

38. Allen F. Isaacman, *The Tradition of Resistance in Mozambique: Anti-Colonial Activity in the Zambezi Valley, 1850–1921* (Berkeley and Los Angeles, 1976).

39. See M. Samuel, "Les Villages communautaires au Mozambique," seminar at the Research Center Connaissance du Tiers-Monde, Université Paris VII.

40. Conference held on the occasion of the inauguration of the School of the Party, Maputo, September 1975.

41. See the census of communal villages published on 4 March 1978, quoted in *Mozambique Information,* no. 11 (1979), and no. 17 (1980).

42. J. Bureau, "Réforme agraire en Ethiopie," *Esprit* n.s. 2, no. 26 (February 1979): 25–36, and Madame Tadesse Zenebeworke (pers. comm.). See also René Lefort, *Ethiopia: An Heretical Revolution* (London, 1983).

43. Klaus Ernst, "La Communauté traditionnelle et le progrès social en Afrique subsaharienne," in Abdel Malek, ed., *Sociologie de l'impérialisme* (Paris, 1971), pp. 339–64.

44. Amadou Seydou, director of the Department of Culture at UNESCO, quoted in *L'Essor,* 30 January 1970.

45. Astrid Nypau, "Diffusion of Innovation and Community Leadership in East Africa," paper presented at the Seventh International Congress of Sociology, Varna, 1970.

46. G. Gosselin, *L'Afrique désenchantée: Sociétés et stratégies de transition en Afrique tropicale* (Paris, 1978). Cf. the illustration of this idea in the case studies of

J. P. Chauveau, J. P. Dozon, and J. Richard, "Histoires de riz, histoires d'ignames: Le Cas de la moyenne Côte d'Ivoire," *Africa* 51, no. 2 (1981): 621–58.

47. Jamal Amin at the ACP–EEC Conference, Arusha, March 1980. Quoted by Dumont and Mottin, *Stranglehold on Africa,* chap. 7.

48. This criticism can be applied to the last chapter of Dumont and Mottin's *Stranglehold on Africa.* Agronomical recipes, however sensible they may seem, are less than fully satisfactory.

49. Food and Agriculture Organization, Harare Conference, Harare, July 1984.

Chapter 9

1. According to E. Wolf, *peasants* can be defined as rural holders of land who produce both for their own subsistence and for sale. They are therefore subject to exactions on productivity in the specific form of a rent on land. E. Wolf, *Peasant Wars in the Twentieth Century* (New York, 1969). With regard to sub-Saharan Africa, see M. A. Klein, *Peasants in Africa: Historical and Contemporary Perspectives* (Montreal, 1980).

2. T. O. Ranger, "Connections between Primary Resistance Movements and Modern Mass Nationalism," *Journal of African History* 9, no. 3 (1968): 437–54, and no. 4 (1968): 631–52. See his comment on a first draft of this chapter: Ranger, "Resistance in Africa," in Gary O. Okihiro, ed., *In Resistance* (Amherst, 1986), pp. 37–38, 47–49.

3. G. Clarence-Smith, *Slaves, Peasants and Capitalists in Southern Angola,* p. 79.

4. Union Congolaise Française to the minister of colonies, 28 March 1905, Archives Nationales, Section Outre-Mer, Conc. 25D (1); H. Ziegle, *Afrique Equatoriale Française* (Paris, 1952), p. 100.

5. Account by L. Taverne, Sarlat, 22 February 1905, Archives Nationales, Section Outre-Mer, Paris, Fonds Brazza. 1905–II. Cf. C. Coquery-Vidrovitch, *Le Congo au temps des grandes compagnies concessionaires* (Paris, 1972), p. 199.

6. C. Coquery-Vidrovitch, "Wongo," *Les Africains,* vol. 11, pp. 263–87.

7. See H. D'Almeida-Topor, "La Révolte des Holli," in *Les Résistances contre l'Occident* (Lille, 1981), pp. 81–89. Cf. L. Garcia, "Les Mouvements de résistance au Dahomey," *Cahiers d'Etudes Africaines* 10, no. 37 (1970): 144–78.

8. S. Marks, *Reluctant Rebellion: The 1906–1908 Disturbance in Natal* (Oxford, 1970).

9. R. Pélissier, *Les Guerres Grises: Résistances et révoltes en Angola, 1845–1961,* 2 vols. (Orgeval, 1977, 1978), and *Naissance du Mozambique, 1856–1918: Résistance et révolte anti-coloniale,* 2 vols. (Orgeval, 1983).

10. C. Roche, *Conquête et résistance des peuples de Casamance* (Dakar, 1979).

11. B. Jewsiewicki, "La Contestation sociale et la naissance du prolétariat au Bas-Zaïre," *Canadian Journal of African Studies,* 10, no. 1 (1976): 47–70.

12. M. Michel, *L'Appel à l'Afrique* (Paris, 1982), pp. 100–120.

13. See R. G. Thomas, "The 1916 Bongo Riots and Their Background," *Journal of African History* 24, no. 1 (1983): 57–75. Cf. similar rebellions in Nigeria: J. L. Ausman, "The Disturbances in Abeokuta in 1918," *Canadian Journal of African Studies* 5, no. 1 (1971): 45–60; O. Akinjide, "Disaffection and Revolts in Nigeria

during the First World War, 1914–1918," *Canadian Journal of African Studies* 5, no. 2 (1971): 171–92.

14. See F. Mukamba-Mwiluya, "Contribution à l'étude de la révolte des Bapende (mai-sept. 1931)," *Cahiers du CEDAF* (Brussels), no. 1 (1971), and J.-P. Chrétien, "Une Révolte au Burundi en 1934," *Annales ESC* 25, no. 6 (1970): 1678–1717.

15. Note from Commandant Angoulvant to the supreme commander of the troops of French West Africa, National Archives of Abidjan, X–34–17.

16. Commandant Harmand, "Quelques Réflexions sur la guerre et la conquête coloniale," *Revue Bleue,* 16 and 23 September 1910.

17. Idrissa Kimba, *Guerres et sociétés: Niger occidental, 1896–1900* (Niamey, 1979).

18. Ranger, "Connections between Primary Resistance."

19. R. Nzabakomada, *La Révolte Kongo-Warra* (Paris, 1985); Thierno Ba, "Karnou et l'insurrection des Gbaya," *Afrika Zamani,* no. 3 (1974): 105–63; P. Burnham and T. Christensen, "Karnu's Message and the War of the Hoe Handle," *Africa* 53, no. 4 (1983): 5–22.

20. R. Buijtenhuis, *Le Mouvement Mau-Mau: Une Révolte paysanne et anti-coloniale en Afrique noire* (Paris, 1971). Cf. Frank Furedi, "The African Crowd in Nairobi: Popular Movements and Elite Politics," *Journal of African History* 14, no. 2 (1973): 275–90.

21. J. Lonsdale, "A State of Agrarian Unrest: Colonial Kenya," in T. Aston, ed., *Agrarian Unrest in British and French Africa, British India and French Indochina* (Oxford, 1982); S. Stichter, *Migrant Labour in Kenya: Capitalism and African Response, 1895–1975* (London, 1982).

22. M. Lovens, "La Révolte de Masisi-Lubutu (Congo belge, janvier-mai 1944)," *Cahiers du CEDAF,* nos. 3–4 (1974). For an account of the succession of revolts in the Belgian Congo since the beginning of the twentieth century, see Jean-Luc Vellut, "L'Histoire des résistances au Congo Belge, ca. 1876–1965," in C. Coquery-Vidrovitch, A. Forest, and H. Weiss, eds., *Rébellion/Révolution au Zaïre (1960–1965)* (Paris, 1987), pp. 24–73.

23. Cf. B. Verhaegen, *Rébellions au Congo,* 2 vols. (Brussels, 1966, 1969); C. Young, *Politics in the Congo: Decolonization and Independence* (Princeton, 1965); and see Coquery-Vidrovitch et al., *Rébellion/Révolution.*

24. M. Michel, *L'Appel à l'Afrique.* Cf. F. Quinn, "An African Reaction to World War I," *Cahiers d'Etudes Africaines* 13, no. 52 (1973): 775–78; and A. Summers and R. W. Johnson, "World War I and Social Change in Guinea," *Journal of African History* 19, no. 1 (1978). For a more general study, see A. I. Asiwaji, "Migrations as Revolt," *Journal of African History* 17, no. 4 (1976): 577–96.

25. For discussions of social banditry in Africa, see A. Isaacmann, "Social Banditry in Zimbabwe (Rhodesia) and Mozambique, 1894–1907," *Journal of Southern African Studies* 55, no. 1 (1977): 1–30; Clarence-Smith, *Slaves, Peasants and Capitalists in Southern Angola,* 82–89; E. Kaller, "A Twentieth-Century Model: The Mau-Mau Transformation from Social Banditry to Social Rebellion," *Kenya Historical Studies* 2 (1973): 189–206; and D. Crummey, ed., *Banditry, Rebellion, and Social Protest in Africa* (London, 1986). More general studies include E. J. Hobsbawm, *Social Bandits* (London, 1969); B. Vincent, ed., *Les Marginaux dans l'histoire* (Paris, 1979); G. Rudé, *Ideology and Popular Protest* (New York, 1980).

26. R. A. Kea, *Settlements, Trade and Politics in the 17th Century Gold Coast* (Baltimore, 1982), pp. 179–82.

27. Ralph A. Austen, "Social Bandits and Other Heroic Criminals: Western Models of Resistance and Their Relevance for Africa," in D. Crummey, ed., *Banditry, Rebellion, and Social Protest in Africa,* pp. 89–108.

28. M. Wilson, "Mhlakaza," *Les Africains,* vol. 5, pp. 203–30.

29. R. I. Rotberg, *The Rise of Nationalism in Central Africa* (Cambridge, Mass., 1965).

30. A. M. Vergiat, *Les Rites secrets des primitifs de l'Oubangui* (Paris, 1951; first ed. 1921), pp. 149–50.

31. B. Jewsiewicki, "La Contestation sociale."

32. F. Fanon, *The Wretched of the Earth* (New York, 1965).

33. G. Balandier, "Les Mythes politiques de la colonisation et de la décolonisation en Afrique," *Cahiers Internationaux de Sociologie* 33 (1962): 85–96; Jean Merlo, "Sources populaires de l'idéologie de l'indépendance en Afrique noire: Mythes africains de la colonisation," Thèse de 3ᵉ cycle, Ecole Pratique des Hautes Etudes, 1967.

34. G. Haliburton, *The Prophet Harris* (London, 1971).

35. Cf. M. Sinda, *Le Messianisme congolais* (Paris, 1972); G. Balandier, *Sociologie actuelle de l'Afrique noire* (Paris, 1963), pp. 417–520.

36. Cf. Rotberg, *Rise of Nationalism,* pp. 136–42; T. Ranger, ed. *The Historical Study of African Religion* (Berkeley and Los Angeles, 1972).

37. J. P. Langellier, "Malawi: Les Héritiers noirs de Victoria," *Le Monde,* 21 and 22 August 1983.

38. Sinda, *Messianisme congolais.*

39. J. L. Triaud, *Les Résistances contre l'Occident* (Paris, 1979), pp. 45–52.

40. As was often the case in Africa, the colonists imposed the name Mauritania. The Muslim literate classes generally used the term Shingit, from the name of local ancient cities, to describe the region.

41. Colonial dispatch, 20 June 1910. Cf. A. I. Ba, "Les Mauritaniens face à la pénétration française," M.A. thesis, Université Paris VII, 1975.

42. A. Le Grip, "Le Mahdisme en Afrique noire," *L'Afrique et l'Asie,* no. 18 (1952): 3–16; T. Hodkin, "Mahdism, messianisme et marxisme dans le contexte africain," *Présence Africaine,* no. 74 (1970): 128–53; and *L'Encyclopédie de l'Islam,* s.v. "Mahdi."

43. A. Duperray, *Les Gourounsi de Haute-Volta, 1896–1933* (Stuttgart, 1984).

44. F. Fuglestad, "Les Révoltes des Touaregs du Niger," *Cahiers d'Etudes Africaines* 13, no. 49 (1973): 82–120; J. L. Dufour, "Le Révolte touarègue," *Relations Internationales* 1, no. 3 (1975): 55–77; A. Salifou, *Kouassan ou la révolte Senoussiste* (Niamey, 1973).

45. The phrase is taken from a memorandum by Governor-General William Ponty, Journal Officiel de l'A.O.F., 22 September 1909.

46. Bachar Moukhtar-Bachar, "Le Ouaddaï de 1850 à 1920," M.A. thesis, Université Paris VII, 1978.

47. C. Roche, *Conquête et résistance,* vol. 2.

48. Cf. the transcripts by G. Vieillard in the *Bulletin du Comité d'Etudes Historiques et Scientifiques de l'AOF* (1937): 225–310.

49. D. Cruise O'Brien, *The Mourides of Senegal* (Oxford, 1971); J. Copans, *Les Marabouts de l'arachide* (Paris, 1980).

50. J. L. Triaud, "La Question musulmane en Côte d'Ivoire," *Revue Française d'Histoire d'Outre-Mer* 61, no. 225 (1974): 542–71.

51. Triaud, *Résistances contre l'Occident;* P. Alexandre, "Hamallism in French West Africa," in R. I. Rotberg and A. A. Mazrui, eds., *Protest and Power in Black Africa* (Oxford, 1970), pp. 497–512; Alioune Traoré, "Cheikh Hamaoullah," *Les Africains,* vol. 11, pp. 81–108, and his *Islam et Colonisation en Afrique: Cheikh Hamahoullah, Homme de foi et résistant* (Paris, 1983).

52. *Les Mouvements paysans dans le monde contemporain,* 3 vols. (Naples, 1976). See Y. Rinaudo's review in *Mouvement Social,* no. 113 (1980): 114–17.

53. Fanon, *Wretched of the Earth;* E. Wolf, *Peasant Wars in the Twentieth Century* (New York, 1969).

54. R. Cohen, P. Gutkind, and P. Brazier, eds., *Peasants and Proletarians: The Struggles of Third World Workers* (New York, 1979), Introduction; J. S. Migdal, *Peasants, Politics and Revolution* (Princeton, 1974).

55. Kusum Datta, "Roots of Popular Protest among the Ushi-Kabendo of Colonial Zambia (1947–1953)"; conference proceedings, *Les Réactions Africaines à la Colonisation en Afrique Centrale* (Ruhengeri, 1986), pp. 357–96.

56. Cohen et al., eds., *Peasants and Proletarians;* cf. S. P. Huntington, *Political Order in Changing Societies* (New Haven, 1968), pp. 274–75, 435.

57. G. Chaliand, *La Lutte armée en Afrique* (Paris, 1967).

58. J. K. Galbraith, *The Nature of Mass Poverty* (Cambridge, Mass., 1979).

PART 4

1. M. Coquery, *La Coopération face aux problèmes posés par l'urbanisation dans le Tiers-Monde,* report to the minister of cooperation, 1983, pp. 4–6; M. Coquery et al., *Le Monde actuel en question* (Paris, 1983), pp. 312–13.

Chapter 10

1. A. Frishmann, "The Population Growth of Kano, Nigeria," in *African Historical Demography,* vol. 1, pp. 212–50.

2. R. J. Gordon, *Mines, Masters and Migrants: Life in a Namibian Compound* (Johannesburg, 1977), p. 245.

3. Gordon, *Mines, Masters and Migrants,* pp. 244–47; Colin Murray, *Families Divided: The Impact of Migrant Labour in Lesotho* (Cambridge, England, 1981). Murray's is one of the very few works to treat the problem from a historical point of view, dealing with the family unit that has remained in the village as well as with the migrant worker at work.

4. C. Van Onselen, "Workers' Consciousness in Black Miners: Southern Rhodesia, 1900–1920," in Cohen et al., eds., *Peasants and Proletarians,* pp. 108–9.

5. C. Liauzu and R. Gallissot study this development in Tunisia and Morocco in "L'Afrique et la crise de 1930," *Revue Française d'Histoire d'Outre-Mer* 63, no. 232–233 (1976): 477–91, 607–21; cf. C. Coquery-Vidrovitch, ibid., 386–424.

6. S. Amin, *Modern Migrations in West Africa* (Oxford, 1974), pp. 65–174; J. L. Amselle, ed., *Les Migrations africaines* (Paris, 1976).

7. G. Arrighi, *The Political Economy of Rhodesia* (The Hague, 1967).

8. Cf. R. Sandbrook, *The Politics of Basic Needs: Urban Aspects of Assaulting Poverty in Africa* (London, 1982), pp. 47–49.

9. "L'Afrique court à la catastrophe," FAO, Harare Conference. This is particularly true in Rwanda, Burundi, eastern Uganda, the Sahel countries, Lesotho, the Ibo region (Nigeria), Bamileke (Cameroon), and parts of Sierra Leone, Ghana, Togo, Benin, Zambia, and Botswana.

10. R. Sabot, *Urban Migration in Tanzania.* Vol. 2: *National Urban Mobility* (Dar es Salaam, 1972).

11. James Waweru et al., "Low-Cost Housing and Squatter Upgrading Study," *Progress Report No. 5: Results of the Socio-Economic Survey,* Report to the Government of Kenya and World Bank, August 1976.

12. Gordon, *Mines, Masters and Migrants,* particularly pp. 5–6, 8–10, 218–19; G. Cronje and S. Cronje, *The Workers of Namibia* (London, 1979); F. Wilson, *Migrant Labour in South Africa* (Johannesburg, 1972).

13. Cf. M. Castells, "Immigrant Workers and Class Struggles in Advanced Capitalism: The Western European Experience," in Cohen et al., eds., *Peasants and Proletarians,* pp. 353–79. Cf. also M. Buroway, "The Functions and Reproduction of Migrant Labor: Comparative Material from Southern Africa and the United States," *American Journal of Sociology* 81, no. 5 (1974): 1050–87 (a comparison with the use of Mexican labor in the plantations of California).

14. Iba der Thiam, "L'Evolution politique et syndicale du Sénégal colonial de 1840 à 1936," state thesis, Université Paris I, 1983, vol. 2, pp. 779–80.

15. That of the corporation of the Kru canoe-paddlers in the Gold Coast, however, was far older; they had gone on strike in 1753: M. Priestley, "An Early Strike in Ghana," *Ghana Notes and Queries,* no. 7 (1965): 24.

16. A. G. Hopkins, "The Lagos Strike of 1897: An Exploration in Nigerian Labour History," *Past and Present,* no. 35 (1966). Republished in Cohen et al., eds., *Peasants and Proletarians,* pp. 87–106.

17. Audrey I. Richards, ed., *Economic Development and Tribal Change: A Study of Immigrant Labour in Buganda* (Cambridge, England, [ca. 1952]).

18. J. Lonsdale, "A State of Agrarian Unrest: Colonial Kenya," in T. Aston, ed., *Agrarian Unrest in British and French Africa, British India and French Indochina* (Oxford, 1982) (cf. Chapter 9 above); Kitching, *Class and Economic Change in Kenya.*

19. B. Lachartre, *Luttes ouvrières et libération en Afrique du Sud* (Paris, 1977).

20. Bruce Fetter, "L'U.M.H.K., 1920–1940," *Cahiers du CEDAF,* no. 6 (1973); P. de Dekker, "Economie et politique au Rwanda entre les deux guerres," M.A. thesis, Université Paris VII, 1974.

21. Cf. R. Cohen, "Resistance and Hidden Forms of Consciousness among African Workers," *Review of African Political Economy,* no. 19 (1980): 8–22.

22. Cf. N. Z. Davies's studies on the charivaris of groups of young people in France in the sixteenth century and particularly those of S. Alexander on the role of fairs in the formation of English working society in the nineteenth century: Davies, "The Reasons of Misrule: Youth Groups and Charivaris in 16th Century France," *Past and Present,* no. 50 (1971): 41–75; Alexander, *St. Giles' Fair, 1830–1914: Popular Culture and the Industrial Revolution in 19th Century Oxford* (Oxford, 1970). Cf. F. A. Isambert, *Le Sens du sacré: Fête et religion populaire* (Paris, 1982); and P. Burke, *Popular Culture in Early Modern Europe* (London, 1978).

23. Recommendation of the commission, incorporated into the Labor Code of the Portuguese Colonies of 14 October 1914.

24. Code du Travail of 1911, quoted in *Le Régime et l'organisation du travail des indigènes dans les colonies tropicales* (Brussels, 1929), pp. 224–315.

25. Avis du G. G. Antonetti, *Journal Officiel de l'AEF* 1, no. 6 (1926); ibid., 1, no. 12 (1927).

26. H. Léonard, *Le Contrat de travail au Congo belge* (Brussels, 1935).

27. On these phenomena, see Carlos Weiss, "A Labour Question em Nossa Terra," *Boletim da Sociedade de Geografia de Lisboa* 10 (1981): 241; I. Isaacmann and B. Isaacmann, "Resistance and Collaboration in Southern and Central Africa," *International Journal of African Historical Studies* 10 (1977): 51. Cf. Richard Price, *Maroon Societies* (New York, 1973), pp. 1–30; C. Van Onselen, "Workers' Consciousness in Black Miners: Southern Rhodesia, 1900–1920," *Journal of African History* 14, no. 2 (1973): 237–56.

28. Isaacman and Isaacman, "Resistance and Collaboration."

29. S. Stichter, "The Formation of a Working Class in Kenya," in R. Sandbrook and R. Cohen, eds., *The Development of an African Working Class* (London, 1975), pp. 21–48; M. Mason, "Forced Labour and the Railway: Northern Nigeria, 1907–1912," in R. Cohen, P. Gutkind, and J. Copans, *African Labor History* (London, 1978), pp. 56–79; G. Sautter, "Le Chemin de fer Congo-Océan, 1921–1934," *Cahiers d'Etudes Africaines* 7, no. 26 (1967): 219–99; C. Van Onselen, *Chibaro: African Mine Labour in Southern Rhodesia, 1900–1933* (London, 1976); M. Echenberg, "Paying the Blood Tax: Military Conscription in French West Africa, 1914–1929," *Canadian Journal of African Studies* 9, no. 9 (1975): 171–92.

30. Van Onselen, "Workers' Consciousness," p. 245.

31. Gordon, *Mines, Masters and Migrants,* p. 237.

32. Cf. Van Onselen, "Workers' Consciousness," p. 250; Isaacman, *Tradition of Resistance, Mozambique,* chap. 5; and Cronje, *Workers of Namibia,* p. 55.

33. Van Onselen, *Chibaro,* p. 241.

34. Gordon, *Mines, Masters and Migrants,* pp. 210–13.

35. Ibid., p. 127.

36. R. D. Grillo, *African Railwaymen: Solidarity and Opposition in an East African Labour Force* (Cambridge, England, 1973).

37. T. O. Ranger, *Dance and Society in Eastern Africa, 1890–1970: The Beni Ngoma* (Berkeley and Los Angeles, 1975), p. 118.

38. Van Onselen, *Chibaro,* pp. 199–200.

Chapter 11

1. P. L. Bonner, "The 1920 Black Mine Workers' Strike: A Preliminary Account," in B. Bozzoli, ed., *Labour, Townships and Protest* (Johannesburg, 1979), pp. 273–97.

2. K. Gottschalk and J. Swalberger, "The Earliest Known Strikes by Black Workers in South Africa," *South African Labour Bulletin,* 3, no. 7 (June–July 1977): 73–74; P. Warwick, "Black Industrial Protest on the Witwatersrand, 1901–1902," Centre for South African Studies, University of York, 1973 (mimeo.).

3. Cf. R. Palmer and N. Parsons, eds., *The Roots of Rural Poverty in Central and Southern Africa* (London, 1977).

4. F. A. Johnstone, "The IWA on the Rand: Socialist Organizing among Black Workers on the Rand, 1917–1918," in Bozzoli, ed., *Labour, Townships and Protest*, pp. 248–78.

5. Van Onselen, *Chibaro*, p. 99.

6. "South African Communist Party, 1921–1981," special issue of *African Communist*, no. 86 (third trimester 1981); R. Davies, "The 1922 Strike on the Rand: White Labor and the Political Economy of South Africa," in Cohen et al., eds., *African Labor History*, pp. 80–108.

7. Davies, "The 1922 Strike on the Rand."

8. Cf. R. Cohen, "Albert Nzula," in Bozzoli, ed., *Labour, Townships and Protest*, pp. 325–40.

9. D. O'Meara, "The 1946 African Mine Workers' Strike in the Political Economy of South Africa," in P. L. Bonner, ed., *Working Papers in Southern African Studies* (London, 1974), pp. 179–275.

10. D. Du Toit, *Capital and Labour in South Africa* (London, 1981), p. 116.

11. This optimistic view was advanced by liberal South African economist F. Wilson, in *Labour in the South African Gold Mines, 1911–1969* (Cambridge, England, 1966).

12. Cf. Du Toit, *Capital and Labour.* For a comprehensive account, see P. Bonner, *Strikes in South Africa* (Bloemfontein, 1980).

13. See the list of strikes in Du Toit, *Capital and Labour,* p. 243.

14. Ibid., p. 274.

15. B. Lachartre, *Luttes ouvrières et libération en Afrique du Sud* (Paris, 1977), pp. 188–90.

16. Cf. A. W. Stadler, "Birds in the Cornfields: Squatter Movements in Johannesburg, 1944–1947," in Bozzoli, ed., *Labour, Townships and Protest*, pp. 19–48. The movement then expressed the protest of the Blacks at the shortage of authorized housing. A period of intense urbanization had occurred when a serious crisis of subsistence, aggravated by rising food prices, made it necessary for the peasants of the Rand to look for jobs that paid wages, even though they could not earn enough to support a family and pay rent. Thus 60,000 to 90,000 squatters lived in 1947 in a city whose population had risen from 230,000 to 380,000 inhabitants in ten years. The movement was remarkable not only because of its scale, duration, and success, but because of its structure and organization, which revealed a spontaneous awareness of the contradictions of the South African political economy.

17. Steve Biko, "Black Consciousness and the Quest for True Humanity," *Reality* (March 1972).

18. Du Toit, *Capital and Labour,* pp. 172–80.

19. "Black Mine Workers' Strike," *Southern Africa* 15, no. 2 (September 1982).

20. Du Toit, *Capital and Labour,* pp. 197–98; *Financial Mail,* 19 September 1975 and 16 July 1976.

21. Michel Bole-Richard in *Le Monde,* 2 September 1987.

22. Cf. B. Fetter, "L'U.M.H.K., 1920–1940: La Naissance d'une sous-culture totalitaire," *Cahiers du CEDAF,* no. 6 (1973); and C. Perrings, *Black Miners in Central Africa* (London, 1979), a comparative study of the Zaire and Zambian Copperbelts.

23. Fetter, "L'U.M.H.K."

24. Ibid., p. 25.

25. The information on the Zambian mines is derived from C. Perrings, "Consciousness, Conflict and Proletarianization: An Assessment of the 1935 Mine Workers' Strike," *Journal of Southern African Studies* 4, no. 1 (1977): 31–51; and C. Perrings, *Black Miners in Central Africa*.

26. The information on Sierra Leone is derived from H. E. Conway, "Labour Protest Activity in Sierra Leone during the Early Part of the 20th Century," *Labour History*, no. 15 (November 1968): 49–63.

27. H. Brunschwig, *Noirs et Blancs dans l'Afrique noire française, 1970–1914* (Paris, 1983). This book examines the Ivory Coast from the point of view expressed in the text. For a more general history of land ownership under the colonial regime, see Coquery-Vidrovitch, *Enjeux fonciers en Afrique noire*, pp. 65–83.

28. Allen F. Isaacman, *The Tradition of Resistance in Mozambique, 1850–1921* (London, 1976).

29. See A. Hugues and R. Cohen, "An Emerging Nigerian Working Class: The Lagos Experience, 1897–1939," in Cohen et al., eds., *African Labor History*, pp. 31–55.

30. Iba der Thiam, "L'Evolution politique et syndicale du Sénégal de 1840 à 1936," Thèse d'Etat, Université Paris I, 1983.

31. H. E. Conway, "Labour Protest Activity," and J. G. Wyse, "The 1926 Railway Strike and Anglo-Krio Relations: An Interpretation," *International Journal of African Historical Studies* 14, no. 1 (1981): 93–123.

32. Cf. M. Michel, *L'Appel à l'Afrique* (Paris, 1983).

33. Cf. N. Bernard-Duquenet, *Le Sénégal et le Front Populaire* (Paris, 1986).

34. Iba der Thiam, "La Grève des cheminots au Sénégal de septembre 1938," M.A. thesis, Université de Dakar, 1972.

35. J. Suret-Canale, "The French West African Railway Workers' Strike, 1947–1948," in Gutkind et al., *African Labor History*, pp. 129–54.

36. One C.F.A. franc was equivalent to 1.70 French francs (.017 "new" francs) in 1946–1947 and 2 French francs (.02 "new" francs) the following year (from a French devaluation).

37. The strike was painted rather fancifully in Sembene Ousmane's otherwise admirable novel, *God's Bits of Wood,* which describes the difficulties of survival of the families of strikers. In this connection see Suret-Canale, "French West African Railway Workers' Strike."

Chapter 12

1. J. Ballard, "The Porto-Novo Incidents of 1923," *Odu*, no. 2 (1965): 52–75.

2. *La Voix du Dahomey,* nos. 70–71, November–December 1932.

3. Cf. C. B. Codo, "La Voix du Dahomey," Thèse de 3ᵉ cycle, Université Paris VII, 1978, and S. Anignikin, "Aux origines du nationalisme au Benin," thèse de 3ᵉ cycle, Université Paris VII, 1980.

4. Confidential memorandum, November 1933, Benin National Archives, quoted by Codo, "Voix du Dahomey," p. 233.

5. M. Merlier, *Le Congo de la colonisation belge à l'indépendance* (Paris, 1962), pp. 198–201; P. Lumumba, *Le Congo, terre d'avenir, est-il menacé?* (Brussels, 1961).

6. M.A. theses of O. Sagna and I. Sy (Paris VII) and N. Saw (Paris I), 1979 and 1981; and C. Liauzu, *Aux origines des tiers-mondismes, 1919–1939* (Paris, 1982); pp. 267–70.

7. A. Owona, "A l'aube du nationalisme Camerounais," *Revue Française d'Histoire d'Outre-Mer* 56, no. 204 (1969): 199–235.

8. Archives Nationales, Section Outre-Mer, Fonds Slotfom, III, 53.

9. J. Suret-Canale, lecture at the Institut d'Histoire du Temps Present (Groupe Décolonisation), CNRS, Paris, February 1983.

10. C. Coquery-Vidrovitch, "Vichy et l'industrialisation aux colonies," *Revue d'Histoire de la Seconde Guerre Mondiale* 29, no. 114 (1979): 69–94; C. Cotte, "La Politique économique coloniale de la France en Afrique noire 1936–1946," Thèse de 3ᵉ cycle, Université Paris VII, 1981.

11. Birgit Muller, "Réaction des femmes Igbo à l'emprise coloniale: Les Révoltes de 1925 et 1929," M.A. thesis, Université Paris VII, 1981; Nina M. Mba; *Nigerian Women Mobilized: 1900–1965* (Berkeley and Los Angeles, 1982).

12. M. Aduayom and G. Kponton, "La Place des revendeuses de tissus dans l'économie togolaise," *Entreprises et Entrepreneurs en Afrique*, (Paris, 1983), vol. 2, pp. 385–400.

13. Der Thiam, *L'Evolution politique*, vol. 8, pp. 3521–24. On South Africa, cf. Judith Wells, *African Women's Protest in South Africa* (New York, 1976); recently, "Black Women Battle Police near Cape Town," *Globe and Mail* (Toronto), 24 September 1983.

14. Der Thiam, *L'Evolution politique*, vol. 4, pp. 1653–56.

15. G. B. Kay, ed., *The Political Economy of Colonialism in Ghana* (Cambridge, England, 1972). In this connection cf. K. Arhin, P. Hesp, and L. van der Laan, eds., *Marketing Boards in Tropical Africa* (Boston, 1985). See also L. van der Laan, "Marketing West Africa's Export Crops: Modern Boards and Colonial Trading Companies," *Journal of Modern African Studies* 21, no. 1 (1987): 1–24.

16. Dharan P. Ghai, "The Bugandaian Trade Boycott: A Study in Tribal, Political and Economic Nationalism," in R. Rotberg and Ali Mazrui, eds., *Protest and Power in Black Africa* (Oxford, 1970), pp. 755–70.

17. Cf. J. Suret-Canale, *Afrique noire*. Vol. 3: *1945–1960* (Paris, 1972), pp. 14, 18, 27; M. Echenberg, "Tragedy at Thiaroye: The Senegalese Soldiers' Uprising of 1944," in Cohen et al., eds., *African Labor History*, pp. 109–28.

18. R. A. Joseph, "Settlers, Strikers and 'Sans-travail': The Douala Riots of 1945," *Journal of African History* 15, no. 4 (1974): 669–87; R. A. Joseph, *Radical Nationalism in Cameroon* (Oxford, 1977), on the disturbances of 1955; and P. Alexandre, "Problème de détribalisés urbains Douala," *CHEAM* 103, no. 2 (undated): 441.

19. Cf. F. Mulambu-Mvuluya, "Contribution à l'étude de la révolte des Bapende (mai-sept. 1931)," *Cahiers du CEDAF*, no. 1 (1971): 1–52.

20. Quoted from B. Jewsiewicki, "La Contestation sociale et la naissance du prolétariat au Zaïre," *Canadian Journal of African Studies* 10, no. 1 (1976): 47–70. Cf. "Documents pour servir à l'histoire sociale du Zaïre: Grèves dans le Bas-Congo, 1945," *Etudes d'Histoire Africaine*, no. 5 (1973): 155–88.

21. M. Lovens, "La Révolte de Masisi-Lubutu, janv.–mai 1944," *Cahiers du CEDAF*, no. 3–4 (1974): 1–154.

22. The following account is derived from L. Gagbo, *Économies et sociétés à la veille de l'indépendance en Côte-d'Ivoire (1940–1960)* (Paris, 1982).

23. See R. Cohen, *Labour and Politics in Nigeria, 1945–1971* (London, 1974);

P. Waterman, *Division and Unity among Nigerian Workers: 1940s–1960s* (The Hague, 1983).

24. R. Nelson, "Nigerian Politics and the General Strike of 1964," in Rotberg and Mazrui, *Protest and Power,* pp. 771–87.

25. A. Peace, "Industrial Protest in Nigeria," in Cohen et al., eds., *Peasants and Proletarians,* pp. 418–40.

26. See Sharon Stichter, "Trade Unionism in Kenya, 1947–1952," in Cohen et al., eds., *African Labor History,* pp. 155–74; A. Clayton and D. C. Savage, *Government and Labour in Kenya, 1895–1963* (London, 1974); G. Kitching, *Class and Economic Change in Kenya, 1905–1970* (New Haven, 1980); R. Sandbrook, *Proletarians and African Capitalism: The Kenyan Case, 1960–1972* (Cambridge, England, 1975); Frank Furedi, "The African Crowd in Nairobi: Popular Movements and Elite Politics," *Journal of African History* 14, no. 2 (1973): 275–90.

27. See S. Stichter, *Migrant Labour in Kenya, 1895–1975* (London, 1982).

28. R. Devauges, *Le Chômage à Brazzaville* (Paris, 1963).

29. P. Vennetier, "L'Urbanisation et ses conséquences au Congo-Brazzaville," *Cahiers d'Outre-Mer,* no. 63 (1963): 263–80.

30. See D. Bassoueka, "Le Mouvement populaire des 13–14–15 août 1963 au Congo-Brazzaville," Thèse de 3ᵉ cycle, Université Paris VII, 1979.

Chapter 13

1. J. M. Gibbal, *Citadins et villageois dans la ville africaine: L'Exemple d'Abidjan* (Paris, 1974).

2. Cf. I. Deblé and P. Hugon, *Vivre et survivre dans les villes africaines* (Paris, 1982); the pioneering synthesizing work by R. Sandbrook, *The Politics of Basic Needs: Urban Aspects of Assaulting Poverty in Africa* (London, 1982), to which this chapter owes much; and P. Lloyd, *A Third World Proletariat* (London, 1982).

3. M. Miracle and B. Fetter, "Backward Sloping Labor Supply Functions and African Economic Behavior," *Economic Development and Cultural Change* 17, no. 2 (1970): 240–41.

4. Sandbrook, *Politics of Basic Needs,* p. 124.

5. Jane Bujra, *Pumwani: The Politics of Property—A Study of an Urban Settlement in Nairobi* (Nairobi, 1973); P. C. W. Gutkind, "The View from Below: Political Consciousness of the Urban Poor in Ibadan," *Cahiers d'Etudes Africaines* 15, no. 1 (1975): 5–35; Sandbrook, *Politics of Basic Needs,* p. 124.

6. S. V. Sethuraman, ed., *The Urban Informal Sector in Developing Countries* (Geneva, 1981).

7. A. Marie, "Marginalité et conditions sociales du prolétariat urbain," *Cahiers d'Etudes Africaines* 21, no. 81–83 (1981): 363.

8. G. Salem, *De Dakar à Paris: Des Diasporas d'artisans et de commerçants* (Paris, 1981).

9. A. Hake, *African Metropolis: Nairobi's Self-Help City* (New York, 1977).

10. C. Hutton, "How the Unemployed Survive in Town: Kampala and Jinja, Uganda," *Manpower and Unemployment Research in Africa* 3, no. 2 (1970): 11, 12; M. Peil, "Male Unemployment in Lagos, 1971," ibid. 5, no. 2 (1972): 23; C. Gerry, "The Wrong Side of the Factory Gate: Casual Workers and Capitalist Industry in Dakar," ibid. 9, no. 2 (1976): 17–28.

11. M. B. Clinard and D. J. Abboh, *Crime in Developing Countries* (New York, 1973), p. 97; P. Satge et al., "Le Problème des jeunes," in *Dakar en devenir* (Paris, 1968), pp. 337–38; D. N. A. Nortey, "Crime in Ghana," *Ghana Social Science Journal* 7, no. 1 (1977): 102–16. All are quoted in Sandbrook, *Politics of Basic Needs,* p. 179.

12. Marie, "Marginalité," p. 368.

13. G. Gerry, "Petite Production marchande ou salariat déguisé? Quelques réflexions," *Tiers-Monde* 21, no. 82 (1980): 393–94.

14. A. Dubresson, "Industrialisation et urbanisation en Côte d'Ivoire," ORSTOM-Abidjan, 1983 (mimeo.).

15. Cf. P. Hugon, "Le Secteur 'non structuré' dans les villes du Tiers Monde," *Bulletin de la Société Languedocienne de Géographie* 16, nos. 1–2 (1982): 88.

16. Ibid., pp. 85–86.

17. It should be noted that P. Bairoch, *Révolution industrielle et sous-développement,* discussed in *Le Tiers-Monde dans l'impasse* (Paris, 1971), attributes the Third World's failure to industrialize to geographical factors such as climate and demography and to historical factors (the industrialization of some countries has, practically speaking, prevented the industrialization of others) rather than to structural differences.

18. M. Coquery, *La Coopération face aux problèmes posés par l'urbanisation dans le Tiers-Monde,* report to the minister of cooperation, 1983.

19. M. J. Daunton, "Towns and Economic Growth in 18th Century England," *Town in Societies: Essays in Economic History and Historical Sociology* (Cambridge, England, 1978), pp. 245–77.

20. E. Antheaume, "Contribution à l'étude de l'artisanat à Lomé," M.A. thesis, Nanterre, 1973.

21. Marie, "Marginalité," pp. 364–66; Gerry, "Petite Production marchande?" p. 390.

22. See B. Granotier, *Le Planète des Bidonvilles* (Paris, 1980).

23. See Chapter 12.

24. See Chapter 6.

25. See Marie, "Marginalité," pp. 368–78.

26. Ali Mazrui, *Political Values and the Educated Class in Africa* (London, 1978), pp. XI–XII.

27. See Kitching, *Class and Economic Change in Kenya.* Cf. Chapter 10.

28. C. Hutton, "Rates of Labour Migration," in J. Gugler, ed., *Urban Growth in Sub-Saharan Africa,* Nkanga no. 6 (Kampala, 1970), pp. 16–17; Sandbrook, *Politics of Basic Needs,* pp. 47, 72.

29. Contrary to the assumption of G. Arrighi, who claimed that there was a difference of 1 to 3 or 1 to 5 between the wages of unskilled and skilled labor in Rhodesia: G. Arrighi and J. Saul, *Essays on the Political Economy of Africa* (New York, 1973), chaps. 1 and 2, reconsidered in J. B. Saul, "The Labour Aristocracy Thesis Reconsidered," in Sandbrook and Cohen, eds., *Development of an African Working Class,* pp. 303–10.

30. See a comparative inquiry into differences of income in the cities and rural areas in Senegal, Zaire, Ghana, Zambia, Kenya, Tanzania, and Botswana: C. Allen,

"Unions, Incomes and Development," in his *Developmental Trends in Kenya* (Edinburgh, 1972), quoted in Sandbrook, *Politics of Basic Needs.*

31. P. L. Esparre, "Le Travailleur en Côte d'Ivoire: Une Intégration difficile à la société industrielle," *Genève-Afrique* 6, no. 2 (1967): 181–92.

32. S. Stichter, "Workers, Trade Unions and the Mau-Mau Rebellion," *Canadian Journal of African Studies* 9, no. 2 (1975); R. D. Jeffries, "Populist Tendencies in the Ghanaian Trade Union Movement," in Sandbrook and Cohen, eds., *Development of an African Working Class,* pp. 261–80.

33. See, e.g., P. Waterman, *Division and Unity Among Nigerian Workers* (The Hague, 1982).

34. See A. Dubresson, "La Localisation des industries à Abidjan," ORSTOM-Abidjan, 1983 (mimeo.).

35. John Wiseman, "Urban Riots in West Africa, 1977–1985," *Journal of Modern African Studies* 24, no. 3 (1986): 509–18.

36. For this reason I am currently engaged in comprehensive research on the historical process of urbanization and the making of urban social components in Africa. See, e.g., Catherine Coquery-Vidrovitch, ed., *Processus d'urbanisation en Afrique* (Paris: L'Harmattan, forthcoming), and Catherine Coquery-Vidrovitch, "Ville africaine et histoire des Africains," *XXe siècle: Revue d'histoire,* no. 19 (July–Sept. 1988).

Appendix

1. C. Wrigley, "Population and History," in *African Historical Demography,* vol. 2, pp. 17–32.

2. Jill R. Dias, "Famine and Disease in the History of Angola," *Journal of African History* 21, no. 3 (1981): 349–78.

3. *Tarikh es-Sudan,* trans. O. Houdas (Paris, 1964); *Tedskiret en-Nisian fi Akbar Mulouk es-Sudan,* trans. O. Houdas (Paris, 1966).

4. See M. Tymowski, "Famines et épidémies à Oulata et à Tichit," *Africana Bulletin* (Warsaw), no. 27 (1978): 35–53.

5. J. C. Miller, "The Significance of Drought, Disease and Famine in West-Central Africa," *Journal of African History* 23, no. 1 (1982): 17–61.

6. D. D. Cordell and J. W. Gregory, "Historical Demography and Demographic History in Africa," *Canadian Journal of African Studies* 14, no. 3 (1980): 389–416.

7. P. J. Munson, "Archaeological Data," and D. V. Ellis, "The Advent of Plant Cultivation," in B. K. Swartz and R. E. Dumett, eds., *West African Culture Dynamics* (The Hague, 1980), pp. 101–37.

8. H. Greenberg, *The Languages of Africa* (Bloomington, Indiana, 1963); Malcolm Guthrie, *Comparative Bantu* (London, 1967).

Bibliography

NON-AFRICAN SOCIAL SCIENCE AND HISTORY

Abrams, Philip, and Edward A. Wrigley, eds. *Towns in Societies: Essays in Economic History and Historical Sociology.* Cambridge, England: Cambridge University Press, 1978.

Burke, Peter. *Popular Culture in Early Modern Europe.* London: Harper and Row, 1978.

Chaunu, Pierre. *La Civilisation de l'Europe classique.* Paris: Arthaud, 1966.

Hobsbawm, Eric J. *Bandits.* London: Weidenfeld and Nicholson, 1979.

Isambert, François A. *Le Sens du sacré: Fête et religion populaire.* Paris: Editions de Minuit, 1982.

Léon, Pierre, ed. *Histoire économique et sociale du monde.* Paris: Colin, 1977.

Mendras, Henri. *Theories and Methods in Rural Community Studies.* New York: Pergamon, 1982.

Rudé, Jean. *Ideology and Popular Protest.* New York: Pantheon, 1980.

Simiand, François. *Le Salaire, l'évolution sociale et la monnaie.* 3 vols. Paris: Alcan, 1932.

Vincent, Bernard, ed. *Les Marginaux dans l'histoire.* Paris: Cahiers Jussieu, 10/18, 1979.

Wolf, Eric. *Europe and the People without History.* Berkeley and Los Angeles: University of California Press, 1982.

AFRICA: GENERAL HISTORY AND ANTHROPOLOGY, ECONOMIC HISTORY, COLONIAL HISTORY, CASE STUDIES

"L'Afrique et la crise de 1930." *Revue Française d'Histoire d'Outre-Mer,* special issue, no. 232–33 (1976).

Amin, Samir. *Le Développement du capitalisme en Côte d'Ivoire.* Paris: Editions de Minuit, 1967.

Arhin, Kwame, Paul Hesp, and Laurens van der Laan, eds. *Marketing Boards in Tropical Africa.* Boston: Routledge and Kegan Paul, 1985.

Arrighi, Giovanni. *The Political Economy of Rhodesia.* The Hague: Mouton, 1967.

Augé, Marc. *Génie du Paganisme.* Paris: Gallimard, 1982.

Austen, Ralph A. "The Metamorphoses of Middlemen: The Duala, Europeans, and the Cameroon Hinterland, ca. 1800–ca. 1960." *International Journal of African Historical Studies* 16, no. 1 (1983): 1–24.

Baier, Stephen. *An Economic History of Central Niger.* Oxford: Clarendon Press, 1980.

Baker, William J., and James A. Mangan, eds. *Sport in Africa: Essays in Social History.* New York: Africana, 1987.

Balandier, Georges. *Sociologie actuelle de l'Afrique noire.* Paris: Presses Universitaires de France, 1963.

———. *Anthropologie politique.* Paris: Presses Universitaires de France, 1967.

Beach, D. N. *The Shona and Zimbabwe, 900–1850.* London, Heinemann, 1980.

Biarnes, Philippe. *L'Afrique aux Africains.* Paris: Colin, 1981.

Birmingham, David, and Phyllis Martin, eds. *A History of Central Africa.* 2 vols. London: Longman, 1983.

Bohannan, Paul, and George Dalton, eds. *Markets in Africa.* Evanston, Ill.: Northwestern University Press, 1962.

Booth, Alan R. *Swaziland: Tradition and Change in a Southern African Kingdom.* Boulder, Colo.: Westview Press, 1983.

Brett, E. *Colonization and Underdevelopment in East Africa.* London: Heinemann, 1973.

Brunschwig, Henri. *Noirs et Blancs dans l'Afrique noire française, ou comment le colonisé devint colonisateur (1870–1914).* Paris: Flammarion, 1983.

Christopher, A. J. *Colonial Africa.* London: Croom Helm, 1986.

Clarence-Smith, Gervase. *Slaves, Peasants and Capitalism in Southern Angola, 1840–1926.* Cambridge, England: Cambridge University Press, 1979.

———. *The Third Portuguese Empire, 1825–1975: A Study in Economic Imperialism.* Manchester: Manchester University Press, 1985.

Cooper, Frederick. *From Slaves to Squatters: Plantation Labor and Agriculture in Zanzibar and Coastal Kenya, 1890–1925.* New Haven: Yale University Press, 1980.

Coquery-Vidrovitch, Catherine. "La Fête des coutumes au Dahomey: Historique et essai d'interprétation." *Annales ESC*, no. 4 (1964): 696–716.

———. *Le Congo (A.E.F.) au temps des grandes compagnies concessionaires, 1898–1930.* The Hague: Mouton, 1972.

———. "La Mise en dépendance de l'Afrique noire: Essai de périodisation, 1800–1970." *Cahiers d'Etudes Africaines* 16, no. 61–62 (1976): 7–58.

———, ed. *Entreprises et entrepreneurs en Afrique, XIXᵉ et XXᵉ siècles.* 2 vols. Paris: L'Harmattan, 1983.

Coquery-Vidrovitch, Catherine, and Henri Moniot. *L'Afrique noire de 1800 à nos jours.* Revised edition. Paris: Presses Universitaires de France, 1984.

Cornevin, Marianne. *L'Afrique du Sud en sursis.* Paris: Hachette, 1977.

Crummey, Donald, and Charles Cameron Stewart, eds. *Modes of Production in Africa: The Precolonial Era.* London: Sage, 1981.

Curtin, Philip, et al. *History in Africa.* Madison: University of Wisconsin Press, 1978.

Dampierre, Eric de. *Un Royaume Bandia du Haut-Oubangui.* Paris: Plon, 1967.

Decraene, Philippe. *Le Panafricanisme*. Paris: Presses Universitaires de France, 1970.

Dresch, Jean. *Un Géographe au déclin des empires*. Paris: Maspero, 1979.

Duperray, Annie. *Les Gourounsi de Haute-Volta: Conquête et colonisation, 1886–1933*. Stuttgart: Franz Steiner, 1984.

Echenberg, Myron. "Paying the Blood Tax: Military Conscription in French West Africa, 1914–1929." *Canadian Journal of African Studies*, no. 9 (1975): 171–92.

Fage, John D. *A History of Africa*. London: Hutchinson, 1978.

Feierman, Steven. *The Shambaa Kingdom*. Madison: University of Wisconsin Press, 1974.

Fetter, Bruce. "L'Union Minière du Haut-Katanga, 1920–1940." *Cahiers d'Etudes et de Documentation sur l'Afrique Noire*, no. 6 (1973): 2–40.

Freund, Bill. *The Making of Contemporary Africa: The Development of African Society since 1800*. Bloomington: Indiana University Press, 1984.

Gaily, Harry A. *The Road to Aba: A Study of British Administrative Policy in Eastern Nigeria*. New York: New York University Press, 1970.

Gbagbo, Laurent. *La Côte d'Ivoire: Economie et société à la veille de l'indépendance, 1940–1960*. Paris: L'Harmattan, 1982.

Gershoni, Yekutiel. *Black Colonialism: The Americo-Liberian Scramble for the Hinterland, 1900–1930*. Boulder, Colo.: Westview Press, 1985.

Greenberg, Joseph H. *The Languages of Africa*. Bloomington: Indiana University Press, 1963.

Guthrie, Malcolm. *Comparative Bantu*. 4 vols. Boston: Gregg, 1967.

Héritier, Françoise. *L'Exercice de la parenté*. Paris: Gallimard, 1981.

Herskovitz, Melville J. *Dahomey, an Ancient West African Kingdom*. 2 vols. New York: Augustin, 1938.

Hopkins, Anthony G. "Economic Imperialism in West Africa: Lagos, 1880–1892." *Economic History Review* 21, no. 3 (1968): 580–606.

Horowitz, Michael M., and Thomas M. Painter, eds. *Anthropology and Rural Development in West Africa*. Boulder, Colo.: Westview Press, 1985.

Iliffe, John. *The African Poor*. Cambridge, England: Cambridge University Press, 1987.

Isaacmann, Allen, and Barbara Isaacmann. *Mozambique: From Colonialism to Revolution, 1900–1982*. Boulder, Colo.: Westview Press, 1983.

Julien, Charles-André, Catherine Coquery-Vidrovitch, Magaly Morsy, and Yves Person, eds. *Les Africains*. 12 vols. Paris: Jeune Afrique, 1977–1978.

Kay, Geoffrey B., ed. *The Political Economy of Colonialism in Ghana: A Collection of Documents and Statistics, 1900–1960*. Cambridge, England: Cambridge University Press, 1972.

Kennedy, Dane K. *Islands of White: Settler Society and Culture in Kenya and Southern Rhodesia, 1889–1939*. Durham, N.C.: Duke University Press, 1987.

Kitching, Gavin. *Class and Economic Change in Kenya: The Making of an African Petite-Bourgeoisie, 1915–1970*. New Haven: Yale University Press, 1980.

Ki-Zerbo, Joseph. *Histoire de l'Afrique noire*. Paris: Hatier, 1972.

Kjekshus, Helge. *Ecology Control and Economic Development in East Africa: The Case of Tanganyika, 1850–1950*. London: Heinemann, 1977.

Klein, Martin A. *Islam and Imperialism in Senegal: Sine Saloum, 1847–1914*. Stanford: Stanford University Press, 1968.

Lumumba, Patrice. *Le Congo, terre d'avenir: Est-il menacé?* Brussels: Office de Publicité, 1961.

Lystad, Robert, ed. *The African World: A Survey of Social Research.* London: Pall Mall Press, 1965.

McCarthy, Mary. *Social Change and the Growth of British Power in the Gold Coast: The Fante States, 1807–1974.* Lanham, Md.: University Press of America, 1983.

Manning, Patrick. *Slavery, Colonialism and Economic Growth in Dahomey, 1640–1960.* Cambridge, England: Cambridge University Press, 1982.

Marks, Shula, and Anthony Atmore, eds. *Economy and Society in Pre-industrial South Africa.* London: Longman, 1980.

M'Bokolo, Elikia. *Le Continent convoité: L'Afrique du XXe siècle.* Paris: Axes, 1980.

Meillassoux, Claude. "Essai d'interprétation du phénomène économique dans les sociétés traditionnelles d'auto-subsistance." *Cahiers d'Etudes Africaines* 1, no. 4 (1961): 38–69.

———, ed. *The Development of Indigenous Trade and Markets in West Africa.* London: Oxford University Press, 1971.

Merlier, Michel. *Le Congo de la colonisation belge à l'indépendance.* Paris: Maspero, 1962.

Michel, Marc. *L'Appel à l'Afrique: Contribution et réactions à l'effort de guerre en A.O.F., 1914–1919.* Paris: Editions de la Sorbonne, 1982.

Mondjannagni, Alfred. *Campagnes et villes au Sud de la République Populaire du Bénin.* The Hague: Mouton, 1977.

Person, Yves. *Samori—une révolution Dyula.* 3 vols. Dakar: Institut Fondamental d'Afrique Noire, 1968–1975.

Ranger, T. O. "The Invention of Tradition in Colonial Africa." In *The Invention of Tradition,* edited by Eric Hobsbawm and T. O. Ranger, 211–62. Cambridge, England: Cambridge University Press, 1984.

Rotberg, Richard I. *The Rise of Nationalism in Central Africa: The Making of Malawi and Zambia, 1873–1964.* Oxford: Oxford University Press, 1966.

Sarraut, Albert. *La Mise en valeur des colonies françaises.* Paris: Payot, 1923.

Sautter, Gilles. "Le Chemin de fer Congo-Océan, 1921–1934." *Cahiers d'Etudes Africaines* 7, no. 26 (1967): 219–99.

Shenton, Robert. *The Development of Capitalism in Northern Nigeria.* London: J. Currey, 1986.

Sheriff, Abdul. *Slaves, Spices, and Ivory in Zanzibar: Integration of an East African Commercial Empire into the World Economy, 1770–1783.* Athens: Ohio University Press, 1987.

Snyder, Francis G. *Capitalism and Legal Change: An African Transformation.* New York: Academic Press, 1981.

Suret-Canale, Jean. *French Colonization in Tropical Africa, 1900–1945.* New York: Pica Press, 1971.

Swainson, Nicholas. *The Development of Corporate Capitalism in Kenya, 1918–1977.* Berkeley and Los Angeles: University of California Press, 1980.

Swartz, B. K., and Raymond E. Dumett, eds. *West African Culture Dynamics: Archeological and Historial Perspectives.* The Hague: Mouton, 1980.

Terray, Emmanuel. *L'Organisation sociale des Dida de Côte-d'Ivoire.* Abidjan: Annales de l'Université d'Abidjan, series F, vol. 1, no. 2, 1969.

Thornton, John K. *The Kingdom of Kongo: Civil War and Transition, 1641–1718.* Madison: University of Wisconsin Press, 1983.

Vail, Leroy, and Landeg White. *Capitalism and Colonialism in Mozambique: A Study of Quelimane District.* London: Heinemann, 1980.

Vansina, Jan. "Towards a History of Lost Corners in the World." *Economic History Review* 35, no. 2 (1982): 165–78.

———. *Oral Tradition as History.* London: J. Currey, 1985.

van Zwanenberg, Roger M. A., with Anne King. *An Economic History of Kenya and Uganda, 1800–1970.* London: Macmillan, 1975.

POPULATION HISTORY:
DEMOGRAPHY, CLIMATE AND DROUGHT,
EPIDEMICS AND HEALTH, SLAVERY

African Historical Demography Vols. 1, 2. Edinburgh: Center of African History, University of Edinburgh, 1977, 1981.

The African Slave Trade from the Eighteenth to the Nineteenth Century. The General History of Africa, Studies and Documents, vol. 2. Paris: UNESCO, 1979.

Akhtar, Rais, ed. *Health and Disease in Tropical Africa: Geographical and Medical Viewpoints.* London: Harwood Academic Publishing, 1987.

Alpers, Edward. *Ivory and Slaves: Changing Patterns of International Trade in East Central Africa in the Later Nineteenth Century.* Berkeley and Los Angeles: University of California Press, 1975.

Beachey, Richard W. *The Slave Trade of Eastern Africa.* London: Collings, 1976.

Becker, Charles. "Note sur les chiffres de la traite atlantique française au 18ᵉ siècle," *Cahiers d'Etudes Africaines* 24, no. 4 (1986): 633–80.

Bideau, Alain. "Les Mécanismes autorégulateurs des populations traditionnelles." *Annales ESC*, no. 5 (1983): 1040–57.

Boserup, Esther. *Population and Technological Change: A Study of Long-Term Trends.* Chicago: University of Chicago Press, 1981.

Bouche, Denise. *Les Villages de liberté en Afrique noire française (1887–1910).* The Hague: Mouton, 1968.

Caldwell, John C. "The Sahelian Drought and Its Demographic Implications." American Council of Education, O.L.C., paper 8, Washington, D.C., 1975.

Carlson, Dennis G. *African Fever: A Study of British Science, Technology, and Politics in West Africa, 1787–1864.* New York: Science History Publications, 1984.

Chastenet, Monique. "Les Crises de subsistance dans les villages Soninke du cercle de Bakel, 1858–1945." *Cahiers d'Etudes Africaines* 23, no. 89–90 (1983): 5–36.

Cissoko, S. Mody. "Famines et épidémies à Tombouctou et dans la boucle du Niger entre le XVIᵉ et le XVIIIᵉ siècle." *Bulletin de l'Institut Français d'Afrique Noire* 30B (1968): 806–21.

Comité Information Sahel. *Qui se nourrit de la famine en Afrique? Le Dossier politique de la faim au Sahel.* Paris: Maspero, 1974.

Cooper, Frederick. "The Problem of Slavery in African Studies." *Journal of African History* 2, no. 1 (1979): 103–25.

Copans, Jean, ed. *Sécheresses et famines au Sahel.* 2 vols. Paris: Maspero, 1975.

Cordell, Denis D. *Dar al Kuti and the Last Years of the Trans-Saharan Slave Trade.* Madison: University of Wisconsin Press, 1985.

Cordell, Denis, and Joel W. Gregory, eds. *African Population and Capitalism.* Boulder, Colo.: Westview Press, 1987.

Curtin, Philip. *The Atlantic Slave Trade: A Census.* Madison: University of Wisconsin Press, 1969.

———. "Medical Knowledge and Urban Planning in Tropical Africa." *American Historical Review* 3 (1985): 4–613.

———. "Nutrition in African History." In *Hunger and History: The Impact of Changing Food Production and Consumption Patterns of Society,* edited by Robert I. Rotberg and Theodore K. Rabb, 173–84. Cambridge, England: Cambridge University Press, 1985.

Daget, Serge, ed. *Actes du Colloque international sur la traite des Noirs (Nantes, 1985).* Paris: Société Française d'Histoire d'Outre-Mer, 1988.

Dalby, David, R. J. Harrison Church, and Fatima Bezzaz, eds. *Drought in Africa.* 2 vols. London: International African Institute, 1974, 1977.

"Démographie historique." *Cahiers d'Etudes Africaines,* special issue, 27, no. 105–106 (1987).

Dias, Jill R. "Famine and Disease in the History of Angola, c. 1830–1930." *Journal of African History* 21, no. 3 (1981): 349–78.

Diop, Louise M. "Le Sous-peuplement de l'Afrique noire." *Bulletin de l'Institut Français d'Afrique Noire* 40B, no. 4 (1978): 718–862.

Domergue, Danielle. *La Santé en Côte d'Ivoire, 1905–1958.* Toulouse: Académie des Sciences d'Outre-Mer et Université de Toulouse, 1987.

Egg, J., et al., eds. *Analyse descriptive de la famine de 1931 au Niger et implication méthodologique.* Paris: Institut National de Recherches Agronomiques, 1975.

Emmer, P. C., Jean Mettas, and Jean-Claude Nardin, eds. "La Traite des Noirs par l'Atlantique: Nouvelles Approches." *Revue Française d'Histoire d'Outre-Mer,* special issue, no. 62 (1975).

"Etudes épidémiologiques et approches géographiques des maladies en Afrique tropicale." *Cahiers d'Etudes Africaines,* special issue, 22, no. 85–86 (1982).

Feierman, Steven. "Struggles for Control: The Social Roots of Health and Healing in Modern Africa." *African Studies Review* 28 (1985): 73–148.

Feierman, Steven, and John Janzen, eds. *The Social Basis of Health and Healing in Africa.* Forthcoming.

Fisher, Allen G. B., and Humphrey J. Fisher. *Slavery and Muslim Society in Africa.* London: C. Hurst, 1970.

Fogel, Robert W., and Stanley L. Engerman. *Time on the Cross: The Economics of American Negro-Slavery.* Boston: Little, Brown, 1974.

Ford, John. *The Role of Trypanosomiases in African Ecology.* Oxford: Clarendon Press, 1971.

Franke, Richard W., and Barbara H. Chasin. *Seeds of Famine: Ecological Destruction and the Development Dilemma in the West African Sahel.* New York: Universe, 1980.

Fuglestad, Finn. "La Grande Famine de 1931." *Revue Française d'Histoire d'Outre-Mer* 61, no. 22 (1974): 18–33.

Gemery, Henry A., and Jan S. Hogendorn, eds. *The Uncommon Market: Essays in the Economic History of the Atlantic Slave Trade*. New York: Academic Press, 1979.

Guyer, Jane. "The Food Economy and French Colonial Rule in Central Cameroun." *Journal of African History* 19, no. 4 (1978): 577–98.

Hance, William A. *Population, Migration and Urbanization in Africa*. New York: Columbia University Press, 1970.

Hansen, Art, and Della E. McMillan, eds. *Food in Sub-Saharan Africa*. Boulder, Colo.: Lynne Rienner, 1986.

Harms, Robert W. *River of Wealth, River of Sorrow: The Central Zaire Basin in the Era of Slave and Ivory Trade, 1500–1891*. New Haven: Yale University Press, 1981.

Harting, G. W. "Demographic Considerations in East Africa during the Nineteenth Century." *International Journal of African Historical Studies* 12, no. 4 (1979): 5–44.

Hartwig, Gerald W., and Karl David Patterson, eds. *Disease in African History: An Introductory Survey and Case Studies*. Durham, N.C.: Duke University Press, 1978.

Hill, Allan G., ed. *Population Health and Nutrition in the Sahel*. London: KPI, 1985.

Inikori, J. E., ed. *Forced Migrations: The Impact of the Export Slave Trade on African Societies*. London: Hutchinson, 1982.

Jones, Adam. *From Slaves to Palm Kernels: A History of the Galinhas Country (West Africa), 1730–1890*. Wiesbaden: Franz Steiner, 1983.

Klein, H. S. *The Middle Passage: Comparative Studies in the Atlantic Slave Trade*. Princeton: Princeton University Press, 1978.

Lawrence, Peter R., ed. *World Recession and the Food Crisis in Africa*. London: James Currey, 1987.

Lovejoy, Paul E. *Transformations in Slavery: The History of Slavery in Africa*. Cambridge, England: Cambridge University Press, 1983.

McSheffrey, Gerald M. "Slavery, Indentured Servitude, Legitimate Trade and the Impact of Abolition in the Gold Coast, 1874–1901: A Reappraisal." *Journal of African History* 24, no. 3 (1983): 349–68.

Manning, Patrick. "The Enslavement of Africans: A Demographic Model." *Canadian Journal of African Studies* 15, no. 3 (1981): 499–526.

Martin, G., Leboeuf, and Rambaud. *Rapport de la mission d'études de la maladie du sommeil au Congo français, 1906–1908*. Paris: Masson, 1909.

Mason, Michael. "Population Density and Slave-Raiding: The Case of the Middle Belt of Nigeria." *Journal of African History* 10, no. 4 (1969): 551–64.

M'Bokolo, Elikia. "Peste et société urbaine à Dakar: L'Epidémie de 1914." *Cahiers d'Etudes Africaines* 22, no. 85–86 (1982): 13–46.

Meillassoux, Claude. "Le Rôle de l'esclavage dans l'histoire de l'Afrique occidentale." *Anthropologie et Société* (Quebec) 2, no. 1 (1979): 117–48.

———. *Anthropologie de l'esclavage: Le Ventre de fer et d'argent*. Paris: Presses Universitaires de France, 1986.

———, ed. *L'Esclavage en Afrique pré-coloniale*. Paris: Maspero, 1975.

Miers, Suzanne, and Igor Kopytoff. *Slavery in Africa: Historical and Anthropological Perspectives*. Madison: University of Wisconsin Press, 1977.

Miers, Suzanne, Richard Roberts, and Igor Kopytoff. *The Ending of Slavery in Africa*. Forthcoming.

Miller, Joseph C. "The Significance of Drought, Disease, and Famine in the Agriculturally Marginal Zones of West-Central Africa." *Journal of African History* 23,
no. 1 (1982): 17–61.

Ohadike, D. C. "The Influenza Pandemic of 1918–19 and the Spread of Cassava Cultivation on the Lower Niger: A Study in Historical Linkages." *Journal of African
History* 22, no. 3 (1981): 379–91.

Patterson, K. David. *Health in Colonial Ghana: Disease, Medicine and Socioeconomic Change, 1900–1955.* Waltham, Mass.: Crossroads Press, 1981.

Polanyi, Karl. *Dahomey and the Slave Trade: An Analysis of an Archaic Economy.*
Seattle: University of Washington Press, 1966.

Ransford, Oliver. *"Bid the Sickness Cease": Disease in the History of Africa.* London: J. Murray, 1983.

Rathbone, Richard J., and Rowland P. Moss, eds. *The Population Factor in African
Studies.* London: University of London Press, 1975.

Retel-Laurentin, Anne. *Un Pays à la dérive: Une Société en régression démographique—les Nzakara de l'Est centrafricain.* Paris: J. P. Delage, 1979.

Richard, Paul, ed. *African Environment: Problems and Perspectives.* London: International African Institute, Oxford University Press, 1975.

"The Roots of Famine." *Review of African Political Economy,* special issue, 15–16
(1979).

Ross, Robert. *Cape of Torments: Slavery and Resistance in South Africa.* London:
Routledge and Kegan Paul, 1983.

Rotberg, Robert I., ed. *Imperialism, Colonialism and Hunger: East and Central Africa.* Lexington, Mass.: Lexington Books, 1983.

Salifou, André. "Quand l'histoire se répète: La Famine de 1931 au Niger." *Environ-
nement Africain* 1, no. 2 (1975): 25–53.

Sautter, Gilles. *De l'Atlantique au fleuve Congo: Une Géographie du sous-peuplement.* Paris: Mouton, 1966.

Somerville, Carolyn M. *Drought and Aid in the Sahel: A Decade of Development
Cooperation.* Boulder, Colo.: Westview Press, 1986.

Stein, R. *The French Slave Trade in the Eighteenth Century: An Old Regime Business.* Madison: University of Wisconsin Press, 1979.

Tabutin, Daniel, ed. *Les Populations de l'Afrique subsaharienne: Analyse des dyna-
miques démographiques et sociales.* Paris: L'Harmattan, forthcoming.

Terry, E. R., K. A. Oduro, and Fields Caveness, eds. *Tropical Root Crops: Research
Strategies for the 1980's.* Ottawa: International Development Research Centre,
1981.

Thornton, John. "The Slave Trade in Eighteenth Century Angola: Effects on Demographic Structure." *Canadian Journal of African Studies* 14, no. 3 (1980): 417–27.

Turshen, Meredeth. *The Political Ecology of Disease in Tanzania.* New Brunswick,
N.J.: Rutgers University Press, 1984.

Tymowski, Michal. *Le Développement et la régression chez les peuples de la boucle
du Niger à l'époque pré-coloniale.* Warsaw: Wydawnictwa Uniwersytetu Warszawskiego, 1974.

———. "Famines et épidémies à Oualata et à Tichit au XIXᵉ siècle." *African Bulletin*
(Warsaw), no. 27 (1978): 35–53.

Walvin, James, and David Eltis, eds. *The Abolition of the Atlantic Slave Trade: Ori-*

gins and Effects in Europe, Africa and the Americas. Madison: University of Wisconsin Press, 1981.

Watts, Michael J. Silent Violence: Food, Famine and Peasantry in Northern Nigeria. Berkeley and Los Angeles: University of California Press, 1983.

Webster, James B., ed. Chronology, Migration and Drought in Interlacustrine Africa. New York: Holmes and Meier, 1979.

Zachariah, Kunni C., and Julian S. Conde. Migration in West Africa: The Demographic Aspects. Oxford: Oxford University Press, 1982.

POWER AND THE STATE

Adler, Alfred. La Mort est le masque du roi: La Royauté sacrée des Moundang du Tchad. Paris: Payot, 1982.

Allen, Christopher. "Tanzanie, les illusions du socialisme." Esprit, no. 26 (1979): 37–50.

Amselle, Jean-Loup, and Elikia M'Bokolo. Au Coeur de l'ethnie: Ethnie, tribalisme et état en Afrique. Paris: La Découverte, 1985.

Balandier, Georges. "Les Mythes politiques de la colonisation et de la décolonisation en Afrique." Cahiers Internationaux de Sociologie 33 (1962): 85–86.

Bates, Robert H. Markets and States in Tropical Africa: The Political Basis of Agricultural Politics. Berkeley and Los Angeles: University of California Press, 1981.

Bayart, Jean-François. L'Etat au Cameroun. Paris: Foundation Nationale des Sciences Politiques, 1979.

Bazin, Jean, and Emmanuel Terray, eds. Guerres de lignages et guerres d'états en Afrique. Paris: Edition des Archives Contemporaines, 1982.

Bonner, Paul L. Kings, Commoners and Concessionaires: The Evolution and Dissolution of the Nineteenth Century Swazi State. Cambridge, England: Cambridge University Press, 1983.

Bulaimu, Abemba. "Le Mode de production lignager face à la traite arabe et à la colonisation . . . au Maniema." Cahiers d'Etudes et de Documentation sur l'Afrique Noire, special issue, no. 6–7 (1979).

Chanock, Martin. Law, Custom and Social Order: The Colonial Experience in Malawi and Zambia. Cambridge, England: Cambridge University Press, 1985.

Clayton, Anthony. Zanzibar, Revolution and Its Aftermath. London: Hurst, 1981.

Coquery-Vidrovitch, Catherine, ed. Décolonisation et nouvelles dépendances: Modèles et contre-modèles idéologiques et culturels. Lille: Presses Universitaires de Lille, 1986.

Delavignette, Robert. Les Vrais Chefs de l'Empire. Paris: Gallimard, 1939.

Diabaté, Henriette. "Le Sannvin: Un Royaume akan de Côte d'Ivoire (1700–1901)." Thèse d'Etat, Université Paris I, 1984.

Dupré, Georges. Un Ordre et sa destruction: Les Nzabi du Congo. Paris: ORSTOM, 1982.

———. La Naissance d'une société: Espace et historicité chez les Beembe du Congo. Paris: ORSTOM, 1985.

Eisenstadt, Shmuel Noah, and René Lemarchand, eds. Political Clientism, Patronage and Development. Beverly Hills, Calif.: Sage, 1981.

Evans-Pritchard, E. Evan, and Meyer Fortes. *African Political Systems*. London: Oxford University Press, 1940.

Finucane, James. *Rural Development and Bureaucracy in Tanzania*. Uppsala: Scandinavian Institute of African Studies, 1974.

Garlake, Peter. *Kingdoms of Africa*. London: Phaidon, 1978.

———. *Life at Great Zimbabwe*. Harare: Mambo Press, 1982.

Hyden, Goran. *Beyond Ujamaa in Tanzania: Underdevelopment and an Uncaptured Peasantry*. London: Heinemann, 1982.

Izard, Michel. *Gens du pouvoir, gens de la terre: Les Institutions politiques de l'ancien royaume du Yatenga (Bassin de la Volta Blanche)*. Paris: Cambridge University Press/CNRS, 1985.

Jackson, Robert H., and Carl G. Rosberg. *Personal Rule in Black Africa: Prince, Autocrat, Prophet, Tyrant*. Berkeley and Los Angeles: University of California Press, 1982.

Joinet, Bernard. *Tanzanie: Manger d'abord*. Paris: Karthala, 1981.

Joseph, Richard. *Democracy and Prebendal Politics in Nigeria: The Rise and Fall of the Second Republic*. Cambridge and New York: Cambridge University Press, 1987.

Kea, Ray A. *Settlements, Trade and Polities in the Seventeenth Century Gold Coast*. Baltimore: Johns Hopkins University Press, 1982.

Keller, Edmond, and Donald Rothchild, eds. *Afro-Marxist Regimes: Ideology and Public Policy*. Boulder, Colo.: Lynne Rienner, 1987.

Lefort, René. *Ethiopia: An Heretical Revolution*. London: Zed Press, 1983.

McGowan, Pat, and Thomas H. Johnson. "African Military Coups d'Etat and Underdevelopment: A Quantitative Historical Analysis." *Journal of Modern African Studies* 22, no. 4 (1984): 633–56.

———. "Sixty Coups in Thirty Years: Further Evidence regarding African Military Coups d'Etat." *Journal of Modern African Studies* 24, no. 3 (1986): 539–46.

Meillassoux, Claude. *Les Derniers Blancs: Le Modèle sud-africain*. Paris, Maspero, 1979.

Mworoha, Emile. *Peuples et rois de l'Afrique des Lacs: Le Burundi et les royaumes voisins au XIXe siècle*. Dakar: Les Nouvelles Editions Africaines, 1977.

Nyerere, Julius K. *Ujamaa: Essays on Socialism*. Oxford: Oxford University Press, 1968.

———. *Freedom and Socialism: Uhuru na Ujamaa—A Selection from Writings and Speeches, 1965–1967*. Oxford: Oxford University Press, 1973.

Peel, John D. Y. *Ijeshas and Nigerians: The Incorporation of a Yoruba Kingdom, 1890's–1970's*. New York: Cambridge University Press, 1983.

Perrot, Claude-Hélène. *Les Ani-Ndenye et le pouvoir aux XVIIIe et XIXe siècles en Côte d'Ivoire*. Paris: Editions de la Sorbonne, 1982.

Person, Yves, ed. "Pouvoir et Etat en Afrique noire." *Revue Française d'Histoire d'Outre-Mer*, special issue, 68, no. 250–53 (1981).

"Les Pouvoirs africains." *Pouvoirs*, special issue, no. 25 (1983).

"La Problématique de l'Etat en Afrique noire." *Présence Africaine*, special issue, no. 127–28 (1983).

Quinn, Francis. "Charles Atangana of Yaoundé." *Journal of African History* 21, no. 4 (1980): 485–95.

Raison-Jourde, Françoise, ed. *Les Souverains de Madagascar: L'Histoire royale et ses résurgences contemporaines.* Paris: Karthala, 1983.

"Relations de clientèle et de dépendance personnelle." *Cahiers d'Etudes Africaines,* special issue, no. 35 (1969): 345–508.

Rennie, J. K. "The Precolonial Kingdom of Rwanda: A Reinterpretation." *Transafrican Journal of History,* no. 2 (1972): 11–54.

Reyntjens, Filip. *Pouvoir et droit au Rwanda: Droit public et évolution politique, 1916–1973.* Tervuren: Musée Royal de l'Afrique Centrale, 1985.

Roberts, A. D. "The Sub-Imperialism of Buganda." *Journal of African History* 3, no. 3 (1962): 435–50.

Shivji, Issa. *Class Struggles in Tanzania.* New York: Monthly Review Press, 1976.

Stevenson, Richard F. *Population and Political Systems in Tropical Africa.* New York: Columbia University Press, 1968.

Suret-Canale, Jean. "La Fin de la chefferie en Guinée." *Journal of African History* 7, no. 3 (1966): 459–94.

"Systèmes étatiques africains." *Cahiers d'Etudes Africaines,* special issue, 22, no. 87–88 (1982).

Terray, Emmanuel. "Une Histoire du royaume Abron de Gyiaman des origines à la fin du XIXᵉ siècle." Thèse d'Etat, Université Paris V, 1985.

Thiam, Iba der. "L'Evolution politique et syndicale du Sénégal colonial de 1840 à 1936." Thèse d'Etat, Université Paris I, 1983.

Tymowski, Michal. *L'Armée et la formation des Etats en Afrique occidentale au 19ᵉ siècle: Samori et le Kenedougou.* Warsaw: Wydawnictwa Uniwersytetu Warszawskiego, 1987.

Urfer, Sylvain. *Une Afrique socialiste: La Tanzanie.* Paris: Les Editions Ouvrières, 1976.

Vansina, Jan. *The Children of Woot: A History of the Kuba Peoples.* Madison: University of Wisconsin Press, 1978.

Wilks, Ivor. *Asante in the Nineteenth Century: The Structure and Evolution of a Political Order.* Cambridge, England: Cambridge University Press, 1975.

Yeager, Rodger. *Tanzania: An African Experiment.* Boulder, Colo.: Westview Press, 1982.

Young, Christopher. *Politics in the Congo: Decolonization and Independence.* Princeton: Princeton University Press, 1965.

Young, Crawford. "Zaire: Is There a State?" *Canadian Journal of African Studies* 18, no. 1 (1984): 80–82 (special issue on Zaire).

RELIGION: MILLENARIANISM, CHRISTIANITY, AND ISLAM

Adas, M. *Prophets of Rebellion: Millenarian Protest Movements against the European Colonial Order.* Reprint. Cambridge, England: Cambridge University Press, 1987.

Asch, Susan. *L'Eglise du prophète Kimbangu: De ses origines à son rôle actuel au Zaïre (1920–1981).* Paris: Karthala, 1983.

Bak, Janos M., and Gerhard Benecker, eds. *Religion and Rural Revolt*. Manchester: Manchester University Press, 1984.

Berger, Iris. *Religion and Resistance: East African Kingdoms in the Precolonial Period*. Tervuren, 1981.

Bhebe, Nywabi. *Christianity and Traditional Religion in Western Zimbabwe, 1859–1923*. London: Longman, 1979.

Clarke, Peter B. *West Africa and Islam (Eighth to Twentieth Century)*. London: E. Arnold, 1982.

Comaroff, Jean. *Body of Power, Spirit of Resistance: The Culture of a South African People*. Chicago: University of Chicago Press, 1985.

Constantin, François. *Les Musulmans d'Afrique orientale*. Paris: Centre de Recherches et d'Etudes Politiques sur l'Afrique Orientale, 1981.

Copans, Jean. *Les Marabouts de l'arachide*. Paris: Le Sycomore, 1980.

Coulon, Christian. *Les Musulmans et le pouvoir en Afrique noire*. Paris: Karthala, 1983.

Cruise O'Brien, Donal. *The Mourides of Senegal*. Oxford: Oxford University Press, 1971.

Ekechi, F. K. "Colonialism and Christianity in West Africa: The Igbo Case, 1900–1915." *Journal of African History* 12, no. 1 (1971): 103–16.

Etherington, Norman. *Preachers, Peasants and Politics in South-East Africa, 1835–1880*. London: Royal Historical Society, 1978.

Fields, Karen E. *Revival and Rebellion in Colonial Central Africa*. Princeton: Princeton University Press, 1985.

Gellar, Sheldon. *Senegal: An African Nation between Islam and the West*. Boulder, Colo.: Westview Press, 1982.

Haliburton, Gordon M. *The Prophet Harris*. London: Oxford University Press, 1971.

Hansen, Holger B. *Mission, Church and State in a Colonial Setting: Uganda, 1890–1925*. London: Heinemann, 1984.

Hastings, Adrian. *History of African Christianity, 1850–1975*. Cambridge, England: Cambridge University Press, 1979.

Hiskett, Mervyn. *The Development of Islam in West Africa*. London: Longman, 1980.

Hodgkin, Thomas. "Mahdisme, messianisme et marxisme dans le contexte africain." *Présence Africaine*, no. 74 (1970): 128–53.

Kapteijns, Lidwien. *Mahdist Faith and Sudanic Tradition: The History of the Masalit Sultanate, 1870–1930*. London: Kegan Paul International, 1985.

Le Grip, A. "Le Mahdisme en Afrique noire." *L'Afrique et l'Asie*, no. 18 (1952): 3–16.

Linden, Ian. *Catholics, Peasants and Chewa Resistance in Nyasaland, 1889–1939*. London: Heinemann, 1974.

———. *Church and Revolution in Rwanda*. Manchester: Manchester University Press, 1977.

———. *The Catholic Church and the Struggle for Zimbabwe*. London: Longman, 1980.

MacDonald, D. B. "Mahdi." In *Encyclopédie de l'Islam*, first edition, 3: 116–20. Leiden: Brill, 1936.

Nicholas, Guy. *Dynamique de l'Islam au Sud du Sahara*. Paris: Publications Orientalistes de France, 1981.

Ranger, T. O. "Religious Movements and Politics in Sub-Saharan Africa." Research Overview Paper, *African Studies Review* 29, no. 2 (1986): 1–70 (see pp. 59–70 for further references).

———, ed. *The Historical Study of African Religion*. Berkeley and Los Angeles: University of California Press, 1972.

Saad, Elias N. *Social History of Timbuktu: The Role of Muslim Scholars and Notables, 1400–1900*. Cambridge, England: Cambridge University Press, 1983.

Sanneh, Lamin O. *West African Christianity: The Religious Impact*. London: Hurst, 1983.

Shank, David A. "The Prophet Harris: A Historiographical and Bibliographical Survey." *Journal of Religion in Africa* 14, no. 2 (1983): 130–60.

Sinda, Martial. *Les Messianismes congolais*. Paris: Payot, 1972.

Traore, Alioune. *Islam et colonisation en Afrique: Cheikh Hamahoullah, homme de foi et résistant*. Paris: Maisonneuve et Larose, 1983.

Triaud, Jean-Louis. "La Question musulmane en Côte d'Ivoire." *Revue Française d'Histoire d'Outre-Mer* 61, no. 225 (1974): 542–71.

———. "L'Islam en Afrique de l'Ouest." Symposium of the Association pour l'Avancement des Etudes Islamiques, March 1981.

Tubiana, Marie-José. *Abd-el-Karim, propagateur de l'Islam et fondateur du royaume du Ouaddaï*. Paris: CNRS, 1978.

Turner, Harold W., Wim Van Binsberger, and Matthew Schoffeleers, eds. *Theoretical Explanations in African Religion*. London: RKP, 1985.

Vansina, Jan. "Les Mouvements religieux Kuba [Kasaï] à l'époque coloniale." *Etudes d'Histoire Africaine* 2 (1971).

———. "Lukoshi/Lupambula: Histoire d'un culte religieux dans les régions du Kasaï et du Kwango (1920–1970)." *Etudes d'Histoire Africaine* 5 (1973): 51–98.

Verbeek, L. "Kitawala et détecteurs de sorciers dans la botte de Sakania (1925–1975)." *Enquêtes et Documents d'Histoire Africaine* 2 (1977): 86–107.

Vergiat, A. M. *Les Rites secrets des primitifs de l'Oubangui*. Paris: Payot, 1936.

Vieillard, G. *Bulletin du Comité d'Etudes Historiques et Scientifiques de l'A.O.F.* 20, no. 3 (1937): 225–311.

Walker, S. *Religious Revolution in the Ivory Coast*. Chapel Hill: University of North Carolina Press, 1984.

RURAL HISTORY, REVOLTS, AND RESISTANCE

See also Crummey (below), pp. 22–29nn., for further references.

"Afrique du Sud." *Canadian Journal of African Studies*, special issue, 17, no. 3 (1983).

"Agrarian History and Society." *Journal of Southern African Studies*, special issue, 5, no. 1 (1978).

Akinjide, Osuntokun. "Disaffection and Revolts in Nigeria during the First World War, 1914–1918." *Canadian Journal of African Studies* 5, no. 2 (1971): 171–92 (special issue: "Politique et Contestation en Afrique").

Amin, Samir, et al. *L'Agriculture africaine et le capitalisme.* Dakar: Anthropos-IDEP, 1975.

Asiwaji, A. I. "Migrations as Revolt." *Journal of African History* 17, no. 4 (1976): 577–96.

Aston, T., ed. *Agrarian Unrest in British and French Africa, British India and French Indochina.* Oxford: Past and Present Society, 1982.

Aubertin, Catherine. *Le Programme sucrier ivoirien: Une Industrialisation régionale volontariste.* Paris: ORSTOM, 1983.

Ausman, J. L. "The Disturbances in Abeokuta in 1918." *Canadian Journal of African Studies* 5, no. 1 (1971): 45–60.

Austen, Ralph. "Social Bandits and Other Heroic Criminals: Western Models of Resistance and Their Relevance for Africa." In *Banditry, Rebellion, and Social Protest in Africa,* edited by Donald Crummey, 89–108. London: J. Currey and Heinemann, 1986.

Ba, Thierno. "Karnou et l'insurrection des Gbaya." *Afrika Zamani,* no. 3 (1974): 105–63.

Ballard, Jacques. "The Porto-Novo Incidents of 1923." *Odu* 2 (1965): 62–75.

Barker, Jonathan, ed. *The Politics of Agriculture in Tropical Africa.* London: Sage, 1984.

Bates, Robert H. *Essays on the Political Economy of Rural Africa.* Cambridge, England: Cambridge University Press, 1983.

Belloncle, Guy. *Participation paysanne et aménagements hydro-agricoles.* Paris: Karthala, 1985.

Bernard-Duquenet, Nicole. *Le Sénégal et le Front Populaire.* Paris: L'Harmattan, 1986.

Bernart, William, and Colin Bundy. *Hidden Struggles in Rural South Africa: Politics and Popular Movements in the Transkei and Eastern Cape, 1890–1930.* Berkeley and Los Angeles: University of California Press, 1986.

Berry, Sara S. *Cocoa Custom and Socio-Economic Change in Rural Western Nigeria.* Oxford: Clarendon Press, 1975.

———. "The Food Crisis and Agrarian Change in Africa: A Review Essay." *African Studies Review* 27, no. 2 (1984): 59–112.

Boserup, Esther. *The Conditions of Agricultural Growth.* New York: Aldine, 1965.

Brantley, Cynthia. *The Giriama and Colonial Resistance in Kenya, 1800–1920.* Berkeley and Los Angeles: University of California Press, 1981.

Buijtenhuis, Roger. *Le Mouvement Mau-Mau: Une Révolte paysanne et anticoloniale en Afrique noire.* The Hague: Mouton, 1971.

Bundy, Colin. *The Rise and Fall of the South African Peasantry.* Berkeley and Los Angeles: University of California Press, 1979.

Bunker, Stephen G. *Peasants against the State: The Politics of Market Control in Bugisu, Uganda, 1900–1983.* Evanston: University of Illinois Press, 1987.

Bureau, Jacques. "Réforme agraire en Ethiopie." *Esprit,* no. 26 (1979): 25–36.

Chaliand, Gérard. *Armed Struggle in Africa.* New York: Monthly Review Press, 1969.

Chrétien, Jean-Pierre. "Une Révolte au Burundi en 1934." *Annales ESC,* no. 6 (1970): 1678–1717.

———. "La Révolte de Ndungtse (1912): Forces traditionnelles et pression coloniale au Rwanda allemand." *Revue Française d'Histoire d'Outre-Mer* 59, no. 217 (1972): 645–80.

————, ed. *Histoire rurale de l'Afrique des Grands Lacs*. Paris: Afera-Karthala, 1983.

Clark, J. Desmond, and Steven A. Brandt, *From Hunters to Farmers: The Causes and Consequences of Food Production in Africa*. Berkeley and Los Angeles: University of California Press, 1982.

Cleave, John H. *African Farmers: Labor Use in the Development of Smallholder Agriculture*. New York: Praeger, 1974.

Coquery-Vidrovitch, Catherine, ed. *Sociétés paysannes du Tiers-Monde*. Lille: Presses Universitaires de Lille, 1981.

Coquery-Vidrovitch, Catherine, Alain Forest, and Herbert Weiss, eds. *Rébellions/ Révolution au Zaïre (1960–1965)*. Paris: L'Harmattan, 1987.

Crowder, Michael, ed. *West African Resistance: The Military Response to Colonial Occupation*. London: Hutchinson, 1971.

Crummey, Donald, ed. *Banditry, Rebellion, and Social Protest in Africa*. London: J. Currey and Heinemann, 1986.

D'Almeida-Topor, Hélène. "La Révolte des Holli." In *Sociétés paysannes du Tiers-Monde*, edited by Catherine Coquery-Vidrovitch, 81–90. Lille: Presses Universitaires de Lille, 1981.

Derrienic, Hervé. *Famines et dominations en Afrique noire: Paysans-éleveurs du Sahel sous le joug*. Paris: L'Harmattan, 1977.

Dewitte, Philippe. *Les Mouvements nègres en France, 1919–1939*. Paris: L'Harmattan, 1985.

Dinham, Barbara, and Colin Hines. *Agribusiness in Africa*. London: Earth Resources Research, Third World Publications, 1982.

Dufour, Jean-Louis. "La Révolte Touarègue." *Relations Internationales*, no. 3 (1975): 55–77.

Dumont, René. *False Start in Africa*. New York: Praeger, 1966.

Eicher, Carl K., and Doyle Baker. *Research on Agricultural Development in Sub-Saharan Africa*. East Lansing: Michigan State University Press, 1982.

Ellis, Stephen. *The Rising of the Red Shawls: A Revolt in Madagascar, 1895–1899*. Cambridge, England: Cambridge University Press, 1985.

Fanon, Frantz. *The Wretched of the Earth*. New York: Grove Press, 1963.

Frelastre, Guy. "Une Etape importante dans le développement rural africain: Le Séminaire de Zinder (nov. 1982) et la nouvelle stratégie de la République du Niger." *Le Mois en Afrique*, no. 212 (1983): 69–106.

Fuglestad, Finn. "Les Révoltes des Touaregs du Niger." *Cahiers d'Etudes Africaines* 13, no. 49 (1973): 82–120.

Garcia, Luc. "Les Mouvements de résistance au Dahomey." *Cahiers d'Etudes Africaines* 10, no. 37 (1970): 144–78.

Gourou, Pierre. "Une Expérience d'agriculture mécanisée en Afrique orientale: Le Plan des arachides." *Cahiers d'Outre-Mer* 8 (1955): 105–18.

Grove, Alfred T., and F. M. G. Klein. *Rural Africa*. Cambridge, England: Cambridge University Press, 1979.

Halliday, Fred, and Maxine Molyneux. *The Ethiopian Revolution*. London: Verso, 1981.

Hart, Keith. *The Political Economy of West African Agriculture*. Cambridge, England: Cambridge University Press, 1982.

Hill, Polly. *Studies in Rural Capitalism in West Africa*. Cambridge, England: Cambridge University Press, 1970.

Hogendorn, Jan S., and K. M. Scott. "The East African Groundnut Scheme." *African Economic History*, no. 10 (1981): 81–115.

Idrissa, Kimba. *Guerres et sociétés: Les Populations du Niger occidental et leurs réactions face à la colonisation, 1896–1906*. Niamey: Institut de Recherches en Sciences Humaines, 1979.

Isaacmann, Allen. *The Tradition of Resistance in Mozambique, 1850–1921*. London: Heinemann, 1976.

———. "Social Banditry in Zimbabwe (Rhodesia) and Mozambique, 1894–1907." *Journal of Southern African Studies* 4, no. 1 (1977): 1–30.

Isaacmann, Allen, and Barbara Isaacmann. "Resistance and Collaboration in Southern and Central Africa, 1850–1920." *International Journal of African Historical Studies* 10, no. 1 (1977): 31–62.

Isaacmann, Allen, et al. "Cotton Is Mother of Poverty: Peasant Resistance to Forced Cotton Production in Mozambique." *International Journal of African Historical Studies* 13, no. 4 (1980): 581–615.

Keller, E. "A Twentieth-Century Model: The Mau-Mau Transformation from Social Banditry to Social Rebellion." *Kenya Historical Studies* 11 (1973): 189–206.

Klein, Martin A., ed. *Peasants in Africa: Historical and Contemporary Perspectives*. Beverly Hills, Calif.: Sage, 1980.

Lan, David. *Guns and Rain: Guerrillas and Spirit Mediums in Zimbabwe*. Berkeley and Los Angeles: University of California Press, 1985.

Lassailly, Véronique. *Espace utile et transfert de population en amont du barrage de Kossou (Côte d'Ivoire)*. Paris: CNRS, 1980.

Le Bris, Emile, François Leindorfer, and Etienne Le Roy, eds. *Enjeux fonciers en Afrique noire*. Paris: Karthala, 1983.

Levi, John, and Michael A. Havirden. *Economics of African Agriculture*. London: Longman, 1982.

Lewinger, Joyce Moock, ed. *Understanding Africa's Rural Households and Farming Systems*. Boulder, Colo.: Westview Press, 1986.

Lovens, Maurice. "La Révolte de Masisi-Lubutu (Congo belge, janvier–mai 1944)." *Cahiers d'Etudes et de Documentations sur l'Afrique Noire*, no. 3–4 (1974).

McCann, James. "The Political Economy of Rural Rebellion in Ethiopia: Northern Resistance to Imperial Expansion, 1928–1935." *International Journal of African Historical Studies* 18, no. 4 (1984): 601–24.

Marks, Shula. *Reluctant Rebellion: The 1906–1908 Disturbance in Natal*. Oxford: Clarendon Press, 1970.

Maton, Guy. "La Politique des grands barrages hydro-agricoles." *Actuel-Développement*, no. 3 (1974): 32–37.

Migdal, Joel S. *Peasants, Politics and Revolution: Pressures toward Political and Social Change in the Third World*. Princeton: Princeton University Press, 1974.

Miracle, Marvin. *Maize in Africa*. Madison: University of Wisconsin Press, 1966.

Mubambu-Mouluya, F. "Contribution à l'étude de la révolte des Bapende (mai–sept. 1931)." *Cahiers d'Etudes et de Documentation sur l'Afrique Noire*, no. 1 (1971): 4–154.

Newbury, Catharine. "Ebutumwa Bw'Emiogo: The Tyranny of Cassava—A Women's Tax Revolt in Eastern Zaire." *Canadian Journal of African Studies* 18, no. 1 (1984): 35–54.

Nzabakomada, Raphaël. *L'Afrique centrale insurgée: La guerre de Kongo-Warra, 1928–1931*. Paris: L'Harmattan, 1985.

Okihiro, Gary Y., ed. *In Resistance: Studies in African, Caribbean, and Afro-American History*. Amherst: University of Massachusetts Press, 1986.

O'Toole, Thomas. "The 1928–1931 Gbaya Insurrection in Ubangi-Shari: Messianic Movement or Village Self-Defense?" *Canadian Journal of African Studies* 18, no. 1 (1984): 329–44.

Owona, A. "A l'aube du nationalisme camerounais." *Revue Française d'Histoire d'Outre-Mer* 56, no. 204 (1969): 199–235.

Palmer, Richard, and Neil Parsons, eds. *The Roots of Rural Poverty in Central and Southern Africa*. London: Heinemann, 1977.

Pélissier, Paul. *Les Paysans du Sénégal*. Saint-Yrieix: Imprimerie Fabrègue, 1966 (published by the author).

Pélissier, René. *Les Guerres grises: Résistance et révoltes en Angola, 1845–1941*. 2 vols. Orgeval, 1970 (published by the author).

———. *Naissance du Mozambique, 1854–1918: Résistance et révolte anti-coloniale*. 2 vols. Orgeval, 1983 (published by the author).

Phiminster, Ian R., and Charles Van Onselen. "The Political Economy of Tribal Animosity: A Case Study of the 1929 Bulawayo Location 'Faction Fight.'" *Journal of Southern African Studies* 6, no. 1 (1976): 1–43.

Quinn, Frederick. "An African Reaction to World War I." *Cahiers d'Etudes Africaines* 13, no. 52 (1973): 775–78.

Ranger, T. O. "Connections between Primary Resistance Movements and Modern Mass Nationalism." *Journal of African History* 9, no. 3 (1968): 437–54, and no. 4 (1968): 631–42.

———. *Dance and Society in Eastern Africa, 1890–1970: The Beni Ngona*. London: Heinemann, 1975.

———. *Peasant Consciousness and Guerrilla War in Zimbabwe: A Comparative Study* [with Kenya and Mozambique]. Berkeley and Los Angeles: University of California Press, 1985.

Richards, Paul. *Indigenous Agricultural Revolution: Ecology and Food Production in West Africa*. Boulder, Colo.: Westview Press, 1985.

Roche, Christian. *Conquête et résistance des peuples de Casamance*. Dakar: Nouvelles Editions Africaines, 1979.

Rotberg, Robert I., and Ali A. Mazrui, eds. *Protest and Power in Black Africa*. Oxford: Oxford University Press, 1970.

Sabot, Richard H. *Economic Development and Urban Migration: Tanzania, 1900–1971*. Oxford: Clarendon Press, 1978.

Salifou, André. *Kouassan ou la révolte Senoussiste*. Niamey: Institut de Recherches en Sciences Humaines, 1973.

Steinhart, E. I. *Conflict and Collaboration: The Kingdoms of Western Uganda, 1890–1907*. Princeton: Princeton University Press, 1977.

Summers, Anne, and R. W. Johnson. "World War I Conscription and Social Change in Guinea." *Journal of African History* 19, no. 1 (1978): 25–38.

Thomas, R. G. "The 1916 Bongo Riots and Their Background: Aspects of Colonial Administration and African Response in Eastern Upper Ghana." *Journal of African History* 24, no. 1 (1983): 57–75.

Tymowski, Michal. "Les Domaines des princes du Songhaï (Soudan occidental): Comparaison avec la grande propriété foncière en Europe au début de l'ère féodale." *Annales ESC*, no. 6 (1970): 1637–58.

Vanhaeverbeke, André. *Rémunération du travail et commerce extérieur: Essor d'une économie exportatrice et termes de l'échange des producteurs d'arachides au Sénégal*. Louvain: Centre de Recherches des Pays en voie de Développement, Université Catholique de Louvain, 1970.

Venema, L. *The Wolof of Saloum: Social Structure and Rural Development in Senegal*. Wageningen: Center for Agricultural Publications, 1978.

Verhaegen, Benoît. *Rébellions au Congo*. 2 vols. Brussels: Centre de Recherche International en Science Politique, 1966, 1969.

Videgla, D. K. Michel, and A. Felix Iroko. "Nouveau Regard sur la révolte de Sakete en 1905." *Cahiers d'Etudes Africaines* 24, no. 93 (1984): 51–70.

Wilcock, David C. *Political Economy of Grain Marketing and Storage in the Sahel*. East Lansing: Michigan State University Press, 1978.

Wipper, Audrey. *Rural Rebels: A Study of Two Protest Movements in Kenya*. Oxford: Oxford University Press, 1977.

Wolf, Eric. *Peasant Wars in the Twentieth Century*. New York: Harper and Row, 1969.

Wondji, Christophe. "Quelques Caractéristiques des résistances populaires en Afrique noire, 1900–1931." In *Etudes africaines offertes à H. Brunschwig*, 333–46. Paris: Ecole des Hautes Etudes en Sciences Sociales, 1982.

LABOR HISTORY AND LABOR MIGRATIONS

Amin, Samir, ed. *Modern Migrations in Western Africa*. London: Oxford University Press, 1974.

Amin, Samir, and Robin Cohen. *Class and Class-Struggle in Africa*. Lagos: Afrograffika, 1977.

Berger, Elena. *Labour, Race and Colonial Rule: The Copperbelt from 1924 to Independence*. Oxford: Clarendon Press, 1974.

Boning, R. W., ed. *Black Migrations to South Africa: A Selection of Policy-Oriented Research*. Geneva: International Labour Organization, 1981.

Bonner, Paul L., ed. *Working Papers in Southern African Studies*. London: Frank Cass, 1974.

Bozzoli, Belinda, ed. *Labour, Townships and Protest: Studies in the Social History of the Witwatersrand*. Johannesburg: Ravan Press, 1979.

Burawoy, Michael. "The Functions and Reproduction of Migrant Labor: Comparative Material from Southern Africa and the United States." *American Journal of Sociology* 81, no. 5 (1974): 1050–87.

Caldwell, John C. *African Rural-Urban Migration: The Movement to Ghana's Towns*. New York: Columbia University Press, 1969.

Callinicos, Luli. *Gold and Workers, 1886–1924: A People's History of South Africa*. Johannesburg: Ravan Press, 1980.

Clarke, John I., and Lescek A. Kosinski, eds. *Redistribution of Population in Africa*. London: Heinemann, 1982.

Clayton, Anthony, and Donald C. Savage. *Government and Labour in Kenya, 1895– 1963*. London: Frank Cass, 1974.

Cohen, Robin. *Labour and Politics in Nigeria, 1945–1971*. London: Heinemann, 1974.

———. "Resistance and Hidden Forms of Consciousness among African Workers." *Review of African Political Economy*, no. 19 (1980): 8–22.

Cohen, Robin, Peter Gutkind, and Philip Brazier, eds. *Peasants and Proletarians: The Struggles of Third World Workers*. New York: Monthly Review Press, 1979.

Cohen, Robin, Peter Gutkind, and Jean Copans, eds. *African Labor History*. London: Sage, 1978.

Colvin, Lucy G., ed. *Uprooted of the Western Sahel: Migrants' Quest for Cash in the Senegambia*. New York: Praeger, 1981.

Conway, H. E. "Labour Protest Activity in Sierra Leone during the Early Part of the Twentieth Century." *Labour History*, no. 15 (1968): 49–63.

Cooper, Carole. *The Durban Strikes, 1973*. Johannesburg: Ravan Press, 1974.

Cooper, Frederick. *On the African Waterfront: Urban Disorder and the Transformation of Work in Colonial Mombasa*. New Haven: Yale University Press, 1987.

———, ed. *Struggle for the City: Migrant Labor, Capital and the State in Urban Africa*. London: Sage, 1983.

Coquery-Vidrovitch, Catherine, and Paul Lovejoy, eds. *The Workers of Long-Distance Trade in Pre-Colonial Africa*. Beverly Hills, Calif.: Sage, 1985.

Crisp, Jeff. *The Story of an African Working Class: Ghanaian Miners' Struggle, 1870–1980*. London: Zed Press, 1984.

Cronje, Gillian, and Suzanne Cronje. *The Workers of Namibia*. London: International Defense and Aid Fund, 1979.

David, Pierre. *Les Navetanes: Histoire des migrants saisonniers de l'arachide en Sénégambie*. Dakar: Nouvelles Editions Africaines, 1980.

Deniel, Raymond. *De la savane à la ville: Essai sur la migration des Mossi vers Abidjan et sa région*. Paris: Aubier, 1968.

Du Toit, Darcy. *Capital and Labour in South Africa: Class Struggle in the 1970s*. London: Routledge and Kegan Paul, 1981.

Esparre, P. L. "Le Travailleur en Côte d'Ivoire: Une Intégration difficile à la société industrielle." *Genève-Afrique* 6, no. 2 (1967): 181–92.

First, Ruth. *Black Gold: The Mozambican Miner Proletariat and Peasant*. New York: St. Martin's, 1983.

Freund, Bill. *Capital and Labor in the Nigerian Tin Mines*. Harlow: Longman, 1981.

———. "Labor and Labor History in Africa: A Review of the Literature." *African Studies Review* 27, no. 2 (1984): 1–58.

Gordon, Richard J. *Mines, Masters and Migrants: Life in a Namibian Compound*. Johannesburg: Ravan Press, 1977.

Grillo, Ralph D. *African Railwaymen: Solidarity and Opposition in an East African Labor Force*. Cambridge, England: Cambridge University Press, 1973.

Gugler, Josef, ed. *Urban Growth in Sub-Saharan Africa*. Kampala: Institute of Social Research, 1971.

Hemson, David. "Dock Workers, Labour Circulation and Class Struggles in Durban, 1940–1959." *Journal of Southern African Studies* 4 (1977): 88–124.

Jeeves, Alan H. *Migrant Labour in South Africa's Mining Economy, 1890–1920.* Montreal: McGill University Press, 1985.

Jeffries, Richard. *The Railwaymen of Sekondi-Takoradi.* Beverly Hills, Calif.: Sage, 1982.

Jewsiewicki, Bogumil. "La Contestation sociale et la naissance du prolétariat au Bas-Zaïre." *Canadian Journal of African Studies* 10, no. 1 (1976): 47–70.

Jewsiewicki, Bogumil, Kilola Keme, and Jean-Luc Vellut. "Documents pour servir à l'histoire sociale au Zaïre: Grèves dans le Bas-Congo (1945)." *Etudes d'Histoire Africaine* 5 (1973): 155–88.

Johnstone, Fred A. *Class, Race and Gold: A Study of Class Relations and Racial Discrimination in South Africa.* London: Routledge and Kegan Paul, 1976.

Joseph, Richard. *Radical Nationalism in Cameroon: Social Origins of the U.P.C. Rebellion.* Oxford: Oxford University Press, 1977.

Lachartre, Bernadette. *Luttes ouvrières et libération en Afrique du Sud.* Paris: Syros, 1977.

Lakroum, Monique. *Le Travail inégal: Paysans et salariés sénégalais face à la crise des années 30.* Paris: L'Harmattan, 1983.

Lee, Richard Borshay. *The !Kung San: Men, Women and Work in a Foraging Society.* Cambridge, England: Cambridge University Press, 1979.

Leonard, Henri. *Le Contrat de travail au Congo belge.* Brussels: Larcier, 1935.

Levy, Norman. *The Foundations of the South African Cheap Labour System.* London: Routledge and Kegan Paul, 1982.

Lloyd, Peter. *A Third World Proletariat.* London: Allen and Unwin, 1982.

Martens, George R. *African Trade Unionism: A Bibliography (1885–1963) with a Guide to Trade Union Organizations and Publications.* Boston: G. K. Hall, 1977.

Murray, Colin. *Families Divided: The Impact of Migrant Labour in Lesotho.* Cambridge, England: Cambridge University Press, 1981.

Odendaal, André. *Black Protest Politics in South Africa to 1912.* New York: Barnes and Noble, 1984.

Parpart, James. *Capital and Labor on the African Copperbelt.* Philadelphia: Temple University Press, 1983.

Peil, Margaret. *The Ghanaian Factory Worker: Industrial Man in Africa.* Cambridge, England: Cambridge University Press, 1972.

Perrings, Charles. *Black Miners in Central Africa: Industrial Strategies and the Evolution of an African Proletariat in the Copperbelt, 1911–1941.* London: Heinemann, 1979.

Phiminster, Ian R., and Charles Van Onselen, eds. *Studies in the History of African Mine Labour in Colonial Zimbabwe.* Salisbury [Harare], Rhodesia: Mambo Press, 1978.

Priestley, Margaret. "An Early Strike in Ghana (1753)." *Ghana Notes and Queries,* no. 7 (1965): 24.

Richards, Audrey I., ed. *Economic Development and Tribal Change: A Study of Immigrant Labour in Buganda.* Cambridge, England: Heffer and Sons, [ca. 1952].

Sabot, Richard. *Urban Migration in Tanzania.* Vol. 2: *National Urban Mobility.* Dar es Salaam: University of Dar es Salaam, 1972.

Salem, Gérard. *De Dakar à Paris: Des Diasporas d'artisans et de commerçants*. 2 vols. Paris: ORSTOM, 1981.

Sandbrook, Richard. *Proletarians and African Capitalism: The Kenyan Case, 1960–1972*. Cambridge, England: Cambridge University Press, 1975.

Sandbrook, Richard, and Robin Cohen, eds. *The Development of an African Working Class: Studies in Class Formation and Action*. Toronto: University of Toronto Press, 1975.

Shijvi, Issa G. *Law, State, and the Working Class in Tanzania, c. 1920–1964*. London, 1986.

Simpson, Richard L., and I. Harper Simpson, eds. Discussion of African problems, pp. 1–104 in *Research in the Sociology of Work: A Research Annual*. Vol. 1. Connecticut: Jai Press, 1981.

"South African Communist Party, 1921–1981." *African Communist*, special issue, no. 86 (1981).

Spencer, John. *The Kenya African Union*. London: KPI, 1985.

Stichter, Sharon. "Workers, Trade Unions and the Mau-Mau Rebellion." *Canadian Journal of African Studies* 9, no. 2 (1975): 259–75.

———. *Migrant Labour in Kenya: Capitalism and African Response, 1905–1975*. London: Longman, 1982.

———. *Migrant Labourers*. Cambridge, England: Cambridge University Press, 1985.

Suret-Canale, Jean. "The French West African Railway Workers' Strike, 1947–1948." In *African Labor History*, edited by Peter C. W. Gutkind et al., 129–54. Beverly Hills, Calif.: Sage, 1978.

Swindell, Kenneth. "Farmers, Traders and Labourers: Dry Season Migration from North-West Nigeria, 1900–1933." *Africa* 54, no. 1 (1984): 3–19.

Van Onselen, Charles. *Chibaro: African Mine Labour in Southern Rhodesia, 1900–1933*. London: Pluto Press, 1976.

Van Zwanenberg, Roger. *Colonial Capitalism and Labour in Kenya, 1919–1939*. Kampala: East African Literature Bureau, 1975.

Waterman, Paul. *Division and Unity among Nigerian Workers: Lagos Trade-Unionism, 1940s–1960s*. The Hague: State Sociological Institute, 1982.

Wicknis, P. L. *The Industrial and Commercial Workers' Unions of Africa*. Oxford: Oxford University Press, 1978.

Wilson, Francis. *Labour in the South African Gold Mines, 1911–1969*. Cambridge, England: Cambridge University Press, 1972.

Wyse, Akintola J. G. "The 1926 Railway Strike and Anglo-Krio Relations: An Interpretation." *International Journal of African Historical Studies* 14, no. 1 (1981): 93–123.

URBANIZATION AND DEVELOPMENT PROBLEMS

Abdel Malek, Anouar, ed. *Sociologie de l'impérialisme*. Paris: Anthropos, 1971.

Amin, Samir. *Neo-Colonialism in West Africa*. New York: Monthly Review Press, 1974.

———. *Unequal Development*. New York: Monthly Review Press, 1976.

Arrighi, Giovanni, and John Saul. *Essays on the Political Economy of Africa*. New York: Monthly Review Press, 1973.

Bairoch, Paul. *Révolution industrielle et sous-développement*. Paris: Sedes, 1963.

———. *Le Tiers-Monde dans l'impasse*. Paris: Gallimard, 1971.

———. *The Economic Development of the Third World since 1900*. Berkeley and Los Angeles: University of California Press, 1975.

Baker, Pauline Halpern. *Urbanization and Political Change: The Politics of Lagos, 1917–1967*. Berkeley and Los Angeles: University of California Press, 1974.

Bruckner, Pascal. *The Tears of the White Man: Compassion as Contempt*. New York: Free Press, 1986.

Bujra, Janet. *Pumwani, the Politics of Property: A Study of an Urban Settlement in Nairobi*. Dar es Salaam: University of Nairobi, 1973.

Chaliand, Gérard. *Struggle for Africa: Conflict of the Great Powers*. London: Macmillan, 1982.

Chesneaux, Jean. *De la modernité*. Paris: Maspero, 1984.

Clinard, Marshall B., and Daniel J. Abboh, eds. *Crime in Developing Countries*. New York: Wiley and Sons, 1973.

Connaissance du Tiers-Monde: Approche pluri-disciplinaire. Laboratoire Connaissance du Tiers-Monde, Université Paris VII. Paris: 10/18, 1978.

Coquery, Michel. "La Notion de mode de composition urbaine: Un Outil opératoire (le cas de l'Afrique noire)." *Bulletin de la Société Languedocienne de Géographie* 16, no. 1–2 (1982): 123–44.

———. *La Coopération face aux problèmes posés par l'urbanisation dans le Tiers-Monde*. Paris: Report to the Ministre de la Coopération et du Développement, 1983.

Deblé, Isabelle, and Philippe Hugon. *Vivre et survivre dans les villes africaines*. Paris: Presses Universitaires de France, 1982.

Devauges, Roland. *Le Chômage à Brazzaville: Etude sociologique*. Paris: ORSTOM, 1959.

Dumont, René, and Marie-Claude Mottin. *Stranglehold on Africa*. London: André Deutsch, 1983.

Epstein, A. L. *Urbanization and Kinship: The Domestic Domain on the Copperbelt of Zambia, 1950–1956*. New York: Academic Press, 1981.

Galbraith, John Kenneth. *The Nature of Mass Poverty*. Cambridge, Mass.: Harvard University Press, 1979.

Gibbal, Jean-Marie. *Citadins et villageois dans la ville africaine: L'Exemple d'Abidjan*. Paris: Maspero, 1974.

Gran, Guy, ed. *Zaire: The Political Economy of Underdevelopment*. New York: Praeger, 1979.

Granotier, Bernard. *La Planète des bidonvilles: Perspectives de l'explosion urbaine dans le Tiers-Monde*. Paris: Editions du Seuil, 1980.

Gutkind, Peter C. W. "The View from Below: Political Consciousness of the Urban Poor in Ibadan." *Cahiers d'Etudes Africaines* 15, no. 1 (1975): 5–35.

Guyer, Jane, ed. *Feeding African Cities: Studies in Regional Social History*. Manchester: Manchester University Press, 1987.

Hake, Andrew. *African Metropolis: Nairobi's Self-Help City*. New York: St. Martin's, 1977.

Hugon, Philippe. "Le Secteur 'non structuré' dans les villes du Tiers-Monde." *Bulletin de la Société Languedocienne de Géographie* 16, no. 1–2 (1982): 85–102.

———, ed. "Secteur informel et petite production marchande dans les villes du Tiers-Monde." *Revue Tiers-Monde* 21, no. 82 (1980): 225–245.

Hyden, Goran. *No Shortcuts to Progress: African Development Management in Perspective*. London: Heinemann, 1983.

Iliffe, John. *The Emergence of African Capitalism*. London: Macmillan, 1983.

Joshi, Heather, Harold Lubell, and J. Mouly. *Abidjan: Urban Development and Employment in the Ivory Coast*. Geneva: International Labour Organization, 1976.

Josselin, Gérard. *L'Afrique désenchantée: Sociétés et stratégies de transition en Afrique tropicale*. Paris: Anthropos, 1978.

Mende, Tibor. *From Aid to Recolonization: Lessons of a Failure*. New York: Pantheon, 1973.

Nortey, D. N. A. "Crime in Ghana." *Ghana Social Science Journal* 7, no. 1 (1977): 102–16.

Peil, Margaret. *Cities and Suburbs: Urban Life in West Africa*. New York: Africana, 1981.

Raulin, Henri, and Edgar Raynaud. *L'Aide au sous-développement*. Paris: Presses Universitaires de France, 1980.

Ross, Robert, and Gerard J. Telkamp, eds. *Colonial Cities: Essays on Urbanism in a Colonial Context*. Dordrecht Martinhus Nijhoff, 1985.

Sandbrook, Richard. *The Politics of Basic Needs: Urban Aspects of Assaulting Poverty in Africa*. London: Heinemann, 1982.

Sandbrook, Richard, with Judith Barker. *The Politics of Africa's Economic Stagnation*. Cambridge, England: Cambridge University Press, 1985.

Sesay, Amadu, Olusola Ojo, and Orobola Fasehun. *The Organization of African Unity after Twenty Years*. Boulder, Colo.: Westview Press, 1984.

Sethuraman, S. V., ed. *The Urban Informal Sector in Developing Countries: Employment, Poverty and Environment*. Geneva: International Labour Organization, 1981.

Skinner, Elliott P. *African Urban Life: The Transformation of Ouagadougou*. Princeton: Princeton University Press, 1974.

Vennetier, Pierre. "L'Urbanisation et ses conséquences au Congo-Brazzaville." *Cahiers d'Outre-Mer*, no. 63 (1963): 263–80.

———. *Les Villes d'Afrique tropicale*. Paris: Masson, 1976.

"Villes africaines au microscope." *Cahiers d'Etudes Africaines*, special issue, no. 81–83 (1981).

Warren, Bill. *Imperialism, Pioneer of Capitalism*. London: Verso, 1980.

Ziegler, Jean. *Main basse sur l'Afrique noire*. Paris: Editions de Seuil, 1978.

WOMEN

Bay, Edna G., ed. *Women and Work in Africa*. Boulder, Colo.: Westview Press, 1982.

Callaway, Barbara J. *Muslim Hausa Women in Nigeria: Tradition and Change*. Syracuse, N.Y.: Syracuse University Press, 1987.

Cock, Jacklyn. *Maids and Madams: A Study in the Politics of Exploitation*. Johannesburg: Ravan Press, 1980.

Etienne, Mona, and Eleanor Leacock, eds. *Women and Colonization: Anthropological Perspectives*. New York: Praeger, 1980.

Femmes et politiques alimentaires. Paris: ORSTOM, 1985.

"Des Femmes sur l'Afrique des femmes." *Cahiers d'Etudes Africaines,* special issue, 17, no. 65 (1977).

Hafkin, Nancy J., and Edna G. Bay. *Women in Africa: Studies in Social and Economic Change*. Stanford: Stanford University Press, 1976.

Hay, Margaret J., and Sharon Stichter, eds. *African Women South of the Sahara*. London: Longman, 1984.

Hay, Margaret J., and Marcia Wright, eds. *African Women and the Law*. Boston: Boston University Press, 1982.

Kinsman, Margaret. "'Beasts of Burden': The Subordination of Southern Tswana Women, ca. 1800–1860." *Journal of Southern African Studies* 10, no. 1 (1983): 39–53.

Matsepe, Ivry P. "African Women's Labor in the Political Economy of South Africa, 1880–1978." Ph.D. diss., Rutgers University, 1984.

May, Joan. *Zimbabwean Women in Customary and Colonial Law*. Harare, Zimbabwe: Mambo Press, 1983.

Mba, Nina M. *Nigerian Women Mobilized: Women's Political Activity in Southern Nigeria, 1900–1965*. Berkeley and Los Angeles: University of California Press, 1982.

Meillassoux, Claude. *Maidens, Meal and Money: Capitalism and the Domestic Community*. Cambridge, England: Cambridge University Press, 1981.

Mickelwait, Donald R. *Women in Rural Development: A Survey of the Roles of Women in Ghana, Lesotho, Kenya, Nigeria*. Boulder, Colo.: Westview Press, 1976.

Oboler, Regina Smith. *Women, Power and Economic Change: The Nandi of Kenya*. Stanford: Stanford University Press, 1985.

Oppong, Christine, ed. *Female and Male in West Africa*. London: Allen and Unwin, 1983.

Robertson, Claire. *Sharing the Same Bowl: A Socioeconomic History of Women and Class in Accra*. Bloomington: Indiana University Press, 1984.

Robertson, Claire, and Iris Berger, eds. *Women and Class in Africa*. London: Africana, 1986.

Robertson, Claire, and Martin Klein, eds. *Women and Slavery in Africa*. Madison: University of Wisconsin Press, 1984.

"The Roles of African Women: Past, Present and Future." *Canadian Journal of African Studies* 5, no. 2 (1972): 143–377.

Romero, Patricia, ed. *Life Histories of African Women*. Atlantic Highlands, N.J.: Ashfield Press, 1987.

Shostak, Marjorie. *Nisa: The Life and Words of a !Kung Woman*. New York: Vintage, 1983.

Société Africaine de Culture, ed. *La Civilisation de la femme dans la tradition africaine*. Colloque d'Abidjan, July 1972. Paris: Présence Africaine, 1975.

———. "La Femme noire dans la vie moderne: Images et réalités." *Présence Africaine,* special issue, n.s. no. 141–42 (1987).

Strobel, Margaret. *Muslim Women in Mombasa, 1890–1975*. New Haven: Yale University Press, 1979.

Sweetman, David. *Women Leaders in African History*. London: Heinemann, 1985.
Walker, Cherry. *Women and Resistance in South Africa (1910–1954)*. London: Onyx Press, 1982.
Women in Nigeria Today. London: Zed Press, 1985.
Wright, Marcia. "Technology, Marriage and Women's Work in the History of Maize-Growers in Mazabreka, Zambia: A Reconnaissance." *Journal of Southern African Studies* 10, no. 1 (1983): 55–69.
————, ed. *Women in Peril: Life Stories of Four Captives*. Institute for African Studies, University of Zambia. N.p.: Neczam, Zambia Past and Present, 1984.

LITERATURE, ELITES, EDUCATION

Astier-Loufti, Monique. *Littérature et colonialisme, 1871–1914*. The Hague: Mouton, 1971.
Barnett, Ursula A. *A Vision of Order: A Study of Black South African Literature in English (1940–1980)*. London: Sinclair Browne, 1983.
Blanchet, Gilles. *Elites et changements en Afrique et au Sénégal*. Paris: ORSTOM, 1983.
Bouche, Denise. *L'Enseignement dans les territoires français de l'Afrique occidentale de 1817 à 1920: Mission civilisatrice ou formation d'une élite?* Lille: Université de Lille III, 1975.
Brown, Susan, ed. *Lip from Southern African Women*. Johannesburg: Ravan Press, 1983.
Chemain, Roger, and Arlette Chemain-Degrange. *Panorama critique de la littérature congolaise contemporaine*. Paris: Présence Africaine, 1979.
Figueroa, John J., ed. *Anthology of African and Caribbean Writing in English*. London: Heinemann, 1982.
Kesteloot, Lilyan, ed. *Anthologie négro-africaine*. Verviers: Marabout-Université, Gérard, 1967.
Kom, Ambroise, ed. *Dictionnaire des oeuvres littéraires négro-africaines de langue française*. Paris: Naaman and Agence de Coopération Culturelle et Technique, 1983.
Lindfors, Bernth. *Black African Literature in English: A Guide to Information Sources*. Detroit: Gale Research, 1979.
Lopes, Henri. *Le Pleurer-rire*. Paris: Présence Africaine, 1982.
Ly, Ibrahima. *Toiles d'araignées*. Paris: L'Harmattan, 1982.
Mazrui, Ali. *Political Values and the Educated Class in Africa*. London: Heinemann, 1978.
Mugomba, Agrippah T., and Mougo Nyaggah. *Independence without Freedom: The Political Economy of Colonial Education in Southern Africa*. Oxford: ABC-Clio, 1980.
Mutloatse, Mothabi, ed. *Reconstruction: Ninety Years of Black Historical Literature*. Johannesburg: Ravan Press, 1981.
Ousmane, Sembene. *God's Bits of Wood*. London: Heinemann, 1970.
Robinson, Cedric J. *Black Marxism: The Making of the Black Radical Tradition*. London: Zed Press, 1983.

Sabatier, P. R. "Elite Education in French West Africa: The Era of Limits, 1903–1945." *International Journal of African Historical Studies* 11, no. 2 (1978): 247–66.

Sow, Alfa Ibrahima, ed. *La Femme, la vache, la foi: Ecrivains et poètes du Fouta-Djalon*. Paris: Julliard, 1966.

Tansi, Sony Labou. *La Vie et demie*. Paris: Editions du Seuil, 1979.

Zell, Hans M., Carol Bundy, and Virginia Coulon. *A New Reader's Guide to African Literature* [English, French, Portuguese]. New York: Africana, 1983.

Index

Compositor:	G&S Typesetters, Inc.
Text:	10/12 Sabon
Display:	Optima
Printer:	Maple-Vail Book Mfg. Group
Binder:	Maple-Vail Book Mfg. Group